One Hundred Years of Valor
RESCUE COMPANY 1
New York City Fire Department

By Paul Hashagen

Best wishes from the Big Apple
"Outstanding!"
Paul Hashagen
Rescue Co. 1
FDNY (Ret.)

Julie,
Thanks for all your support over all these years
Love,
Bruce

M.T. Publishing Company, Inc.
P.O. Box 6802
Evansville, Indiana 47719-6802
www.mtpublishing.com

Copyright © 2015
Paul Hashagen

Graphic Designer: Elizabeth A. Dennis

All rights reserved. No part of this publication may be translated, reproduced, or transmitted in any form or by any means, electronic or mechanical, including photocopying and recording, or by any information storage and retrieval system, without expressed written permission of the copyright owner and M.T. Publishing Company, Inc.

The materials were compiled and produced using available information; M.T. Publishing Company, Inc., and the copyright owner regret they cannot assume liability for errors or omissions.

Library of Congress
Control Number: 2015933211

ISBN: 978-1-938730-54-2

First Printing: April 2015
Second Printing: December 2015

Printed in the United States of America

Dedication

This book is dedicated to all the members of Rescue Company 1 FDNY Past, Present and Future Especially those lost in the line-of-duty, and their families.

Contents

Dedication 2

Acknowledgements 4

Preface 5

Chapter 1 – The Beginning 7

Chapter 2 – The Twenties 25

Chapter 3 – The Thirties 47

Chapter 4 – The Forties 57

Chapter 5 – The Fifties 71

Chapter 6 – The Sixties 83

Chapter 7 – The Seventies 103

Chapter 8 – The Eighties 119

Chapter 9 – The Nineties 141

Chapter 10 – The Millennium 163

Chapter 11 – The 2010s 183

Rescue 1 Company Apparatus 196

Rescue 1 Company Members Through The Years ... 202

Rescue 1 Company Appendix 214
   I. Rescue Company 1 FDNY Company Commanders ... 214
   II. Rescue Company 1 Firehouses 214
   III. Rescue Company 1 Awards 215
   IV. Rescue Company 1 Unit Citations 221
   V. Medals Awarded to Members of Rescue Company 1 ... 225

Index 226

"I have no ambition in this world but one, and that is to be a fireman"
Chief Edward F. Croker

Acknowledgements

The stories contained in this book are mostly taken from documented sources such as Official New York City Fire Department Orders, Medal Day books, official reports of meritorious acts, and other department publications, as well as the many newspapers in print at the time. It is not the author's intent to make it appear the work of Rescue 1 was the only thing extinguishing fire and saving lives at these operations. On the contrary, the work of the FDNY since its inception back in 1865 has become legendary in the annals of firefighting.

With this in mind, I would like to thank those who helped me with this quarter-century project. Way back in 1987 when I began the first book, one person stood out, helping me with and showing me how to research: Herb Eysser, FDNY Dispatcher 124 (retired). Thanks for putting me on the right path! Another important mentor was Battalion Chief Jack Calderone. A great fire chief with a wealth of historic data and photos.

My thanks to Fire Commissioner Daniel A. Nigro, for permission to use official FDNY documents and photos for this book. Many thanks to the FDNY Photo Unit especially Katy Clements.

Thanks to the Connecticut Firemen's Historical Society, Inc. Especially, Gary Pinkham and Wayne Crossman. For their super clear copies of photos taken by Hon. Chief Albert Dreyfous.

Several people who have passed on during this project, but that helped me greatly were: Rescue 1 Firemen Dominico DiBenedetto (1930s), Hank Williams (1940s), George Tollefson (1940s-1950s), and William Riley (1970s-1980s). In addition, I'd like to thank my publisher and friend Dennis Campbell, and Honorary FDNY Chiefs Harvey Eisner, John Lee Gill, and Professor Don Cannon. Each of these men had a profound effect on my grasp of writing and researching fire history. I miss them.

Special thanks to Jack Lerch, Danny Maye, and Fred Melahn at the FDNY Mand Library, as well as Gary Urbanowicz, Ed Sere, Bill Noonan, John Norman, David Handschuh, Bill Bennett, Steve Spak, Michael Gomez, Larry Shapiro, Mike Dick, Carl Westbrook, Pete O'Dea, Tom Hurley and Danny Alfonso.

Thanks to all the great rescue firemen I have worked with, especially those that helped so much with their photos and memories. Especially, Bill Bessman, Paul Geidel, Tom Bonamo, John Driscoll, George McGann, Dennis Dale, Mike Geidel, Tom Donnelly, Dave Marmann, Rich Miranda, Andrew Dinkle, Mike Pena, Tim Brown and Kevin Kroth.

Heartfelt thanks to Jules and Gedeon Naudet for their kind permission to use the amazing images taken in the lobby of the World Trade Center.

My publishing team at M.T. Publishing Company, thank you Mark Thompson, Liz Dennis and Alena Kiefer.

Last but not least is my manuscript editor. I am very lucky to have married a woman who has a keen interest in the fire service, history, and also a very sharp pencil. I thank Joanne for all the hours of corrections and wonderful suggestions to make this book better.

Any errors or mistakes in this book are mine, and mine alone.

Rescue men "began where the ordinary fireman left off."
Chief John J. McElligott – January 17, 1934

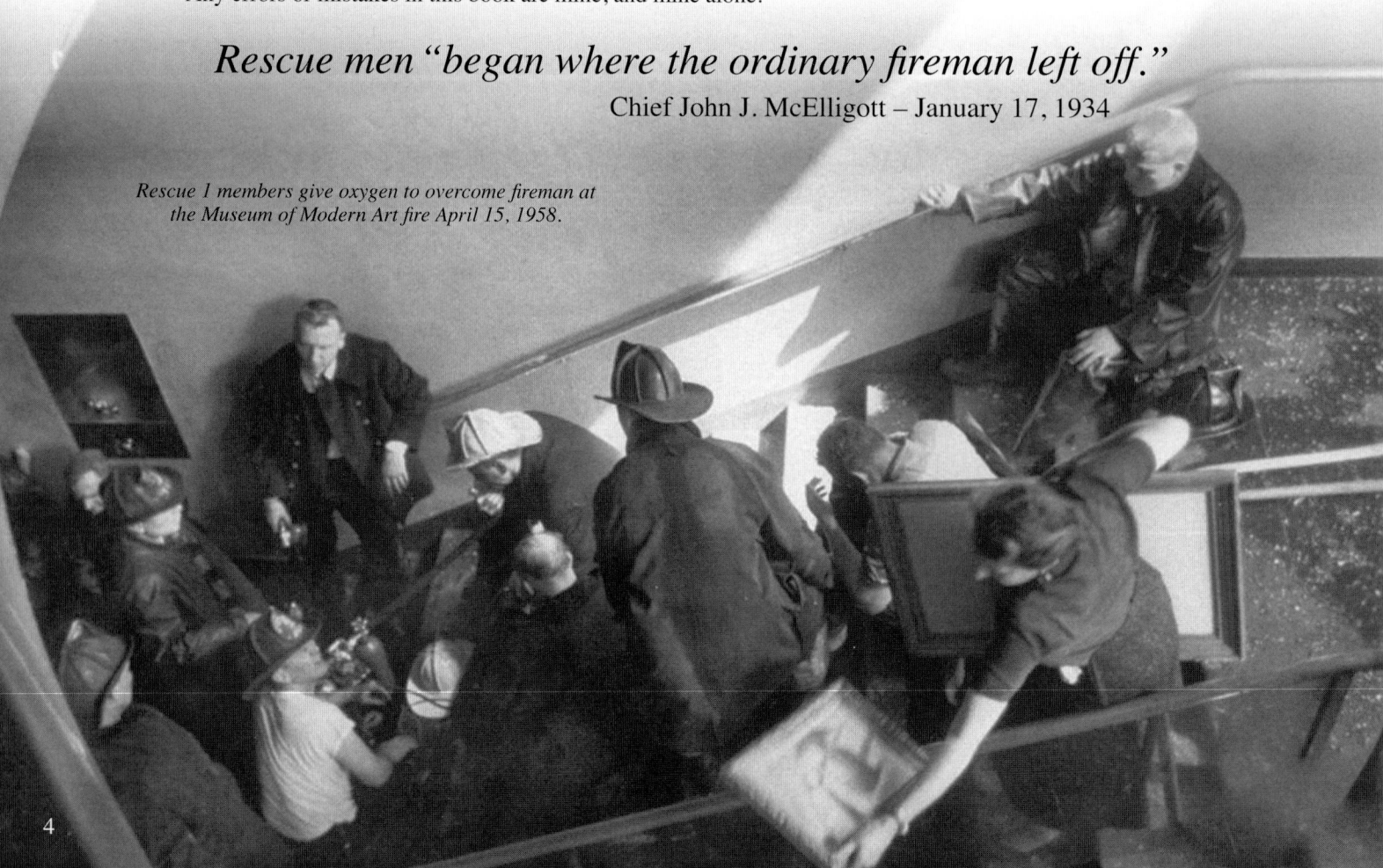

Rescue 1 members give oxygen to overcome fireman at the Museum of Modern Art fire April 15, 1958.

"As long as they speak your name you will never die."
Proverb

Preface

When I began this project, I thought I knew quite a lot about Rescue Company 1, its history, membership, and apparatus. I was mistaken. The pioneering work of the first ten members assigned to the company back in 1915, and those that followed for the next ten years, set a standard that would have historical significance in emergency work around the world. These men and their "state-of-the-art" equipment, primitive by todays standards, allowed them to go places no other humans could survive.

They not only performed extreme firefighting, but accomplished hazardous material control and mitigation. They provided and developed, heavy rescue tools and techniques for building collapses, vehicle wrecks and other accidents. Rescue men delivered aggressive street medicine with their pulmotors and resuscitators, in an era where none of these disciplines existed.

This work was carried on and expanded as Rescue 2 was formed in 1925, followed by Rescues 3, 4 and 5. This new idea, of "rescue firemen", that were specially trained and equipped, was a monumental step forward. Rescue started with a small 1914 Cadillac touring car packed with leather helmeted men and a small array of tools. Today the modern day FDNY Special Operations Command, national Urban Search & Rescue Teams and Haz-Mat Teams expand the boundaries of rescue work.

The dangers they faced, and the traditions they set were amazing. In an era where firefighting was conducted by "iron men and wooden ladders" they took things to a higher level. Their trailblazing work left a legacy for all American fire departments, both large and small.

I would like to note that the stories in this book are only part of this history. Numerous rescue men worked dangerous fires, and made daring rescues that never received official recognition. Their valor and sacrifice is not lost.

Finally, this is a book about Rescue Company 1. Every fire that Rescue responded to was also already being worked by other companies. Where the vast majority of rescues were made by ladder companies and the flames were extinguished routinely by engine companies. Due to their exceptional professionalism, the reputation of the FDNY is known world wide. With the exception of two men, every rescue man has worked in either an engine or ladder or both, before being assigned to the Rescue. The stories in this book simply chronicle the work of one company. A new and special company that began in 1915.

All the FDNY rescue companies operated at this difficult fire onboard the USS Constellation *in the Brooklyn Navy Yard, December 19, 1960.*

This 1916 photo shows rescue man standing by outside a fire building, while a nearby fireman tends the rope attached to helmeted men inside. This safety procedure insured instant help was available to those rescue men operating inside.

Chapter 1

The Beginning

As a result of many unusual situations occurring at fires and emergencies, the New York City Fire Department began contemplating the development of a special unit trained and equipped to handle these special problems. Chief of Department John Kenlon and Fire Commissioner Robert Adamson, hoped to provide the FDNY with a company that could shut off ammonia supplies when pipes burst in cold-storage plants, for entering and ventilating the deadly smoke produced during fires in drug and chemical plants and rescue people overcome during these fires. In addition they could operate in the worst smoke conditions often found in the cellars and sub-cellars in lower Manhattan. Their ability to work under these punishing conditions reduced the terrible toll these fires placed on the regular companies.

Kenlon and a group of trusted associates began a study of all available equipment and methods used in other fire departments around the world and other endeavors such as the rescue work being done by the Government Bureau of Mines. During this study a very successful Wall Street stockbroker and friend of the department, Robert H. Mainzer traveled to Europe and investigated the fire departments of major cities and noted the equipment they utilized. Upon his return, Mainzer, an Honorary FDNY Battalion Chief, reported his findings to Chief Kenlon and strongly urged the formation of a rescue company outfitted with smoke helmets and other unique tools.

This research was instrumental in the development of a plan to equip, train and place in service a specialized unit utilizing the latest innovations and methods in modern firefighting. A call for volunteers went out to all firehouses in the city. Two hundred men volunteered for the assignment. As the list of candidates was compiled Chief Kenlon went ahead with the testing of an integral part of the entire program: the smoke helmets. A particular young officer had caught the chief's eye and was detailed to put the smoke helmets to the test. John J. McElligott, the thirty year-old captain of Ladder 1, stood six-feet tall. He was a solid two hundred pounds when he reported to the sprinkler testing room of the Fire College to familiarized himself with the breathing apparatus under actual smoke conditions. A fire fueled by excelsior, oakum, hay, sulfur and rubbish was then prepared.

The fire was ignited and quickly filled the room with intense heat and dense noxious smoke. McElligott donned the Draeger smoke helmet and entered the room. Driven to the floor by the heat building above him he settled in and tried to get comfortable. During the entire test he was able to report conditions as they occurred using the helmet's built-in telephone system. At regular intervals a hand-held thermometer was extended overhead where temperatures were reaching 300 degrees. The captain remained in the room for one hour, at which point the gauge on the smoke helmet went to zero. Determined to fully test the reserve supply of air, which was still supplying two liters of fresh air per minute, he remained in the room an additional fifteen minutes.

Smoke helmets were cumbersome and provided poor visibility. They did however, allow rescue firemen to work in deadly atmospheres.

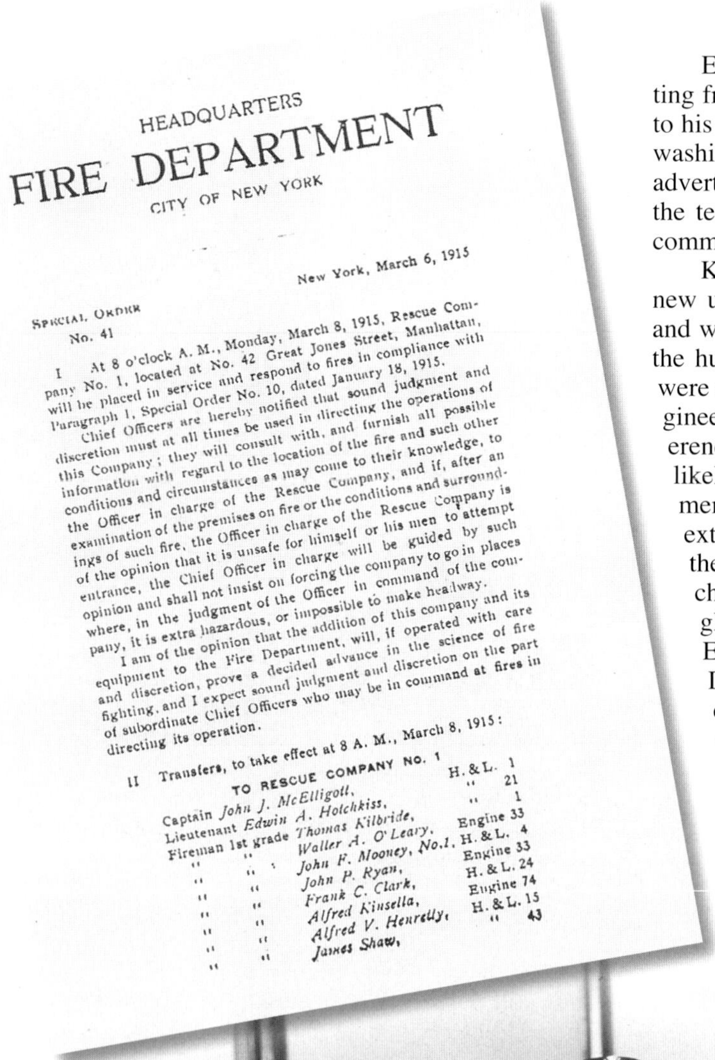

HEADQUARTERS

FIRE DEPARTMENT

CITY OF NEW YORK

New York, March 6, 1915

SPECIAL ORDER
No. 41

I At 8 o'clock A. M., Monday, March 8, 1915, Rescue Company No. 1, located at No. 42 Great Jones Street, Manhattan,
will be placed in service and respond to fires in compliance with
Paragraph 1, Special Order No. 10, dated January 18, 1915.
Chief Officers are hereby notified that sound judgment and
discretion must at all times be used in directing the operations of
this Company; they will consult with, and furnish all possible
information with regard to the location of the fire and such other
conditions and circumstances as may come to their knowledge, to
the Officer in charge of the Rescue Company, and if, after an
examination of the premises on fire or the conditions and surroundings of such fire, the Officer in charge of the Rescue Company is
of the opinion that it is unsafe for himself or his men to attempt
entrance, the Chief Officer in charge will be guided by such
opinion and shall not insist on forcing the company to go in places
where, in the judgment of the Officer in command of the company, it is extra hazardous, or impossible to make headway.
I am of the opinion that the addition of this company and its
equipment to the Fire Department, will, if operated with care
and discretion, prove a decided advance in the science of fire
fighting, and I expect sound judgment and discretion on the part
of subordinate Chief Officers who may be in command at fires in
directing its operation.

II Transfers, to take effect at 8 A. M., March 8, 1915:

TO RESCUE COMPANY NO. 1 H. & L. 1
Captain *John J. McElligott*, " 21
Lieutenant *Edwin A. Hotchkiss*, " 1
Fireman 1st grade *Thomas Kilbride*, Engine 33
" " *Walter A. O'Leary*, H. & L. 4
" " *John F. Mooney, No. 1*, Engine 33
" " *John P. Ryan*, H. & L. 24
" " *Frank C. Clark*, Engine 74
" " *Alfred Kinsella*, H. & L. 15
" " *Alfred V. Henretty*, " 43
" " *James Shaw*,

Exhausted and drenched in sweat, his clothes actually rotting from the fumes, he stepped from the room. Hair plastered to his head and his hands so blackened it would take weeks of washing to clean them, he was satisfied the helmet worked as advertised and would recommend their use. The helmets passed the test as did the young captain who would find himself in command of the new company as it went into service.

Kenlon was now faced with the formal organization of the new unit. Captain John J. McElligott was an obvious choice and would help chose the members of the new company from the hundreds of firemen who had volunteered. All applicants were checked and members with experience as mechanics, engineers, electricians, ironworkers, riggers etc. were given preference providing they were otherwise fit for the severe work likely to be encountered by the new unit. These prospective members were given exhaustive physical exams due to the extreme operating conditions they were expected to face: they would have to work while wearing an early version of chemical protective clothing (rubber waders, sleeves and gloves) while dealing with chlorine and ammonia leaks. Extensive use of the complicated, heavy and cumbersome Draeger smoke helmets, an early rebreather mask that required almost constant maintenance. After much consideration the list of finalists was drawn up.

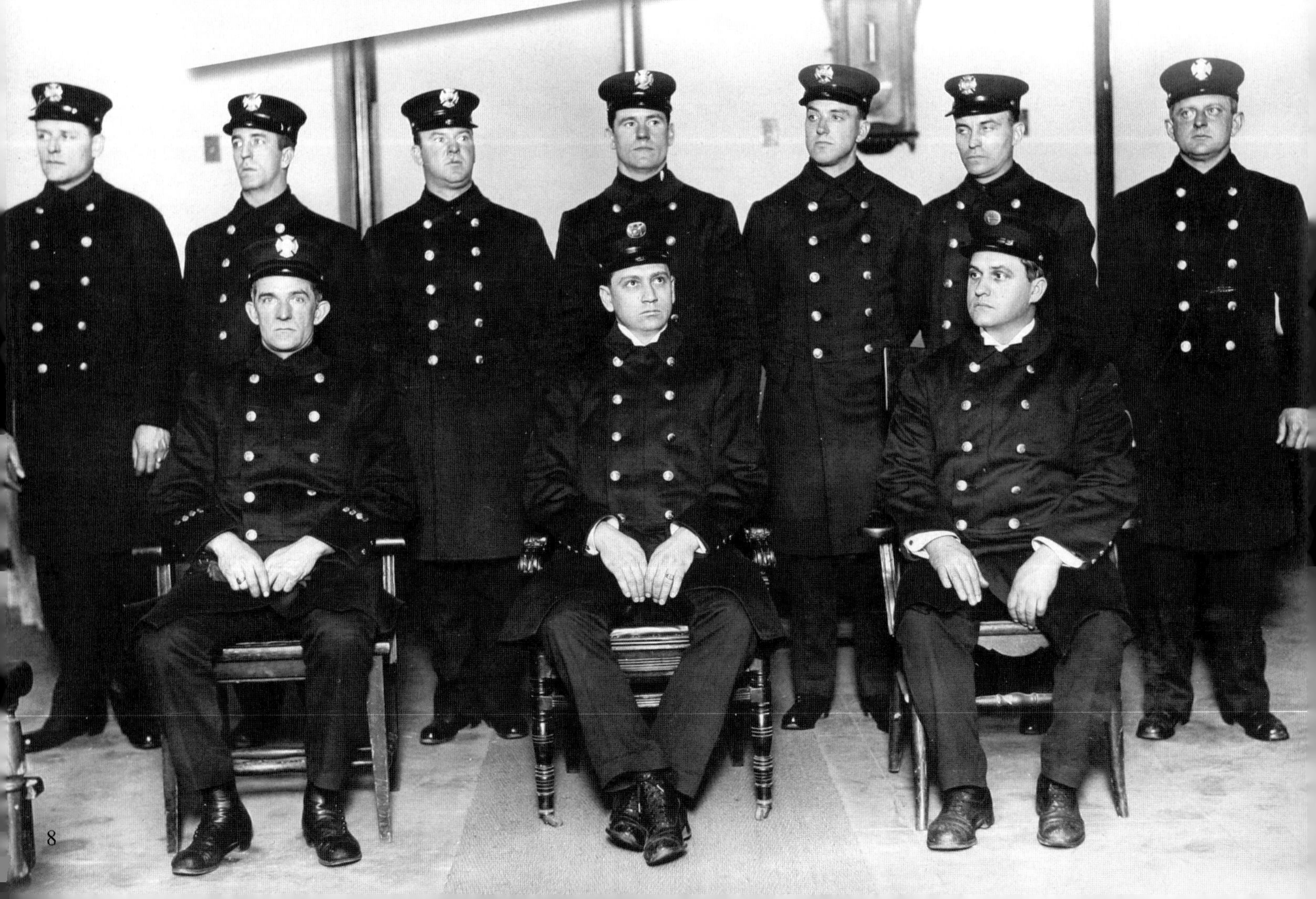

The original members of Rescue Company 1. In service March 8, 1915. (l. to r.) Front: Fireman Thomas Kilbride, Capt. John McElligott, and Lt. Edwin Hotchkiss. Back: Firemen Frank Clark, James Shaw, John Ryan, Walter O'Leary, Alfred Henretty, Alfred Kinsella and John Mooney. (Connecticut Firemen's Historical Society)

The first rescue rig was a custom-rebuilt 1914 Cadillac touring car. This right-hand drive vehicle had two bench seats facing each other in the rear, with a storage space beneath them and a center storage compartment. The gleaming red, high-powered vehicle featured a four-cylinder 32.4 horsepower engine. A large bell and a hand-cranked siren are seen on the dash. There was no windshield. (Connecticut Firemen's Historical Society)

The new rescue men consisted of a captain, lieutenant and eight firemen. They were announced on the department orders and assigned to the FDNY training school on East 67th Street. They started their intensive training at 10 a.m. on January 19, 1915. The specialized instruction covered operation of the unique tools the company would be assigned, use and maintenance of the Draeger smoke helmets, use of cutting torches and advanced first-aid.

The original officers of the company were: John J. McElligott the fast rising young captain of Ladder Company 1 and Lieutenant Edwin Hotchkiss of Ladder 21 who had distinguished himself at the subway fire on January 6, 1915. The firemen were: John Mooney of Ladder 4 who already held both the James Gordon Bennett and the Wertheim Medals, Thomas Kilbride of Ladder Company 1 awarded the Strong and Department Medals in 1912; Firemen Walter O'Leary and John Ryan of Engine 33, Frank Clark of Ladder 24, Alfred Kinsella of Engine 74, Alfred Henretty of Ladder 15 and James Shaw of Ladder 43.

The FDNY shops hurried to complete the rebuilding of the company's new apparatus, a 1914 Cadillac touring car. Rather small by today's standards the right hand steering rig had a huge bell mounted on the center of the dashboard, there was no electrical siren. A spare tire was mounted on the driver's side running board. The shop's bodywork included two bench seats facing each other with storage space beneath them and a center storage compartment. While this was not a tremendous amount of storage space, it was adequate for the time. The list of tools the company started with included Draeger smoke helmets (six were carried on the rig), gas masks, life lines, a Lyle gun (rope rifle), rubber gloves, wading pants, and forcible entry tools. In addition five

New members: (l. to r.) Capt. McElligott, Firemen Clark, Kinsella, O'Leary, Kilbride, Henretty, Shaw, Ryan, Mooney and Lt. Hotchkiss pose with some of the tools carried on the rig: smoke helmet, pulmotor (a resuscitator) oxygen tanks, cutting torch and rope rifle. In addition, the rig also carried: gas masks, life lines, rubber gloves, hydraulic jacks, fire extinguishers and various other tools. Fireman Francis Blessing is seen driving.

hydraulic jacks: 15-10-5 tons, oxygen tanks, two pulmotors (resuscitators), cutting torches, 150-feet signal line, various blocks, wedges, stretchers, fire-extinguishers, axes, first aid kit, rivet cutters, towing cables, claw tools, a telephone set (for the smoke helmets) and an extensive tool kit. This was the "state-of-the-art gear" in 1915. This sturdy little vehicle would remain in-service until 1921.

On the afternoon of March 2, 1915 a large crowd began to gather outside the Municipal Building in lower Manhattan as Battalion Chief Charles S. Demarest, in charge of construction and repairs at the FDNY shops, unveiled the new rescue apparatus. The gleaming red, high powered vehicle, featured a four-cylinder 32.4 horsepower engine. The new rescue rig was examined by Fire Commissioner Adamson and Chief Kenlon, the media and the public, and received high praise.

At the time of Rescue Company 1's establishment, as is still the practice, firefighters were identified on the fire ground by the color of their helmet frontpiece indicating the type of unit to which they were assigned, along with the actual number of the company on the frontpiece. Engine company members had black frontpieces with white company numbers, while ladder company members wore red frontpieces with white company numbers. To distinguish the members of the rescue, blue helmet frontpieces with a white "1" were assigned to them. This "rescue blue" would be assigned to all five rescue companies over the years and the rescues would use blue whenever possible, painting their tools that color, using it on company patches and insignias. As the department established other types of units, each was assigned its own color.

In addition to the frontpiece, a more formal insignia was designed. All company officers in the department wear a uniform cap insignia and collar insignias on each lapel of their uniform jacket. The insignia for the engine company officers is a trumpet for lieutenants and two trumpets for captains. Ladder company lieutenants wear a single axe while captains wear two axes. In addition the company number is affixed to the hat badge. The design for the rescue company officer is unique and consists of a Draeger smoke helmet with the bellows beneath it, a roof rope above it and either one Lyle gun for lieutenants or two Lyle guns for captains. The design varies with one gun behind the smoke helmet or two angled above it. The designer of the insignia and the adoption are unknown, although artist's designs for this insignia and other FDNY designs can be found in the archives of the G.C. Braxmar Company in Manhattan.

The rescue company officer's helmet frontpiece was white with a blue number 1, and depending on the rank either one or two Lyle guns placed above the number. The earliest of the helmet fronts, back in the days of the "high eagle" also featured a blue outline on the edges of the frontpiece either as further identification or as decoration.

Rescue One Goes In-Service

On Monday March 8, 1915, at 8 o'clock in the morning, Captain John J. McElligott picked up the telephone at Engine 33's Great Jones Street firehouse's housewatch desk and advised the Manhattan dispatcher that Rescue Company 1 was in service. The first true heavy rescue company in the United States was now up and running. They would share quarters with the engine and respond to all second alarms south of 59th Street, all third alarms below 125th Street, and on special calls anywhere in the city. It is interesting to note that during its first year of operations Rescue 1 did not respond to first-alarms at all.

The location of the unit on Great Jones Street would allow it a quick response to the heavily commercial districts of lower Manhattan. This area of loft buildings and converted tenements was a very heavy fire area. Chief Kenlon also had an office in this firehouse allowing him to monitor closely the activities and operations of the new unit.

During its first year of operation the company responded to eighty-six alarms. These incidents included removing quantities of nitric and sulfuric acid, a pulmotor case, a subway construction collapse, several cellar fires, a ship fire and five ammonia leaks. The positive publicity surrounding the company as a result of these incidents convinced several other cities that had been operating "flying squadrons" (manpower squads or first-aid squads with no specialized tools) to convert these units into heavy rescue companies rather than manpower auxiliaries.

The rescue rig ready to roll from the quarters they shared with Engine 33, at 42 Great Jones Street. (Connecticut Firemen's Historical Society)

The New York City newspaper *The Evening World* ran this story on March 12, 1915:

> A special call for Rescue Company No. 1 the new smoke helmet organization of the Fire Department, saved Chief Kenlon from having to turn in a second alarm for a serious fire at Nos. 231 and 233 Greene Street at 3 o'clock this morning.
>
> The Chief went to a call box and with a Morse key, and using the Morse code, sent in the Rescue Company's special call- "2- a pause- 2- a pause- 2- a pause- the box number- 1."
>
> Lieut. Edwin Hotchkiss and the Rescue Company men arrived a few minutes later, donned their smoke helmets and started into the cellar of 233. The lieutenant led the way and others followed. Hotchkiss had a rope around his waist and the others clung to that as they groped in the smoke.
>
> They located the "heart" of the fire in the basement of No. 231, returned and got two lines of hose, with which they put out the fire in twenty minutes. The damage was $10,000.

An explosion and fire in a cigar box factory at 637 East 17th Street during the afternoon of April 1, 1915 sent the panicked workers fleeing the building. The fire apparently started in a sawmill on the first floor, the explosion shattering the rear wall. As FDNY companies went to work in the suffocating smoke Commissioner Adamson and Chief Kenlon were on scene to watch as firemen carried an unconscious woman from an adjoining building.

Several minutes later the members of Rescue 1 proved their worth when four firemen, including Battalion Chief McGuire, were overcome on the roof of No. 643. The rescue men, grabbed scaling ladders and climbed up to reach the downed men. They revived the men then helped them to the street.

Five firemen, including a member of Rescue 1, were overcome battling a blaze in a three-story dyehouse at 353 East 58th Street on the afternoon of April 16, 1915. Workers were driven from the basement with cries of "Fire!" Companies arrived and lines were stretched into the building. The thick smoke had a distinct "chemical taste" but the men pressed on until a backdraft drove them out. Several men fell where they were.

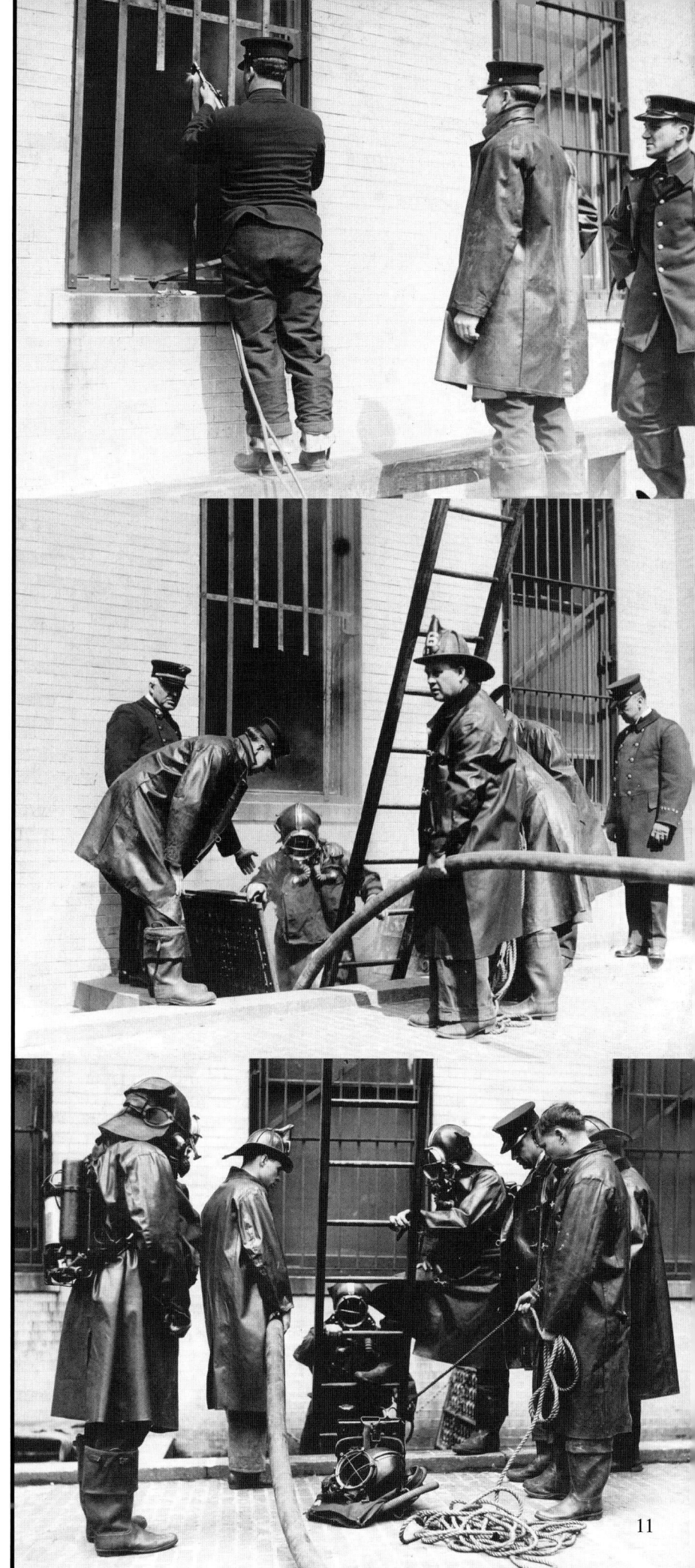

Top: *In a series of photos taken at the Fire College on East 68th Street by Hon. Chief Albert Dreyfous, the rescue men demonstrate their tools and abilities. Above Fireman John Ryan cuts iron window bars using a cutting torch. (Connecticut Firemen's Historical Society)*

Middle: *Capt. McElligott helps a rescue man emerging from a smoke filled cellar wearing Draeger helmet. Note the bars missing above where Ryan had used the torch.*

Bottom: *A smoke helmeted rescue man descends into the cellar. This photo appeared on the front cover of the 1915 FDNY Annual Report. (Connecticut Firemen's Historical Society)*

Rescue 1 arrived and Captain McElligott, Lt. Hotchkiss, Fireman Alfred Kinsella and two other rescue men donned the smoke helmets and entered the blazing basement. They pushed a hand line down a hallway and were driven back by another backdraft. As they tried to regroup Fireman Kinsella's smoke helmet was knocked from his head and he was immediately rendered unconscious. He was helped from the building and quickly revived. Despite some minor burns he re-donned his helmet and joined in the final extinguishment of the stubborn flames.

The method of company operations using the smoke helmets was as simple in design as the helmets themselves were complicated to use and maintain. After the rescue officer conferred with the chief and it was decided the company would operate, several members of the unit would put on the helmets and using a guide rope, enter the fire building. The remaining members would wait outside, monitoring the progress of both the rescue men operating inside, and the fire conditions within the building.

Using the guide rope for communications, a simple system of prearranged tugs kept both the inside team and those outside in touch with each other. Members outside could quickly gear up in their smoke helmets if needed, to relieve or rescue their counterparts inside. This system would be used for many years. The telephone system built in to some of the helmets was only used for the most unusual incidents.

Another acid case was on April 22, 1915 at 206-208 Canal Street. A large quantity of sulfuric and nitric acid had leaked on the third floor of the building. Dense clouds of pungent vapor were formed as flames broke out. Again, first arriving units were forced out of the building by the toxic mixture. Rescue 1 was special called and upon their arrival searched and found a thirty-two-gallon cauldron filled with bubbling chemicals. They formed a bucket brigade, and under the direction of Lt. Hotchkiss bailed the nitric and sulfuric acids out of an immense tank. The acid was then dumped in the street and neutralized. The acid fumes disintegrated the uniforms of the rescue men. Seventeen firemen, including rescue men, were taken ill; one of the first arriving captains was forced to retire from the department due to the effects of the fumes.

Rescue would prove again their worth rather quickly while operating at 442 Pearl Street on April 27, 1915. At the height of the blaze several firemen staggered from the smoke filled cellar and collapsed in the street overcome by a combination of smoke and natural gas that was leaking in the cellar. The quick and effective use of the pulmotors by members of Rescue 1 made the difference for these brothers, who were resuscitated on the spot in an era when street medicine and a public ambulance services did not exist.

> Time after time and fire after fire, the members of Rescue 1 would revive firemen and civilians from the effects of smoky fires, chemical, ammonia and gas leaks.

Time after time and fire after fire, the members of Rescue 1 would revive firemen and civilians from the effects of smoky fires, chemical, ammonia and gas leaks.

The new company's impact was being covered in newspapers across the country as well, as respected journals such as *Scientific American*. In the March 27, 1915 issue of *Scientific American* a full-page story chronicled New York City's need for a rescue squad and the establishment and training of the company. Photos featured members of Rescue 1 wearing their smoke helmets.

Members of the company demonstrate resuscitation using a pulmotor. The company became renowned for their use of these life-saving tools. (Connecticut Firemen's Historical Society)

Members of Rescue 1 wearing smoke helmets march in 1915 Medal Day parade.

Chief Kenlon used the paid department's Fiftieth Anniversary parade and medal ceremony on Saturday June 12th to showcase the new rescue unit and their equipment. The parade was led by former volunteer firemen who drew antique hand pumpers from Fifth Avenue and 45th Street to the Firemen's Monument on Riverside Drive at 100th Street, where a reviewing stand had been erected.

Eight members of the department were singled out for extraordinary heroism during the previous year and were awarded medals to the cheers of the huge crowd. Exhibitions of calisthenics and scaling ladders led into a demonstration of the smoke helmets, cutting torch and pulmotor. A fireboat display in the Hudson across from the monument brought the event to a spectacular conclusion.

Sometime in early 1915, Fireman Francis Blessing of Engine 33, who was one of the most experienced department chauffeurs, was detailed to the company as the primary chauffeur. Blessing who had quite a name for himself after a dramatic scaling ladder rescue attempt at the Equitable Building fire in 1912, had served as Chief Kenlon's chauffeur from 1910 until 1913. Blessing would become noted for his driving skills as he wheeled the high-powered rescue rig through the streets of the city.

The company was also being utilized for other unusual fire situations, such as the ship fire on July 24, 1915. The fire was in the S.S. *Cragside*, docked at the foot of West 23rd Street, North River. The ship, filled with sugar, was bound for Europe when flames broke out in the hold. By the time the first fire units arrived the interior of the ship was so hot and smoky firemen could not approach the opening leading below decks. Rescue 1 arrived and members donned smoke helmets and stretched a line deep into the ship's hold. Under extreme conditions they located the seat of the fire and were able to extinguish the flames.

Rescue 1 fireman pauses on a ladder after operating in the burning cargo hold of the S.S. Cragside. *The fire occurred on July 24, 1915 at the foot of West 23rd Street.*

It was 3:30 in the afternoon on August 15, 1915 when Rescue 1 responded to an ammonia leak in what was said to be the largest ammonia installation in the country—Ruppert's Brewery at 205 East 92nd Street. First arriving units found vast quantities of gas escaping at great pressure. The break was in a two-inch supply pipe on top of some condensers on the first floor. A similar accident had occurred in the plant before, that one taking eight hours to shut off.

Rescue 1 arrived and the men donned their smoke helmets and under the command of Captain McElligott went straight to work. The leak was controlled in ten minutes, but overall control and venting took an hour and a half.

Another special call brought Rescue 1 to the Hotel Biltmore shortly after midnight when an ammonia pipe exploded, far below the street, killing one employee and causing a panic within the famous hotel as the building began to fill with the escaping gas. As soon as Rescue 1 arrived they helmeted up and entered the cellar. They worked their way through the damaged parts of the cellar and were able to shut down the ammonia based refrigeration system. They then turned their attention to recovering the body of the dead worker. It took the rescue men more than a half hour to disentangle the man.

A leaking tank of sulpher chloride drove back first alarm units on September 7, 1915. Rescue 1 responded to the United States Rubber Company's laboratory at 561 West 58th Street and conferred with the chemist outside the building. Dr. Whitleson, the chief chemist, had found the leaking tank after several employees began coughing violently. Despite his warning, that the slightest defect in their helmets might mean death, the company prepared for action. Helmeted rescue firemen entered the cellar, located and raised the tank to the street where it was transferred to a new container and sealed.

A month later, the department battled a difficult blaze fed by films stored in the studio and offices of the Famous Players Film Company, in the old Ninth Regiment Armory Building at 213 West 26th Street. Flames were leaping 200-feet into the air and were visible for miles around the city as the battle commenced. The September 11, 1915 fire severely taxed the men as toxic smoke from the burning celluloid took its toll on firefighters and civilians. Five-alarms were transmitted for Manhattan Box 375 bringing 25 engines, five ladder companies and two water towers. Members of Rescue 1 wearing smoke helmets made their way to the adjoining roof, then climbed ladders to the roof of the blazing building attempting to complete their assignment of roof ventilation. (This is probably the first time in the history of the fire service that roof ventilation was accomplished by firefighters using breathing apparatus).

They had just opened skylights and scuttles when an explosion beneath them caused the roof to begin sagging beneath their feet. They quickly scrambled back to the ladders and climbed to safety as the roof disappeared into the flames below. Water towers were set up and dozens of streams were directed at the doomed structure.

One of the major incidents of 1915 occurred on September 22. A huge explosion occurred at a subway tunnel construction site at 7th Avenue and 23rd Street. The blast caused a huge section of the street to cave-in just as a trolley car filled with passengers approached the scene. The trolley car plunged through the temporary planking on the street crashing into the bottom of the excavation trench. First due fire companies carefully made their way to the dozens of passengers trapped in the tangled wreckage. Rescue 1 went to work with their special tools digging, cutting, jacking and shoring the fractured wooden forms extricating trapped victims from beneath tons of debris. Special calls were transmitted to bring extra manpower without apparatus to help in the rescue effort. In all seven persons were killed and eighty-five were injured at this extended operation.

In 1916, Rescue 1 increased its workload by responding to a greater number of alarms. The company rolled on 253 alarms and worked at 182 "jobs". The company was being used for more and varied assignments. During 1916, Rescue 1 was assigned to thirty-three street boxes on the first alarm. These boxes were in the most dangerous area of the city, the manufacturing and dry goods district. Known ominously to FDNY firemen as "Hell's Hundred Acres". Some of the most difficult and dangerous fires ever fought in the city were battle within the confines of this lower Manhattan neighborhood. These were the days before sprinkler, masks and fire laws were passed to protect citizens and firemen alike.

One of the special tools carried by Rescue 1 was the Blau gas torch (German for blue gas). A cutting torch fueled by a propane-like fuel consisting of hydrogen and other hydrocarbon gases. This very fuel was later used to propel Germany's famed Graf Zeppelin. Although members of the company had spent hours of practice and each had become proficient in its use, the torch had never been used "in anger".

That would change however in the year 1916, when the torch was fired up eight times. The first reported use of the torch was January 20th when it was used to free a horse trapped between a wall and a railing at 1-5 Bond Street. The first recorded life saving use of the cutting device was during a fire at 438-440 Pearl Street on February 6, 1916, just doors away from the location where they had resuscitated overcome firemen months earlier.

During the fire Barney Miles, a member of the Fire Patrol, became lost in the dense smoke in the cellar and was barely able to find a window. Trapped behind iron bars he shouted for help, but firemen could do little to assist him as he fell unconscious a victim of the carbon monoxide laced smoke. Moments later, members of Rescue 1 arrived, the torch was ignited and in a matter of minutes the bars were cut and cleared and the unconscious man was pulled to safety. This was the first of many rescues the company would be credited with.

Several weeks later Rescue 1 was called to another unusual emergency. A thirty year-old man was trying to cross Broadway, between 23rd Street and 24th Streets, when two trolley cars, traveling in opposite directions, reached him at the same time in the middle of the street, wedging him between the cars. The operators brought the cars to screeching halts before inflicting any further injuries to the man. But there he was, pinned between the cars with a broken shoulder and numerous contusions. Rescue 1 arrived and carried various tools to the site. With thousands of pedestrians watching they methodically went to work: a team began first aid, as other members started cutting the steel window bars that entrapped the injured man. As the last bar was cleared, he was carefully hoisted by rope from between the cars to the roof of the trolley car. He was then handed over for medical attention.

The company was at work again on the morning of March 31, 1916 when they were summoned to 76 Pine Street the laboratory of the Bielfoil Chemical Works. The owner, making phosphorous trichloride, was unable to control escaping chlorine gas as tubing of his apparatus became disconnected. The lab filled with the toxic gas and a fire started. Members of Rescue 1 entered the lab wearing their smoke helmets and were able to control the leak and carry the defective apparatus outside.

On April 29, 1916 at 9:40 a.m. FDNY units were sent to 76 Pine Street, The Niagara Chemical Company, for a reported building fire. First due units could not stay inside for very long as clouds of toxic vapor drove them from the building and

Rescue work at subway construction explosion and cave-in 7th Avenue and 23rd Street, September 22, 1915.

Rescue 1 members and other firemen removing the injured from accident site.

out into the street. The five-story building housed a number of chemical companies on the various floors. It became so bad outside the building that FDNY horses were being driven from the area. Chemists forced from the building and others from nearby buildings overwhelmed the fire chief with advice, but no two of the chemists agreed. Many claimed the vapor was chlorine gas, others said sodium oxide, which is created by a mixture of water and metallic sodium. With no actual fire in the building the hoses were withdrawn but remained nearby just in case.

Half of the Rescue 1 crew donned smoke helmets and tied ropes around their waists before entering the toxic cloud. The remaining members of the company, with smoke helmets at the ready, tended the ropes of those inside. The Rescue 1 members were very familiar with this building having handled a chlorine gas leak there a month earlier. Carefully bottles of phosphorus tri chloride were removed. Then bottles, carboys, barrels and other containers filled with chemicals of all kinds were carried to the street. The air began clearing and things returned to normal.

The torch would be used to save another life, this a time a civilian's on May 10, 1916 when the company was called to 82 Beaver Street to help free a 16 year-old messenger boy pinned between an elevator car and the wall between the fifth and sixth floors. A call to the fire department a little before 5 p.m. brought Ladder 15 to the scene, they then special called Rescue 1. As the torch began its work a small fire broke out in the elevator pit adding to the difficulty of the operation. This fire was quickly extinguished as the cutting continued. For more than two hours rescue firemen carefully cut away a steel door piece by piece pulling it from the shaft. Then the flooring of the car was cut away to expose the four-inch thick steel boarder beam imprisoning the trapped youth. A doctor injected morphine into the badly injured boy to ease his pain, as the last of the cuts were made. He was carefully removed and sent to the hospital with two badly broken legs, but amazingly no internal injuries.

> Firemen had their hands full as the dense smoke refused to lift. Deputy Chief "Smoky Joe" Martin transmitted second and third alarms hoping to gain an edge on the stubborn blaze.

One of the company's original members, Fireman John F. Mooney who'd transferred into Rescue 1 from Ladder 4, left Rescue 1 on June 16, 1916 and was assigned to Hook & Ladder 137. Mooney would serve there briefly before retiring. Taking his place was Fireman John W. Donohue who crossed the floor from Engine 33. Fireman James Shaw, another original member, was promoted to Engineer of Steamer on July 7, 1916 and was assigned to Engine 21. Taking his place on the roster Fireman James Smith was transferred from Engine 74. Smith a former Landsman in the United States Navy was the only member of the FDNY to have been awarded the Congressional Medal of Honor. His citation in part read: In action with the relief expedition of the Allied forces in China during the battles of 13, 20, 21, and 22 June 1900. Throughout this period and in the presence of the enemy, Smith distinguished himself by meritorious conduct. This was during the Boxer Rebellion.

On July 13, 1916, Rescue 1 responded to 422 Sumner Avenue in Brooklyn when an ammonia refrigerating machine exploded collapsing the four-story brick building. Helmeted members of Rescue 1 searched the collapsed building trying to locate trapped victims. Conditions were so severe that despite the smoke helmets they could only operate for short periods of time. The company removed at least 5 bodies the first several hours, and continued digging with the assistance of 100 firemen until all were recovered.

A few minutes before six in the evening on July 14, 1916, John Cummings, a private in the National Guard, was mopping the second floor hallway inside the arsenal building at 35th Street and Seventh Avenue in Manhattan. Busy with his custodial duties he was startled to see smoke pouring from a room along the south side of the building. As he moved closer to investigate, fifty rounds of ammunition discharged due to the building heat condition. Cummings dropped his mop and ran to warn the sixty-two other people working in the structure.

Charles Lenz, an engineer working on some rifles nearby, heard the detonation of the cartridges and also went to investigate. Seeing the rapidly developing fire, he dashed directly to the magazine, hoping to avert a catastrophic explosion of the stored munitions. Swinging open the large steel door, he stepped inside and opened the main emergency water valve. Slamming the heavy door closed, he left the water to do its work as he hurried from the building.

Meanwhile, Major W.A. Niver received news of the fire and telephoned the Manhattan fire dispatcher's office directly, then hurried to the street to meet the arriving fire apparatus.

As workers were evacuating the building, two men, Private Andrew Moran and Tom McNally a truck driver, reentered the arsenal and began removing army trucks stored inside. The duo successfully removed several trucks and despite the severe conditions entered the building once again to get more. Clouds of thick noxious smoke pumped throughout the structure and hung over the entire neighborhood in a choking blanket. Moran materialized through the miasma at the wheel of yet another vehicle and pulled it to the curb. Waiting in the street and watching the smoke filled truck door, he realized McNally had not exited after their last foray and quickly reported the missing man to his superiors. One hour later McNally was found by firemen, unconscious and wedged between a truck and a pile of barrels. He was dragged outside, then given the Last Rites after all efforts to resuscitate him failed.

Firemen had their hands full as the dense smoke refused to lift. Deputy Chief "Smoky Joe" Martin transmitted second and third alarms hoping to gain an edge on the stubborn blaze. Fireman John B. Corrigan of Hook & Ladder 4, was venting windows along the third floor when he came across an unconscious fireman slumped on the floor. Corrigan dragged the man to a window and called for help. Below on a ladder Fireman Walter O'Leary of Rescue 1 was operating a high-pressure hose through a straight nozzle when he heard the call for help from above. Calling to the street to shut down the line O'Leary wasted no time and ascended the ladder with the writhing hoseline tucked under his arm. Corrigan was able to lift the unconscious man out the window and across O'Leary's arms.

While controlling the twisting hose and managing the weight of the unconscious man at the same time, O'Leary started down the ladder. Each step was a challenge as the pressure of the hose threatened to topple them both at any time. When O'Leary and the unconscious fireman were about halfway down the ladder the correct high pressure hydrant connection was identified and shut down. The hose went limp making his descent a bit easier. Upon reaching the ground, members of Rescue 1 moved in with a pulmotor and resuscitated the unconscious man. Fireman John P. McNamee of Engine 16 would suffer a throbbing headache but would live to fight many more fires.

It was just after 11 am, on September 16, 1916 when two trains, the Washington Express and an electric engine pulling empty cars, collided in the Pennsylvania Tube, Tenth Avenue between 32nd and 33rd Streets in Manhattan. Fire Department units entered the tube and assessed the situation: Seven passengers and seven train workers were injured, several of them pinned in the wreckage. Rescue 1 moved in and began cutting away the mangled steel and splintered wood of the damaged

A rope rifle being used at the Fire College. This not only became a valuable rescue tool, but the symbol of New York City rescue companies.

railcars. One train worker, Conductor William H. Pierson of Washington D.C. was trapped between the train car and the electric engine. Using their torch, members of Rescue 1 worked for more than an hour carefully cutting away the twisted steel that imprisoned the seriously injured conductor. He was carefully carried from the crash site and taken to a nearby hospital.

The first individual department recognition for valor by a member of Rescue 1 was as a result of actions that occurred on October 25, 1916, during a spectacular fire that swept through a seven-story loft building at 21-23 East Houston Street. Fireman Thomas Kilbride, a ten-year veteran who had been cited for bravery five previous times while assigned to Ladder Company 1, would make another death defying rescue at this fire.

The burning loft building adjoined a tenement at the front, but about twenty feet back from the street an airshaft, fifteen feet wide, separated the walls of the two buildings. This gave the loft the shape of an "L" if viewed from above. Seven men and seven women were trapped on the roof of the burning loft waving and crying for help.

Firemen burst onto the roof of the adjoining building, sizing up the situation across from them. Numerous people were calling for help from the burning building but out of the firemen's reach. Acting Chief Farley took one look at the fire situation and people trapped and ran to the front parapet, calling for ladders to be brought to his location. Behind him, through the heavy smoke the outline of a man began to take shape at a fifth floor window of the fire building, just across the shaft. A frantic man climbed out onto the iron window shutter trying to escape the scalding heat within the blazing building. Clinging there, he looked back and forth to the roof of the building next door, only a dozen feet away. A dozen feet with a five-story drop looming below any false step. Stammering for help, he considered a possible jump, but realized he would never make it.

Thomas Kilbride of Rescue 1 also raced to the roof of the adjoining building. To his left, firemen were at the front of the building, pulling up heavy wooden fire ladders. Just in front of him was the trapped man calling for help. Kilbride quickly scanned the roof top. Then turning back to the trapped man he yelled "Hold on!", as he dashed towards the rear of the roof where an old water tank ladder lay abandoned near some construction debris. Hurrying back to the shaft, he placed the butt of the rickety ladder on the coping tiles of the parapet wall and lowered it towards the shutter and the trapped man. The ladder now bridged the shaft between the fire building and the adjoining structure resting precariously on the iron shutter perpendicular to the building's windows.

Kilbride stepped up onto the ladder and climbed carefully, edging his way upwards to the trapped man as a swirling cloud of smoke enveloped them both. Through the smoke he shouted, "Keep your arms straight ahead, straight ahead!"

Shifting his weight Kilbride reached up blindly through the smoke. As his finger tips found the man the fireman latched onto him with all his might. Blindly, the man took hold of his shoulders as he ordered. Straining, Kilbride lifted the man from the shutter and lowered him to the ladder. Eyes tearing from the hot smoke, he guided the man down stopping only when their vision became totally obscured. Carefully they stepped onto the roof and Kilbride pointed the way to the stairs.

As other firemen made the roof of the adjoining building, a series of unbelievable scaling ladder rescue began. Members of Rescue 1 fired a line of rope from the rope rifle up and over the roof of the blazing structure then a larger rope was pulled up. Several people were able to escape using this rope.

For his actions at this fire Thomas Kilbride found himself on the steps of City Hall on July 17, 1917 where Mayor John Purroy Mitchel pinned a second Department Medal on his chest. This was the first medal awarded to a member of Rescue Company 1.

A smoky fire in the subway on November 7, 1916 left forty persons overcome, with many inside the tunnel near the emergency exit at 104th Street and Central Park West. As firemen guided and carried up victims, Rescue 1 set up a first aid station on the grass of Central Park. Using a pulmotor, they pumped oxygen into the lungs of those overcome. Most were rapidly revived and only three required hospitalization.

On November 13, 1916 Lieutenant Edwin A. Hotchkiss was promoted to Captain and remained in Rescue 1 until he was transferred to Ladder 12 on December 1, 1916. Lieutenant Benjamin F. Parker from Engine 14 would fill the open spot in the rescue company.

The sudden collapse of a concrete garage under construction at 64th Street and Third Avenue had Rescue 1 special called to the box. One worker was killed and seven others were injured by the collapse where Rescue 1 and three engines and two ladder companies worked under the direction of Deputy Chief Hayes.

A serious fire broke out in the subcellar of the Park and Tilford Company located at 72nd Street and Columbus Avenue around 4 o'clock on the afternoon of December 27, 1916. Members of Engines 56 and 74 and Ladder 25 entered the building and made their way to the subcellar. There they confronted a raging fire. Under the direction of Battalion Chief McKenna, the companies began to move in, working hose streams ahead of them. They had managed to push the flames back into one corner of the room when suddenly several carboys (large glass containers) of ammonia, used in an ice making plant, exploded. The explosions toppled the firemen and sent waves of noxious ammonia gas throughout the close quarters of the subcellar.

Fire officers and their men stumbled blindly, the fumes strangling them as they took each breath. Man after man staggered to the street and collapsed, their lungs, throats and eyes burning from the horrid gas. As the last members of Engine 74, closest to the blast and the most seriously effected, helped each other to the street the Rescue reported to the chief.

Captain McElligott and his men, wearing smoke helmets, plunged into the swirling caldron of heat and gas. They conducted a quick search, aiding a few firemen still searching for injured comrades. With the subcellar cleared of injured personnel, Rescue 1 manned the hoselines and began a tense battle with the blazing rooms before them. For nearly an hour, they worked the hoses cooling the searing hot walls and ceilings, and pushing back waves of fire. As the secondary searches were being finished Captain McElligott fell to the floor, overcome with fumes and exhaustion. He had used up all the oxygen in his smoke helmet, but refused to leave until a thorough search was done and the last of the flames were quelled. His men lifted him from the two-and-a-half feet of water and dragged him to the street placing him in the hands of Doctor Archer.

Amazingly no lives were lost at this operation but many firemen, McElligott included, suffered serious injuries due to the conditions they encountered. To allow him some time to recuperate Chief Kenlon detailed Captain McElligott to the fireboats. Kenlon then designated Lieutenant Benjamin Parker company commander.

On February 7, 1917, after speeches by several civic dignitaries, Fire Commissioner Robert Adamson introduced Chief John Kenlon to a crowd of more than 3,000 people filling Carnegie Hall. As part of a spectacular demonstration of how the fire department worked, the chief strolled across the stage and stood before a three-story "building" that would soon have flames projected onto it by moving picture camera. The chief pulled a prop fire alarm box wired directly to the dispatchers for the occasion. Thirty-seven seconds later the crowd could hear Engine 23 responding from their quarters on 58th Street and Broadway. Moments later a line was being stretched up the center aisle and within four minutes the auditorium was swarming with an entire first alarm assignment to the delight of the crowd.

Members of Rescue 1 appeared on stage and cut away steel bars blocking the windows of the mock building. Other rescue men in smoke helmets, entered the building and performed a "rescue". The victim was turned over to other rescue men who revived him using pulmotors. Other firemen ascended the facade using scaling ladders, slid ropes and jumped into life nets behind them. The exhibition was given as part of a Civic Forum showing the department's role as a vital part of city life.

The terminal equipment of the Mexican Telegraph Company, in the basement of 66 Broad Street caught fire during the early morning hours of February 13, 1917. FDNY units were led to the seat of the fire by the building engineer and within minutes the engineer and several firemen lay unconscious on the basement floor. Members of Rescue 1 wearing smoke helmets found the unconscious men and brought them to the street as other firemen vented sidewalk deadlights to help vent the smoke. (Deadlights or vault lights are glass blocks or iron-framed glass bulbs that allowed light to enter basements and cellars through sidewalks, before electricity was used.) When the downed men were all accounted for, the fire was knocked down with hose streams directed through the broken deadlights. Fire companies then moved in and extinguished the remaining pockets of fire.

The janitor of the building at 9 West 28th Street decided to improvise insect control when he set a can of chemicals on fire in the cellar. The space quickly filled with choking smoke driving the man outside. As the fumes filled the building the FDNY was called. The services of Rescue 1 were requested and they, wearing the Draeger helmets, were able to locate and remove the smoking can.

It was clear now, one of the things the Rescue Company could do, that none of the other fire companies could, was operate in noxious fumes. Their smoke helmets gave the protection they needed to utilize their specialized training and tools even in the worst conditions. A case in point was their response March 7, 1917 to a third-alarm at 311 West 59th Street. Five large drums of chlorine gas, damaged by fire, failed and the escaping fumes swept across firemen operating in the building and also drifted into a nearby theatre. Five hundred people were removed from the theatre without incident, but the firemen inside the fire building were not so lucky as man after man fell unconscious. Dozens of men at a time were laid out on the sidewalks outside overcome by the gas. One fireman remarked they had their "first taste of trench warfare." (Chlorine was one of the deadly gases used during the First World War.)

Upon their arrival the rescue men, under the command of Acting Lt. Thomas Kilbride, put on smoke helmets and plunged into the building removing a number of firemen too weak to move and too injured to cry for help. On the roof several firemen were overcome after venting a hole and being overwhelmed by the escaping gas. They had to be lowered by rope to an adjacent roof. A number of men suffered serious effects from the leaking gas but luckily none were killed.

Three young boys were playing a game of marbles on the sidewalk near the electric plant at 14th Street and Avenue C on the sunny afternoon of May 3, 1917. Suddenly the sidewalk beneath them collapsed plunging the three lads into a huge water filled hole that had been undermining the sidewalk for sometime. A street cleaner who was working nearby by heard their cries and summoned help. Then he and another man jumped into the water filled crater and helped keep two of the boys afloat. FDNY units arrived and pulled the men and boys to the street. Rescue 1 arrived and when informed a boy was still missing in the muddy water below Frank Clark wearing a smoke helmet, plunged under the water. For several minutes he searched the mud blackened waters trying to locate the youth without success. As his helmet began to fill with water he was forced to abandon his search. (This was probably the first FDNY underwater rescue attempt). A professional hard-hat diver later found the boy wedged under some bracing.

A fire started in the cupola of City Hall on May 10, 1917. The Fire Commissioner, Robert Adamson, was in the building at the time of the fire and transmitted the alarm by telephone to the Manhattan dispatcher's office. Within minutes first due units rolled up and went to work on the stubborn blaze. Rescue 1 operated for several hours at this fire.

The annual presentation of medals by the FDNY was held in City College Stadium. After a large parade featuring old and new fire apparatus the Medals for valor were presented, including a Department Medal to Rescue 1 Fireman Thomas Kilbride for his dramatic rescue on East Houston Street on October 25, 1916. After the presentation of awards a large demonstration was held in the huge midfield area where a large structure had been built for the occasion.

With the large crowd, including the mayor, fire commissioner, Chief Kenlon and a delegation that included the Russian Ambassador, an exhibition of response and fire fighting followed. It included a demonstration by Rescue 1 who cut iron beams with their torches and then put on smoke helmets, disappearing into the thick smoke inside the temporary building.

The Union League Club, a social and political organization was formed in New York City in 1863 during the Civil War with the twin goals of cultivating "a profound national devotion" and to strengthen "a love and respect for the nation." Early members of the club included: the cartoonist Thomas Nast, John Jay, Teddy Roosevelt, U.S. Grant and a number of former presidents. Their building located at Thirty-ninth Street and Fifth Avenue was designed to be a quiet sanctuary and a relief from the hustle of the city for its members and their guests. This tranquility was disturbed on September 4, 1917, when an employee cleaning the boiler, became trapped inside one of the horizontal tubular sections. After working inside the hot confined space for a time, he found he could no longer fit through the sixteen by twelve inch opening and the 105-degree temperature had an ill effect on him. Other building workers arrived and suggested he remove all his clothes and cover himself with grease. After two attempts to pull him through the opening failed, the building engineer called for Rescue 1.

The company arrived and sized up the job. Acting Lieutenant John Ryan called for the acetylene torch and as a small audience of club members, each a former army and navy officer, watched with professional interest. In a matter of minutes the boilerplate was carefully cut away and the weary man was freed.

Captain John J. McElligott, who'd been detailed to the fireboats since he was almost killed operating in the cellar of the Park & Tilford's store at 72nd and Columbus Avenue the

> It was clear now, one of the things the Rescue Company could do, that none of the other fire companies could, was operate in noxious fumes. Their smoke helmets gave the protection they needed to utilize their specialized training and tools even in the worst conditions.

previous December, was officially transferred to Engine 78 the fireboat moored at East 99th Street and the East River.

The company was special called on September 14, 1917 to the Express Office at 397-401 Tenth Avenue at 2:25 in the morning. Bottles of nitric acid encased in a wooden box were broken and leaking. Nitric acid is a highly corrosive and toxic, strong mineral acid that is used in the production of fertilizers, explosives, etching and the distillation of metals especially gold. The fumes were so strong companies could not enter. Rescue 1 arrived and smoke helmeted members removed the acid to the street and neutralized it. They also vented the building and neutralized the acid which had leaked on the floor. This was an extremely large floor space and was heavily stocked. An enormous loss was prevented by the quick actions of the company.

On November 1, 1917 Francis Blessing, who'd been promoted to Lieutenant the previous June, returned to the company as an officer. The thirty-two year-old Blessing had made quite a reputation for himself since joining the department in 1907. Blessing was already on the Roll of Merit three times, including a Class II for his scaling ladder rescue attempt and other actions at the Equitable fire in 1912. As a fireman he was detailed to Rescue 1 shortly after the company was organized, yet was not officially transferred to the unit until March 16, 1917.

An automobile chauffeur became wedged upside down between the elevator and the shaft wall of the loft building at 504 East 75th Street the evening of November 7, 1917. Rescue 1 and members of Ladder 13 worked together as a priest gave the trapped man the Last Rites. Rescue men cut away the iron supports pinning the man who was imprisoned seventy-five feet above the floor of the shaft. A life net had been placed beneath him as a precaution, and as he was freed the injured man was carefully dropped down to the net below.

The war in Europe was in full swing and German saboteurs were very busy in the United States trying to stop materials bound for the Western Front from ever leaving America. Their destructive efforts were testing the abilities of the FDNY and other fire departments across the nation.

A fire of mysterious origin broke out underneath the Municipal Pier at the foot of East 24th Street on which hundreds of thousands of dollars of naval supplies were stored. The fire, burning under the flooring of the pier 400-feet out from the shoreline was discovered and a first alarm was transmitted. It was late on Thursday evening November 8, 1917. Some pier personnel and Marines, stationed to protect the stores, attempted to fight the fire while help was summoned. Due to the difficult location of the fire the Marines, the first arriving land units and even the fireboat could not hit the flames directly with a hose stream. Rescue 1 with a cache of torches and hand tools, made their way to a position above the seat of the fire and were able to cut through the steel flooring and the wooden pier below it to expose the fire.

Days later November 11, 1917, four separate fires in different locations were set within the five- and six-story Washburn Wire Company factory buildings located at 117th Street and 118th Street along the East River. Just after midnight flames tore through the huge complex and Rescue 1 was assigned to the fire which quickly reached five-alarms. Early in the fire an explosion caused a wall collapse that narrowly missed killing several firemen, many firemen were injured however. The falling bricks also demolished the hose wagon of Engine 58 and Water Tower 3.

Apparently, the war had reached American shores.

As the company's unique abilities became better recognized by the chief officers of the department their roles at fires and emergencies became greater. The city and especially the firefighters suffered through the coldest three-month period in its history during December 1917 through February 1918. The average daily temperature was 25.7 degrees in Central Park. For sixty-seven consecutive days the temperature averaged less than twenty-degrees, and on more than one occasion touched fifteen-degrees below zero. This brought about an unusual congestion of freight on piers and railroad terminals. Many vital sprinkler systems throughout the city were frozen and rendered useless for firefighting.

When a huge ammonia pipe inside the Bellevue Hospital power house burst on January 2, 1918 Rescue 1 was special called to the scene. The temperature inside the hospital had dropped 15-degrees and extra blankets were being placed on the patients as the rescue company devised a plan.

The chief engineer of the plant, Wilmer McInzer, donned a smoke helmet and led members of Rescue 1 through the labyrinth of pipes to the location of the damaged pipe. The rescue men shut off the flowing ammonia and vented the space before the fumes could reach the hospital.

Beginning at 8:30 pm, January 4, 1918, Manhattan fire companies started what would become one of the longest and coldest nights in department history. Units battled a two-alarm fire in a six-story loft building at 444 Broadway under freezing conditions. As this fire was being brought under control another major fire, in a six-story building on Mulberry Street came in. This huge building was filled with cardboard boxes. Chief Kenlon, Deputy Chief Binns and the members of Rescue 1, already coated in ice, responded to the fire. Upon arrival Kenlon transmitted a fourth alarm and began efforts to keep the flames from spreading to nearby buildings.

> The city and especially the firefighters suffered through the coldest three-month period in its history during December 1917 through February 1918. The average daily temperature was 25.7 degrees in Central Park. For sixty-seven consecutive days the temperature averaged less than twenty-degrees, and on more than one occasion touched fifteen-degrees below zero.

A crossfire of water sprays showered the fire ground causing ice to coat the structures, fire apparatus and the firemen. The situation was becoming so bad that firemen had to literally chip the ice off each other, to keep from freezing in place where they stood. In addition, water pressure problems prolonged the operation until 11 o'clock.

Upon their return to quarters on Great Jones Street Chief Kenlon and the men of Rescue 1 were so encrusted in ice that jets of steam were used to free them from their fire coats. The newspapers quoted the new Fire Commissioner Thomas Drennan the next day remarking, "It is difficult to appreciate the terrible conditions under which firemen work. This has been an eye-opener. The job of a fireman is certainly not enviable. The men I have seen working tonight are heroes."

Just after noon on January 16, 1918, a member of the department was walking past the six-story brick building at 343-345 West 36th Street when he noticed smoke coming from the structure. The alarm was transmitted and companies rolled in quickly. Fireman John F. Kocher of Engine 54 pulled the nozzle and a line of hose off his rig and moved towards the fire building as members of his unit continued the stretch behind him. The team waited by the door as the hose was flaked out then Lieutenant John Donaghey called for the line to be charged.

Neighbors had smelled smoke since 8 a.m. that morning, and now watched as dense smoke pumped from the warehouse. The nozzle team prepared to enter the warehouse, which was filled with stored theatrical scenery. Joined by Acting Battalion Chief Murtagh the officer nodded to his men and they all crawled forward disappearing into the smoke. After pressing in about thirty feet the floor began to collapse beneath them. Members of the nozzle team clawed the slopping wood floors calling to each other and shouting for help. Members of Rescue 1 moved in and began to pull the closest members to safety.

Fireman Frank Clark of Rescue 1 was able to reach the engine officer who was hanging on desperately as the pitch of the collapsing floor increased. Rescue officer Lt. Benjamin Parker directed his men into position and called for a hoseline as he pulled one of the trapped firemen clear of the blazing collapse area. Conditions were becoming so severe the continuing rescue effort was conducted under the covering spray of a hose stream. With a fireman holding his legs, Parker was lowered down to where he could reach the trapped acting chief. With extraordinary effort Parker dragged the acting chief up the steep incline. Lt. Parker returned for one more rescue attempt, but the complete collapse of the first floor and the fire conditions forced him back. Sadly one member, Fireman John F. Kocher of Engine 54 was killed as he slid into the blazing cellar.

The members of Rescue 1: Firemen Frank C. Clark, John Mayr, James Smith, John W. Donohue and John C. Conners were placed on the Roll Of Merit with Class II awards. Lt. Benjamin Parker was given a Class I and was awarded a Department Medal and the Thomas A. Kenny Memorial Medal. This was the first time this medal was ever awarded.

The company's special training and equipment came into play on April 11, 1918, when Rescue 1 was special called to Charles Street and the North River. Moored just off shore was the U.S.S. *Frank H. Buck*, a 6076 gross ton tanker built in 1914, owned by the Associated Oil Company until acquired by the Navy in 1918. Two pipe fitters were lowered into the ships hold and began making repairs. A navy quartermaster, Felix Taskowsky, who'd become concerned when the workers were not heard from, lowered himself into the hold. Several tense minutes later he signaled to be hauled up. Just as he approached the deck his strength gave out and he slipped from the noose of the rope.

The fire department responded, and wearing smoke helmets members of Rescue 1 under the command of Acting Lt. John Ryan were lowered into the hold. Searching, they found a compartment separating the engine room and the oil tank. The compartment, filled with deadly fumes, is where the overcome workers were located on the floor. The men were dragged back to the rope and each was hoisted to the deck, but all three could not be revived. For their dangerous confined space rescue operation Firemen John W. Donohue, John C. Conners and John P. Ryan were placed on the Roll of Merit with Class II awards.

A fire, followed by a series of explosions of ammonia fumes, rocked the new eleven-story Merchant's Refrigeration Company, a concrete refrigerating plant on Sixteenth Streets and the North River (Hudson). It was 7:32 p.m., on May 11, 1918 when James Vincent, an assistant engineer in the plant, turned in the alarm. He became asphyxiated by the fumes when a 225-ton compressor exploded, rupturing an ammonia pipe. The first arriving units were faced with a huge building covering an entire square block. Inside a major fire was burning compounded by a serious uncontrolled ammonia leak in the basement. To add to the problems, the assistant engineer had not escaped and was believed to still be inside.

Assistant Chief "Smoky Joe" Martin immediately transmitted a third alarm and special called Rescue 1 to the scene. Under the command of Lt. Parker the men using smoke helmets, split into teams, preparing to enter the basement from three different sides. Before they could begin, a huge explosion tore a twelve-foot square three hundred pound door across Eleventh Avenue injuring members of Ladder 12 and a score of soldiers who had been guarding the military stores within the plant.

Heavy ammonia fumes blanketed the street. Many firemen were overcome where they stood and operations were suspended for almost an hour before Chief Martin would allow Rescue to enter the building. The company was then able to shut off the flow of ammonia and locate and remove the dead worker.

The following day the Rescue was special called to Staten Island for a stubborn fire aboard a new freight ship moored at the pier of the Atlantic Dock Company in Tompkinsville. The company was taken by fireboat to the scene and members again wearing smoke helmets, climbed down into the hold of the ship. They were able to locate a difficult to reach fire in the coal bunkers, and immediately water was directed into the area. The company took up and returned to Manhattan by fireboat.

One of the most difficult and dangerous operations under taken by the members of Rescue 1 during the early years, or perhaps any year, took place on Saturday October 5, 1918. For security reasons the Navy Department did not make the story public until years later.

The Brooklyn Navy Yard was in full swing, its piers crowded with ships of all types, most of these laden with ammunition. At Pier 12, one of the largest types of submarines, an "O-class", was preparing to put out to sea; on board was its full complement of ordnance. Together with a nearby powder magazine and the other ships, there were enough munitions to wreck the Williamsburg Bridge and a good portion of Brooklyn—not to mention what a chain reaction would do to the nation's war fleet. Things were about to go wrong.

Submarine O-5 was built at the Fore River Ship Building Company of Quincy, Massachusetts, and was commissioned on June 8, 1918, with Lt. Commander George A. Trevor a Naval Academy graduate as its skipper.

O-5 had been operating prior to its New York arrival, patrolling along the Atlantic Coast from Cape Cod to Key West. It came to the Navy Yard to be readied for an Atlantic crossing with its division.

As preparations for the trip were underway, somehow the ventilator to the battery room was accidentally left closed. While trying the port engine on battery power, Lt. Comm. Trevor became aware of the build-up of hydrogen gas (created under certain conditions when the batteries were charging – a four percent mixture of hydrogen in the atmosphere would create a powerful explosive). Along with Ensign W. J. Sharkey, the skipper attempted to avert the pending disaster.

Suddenly, the after-battery exploded! Trevor, seriously injured, was forced from the area by the ensuing fire. Sharkey was missing and feared dead in the battery compartment area.

The crew, still under Lt. Comm. Trevor's command, made valiant efforts to control the flames. Extreme heat was building up, and the batteries began generating chlorine gas (formed when water mixed with the sulfuric acid in the batteries). Unable to cope with the deteriorating conditions, the sailors were forced to withdraw.

Realizing the need for assistance, Navy Yard officials called the New York City Fire Department. First-due units were confronted with a situation beyond their capabilities. Arriving at the scene, Deputy Chief Patrick Maher of Division 11 sized up the escalating conditions and special called Rescue Company 1.

The on-duty members: Firemen Thomas Kilbride, John Donohue, John Ryan, Frank Clark, James Smith and John Mayr — with Lieutenant Francis Blessing at the wheel raced from their quarters on Great Jones Street, Manhattan in the company's original rig, the 1914 Cadillac touring car.

A newspaper illustration shows the blazing submarine moored at the Brooklyn Navy Yard, on October 5, 1918. The members of Rescue 1 rescued crew members, off-loaded munitions and extinguished the fire.

Meanwhile D.C. Maher was discussing tactics and the chain-of-command with naval officials. Since the FDNY would be doing the firefighting, Maher stated he would be in charge. The naval officials reluctantly agreed.

When Rescue arrived, the chief advised Blessing of the situation: fire was raging in the battery and dynamo rooms and was venting through the front hatch, exposing a nearby powder magazine. There was also 20,000 gallons of diesel fuel on board and, to compound matters, Ensign Sharkey and two other sailors were missing below decks.

Blessing and two volunteers, Firemen Kilbride and Donohue, donned Draeger smoke helmets. They started down the rear hatch ladder into the sub, stretching a hoseline as they went. Two naval officers, also wearing smoke helmets accompanied them apparently to guide them through the unfamiliar submarine.

Meanwhile, on the pier, the other members of Rescue 1 began the dangerous task of unloading the powder magazine.

The advancing fire, dense smoke, deadly gases, lack of ventilation, and constant threat of another explosion confronted the men inside the sub as Lt. Blessing led them toward the fire area. They located two sailors overcome by the noxious atmosphere and were able to remove them to safety, then continued searching where they could as the hose was pulled into position.

The deadly flames were knocked down creating a scalding heat. Fireman Thomas Kilbride pressed ahead and located Ensign Sharkey, dead, in the aft battery compartment. The injured were rushed to the hospital. Unfortunately Lt. Comm. Trevor succumbed to his injuries nine days later. (Both men were posthumously awarded the Navy Cross.)

For their heroic actions, the FDNY placed Blessing, Kilbride and Donohue on the Roll of Merit with Class I ratings. Class II awards were given to Mayr, Clark, Ryan and Smith. On Medal Day Lt. Francis Blessing was awarded the Bennett and Department Medals, and Kilbride and Donohue were presented Department Medals.

A subway employee was killed and four others were severely injured when a two-car Lenox Avenue shuttle train jumped the tracks at 142nd Street and crashed into the iron pillars supporting the roof of the subway tunnel. It was 8 a.m., on December 8, 1918 when the train, traveling at a high rate of speed derailed with catastrophic results. The first car shot up at an extreme angle and almost broke in half, the second car rolled onto its side after shearing four steel pillars, then burst into flames. Rescue 1 was assigned and with Lt. Blessing at the wheel traveled from Great Jones Street to the crash site in fourteen minutes. The company immediately went to work with the oxyacetylene torch and cut the dead motorman out of the car in fifteen minutes.

Two weeks later, on December 16, 1918, Rescue 1 raced from Great Jones Street northward to the Upper Westside responding to a chemical fire that had broken out on the first floor of Havemeyer Hall in Columbia University. Students attempted to fight the blaze with extinguishers, but were driven back by the noxious gases generated by the combustion of the chemicals. First arriving fire companies faced the same problem and several firemen were knocked out as they ventured into the gas laced smoke. Rescue 1 arrived and equipped with their smoke helmets, were able to control the fire and separate the chemicals involved. The unconscious firemen were quickly revived and went back to work.

Without benefit of breathing protection the firefighters of New York City faced not only the deadly gases mixed in the smoke of burning materials, but leaks of illumination gas mixed in with the smoke would take a man to his knees in seconds and render him unconscious in less than a minute. Ammonia leaks left the arriving units nearly helpless, as it is next to impossible to enter a high concentration of ammonia and survive without breathing protection. The only reliable breathing protection available to the members of the FDNY, were the smoke helmets used almost exclusively by Rescue 1.

A case in point occurred on February 17, 1919 when thirty firemen were overcome while fighting a fire in a four-story warehouse on East 48th Street formerly used by a flour company, but now being used by the government. The fire originated in bales of jute (a coarse fiber used in making sacks or ropes) and spread to stored bags of sulfur on the second floor. A near lethal mix of gases began to permeate the building and caused an explosion that blew off the metal shutters on second floor windows.

The smoke rendered two firemen unconscious on the first floor. These men were dragged to safety by their comrades. Waves of firemen trudged into the building only to stagger out moments later. Chief Kenlon tried sending in five man teams for no more than seven minutes at a time, but even this proved to be too long exposed to the toxic fumes. An aide station was set-up and doctor Archer and Honorary Battalion Chief Robert Mainzer began resuscitating the overcome men as they were removed. Despite dangerous conditions, even in the street, the duo continued.

Finally, members of Rescue 1 were able to make the second floor wearing their smoke helmets. As stated in the official report of the Board of Merit: "mask equipped, they operated under the most hazardous and trying conditions until weakened to a point of exhaustion, in stretching and operating lines… for five and a half hours. Fireman Smith was removed to the hospital." For their bravery Acting Lieutenant John P. Ryan and Firemen Thomas Kilbride, John W. Donohue, John C. Conners, William A. Dorritie, William T. Hutcheon and James Smith were all placed on the Roll of Merit with Class A awards. Several days later Chief John Kenlon promoted both Doctor Archer and Robert Mainzer to Honorary Deputy Chiefs for subjecting themselves to unusually severe hazards while resuscitating thirty firemen who had been overcome by the deadly fumes.

Ship fires have always proven difficult and dangerous for firemen for a number of reasons both known and unknown. First the unknowns: How extensive is the fire? How much water can be used before making the vessel unstable? The knowns: The great difficulty in stretching hoselines to the seat of the fire. Little or no ventilation of smoke and gases. And, the unfamiliar nature of a ship and its inner workings and features.

A steward onboard the White Star liner *Cedric*, tied up Pier 6 at the foot of West 20th Street, noticed smoke coming from one of the hatches of holds 5 and 6 in the aft part of the ship at 6:45 p.m., on July 24, 1919 and the ship's fire crew were summoned. As the hatch was opened escaping vapors enveloped the men one of whom fell unconscious into the hold. After several rescue attempts failed his comrades called the fire department.

Firemen from land based and marine units arrived at the dock and began operations. Five members from the fireboat *Thomas Willett* went into the hold to rescue the missing crew member. After several anxious minutes the firemen were not heard from and three more firemen were sent to check on the first team. The moment they reached the bottom of the hold they requested to be hauled up as conditions were too severe to operate.

As the last of these men were pulled to fresh air, Rescue 1 arrived on the ship under the command of Acting Lt. John Ryan. Four rescue firemen donned their smoke helmets and disappeared into the swirling smoke. With the aide of electric lanterns they located and removed the five unconscious members of the fireboat, then found and removed the dead crewman. It was later determined that a large shipment of mattresses stored in the hold were the cause of the dense smoke. Four members of Rescue 1: Firemen Charles Roggencamp, Paul Maron, John Ryan and Joseph Horacek were placed on the Roll of Merit with Class "B" awards for their life saving actions.

Rescue 1 was special called to the Standard Arcade Building at 50 Broadway for a workman who'd caught his arm under an elevator. The elevator repairman had lifted the car some distance up the shaft to make a repair when a faulty mechanism caused the car to lower. The worker was able to get most of himself clear of the car, except for his arm that became pinned between the car floor and the shaft wall.

Rescue arrived quickly and was able to cut away a fifteen foot section of the flooring to free the trapped worker.

Thomas Kilbride, one of the original members of Rescue 1 was promoted to lieutenant on August 1, 1919 and remained in the company taking the place of Benjamin Parker who was promoted to captain on the same day and given command of Hook & Ladder 16. The officers of Rescue 1 were now Lieutenant (in command) Francis Blessing and Lieutenant Thomas Kilbride.

The company was again making rescues on board docked ships when on August 5, 1919 they were special called to North River Pier 63 at the foot of West 21st Street. Lt. Francis Blessing at the wheel of the rescue rig made record breaking time responding to the scene. Blessing and Fireman John Milward wearing smoke helmets were quickly lowered by rope into the hold of the Steamship *West Indian*. They were able to locate and remove the lifeless bodies of two members of the crew overcome by fumes below decks. One man was resuscitated by rescue men using pulmotors. The second man could not be revived despite the strenuous efforts of the rescue men.

On Saturday September 13, 1919, at about 2 p.m. a fire was noticed in Tank No. 36 in the Standard Oil Company refining yard on Newtown Creek in the Greenpoint section of Brooklyn. The sprawling complex was more than 20 acres in size, with numerous tanks—some as large as 35,000 barrels in capacity. The yard held large quantities of naptha, gasoline, oil, and alcohol, and over a thousand barrels of flammable and explosive liquids in the yard. These burning and exploding barrels prevented a close-in attack and limited the department's ability to control the growing flames. The department battled the flames for four days.

Speed Record Shattered By Fire Department

Rescue Squad Covers Ten Miles Through City Traffic in Fourteen Minutes

All records for prompt responses to alarms were broken early yesterday when the Fire Department Rescue Squad covered the ten miles between its headquarters on Great Jones Street and a motion picture theatre at 368 East 149th Street, The Bronx, in fourteen minutes.

The time required by the firemen for dressing and getting their apparatus to the street is included in the fourteen minutes, and it is believed that a speed of more than a mile a minute was attained, all of it through streets well traveled at that hour.

The Rescue Squad was summoned by Deputy Chief Thomas Hayes, when the firemen fighting the blaze were driven to the street by gas fumes. The gas company employees had been summoned but were unable to find the break in the main or the street cut-out.

When Lieutenant Francis Blessing, commanding the rescuers, arrived at the scene he donned a smoke helmet and with two of his men went into the building. They found the leak and did some hurried plumbing to stop the flow.

The burned building was occupied by several stores.

The *New York Tribune* ran this story on December 5, 1919.

Medal Day 1919 at City Hall. From left: Chief John Kenlon, Rescue 1 Lt. Francis Blessing with James Gordon Bennett and Department Medals. Lt. John Coffey of Engine 33 (later an officer in Rescue 1), Lt. Benjamin Parker of Rescue 1 with Kenny & Department Medals. Fourth from right, Fr. Thomas Kilbride with Department Medal and third from right, Fr. John Donohue with Department Medal.

Lt. Francis Blessing

Fireman Thomas Kilbride

Fireman John Donovan

Lt. Benjamin Parker

Fireman Kilbride receiving his medal.

In the official report to the Board of Merit, Assistant Chief Martin and his committee stated: "that the duty performed at the fire in the Standard Oil Plant…is deserving of the highest commendation for the energy, efficiency, courage and fidelity displayed and the effective service rendered under the most hazardous and trying conditions…"

Service Rating Class "A" was awarded to 409 officers and firemen including seven members of Rescue 1 under the command of Lt. Francis Blessing.

Lt. Thomas Kilbride and Firemen Paul C. Maron, Alfred Kinsella and William A. Dorritie also received Class A awards for actions on October 17, 1919. Under punishing conditions they entered ammonia filled rooms, shutting off valves on compressors and condensers to control the leaks.

As Rescue One's first five years of service was drawing to a close, it had become clear to the department and the public that this special unit had become a very important part of the FDNY's firefighting force. The use of the smoke helmets and special tools carried by the company were becoming more and more frequent. In an era of leather lungs and wooden ladders the origins of technical and heavy rescue and breathing equipped firefighting were being established.

Chapter 2

The Twenties

As the new decade began, Rescue Company 1 was having a major impact at fires and emergencies with greater frequency, as the chief officers in command of their operations had a better idea of what the company could do. Their expanding experience with, and creative utilization of their specialized tools and equipment was simplifying previously Herculean tasks, it seemed as if they could do most anything. The company was proving the old military proverb correct: "The difficult we do immediately; the impossible takes a little longer."

On January 22, 1920 units responded to a smoky fire in the ballroom of the Ritz-Carlton Hotel on 46th Street and Madison Avenue. A fire started in an insulated vault and spread to the ballroom halting a wedding that was in progress. The flames also extended to a three-story addition to the hotel. Fireman after fireman fell to the dense smoke and heat and were moved to a temporary emergency station set up in the hotel's main corridor. Conditions were so severe that a battalion chief was sent home suffering from temporary blindness brought on by the acrid smoke. Rescue 1 arrived under the command of Lt. Blessing. They snugged down their smoke helmets and went to work. Tank after tank of oxygen was changed as the rescue firemen worked in relays for seven hours extinguishing the fire. In all, the rescue men changed out 22 tanks for the smoke helmets. Several rescue men suffered blistered necks and ears. But the fire was extinguished despite the dense smoke and extreme heat conditions.

The department and the city faced blizzard-like conditions on February 11, 1920. The streets were filled with deep snow and were impassable in certain areas. Chief Kenlon said, "New York was facing the greatest fire hazard it has ever confronted in the history of the present Fire Department." The streets especially in lower Manhattan were not only snow filled but blocked by numerous vehicles stuck in the snow.

During the night a three-alarm blaze in a loft building at 145 Spring Street was battled and as the four engines, two ladders and rescue wagon responded only one engine reached the fire. The remaining companies were stalled in the streets blocked by trucks, cars and snow. Members jumped from the trapped rigs, grabbed tools and ladders, and plodded on foot to the fire.

The companies faced similar conditions several hours later when they responded to another third-alarm at 321 Broadway. Only one-third of the assigned units arrived at the blaze.

As the frequency and severity of fire duty on lower west side Manhattan increased, Rescue 1 was moved from Great Jones Street to the quarters of Engine 30 at 278 Spring Street. They moved in on February 18, 1920. The third section of Engine 30 had been disbanded and only two sections remained in service. This placed the company in the Fifth Battalion, about a mile west of their previous location. This three bay firehouse, now the home of the Fire Museum, allowed more room for the special tools of the company and a faster response to the heart of the dry goods district, a neighborhood filled with warehouses, converted tenements and factories. FDNY firemen called this area Hell's Hundred Acres. So named because of the terrible death toll it took on civilians and firemen alike.

> The company was proving the old military proverb correct: "The difficult we do immediately; the impossible takes a little longer."

The 1920's started on a sad note for the members of Rescue 1 and the department. The company's commander, Lieutenant Francis Blessing, passed away on March 15, 1920 at St. Lawrence Hospital in Brooklyn. The thirty-five year old fire officer had spent two weeks in the hospital and died from pneumonia. Upon the organization of Rescue Company 1, Blessing was the first fireman to join the company after the original members were chosen. He was an experienced motor mechanic when he entered the department and was specifically brought to the rescue company to drive the rig. He had been the chauffeur of Chiefs Kenlon, Croker, and Martin. According to the *N.Y. Evening World's* article about his death:

"He was assigned to the Rescue Squad as first chauffeur when it was organized six years ago and continued to drive for the squad after he was promoted to be lieutenant and commander. He had a record of taking the apparatus seven miles into the Bronx in ten minutes one night last winter."

His name appeared on the Roll of Merit seven times for his valor, including the Bennett Medal.

To fill the vacant position John A. Coffey was promoted to Lieutenant and assigned to Rescue 1. Lt. Thomas Kilbride became the company commander.

On the night of March 28, 1920 three alarms were transmitted for a fire in the Fidelity Storage and Warehouse Company at 280 South Street and 565 Water Street. The interconnected five and six story warehouses were filled with thousands of bags of pepper, spices, coffee and fireworks. Members of Rescue 1 wearing smoke helmets, plunged into the burning building.

Bag after bag was hauled out to the street under the direction of Acting Chief Smoky Joe Martin. Engine men and truckies aided the helmeted rescue men as best they could as bags were removed. Despite their energetic work the flames proved to be faster than the removal efforts. Spurred by exploding fireworks the fire spread across the vast piles of stored spices. Flames were soon shooting through the roof drawing large curious crowds that lined the waterfront and watched from the East River bridges. As the fire reached each of the different stored spices the smell and quality of the smoke changed dramatically. The sweet aroma of coffee gave way to the pungent biting taste of pepper. Firemen suffered greatly as the pepper laced smoke tore at their eyes, throats and lungs.

Setting up an aid station, Doctor Archer called for milk to soothe the pepper's effects. Despite the spectacular flames blazing through the roof, the acrid peppery smoke drove the crowds away from the fire. The streets were soon empty as handkerchiefs were pressed to the faces of the fleeing spectators. Eventually the building collapsed inwards on itself and the smoldering ruins continued to pump acrid smoke into the air.

Rescue 1 and nine Manhattan engine companies responded to Staten Island on board two ferry boats to help battle a blaze at the National Lead Company. This May 2, 1920 fire went to three alarms and was the first time Manhattan companies ever responded to the Borough of Richmond.

The smoke helmets would once again prove their value on June 23, 1920, as Rescue responded to the Thompson Warehouse at 521 Broome Street. It was just after 11 p.m., when two hundred families in the neighborhood were being driven from their homes by greenish-yellow clouds of chlorine gas pumping from inside the warehouse. Deputy Chief Helm and the members of Rescue 1 entered the contaminated area to find a one-inch hole in one of the tanks. Under extreme conditions they were able to plug the hole and check the remaining tanks for any other leaks. Despite using the smoke helmets the chlorine gas had severe effects on the rescue firemen. Four members of Rescue 1 were taken to the hospital by Doctor Archer. For their valiant efforts Lt. Thomas Kilbride and Firemen Frank Clark, Walter Lamb, Charles Roggencamp, John Kistenberger, Frank Joseph and Joseph Horacek were placed on the Roll of Merit with Class "A" awards.

The superintendent of the twelve story apartment house at 600 West End Avenue, smelled ammonia leaking from a fifty pound refrigeration tank in the

> The super was amazed saying it was the fastest work he'd ever seen. The Rescue had responded five and a half miles from their quarters on Spring Street to the upper westside building and completed the dangerous job within minutes.

sub-cellar, on the morning of July 4, 1920. After closing the doors to stop the spreading gas, he called the fire department. Nine and a half minutes later Rescue 1 rolled up with their masks on. The members jumped off the rig and hurried into the sub-cellar. They quickly found and stopped the leak, then opened windows to vent the gas.

The super was amazed saying it was the fastest work he'd ever seen. The Rescue had responded five and a half miles from their quarters on Spring Street to the upper westside building and completed the dangerous job within minutes.

A young boy slipped away from his mother while she was shopping in a West 34th Street store on July 28, 1920. The seven year-old boy, entered the empty freight elevator and started it upwards. In his efforts to stop the elevator or while trying to get out, he became caught between the elevator and the wall of the

This 1921 White rescue truck replaced the original rig. Only slightly larger than the Cadillac, this truck had a 50 horsepower engine.

Terrorist bomb explosion on Wall Street, September 16, 1920. A wagon filled with dynamite and sash weights exploded at high noon killing forty-four people and injuring hundreds.

second floor. His screams rang through the building, and Rescue 1 was dispatched. Using torches and hand tools they carefully worked for more than an hour to extracted the boy. He was lifted from the shaftway unconscious, but still alive. The ambulance surgeon took charge of the boy and transported him to New York Hospital. The boy's father, a fire captain in the Bronx, on-duty at the time accident later sent an impassioned letter to Lt. Kilbride and the members of Rescue 1 thanking them for their efforts.

On September 6, 1920, Rescue 1 responded to 160 Fifth Avenue where a building superintendent was trapped between the roof of the elevator car and the sixth floor. Sadly, the super passed away just as the firemen arrived but the Rescue Company spent the next hour cutting away parts of the heavy steel car to free the body of the trapped man.

Ten days later, September 16, 1920, just after the noon hour bells rang from Trinity Church, a wagon filled with explosives detonated on Wall Street outside the J.P. Morgan Company. The first FDNY units rolled into a devastating scene: the streets and sidewalks were covered with dust, debris, splintered wood, shards of glass, burning automobiles and the mangled bodies of the dead, the dying and the injured. A second alarm was immediately transmitted. As the vehicle fires were extinguished, members of Rescue 1 and the other fire companies began treating the injured strewn across the street and sidewalks. First aid stations were organized and ambulances hurried the injured to nearby hospitals. This act of terrorism took a terrible toll: forty-four people were killed and more than one hundred were seriously injured.

The early evening of December 29, 1920 saw Rescue 1 respond to a fire in a seven story loft building at 414 Broadway near Canal Street. There was heavy fire on the fourth floor and Rescue 1, one of the first units on scene, entered the heavily charged floor to conduct a search. Conditions were getting worse by the second when a backdraft shook the floor. Two members of the company Lieutenant John Coffey and Fireman Paul Maron were leveled by the blast of smoke and heat. Realizing their plight, Fireman William Hutcheon grabbed a scaling ladder and made his way to the fourth floor. Hutcheon rolled into the dense smoke and returned with the unconscious Maron. As this was happening, an aerial ladder was placed at an adjacent window and a semi-conscious Coffey was helped out onto the ladder. Once Maron was safely removed, Hutcheon again dove into the heavy smoke and heat searching for any other unconscious firemen. After a few moments he fell unconscious in the smoke and had to be dragged clear.

It was New Year's Eve, five hours until 1921 when Rescue 1 was called to 278 West Broadway, to a crockery store on the fifth floor of the building. First due units rolled in just after 7 p.m. and worked their way towards the top floor fire. Ladder 8 took the rear fire escape as Engine 31 stretched a line of hose up the interior stairs. Both teams were moving in on the fire when it became apparent this wasn't an ordinary fire. They all tumbled backwards, choking on acrid fumes. Members of Rescue 1 using smoke helmets, entered the caustic atmosphere. They found that the gas pipes in the occupancy had melted and the escaping illuminating gas was feeding the flames. They controlled the leaking pipes, then turned their attention to a drum of sulphuric acid that was attached to an apparatus used in the finishing process for the crockery ware.

Rescue men disconnected the drum and carefully carried the hazardous material from the fire area. Companies then commenced an aggressive attack on the flames and had things under control in several minutes.

During the year 1921 the department purchased Rescue 1 a new truck built on a White chassis. This vehicle was quite similar in size and appearance to the original rescue rig and would remain with Rescue 1 until it replaced in 1924. Equipped with a 50 horsepower engine, this open cabbed vehicle was only slightly longer than the Cadillac and did not have cab doors or a windshield. It would serve as a spare for a short time and be assigned to Rescue 2 when the unit was organized in 1925. It would only remain there for a few months until replaced by a new rig, and it would then revert to a spare once again.

Rescue 1 was special called to 492 Throop Avenue in Brooklyn, the site of a building fire and collapse on the night of January 21, 1921. Companies were moving lines in on the first floor of the four-story brick factory building when the floor above them collapsed. Amazingly the way the building collapsed the timbers actually formed an arch and none of the firemen was seriously injured. One man from Engine 235 was found unconscious, knocked out by the thick smoke. He was quickly removed and revived in the street.

On May 19, 1921 the company was called to Ninth Avenue at Thirty-fourth Street where a sixteen year-old boy had fallen beneath an elevated subway car at the station. Rescue 1 brought a priest to administer Last Rites to the trapped boy as they freed him from beneath the wheels of the first car. Sadly, the boy died.

Later that night, a crowd of more than one thousand people watched Rescue 1 work for twenty minutes to extricate a thirty-five year-old man from under the forward trucks of a Third Avenue trolley car at Canal Street and the Bowery. This operation was under the command of Deputy Chief John Binns. While the rescue men worked to free the man, an ambulance surgeon joined them under the car and administered first aid to the pinned man. The man was then rushed to Gouverneur Hospital in critical condition.

Gas leaks, especially ammonia and illuminating gas were fairly common in the 1920's. Ammonia was among the early refrigerants used in large commercial mechanical systems and continued to be used for many years. These refrigeration machines, used in breweries, ice plants and cold storage warehouses, used ammonia within a closed cycle of evaporation, compression, condensation and expansion. The size of the machine and the amount of ammonia being used depended on the size of the area being cooled. Problems arose when the piping or valves used in ammonia refrigeration system leaked or burst.

Ammonia, NH 3, is a colorless gas with a pungent odor. It is potentially toxic, but its average odor threshold is 5 ppm, well below any danger level. This means the smell and the effects it has on human eyes and sinuses drive a person away before any permanent damage can be done. Therefore even the toughest fireman without breathing protection would be forced from any area with a significant ammonia leak. This would then require a special call for Rescue 1 and their Draeger smoke helmets. And these leaks did not only occur in Manhattan, they happened all over the city.

On the night of July 8, 1921 Rescue 1 was special called to Third Avenue and 149th Streets in the Bronx. A cylinder head in the ice manufacturing machinery of John Counes, a confectioner and ice cream dealer, blew out filling the cellar with the noxious vapors. Unable to operate in the area firemen stretched lines to a window and shot water inside diluting the fumes while Rescue 1 responded from lower Manhattan.

In a drill they were very familiar with, Rescue arrived and under the leadership of Lt. John Coffey, put on their smoke helmets and wading trousers, then entered the basement to locate the leak. They shut off the pump and stopped the flow of ammonia. They searched the area, then reported to the chief in the street. Within a few minutes they were on their way back to quarters.

It is interesting to note that Rescue 1 and all FDNY units at this time responded to alarms and responded back to quarters from alarms. The use of sirens and bells in both directions was needed because there were no radios and the companies would be out of service until they could be contacted via the bells or telephone system.

The smoke helmets were used again several days later, June 19th, when fire companies were faced with a large ammonia leak in an artificial ice plant at 453 Hudson Street. Five families living in the building were driven to the street and first due units were helpless until the rescue company arrived with their helmets and protective gear. After forty minutes the leak was repaired and the scene secured. The families safely returned to their apartments.

On July 13th the department was faced with another dangerous gas related emergency. Hydrocyanic acid, which is a solution of hydrogen cyanide in water, is a colorless and extremely deadly poison and was being used to fumigate the hold of a ship moored at the foot of West 30th Street. One worker was overcome and soon the hold was filled with his heroic shipmates trying to reach him. Rescue 1 arrived and immediately donned their masks and dove into the dangerous ships hold. Under the command of Acting Lieutenant Conners the rescue men removed five crewmen from the dark depths of the ship and hurried them to the main deck. Three of them were dead, but two were rushed to Bellevue Hospital.

It was four in the morning on July 18, 1921 when three alarms were transmitted for a stubborn fire in the Phoenix Cheese Company at 345-347 Greenwich Street. Dense acrid smoke pouring from the building filled the streets in the neighborhood and stopped the elevated subway trains. The main body of fire was determined to be inside a huge walk-in refrigerator and a hose was positioned as the door was forced. When the door opened a wave of noxious fumes rolled out driving almost every fireman from the area. The three men on the nozzle crawled into the refrigerator trying their best to get water on the fire. Within moments they were unconscious on the floor. Wave after wave of firemen pressed into the building trying to reach the seat of the blaze. Man after man was dragged out unconscious. Firemen Charles Roggencamp and Charles Kennedy outfitted in smoke helmets began their search. On their hands and knees they pressed forward into the swirling darkness. They located the downed men and called for help. They were joined by Captain David Oliver and Fireman James Mulvaney of Ladder 1, and Fireman James Simonetti of Engine 27as well as the remaining members of Rescue 1.

Fireman Charles Roggencamp

Under extreme conditions the three unconscious members were dragged out of the refrigerator and taken outside to the first aid station. The department awarded Class II's and medals to Captain Oliver, Firemen Mulvaney and Simonetti for their heroic actions. Fireman Charles Roggencamp of Rescue 1 was awarded the Prentice Medal. Lieutenant Thomas Kilbride and Firemen Charles A. Kennedy were also awarded Class II's.

On the afternoon of August 12th a seven-year-old boy who'd just been given a penny for running an errand stood in front of 22 Ludlow Street, between Hester and Canal Streets showing his reward to some friends. One of the boys took the penny and pitched it inside the open outlet of a nearby fire hydrant and ran away laughing. The boy drove his arm deep inside the hydrant in search of his lost penny. After several minutes it became clear to his friends that their friend's arm was now wedged inside the large black fire hydrant. Mechanics from an irons works several doors away arrived with a torch and attempted to cut the bolts away from the hydrants top. They were unsuccessful.

Rescue 1 was called to the scene to find the youngster unconscious and being supported by his distraught mother. Rescue, under the command of Lt. Jones and with help from Ladder 6, began an operation that would take two hours of difficult and careful work. An estimated crowd of two thousand was held back by the police reserves as the rescue men used torches in relays to cut away the hydrant from its base.

During the operation, Fire Commissioner Thomas Drennan arrived to oversee the work. Finally the hydrant was freed and carefully lifted while the boy's hand, now partially visible, was carefully released. He was then treated by a doctor from the Gouverneur Hospital ambulance and allowed to go home with his mother.

The hydrant cap had been removed to allow the quick filling of a tub. These tubs were used by children in many downtown streets to cool off during the sweltering summer days.

It is not known if the penny was recovered.

On the night of September 16, 1921, a blow out in a refrigerating plant machine released six hundred thousand cubic feet of ammonia gas that quickly engulfed the surrounding neighborhood. The Knickerbocker Ice Company located at 77th Street and East End Avenue was nearly surrounded by tenements and in a matter of minutes fifteen hundred people were driven from their homes choking and gasping for breath. At the first sound of the explosion a group of veterans from a nearby VFW post grabbed gas masks and sprang into action searching the fourteen tenements effected by the noxious fumes. As the first fire units arrived, sixty people were unconscious in the street and the fumes were almost impossible for even the toughest fireman to penetrate. Rescue 1 raced to the scene from their quarters on Spring Street under the command of Lieutenant John A. Coffey.

On their arrival the company split into teams: one team entered the plant and began a search. Inside they found the cylinder head of Ice Machine No. 2 had blown off and that the machine was connected to twenty drums, each containing 100 pounds of liquid ammonia that was being fed through the system at 180 psi. The members of Rescue 1 located and shut down the feeder valve stopping the escaping gas, then searched the plant for any possible victims.

The second team spread sheets on the East End Avenue sidewalk between 69th & 70th Streets, seven blocks south of the leak and began tending to those overcome or effected by the fumes. They were forced to stay low as the layered fumes hung about four feet above the sidewalk even at this distance from the leak. Firemen and police officers, without the benefit of breathing apparatus, used wet pillow cases wrapped around their nose and mouth to provide some protection, as they carried victims to the first aid station. Exceptional team work between firemen, the gas masked veterans and police officers averted a potential catastrophe.

A special call sent Rescue 1 to the Bronx on October 10, 1921. A young girl had become wedged in a dumbwaiter inside a building at 668 East 188th Street. Rescue was able to free the child's body by chopping away woodworking around the dumbwaiter casing. Sadly, the child had been riding inside the dumbwaiter when the accident occurred and was killed.

The following week found the company again responding to a fire with firemen down due to mixture of heavy smoke and leaking gas. It was 2 o'clock in the morning on October 15, 1921 when FDNY units arrived at a basement fire in the five-story loft building at 116-118 East 14th Street. Ladder 3 and Engine 72 arrived first under the direction of Acting Battalion Chief Arthur Callagy. Unknown to the men moving into the fire area, the flames had already eaten into the floor beams and melted the couplings at the gas meters. Illuminating gas was flowing into the thick moving smoke. One after another of the unprotected firemen, including the acting chief, were knocked out by the gas and had to be dragged from the cellar. Assistant Chief Martin special called two additional ladder companies, a chemical engine and the Searchlight from Brooklyn.

As the number of unconscious firemen grew, Martin ordered the companies from the basement and directed Rescue 1 to get their smoke helmets and go to work. Lieutenant Thomas Kilbride led the company into the smoke filled basement and went in search of the leaking gas, while other members of the company located the hose line and advanced on the fire. Within a few minutes the gas had been controlled and the advancing hose was making progress against the flames. Outside the number of unconscious firefighters had risen to seventeen, with several taken to nearby hospitals. Others were treated in a makeshift first aid station set up in the lobby of the Fox Theatre across the street. Bottles of milk were brought in from Luchow's Restaurant (a common remedy for smoke and gas inhalation at the time) and administered to the injured firemen.

Bottles of milk were brought in from Luchow's Restaurant (a common remedy for smoke and gas inhalation at the time) and administered to the injured firemen.

Lieutenant Kilbride returned to the street and reported that the gas was shut and the fire extinguished. As Honorary Deputy Chief Edward Kenny and the Searchlight unit lit the area, and overhauling commenced, another fire— in an adjacent building was seen and weary firemen hustled inside to extinguish that blaze.

Rescue 1 responded to another elevator entrapment on November 2, 1921. A worker was wedged between the flooring of the freight elevator and the shaft wall at the Mundet & Company cork factory 65 South 11th Street in Brooklyn. The worker, a 22-year-old man, was still conscious and helped the torch wielding rescue men by directing their efforts around his crushed leg. He assured Lieutenant Kilbride he would not faint as the operation commenced. True to his word, a half-hour later as the last of the metal was cut free, he was lifted onto a stretcher and thanked each of his rescuers.

Forty-eight men were busy constructing the New American Theatre at 779 Bedford Avenue near Park Avenue in the Williamsburg section of Brooklyn at 12:30 p.m. on November 29, 1921 when disaster struck the site. Four steel girders, each weighing several tons, slipped from the brick columns supporting them sending an avalanche of steel, bricks and lumber onto a score of men working below. The falling beams also toppled an entire forty-foot high brick wall onto the unsuspecting workers. A nearby fire alarm box was pulled sending Engines 209, 211 and 230 and Ladder Companies 102, 104 to the scene under the command of Captain Maurice Foley, the Acting Chief of the 34th Battalion. Foley immediately called for more help,

Rescue 1 members: Lt. Coffey, and Firemen Roggencamp and Conners take a break after removing storage boxes of leaking acetylene on December 17, 1921. (Connecticut Firemen's Historical Society)

Ladders 108 and 119 were sent and Rescue 1 was special called from Manhattan. The firemen worked quickly and carefully trying to free the many trapped and injured workers.

While the rescue work was being accomplished the Brooklyn District Attorney, Harry E. Lewis and investigators from his staff arrived at the scene. Eager to determine if any laws had been broken, Lewis ordered a team of police officers to clear the building of everyone except the firemen and cops working. The construction workers, foremen and construction management were escorted from the site and held for questioning.

As the D.A.'s investigation commenced, the dangerous and laborious task of lifting the mangled steel, cutting the fallen timbers, and removing the collapsed brickwork piece by piece was continued. Several trapped workers were rescued by the firemen and hopes were high that others could be recovered. By 6 p.m., a steam shovel was brought in to help lift the heavy debris. Under illumination from the FDNY Searchlight rig, the work to remove all those imprisoned in the rubble continued late into the night. By midnight, six dead workers were in the King's County Morgue and the building's owners and general contractors were under arrest charged with manslaughter for their improper building methods. Seven workers in all were killed in the collapse and more than twenty were injured.

Special Department Order No. 110, dated June 19, 1922 cited the following:

Class A, service rating, awarded to each of the following for their work at collapsed theatre building, 779-787 Bedford Avenue, Brooklyn, on November 29, 1921.

Rescue Co. 1
Lieutenant John A. Coffey
Firemen 1st grade
Wm. T. Hutcheon – Wm. Dorritie – John C. Conners
Joseph D. Sullivan – James A. Devine – Joseph Horacek

Also included were: all the members of Engine 209, 211, 230, H&L 102, 104, 108, 119. Acting Battalion Chief Maurice Foley, Fireman Harry F. Gray H&L 12 (Chief Martin's aide) and Fireman Daniel Healy H&L 24 (Chief Martin's driver "Daredevil Dan")

Another storage box is removed from the Welding Supply Company on Nassau Street. Rescue 1 was "special called" to remove the hazardous materials. (Connecticut Firemen's Historical Society)

The chief officers and firemen had vast experience with heavy smoke laced with various chemicals. They were found in commercial buildings across the city. Leaking natural gas could be expected in cellar fires that burned near the gas meters. But generally speaking, they did not expect these unique hazards while operating in office buildings. The first arriving units that responded to the Vanderbilt Building, at 132 Nassau Street at 9 a.m. on December 17, 1921 did not find a fire on the fifth floor, but rather a cloud of chlorine gas. The gas seemed to be coming from Room 520, the offices of a welding manufacturer and nearly overwhelmed the first due firemen. Battalion Chief Patrick Walsh special called Rescue 1. The company pulled on their smoke helmets and located the source of the leak. The rescue men then carefully removed the sixty-pound tank that was ready to be shipped to Manila.

A stubborn fire in the sub-cellar of the Federal Building (the old Post Office Building just south of City Hall) was fought by firemen on December 18, 1921. The fire was discovered by workers in the newspaper mailing room who attempted to extinguish the blaze without success. First alarm units rolled in and went to work. The smoke was proving so debilitating that a second alarm was transmitted. Before the arrival of those companies, a score of firemen dropped unconscious in the smoke. Conditions were so severe that Acting Chief Martin had the companies working in relays until Rescue 1 could get into position with their smoke helmets. The chief also had holes cut through the pavement on the Park Row side of the building to vent some of the heavy smoke. Nine firemen were overcome in the basement and sub-cellar including seven members of Engine 32. Rescue 1, under the command of Lt. Coffey, helped remove the majority of those unconscious firemen before extinguishing the fire.

Yet another smoky fire in lower Manhattan broke out just after six o'clock on the evening of February 21, 1922 in a warehouse filled with cotton, cotton goods and woolens at 55-57 White Street. While employees were investigating the source of the smoke an automatic fire alarm summoned the fire department. Deputy Chief John Binns arrived and sizing up the level of smoke and the nature of the flammables involved transmitted a second alarm. The acrid smoke from the burning cotton compelled the firemen to work for only brief periods, before being relieved. Twelve firemen fell, knocked out by the dense smoke. They were removed by their comrades and members of Rescue 1 who were using smoke helmets.

Companies made very slow progress. When they reached the stairs to the basement the heat from the blazing cellar was so hot not even the helmeted rescue men could descend. Binns sent Rescue 1 and several truck companies to vent the cellar by opening up the sidewalks. As the smoke chugged from the cellar, hose streams were directed into the blazing cellar.

For more than two hours FDNY companies struggled to extinguish the fire, protect the building's contents, and remove each other as they were overcome by the smoke. Acting Battalion Chief Crawley checked the first floor, where several companies were trying to save a large quantity of baled cotton. The chief decided the floor was unsafe ordering everyone out of the building. Moments later the floor collapsed into the blazing cellar, luckily the chief had just cleared the last of his men.

Although Rescue 1 was routinely handling ammonia and other leaking gas problems, they never took the work for granted. It was difficult and dangerous. On April 26, 1922 the fire department was called to 409 West 14th Street where two machinist's helpers were overcome as they attempted to stop a leak in a large ammonia tank in the building's basement. Seven firemen were severely burned, as they worked to control the leaking ammonia tank including: Lt. John Coffey and Firemen John Milward and Charles Roggencamp of Rescue 1.

The special training given to the members of Rescue 1 could help make a difference in a fire operation, even if the company was not at the scene and the members were not working. A case in point was the evening of June 23, 1920 when off-duty Rescue 1 Fireman Charles Roggencamp came across Brooklyn fire companies at work battling a smoky fire in a three-story building on West Eleventh Street. Suddenly, two unconscious firemen were dragged from the building and were placed on the sidewalk. Roggencamp, identified himself and sprang into action. Roggencamp began administering first aid to the downed men. His efforts were of such a high quality that Deputy Chief Helm recommended him to the Board of Merit for his capability. He was awarded a Class A.

Workmen in the Knickerbocker Ice Company factory at Broome and Elizabeth Streets, accidentally broke an ammonia pipe in the second floor freezing room at around 10 a.m. on the morning of July 15, 1922. Rescue 1 arrived and helmeted Firemen Sullivan and Hutcheon joined the ice company machinist, who was already at work wearing a gas mask, and together were able to close the valves of the ammonia supply system.

The morning of July 18, 1922 started as another beautiful day in New York City. It was just a little after 8 a.m., and the summer sun was just peeking over the top of the Manufacturer's Transit Company's seven-story warehouse on Jane Street in Greenwich Village. Out front, workers were busy loading wooden cases filled with powdered magnesium into the building's freight elevator. A number of additional cases were stacked on the sidewalk adjacent to the opened elevator. Despite the fact that the air was still relatively cool, the workers were building a good sweat as they moved the heavy crates into the building. The huge warehouse, which ran through to the next block, contained large quantities of combustible materials. Stored in the basement and on the various floors were crates of photographic flashlight powder, bonded whiskey, tons of rubber and quantities of rolled paper.

For some unknown reason—maybe a spark caused by friction—one of the cases of magnesium powder suddenly exploded, throwing several of the workers across the cobblestone street. Scrambling to their feet, they were horrified to see flames spreading among the stacked wooden crates. Most of the workers ran for their lives, while several brave men dashed back towards the fire and tried to smother the flames with pails of sand.

The sand was having no effect as the fire spread from the crates on the sidewalk to those in the freight elevator. A second explosion toppled the remaining workers and spread the flames deep into other parts of the warehouse. A Greenwich Avenue merchant watching the activity from his store across the street decided he'd better call for help. He hurried to the nearest fire alarm box and pulled the handle.

At 8:15 a.m. the alarm was received in the Manhattan Fire Dispatcher's Office.

The first firemen to arrive found the flames blazing out of control. The wooden crates of magnesium powder were burning briskly on the sidewalk, while spewing fountains of white sparks into the air. The extending fire roared up the open elevator shaft inside the seven-story building.

The Acting Chief of the New York City Department, Joseph "Smoky Joe" Martin, arrived and took command of the fire. At first, he encouraged his men to bring their fire hoses as close to the flames as possible.

Heavy streams of water bored into the wall of flames, but whenever the stream was moved the flames instantly refilled the empty spot. Sparks and sheets of white-hot flame continued to pour from the wooden crates on the sidewalk, endangering nearby buildings. At times the plume of burning magnesium, which resembled the flaring fountains in a pyrotechnical display, actually reached over the roofs of the three- and four-story houses fronting on Jane Street.

Chief Martin had his men hose down nearby buildings to prevent their ignition. But within the burning warehouse the fire seemed unaffected by the torrents of water firemen were pouring onto it.

With flames bursting through the roof of the warehouse a dense, black, acrid cloud of smoke settled around the building until it became so dark on Jane and West Twelfth Streets that firemen had great difficulty navigating the streets and sidewalks.

At about 8:45 a.m. Engine Company 13 began moving a hose line into the warehouse through a door on the Twelfth-Street side of the building. Suddenly, there was an explosion that far exceeded the magnitude of any of the previous blasts. In a massive gush of white hot flames the entire roof was lifted off and a fifteen foot wide section of wall extending from the fifth floor up was blow outwards.

Chief Martin was lifted off his feet and slammed against a building across the street, burning his face and knocking the wind out of him. Engine 13 was also hurled backwards by the explosion. A large section of elevator machinery and roofing, blew into the sky, then fell to the street crushing the officer. Lt. John Schoppmeyer. He was pulled, unconscious, from the debris, but he never regained consciousness. He died several minutes later.

The fire was declared under control thirty-four hours after it started, but it continued to burn for a total of five days. Finally, one last eruption of the "Greenwich Street Volcano" occurred on the afternoon of July 23rd, sending walls crashing outward and totally destroying two houses. The fire was finally out.

Across the street, Rescue 1 under the command of Lt. Kilbride, operated a hose line from the roof of an adjacent building. Fireman Charles Roggencamp arched the stream across the street into the blazing building. When the explosion occurred, Kilbride, Roggencamp and four other rescue men were thrown from their feet tumbling to the very edge of the roof. Scrambling to regain their footing, their hose slid off the roof, the stream whipping around as it fell to the ground.

A large section of the coping fell onto the tenement next door followed by another tremendous explosion. They were again knocked from their feet and stunned by the explosion. The members of Rescue 1 reorganized and quickly made their way down the front fire escape and dove into the flaming piles of rubble searching for the trapped men.

Martin ordered more manpower and resources to the scene including companies from Brooklyn.

The detonation had driven cases filled with merchandise through the warehouse windows and walls, littering the street with an eclectic assortment of dolls, toys, fancy electric light bulbs, dried peas and other small items, that were quickly washed away by the rivers of fire-hose water cascading down West Twelfth and Jane Streets.

The thick acrid smoke of the Jane Street fire was so dangerous that city officials ordered 2,000 people evacuated from the neighborhood. Despite this precaution, several residents were sickened by the smoke. They were treated at first aid stations set up around the fire area by the local chapter of the American Red Cross.

Scores of firemen and police officers were also overcome by smoke and had to be treated at the Red Cross stations. A battery of six pulmotors were in use at one time at the corner of Greenwich and West 12th Streets, with a score of unconscious and semi-conscious persons laid out on the sidewalk. The street resembled a battlefield.

As Martin's men held their hoses close to the fire, they were pelted by hot ejected materials, and risked being scorched by bursts of flame. For protection Martin ordered them to remove doors from nearby buildings and use them as wooden shields. They continued fighting the fire in this manner for several hours.

The constant eruptions resembled volcanic activity and the fire quickly became known to both firemen and the public as the "Greenwich Street Volcano."

Instead of having his men aim hoses from rooftops, where they would be vulnerable to showers of debris from explosions in the burning building, Martin decided to send his men to new positions inside the buildings surrounding the burning warehouse.

Hose after hose was repositioned under Martin's direction, until water poured from every window and fire escape overlooking the burning building. Eventually, sixty-four streams of water were directed into the fire from different vantage points. More than 216,000 tons of water were pumped into the burning warehouse — the largest volume of water directed at a single fire in the history of the New York City Fire Department. After a bulging wall fell on the Jane Street side of the building, water could more easily reach the seat of the fire.

By midnight the fire was clearly diminishing, although it continued to burn. At that point, over two hundred firemen and police officers had been treated for smoke inhalation, and an additional sixty-one men had been hospitalized with burns, bruises, or lacerations. Two firemen had been killed: one by falling debris, the other had fallen from a truck racing towards the fire.

The fire was declared under control thirty-four hours after it started, but it continued to burn for a total of five days. Finally, one last eruption of the "Greenwich Street Volcano" occurred on the afternoon of July 23rd, sending walls crashing outward and totally destroying two houses. The fire was finally out.

Two days later the company responded to the Bronx where an excavation cave-in took the life of one worker and trapped five others. The work site was for a new apartment building foundation being dug at 174th Street and Macombs Road. Rescue 1 joined a ladder company already at work digging at the scene.

On August 3, 1922 the company responded to a fire in the Vesuvio Restaurant on Mulberry Street in Little Italy. A hose line was pushed into the cellar and members of Engine 9 and Ladder 20 were moving in when a backdraft occurred. As some of the dazed and injured firemen staggered from the cellar, Acting Lt. John Milward and the smoke helmeted rescue men hurried into the cellar. There, amidst the thick smoke and high heat, several unconscious firemen were located and removed with some difficulty. Leaking illuminating gas was also controlled, allowing the fire to be extinguished quickly.

An unusual emergency faced the company on August 18, 1922 when a flood of ammonia threatened the lives of all the aquatic mammals in the New York Aquarium at Battery Park. The aquarium, located inside Castle Clinton (now a National Landmark) had over 100 tanks positioned around the circular design of the fort. Six large pools surrounded the seventh and largest pool in the very center of the structure. It was a very popular venue with tourists and locals alike. Noxious fumes were leaking into the exhibits area from the engine room making the old castle structure uninhabitable. Rescue 1 was called to the scene.

Inside the aquarium, the fish contained in tanks faced no serious problem, but the sea lions, turtles and the lone seal were having difficulty breathing. They huddled near the edges

Background photo: *This very serious Jane Street fire on July 12, 1922 became known as the "Greenwich Village Volcano". A warehouse filled with volatile chemicals, rubber, 400 tons of rolled newspaper and other flammables took the life of a fire officer and burned for days.*

Inset photo right: *The initial explosion of boxes of powdered magnesium caused a partial collapse and ignited a deep-seated fire. Five alarms and a Borough Call were transmitted. (Connecticut Firemen's Historical Society)*

of their enclosure slapping their flippers against the walls and barking in alarm. Despite the fumes the sea mammals resisted all efforts to drive them into the water, where it was thought they would be safer. The alligators however, appeared to be having no problems at all.

The rescue men pulled on their Draeger helmets and made their way to the second floor where the leak was originating. This area housed a refrigeration plant that cooled the stored fish used to feed the mammals. As the leak was investigated Acting Lt. Milward sent two smoke helmeted rescue men back to the main hall to keep an eye on the animals and report back if conditions became worse. After an hour the leak was located and repaired, and the main hall was vented clearing the fumes. The company took up happy to know all the animals were okay.

Another building fire with leaking gas found Rescue 1 saving a husband and wife, both overcome by the fumes and smoke in their apartment inside the five-story building at 211 West 61st Street on October 4, 1922. The unconscious couple were found by helmeted rescue men in their second floor rooms. Two floors below firemen were struggling to extinguish the smoky gas laced cellar fire. After removing the unconscious couple, rescue members joined the battle in the cellar where they found and controlled the leak, then helped extinguish the blaze.

The alarm box at the corner of Washington and Fulton Streets was transmitted after the fourth floor of a six-story brick building at 195 Washington Street collapsed on November 14, 1922. Six men were loading bags of onions when the floor beneath them gave way, plunging four of the men to the ground floor beneath a mass of tangled wreckage. The task of rescue was further complicated by the clouds of onion dust hanging in the air.

Members of Rescue 1 tunneled through the debris to reach several injured men who were carefully removed. All of the trapped men were freed by rescue men, but one would later die in the hospital from his injuries.

As New York City residents were preparing to ring in the New Year of 1923, Rescue 1 heard bells of a different sort—alarm bells! One year would end and the next begin, with some difficult and taxing jobs for the company.

The company faced a real test of endurance as they responded to a leak in a basement vault at 18 East 41st Street early in the afternoon of December 31, 1922. The basement was filled with suffocating fumes as members of Rescue 1 made their way to the vault door. Although the door was closed the fumes were leaking around the door's casing. As they opened the door the air was so heavily laden with the dense acrid fumes that even with their gas masks on they could not stay in the vault for more than fifteen minutes. It was believed the fumes came from improperly sealed carboys (rigid shatter proof glass containers that held 5 to 15 gallons of liquid) filled with sulfuric and muriatic acid.

The fumes were so debilitating that the rescue men had to work in relays. At one point two members, Lt. John Coffey and Fireman Thomas Larkin were overcome and had to be pulled from the vault by other helmeted rescue men. The two unconscious men were taken to the street and were revived by a doctor from Bellevue Hospital. Both men refused sick leave and continued on duty.

Deputy Chief Thomas Murtha assigned members of Ladder 2 to help Rescue 1 with the final part of the operation. For two hours the chemicals were carried to the rear yard and the entire building was vented. Late in the afternoon it was realized there was also a leaking tank of chlorine inside a closet within the vault. Lt. Coffey and Fireman Charles Kennedy removed the tank, which contained about 220 cubic feet of chlorine gas. The tank was taken to the street, and later driven to the East River where the tank was dumped into the water.

At 10:40 the next morning, January 1, 1923 a fire broke out on the 15th floor storeroom within the offices of a brokerage house at 60 Wall Street. The smoldering deep-seated fire created extreme heat and deadly carbon monoxide laced smoke. First alarm units found it impossible to approach the fire area as man after man dropped unconscious from the poisonous smoke. Deputy Chief Helm special called Rescue 1.

An aid station was hastily set up and unconscious firemen were treated by Doctor Peever who'd arrived on board the ambulance from the Beekman Street Hospital. As the room began to fill with what would eventually become 23 unconscious firemen, Dr. Peever sent in his own version of an additional alarm when he requested assistance from St. Vincent's Hospital.

As the helmeted rescue men made their way into the dense smoke chugging from the fifteenth floor storeroom, Chief Helm sent a team to the floor above to bore holes through the floor directly above the fire. Members of Rescue 1 then attempted to push a hose line into the storeroom. But even with masks they could only stay for five minutes or so due to the the tremendous heat. The attack line was backed off and streams were then directed through the holes from above in an attempt to extinguish the fire remotely. A large amount of steam was generated, so additional holes were made and more water was delivered.

Chief Helm stopped all streams and waited a moment to allow the steam to lift before sending Rescue 1 back inside with the attack line. This time they quickly penetrated to the seat of the fire and soon had it under control in several minutes.

It was Good Friday, March 30, 1923 when FDNY units responded to Box 646 for a fast moving fire at First Avenue between 26th and 27th Streets near Bellevue Hospital. The original fire building was a paper box company and the flames, fanned by high winds, were soon extending to an L-shaped building that ran to East 27th Street. This three-story structure, being used as a annex and storehouse for a printing company, was built one hundred years before as a city prison. Flames got into the second floor and were soon through the roof and eating their way down to the first. Additional alarms were quickly transmitted.

Waiting at the doorway of the old prison building were members of Engine 26, with a hose, and members of Ladder 24 standing just to their east. Suddenly a huge backdraft explosion rocked the building, blowing down the exterior wall onto the engine men. The members of Ladder 24, directed by injured men from Engine 26 moved into the rubble and began to extricate the trapped firemen. They were soon joined by other firemen including members of Rescue 1.

The huge draft of flames caused by the collapsing building threatened to sweep across the street. As the last of the trapped firemen were pulled clear an all out attack commenced as firemen attempted to halt the extending flames. Lines were positioned to protect the scorched adjacent properties. After hours of difficult and dangerous work the flames were halted.

Sadly two firemen had been killed in the collapse.

As the companies began overhauling the remains of this five-alarm fire, Rescue 1 and Doctor Archer were special called to Eldridge Street on the lower Eastside where a tenement had collapsed.

It was just before two in the afternoon and a large work crew was demolishing the five-story tenement building at 39 Eldridge Street. A section of the third floor was being used to pile dismantled brickwork and other materials prior to its being taken outside to trucks. This overweighted sectioned collapsed, toppling parts of the building above and sections of the adjacent building as well, injuring nineteen men and trapping three within the rubble.

The men were trapped between scores of large beams and tons of brick. First due units used axes to open a breach in the rubble. Rescue 1 moved in and began to thread their way through the tangled, shifting debris pile. Carefully cutting the large tim-

bers they located the trapped men, pinned beneath the massive lean-to collapse. One was dead, the other two in severe pain. As the area around them was shored Doctor Archer was called for.

Archer removed his hat and coat and rolled up the sleeves of his white shirt. Clutching his medical bag he carefully moved into the collapse pile following the path cleared by Rescue 1. Doctor Archer examined the men before injecting them with morphine to ease their pain. The rescue men then began to cut and shore the imprisoning beams. A priest joined them briefly administering the Last Rites to the pinned men. For an hour the rescue men carefully sawed under the watchful eye of Doctor Archer. Finally the first was freed and carefully carried out on a stretcher. A few minutes later the second was removed — alive.

> **A**rcher removed his hat and coat and rolled up the sleeves of his white shirt. Clutching his medical bag he carefully moved into the collapse pile following the path cleared by Rescue 1.

As the rescuers began exiting, the collapse pile above them moved. The huge beams surrounding them groaned and shifted, dislodging smaller pieces that fell blocking their way out. For the next several minutes the rescue men tunneled through the newly shifted debris. As they went to exit it became apparent that Doc Archer's foot was wedged fast. Archer was able to wiggle his foot free and rather than risk further cutting, his shoe was left in place.

Doctor Archer, his shirt filthy and in tatters and wearing only one shoe joined the men from Rescue 1 who lined up to be congratulated by Mayor Hylan and Chief Kenlon. The impromptu ceremony was over quickly and minutes later the rescue men and other members of the department began the dangerous task of removing the body of the dead worker.

For his heroic work Doctor Archer would be awarded the James Gordon Bennett Medal the following year. (According to the minutes of the Board of Merit dated November 23, 1923, a subcommittee was to be formed to consider the meritorious actions of the officer and eight firemen from Rescue 1, and the officers and members of Hook & Ladders 6, 9 & 18 for their heroic work at this collapse. There is no further mention of these reports in subsequent minutes or department orders. It appears no action was taken and no formal recognition was given to these members.)

Top left: *Good Friday, March 30, 1923, after battling a 5-alarm blaze on East 26th Street, Rescue 1 responded to a building collapse on Eldridge Street. (Connecticut Firemen's Historical Society)*

Bottom left: *Rescue men tunneled, and shored their way into the pile of debris for three hours. Three men were rescued. The dead were also carefully recovered. Rescue men can be seen wearing soft caps and working in close to the opening. (Connecticut Firemen's Historical Society)*

About a month later, April 25, 1923 the company responded to an afternoon fire in a commercial building where street cleaning machines were manufactured. Two alarms were transmitted for this very smoky East 18th Street fire. The fire apparently originated on the fourth floor where bamboo, rattan and hemp were stored. Fireman Charles Kennedy of Rescue 1 and others members were sent to the upper floors to remove some of the smoldering bales of bamboo.

Half smothered by the carbon monoxide laced smoke, Kennedy groped for a window. Dizzy from the toxic smoke he tumbled into an open elevator shaft and fell three stories to the ground floor. The dazed fireman was carried to the street and examined by Doctor Archer. Amazingly Kennedy only suffered cuts and bruises and was sent home to rest for a short time before returning to duty.

It was 6:05 on the morning of August 26, 1923 when the FDNY responded to 281-284 West Street between Watts and Canal Street in Manhattan. The Towers Warehouse Corporation's five-story building was packed tightly with goods from floor to ceiling and the only openings were windows along the front on West Street. The remaining three walls of the solid brick building ran 100-feet deep then made an L-shape that ran another 50-feet.

With little ventilation available teams of firemen pressed forward into the thick acrid smoke only to become overwhelmed and rendered unconscious. Wave after wave of men again and again tried to reach the seat of the fire with no success. Outside the water supply was plentiful as the high pressure system and several fire boats provided more water than the hoses could deliver.

The sidewalks filled with unconscious firemen and additional alarms were transmitted. The fire attack had completely stalled, but thick clouds of smoke continued pumping from the building's limited openings. Chief Smoky Joe Martin called the rescue company's officer over and a few minutes later a smoke-helmeted crew disappeared into the pulsing wall of smoke.

Several times the rescue men re-emerged from the building dragging unconscious firemen behind them only to plunge back into the smoke. Rescue men found the hose line and attempted to press the attack forward only to be driven back. Conditions had become to dangerous even for the smoke helmets. Assured all firemen were accounted for Rescue 1 staggered from the building.

After another brief meeting with Chief Martin, the tactics were changed. Holes were made from adjoining structures onto several floors of the burning building and holes were chopped through the roof. Hoses were then directed into these openings in an attempt to cool off the now raging fire. A dozen lines were operating on the roof where conditions were somewhat better than inside the adjoining buildings. Despite sections of clear air on the roof several firemen forced to work in the dense clouds of smoke were overcome and had to be taken down ladders to the aid station.

The firefighting continued into the night. The fire was defying all efforts of extinguishment. Several times it appeared to be under control only to flair up again. The north wall began to bulge and firefighting positions were relocated. Water cascaded down the stairs inside the blazing structure and poured out onto West Street flooding several nearby cellars.

Finally with the structural stability in question, it was decided to pull all the lines from adjacent roofs and buildings and use only water towers and streams from the street.

In all fifty men were overcome by the dense smoke. A dozen were taken hospitals. With the temporary loss of so many men Martin and his chiefs called for additional men from upper Manhattan, the Bronx and some from Brooklyn. Amazingly the fire was held to the original fire building and only required three alarms.

The fire alarm box at the corner of Broome and Attorney Streets was pulled at 5:30 p.m., on September 26, 1923. As companies scrambled to their rigs a little girl dashed into the quarters of Engine 11 on East Houston Street shouting her brother had fallen into a sewer. Arriving at the box were Engines 15, 17 and 11, with Hook & Ladders 6 & 18. Captain Poggi of Engine 15 called for a scaling ladder and was preparing to enter the manhole as Battalion Chief McElligott arrived.

"Don't go down there without rope around you, Tony!" the chief called to the captain. As a rope was quickly tied around the officer, Rescue 1 was special called to the scene. Chief McElligott ordered firemen to open every manhole cover from Attorney Street to the East River. He also called for help from the Department of Sewers.

Firemen from Ladder 18, Ladder 6 and Rescue 1, entered every manhole along the sewer line and searched the waist-deep water in pitch blackness. Above firemen tended safety lines in case the fireman below encountered any sewer gas or other dangerous situation. After a long fifteen minutes things were starting to look bad when the voice of Fireman James Landers of Ladder 18 could be heard echoing inside the sewer. He'd found the boy between Goerck and Lewis Streets. He climbed up a ladder, the slumped form of the boy over his shoulder and handed the limp child to members of Rescue 1 who'd arrived with a pulmotor. Landers, soaking wet from his trips into the sewer, pitched forward unconscious himself from exertion and gas poisoning. Under the direction of Lt. Kilbride resuscitation efforts on both began.

A huge crowd, originally spread the length of the sewer line, began to congregate around the rescue efforts. Fireman Landers was taken to the hospital unconscious. Meanwhile tank after tank of oxygen was being administered to the boy until on the fourth tank Kilbride thought he detected life signs. With no ambulance on scene the boy was placed in the rescue truck and as resuscitation efforts continued he was rushed to the hospital. Sadly, the child was later pronounced dead.

Five members working in Rescue 1: Lt. Kilbride and Firemen Walsh, Tierney, Fletcher and Sullivan along with three members of Ladder 6, four members of Ladder 18 including Fireman Landers, and Captain Poggi were placed on the Roll of Merit with Class II awards.

On December 1, 1923 Lt. John Coffey was promoted to captain and transferred to Engine 5. On the same day Lt. Walter L. Lamb of Ladder 9 was promoted captain and assigned to Rescue Company 1. Lamb had served as a fireman in Ladder 26 and Rescue 1. The fourteen year veteran, who's name appeared on the Roll of Merit several times, had already served half his career in Rescue 1.

A most unusual response occurred on Christmas Day, December 25, 1923 when Rescue 1 was special called to the base of a 360-foot high smoke stack at the Pennsylvania Rail Road power house in Long Island City. A worker, missing for some time, had apparently been pulled into the flue of one of the huge boilers. The fires were immediately lowered and the fire department requested. Ladder Company 115 and Acting Chief Dewey assisted the rescue men as their equipment was readied.

A scaling ladder was placed and two rescue men wearing "fire-proof clothing" and smoke helmets tied ropes around their waists and descended into the stifling heat. Firemen above poured water down onto the two men cooling them as they worked in the extreme heat. They recovered the worker's body and brought him up.

February 1924 was a leap year, and the evening of the 29th would prove to be very difficult and rather dangerous to Manhattan firemen. At 6:45 p.m., a cop walking his beat on Broadway noticed smoke drifting up through a sidewalk grate on Reade Street. He hurried to the spot and saw a fire in the cellar of 61 Reade Street. Dashing back to the corner he pulled the alarm box. Within minutes companies were rolling to a fire that would knock out forty firemen including two battalion chiefs and Chief Kenlon himself.

The blaze started in the cellar of the five-story building and spread to a first floor shoe and leather establishment. The billowing smoke, now filled with noxious fumes, knocked man after man to his knees then rendered them unconscious. The men were falling so quickly that Doctor Archer set up an emergency hospital in the store adjoining the fire building. Wave after wave of firemen pushed into the walls of smoke only to be battered senseless.

Rescue men showing the smoke helmets and the growing array of tools now being carried on the rig in 1924.

Water accumulating in the cellar and sub-cellar were becoming dangerously high adding the possibility of drowning to growing list of dangers. After both battalion chiefs assigned to the fire had been dragged out unconscious, Chief Kenlon led a team into the sub-cellar to attack the fire. Several of the men around him dropped into the water but quick work by other firemen saved them. Conditions were getting worse by the minute.

"This is one of the toughest cellar fires I have ever had to handle…The fire itself is not hard to handle, but the smoke is certainly proving fearful on my men." Kenlon said.

A number of firemen were in such bad condition that they had to be taken to the hospital. As reported in the *New York Times*: Among the firemen to go to the hospital was Captain Walter Lamb, commanding Rescue Squad No. 1. He carried out eight of his comrades and then pitched to the sidewalk. Physicians at Beekman Street Hospital reported his condition as more alarming than any of the others. (Lamb was one of nine hospitalized.) Three alarms were required to bring the fire under control.

The life of a fireman in any era can cover a wide range of experiences. Some days are slow and boring, others seem to fly at you and go by in a blur. Then there are times where you just can't believe how difficult things are: dangerous, exhausting, and there seems to be no end in sight. Tuesday into Wednesday May 19-20, 1924 was one of those times.

It all started just before 8 o'clock Tuesday evening when Box 199 came in for a building fire at Broadway and Grand, the warehouse of Lord & Taylor. It would require four alarms and many hours to control. Thick clouds of smoke pumped from the building dropping a dark shroud over the neighborhood. Visibility outside the burning building was zero. Firemen had to feel their way along parked apparatus, across the smoke obscured street and sidewalks. Man after man dropped both inside the building and outside.

At one point a deputy chief who'd twice ordered the deckpipe on Engine 30's hose wagon to be shut down and twice received no reply. Sent his aide through the dense smoke to find out why his order had not been carried out. The aide climbed carefully onto the hose wagon and inched towards the huge nozzle. There he found both firemen slumped over the deckpipe, unconscious. The heavily stocked building filled with dry goods defied all attempts to extinguish it.

While this fire was at its height another blaze broke out on Pier A at the Battery on the tip of Manhattan. The fire was in the Iron Steamship Company's base and would also require four alarms to extinguish.

With little rest the exhausted members of Rescue 1 worked these fires then responded to a special call at 217 Mercer Street. Acid fumes had driven a hundred people into the street and would not let firemen even enter the five-story loft building.

Donning gas masks, Rescue 1 under the command of Lieutenant Kilbride entered the cellar and located a drum of muriatic acid. The acid was leaking from the drum then coming into contact with water and creating a stifling steam mixture. The leaking drum was hoisted up by block and tackle and placed on the sidewalk. The acid continued pouring from the drum, steam mushrooming across sidewalk, while the fluid ate through the paving blocks. Rescue men were finally able to stopper the leak.

The exhausted men of Rescue 1 finally found themselves back in quarters reeking of smoke and acid fumes. They changed clothes and began to place fresh smoke helmets on the rig as Lieutenant Kilbride tapped them back in service.

A second alarm was transmitted upon arrival at the Fidelo Brewery on May 29, 1924. The brewery building, built in 1852, took up half the block along First Avenue at 29th Street. It was 2:45 in the afternoon when workers saw flames shooting from the second floor stock room inside the five-story landmark structure, the workers fled the building. With a raging fire inside and a 70,000 pound ammonia tank on the roof, the first due battalion chief transmitted a second alarm upon his arrival. Assistant Chief Martin assumed command and with the danger of the roof tank exploding, companies began to battle the fire defensively from the street, ladders and adjoining buildings.

Rescue 1 rolled in and were advised of the situation. They donned their smoke helmets and entered the smoke filled building hoping to find the shut-offs for the ammonia tank. Twenty hoses were pouring streams into the building from the outside. Firemen could only get close to the building by wearing gas masks. Inside Rescue 1 searched the burning structure and found the body of a worker in a fifth floor fermenting room and another on the fourth floor.

The shut-offs were located and made safe. As Rescue 1 was making their searches of the top floor a team of firemen outside were almost killed as an auxiliary ammonia tank on the 29th Street side of the building collapsed. The men under a heavy curtain of fumes made their way to a set back roof and found fresh air before any were overcome.

The flames were finally extinguished, but not before 25,000 barrels of beer in the process vats was destroyed.

Background photo: On May 24, 1924 a concrete mixing platform collapsed at 129 West 46th Street, trapping numerous construction workers. Firemen and construction workers used a crane to remove the cement mixer, allowing rescue work to begin. (Connecticut Firemen's Historical Society)

With the aid of Ladder 4, Rescue 1 worked in wet concrete and debris to free the imprisoned men. (Connecticut Firemen's Historical Society)

Doctor Archer provided medical care as each of the trapped workers were freed. (Connecticut Firemen's Historical Society)

*This 1924 Mack AC-10 "Bulldog" rescue truck replaced the 1921 White.
This chain-driven truck was slightly larger and more heavy-duty than the previous rigs.*

Rescue Company 1's third apparatus was placed in service on July 19, 1924. It was a Mack chain-driven AC-10 Bulldog that carried Mack registration number 736-866. This rig was slightly larger than the previous two rigs, reflecting the fact that more equipment was being assigned to the company. It was also a more heavy duty design. This 1924 Mack remained in service with Rescue 1 until replaced in 1931. It served as a spare for a few months and was then assigned to Rescue 3 when that unit was organized. Unfortunately, this rig was involved in a fatal accident with Engine 48 while both units were responding to Bronx Box 3192, on May 5, 1938. An explosion and fire resulted from the collision and the rig was destroyed. Captain Joseph Tracy and Fireman James Hughes, both of Engine 48 were killed in this accident.

According to their brochure: The President Liners of the Dollar Steamship Line provided a distinctively higher standard of luxury, comfort and convenience... on a par with those of metropolitan hotels or clubs. One of their liners, *The President Polk* had just moored in Bush Terminal after a world cruise. All the passengers had disembarked and only the ship's crew, a staff of stevedores and a number of Chinese "coolies" who were to be returned to China, were onboard. At about midnight on October 11, 1924, a fire was discovered in the ship's lower deck. As members of the crew attempted to battle the flames, some of the more than 200 workers on the ship at the time, went into a panic and began jumping into the river.

The FDNY arrived and found an advanced fire situation below decks that was difficult to approach due to the extreme heat and noxious smoke. Many of the ship's company had already jumped into the river and the rest were successfully removed from the ship by firemen. As Brooklyn fire companies began an attack, Rescue 1 was special called. After a difficult battle the flames were knocked down and a smoke helmeted search was begun for a missing stevedore. Members of Rescue 1 located his charred remains and completed the search trying to define the extent of damage and any hidden pockets of fire. Damages to the ship and her cargo were estimated at a half million dollars.

Late in January of 1925, Fireman Peter Walsh was promoted to lieutenant and remained in Rescue 1.

A huge building renovation was underway on West 31st Street. The Irving Hall Hotel, soon to be a new women's hostelry was nearing completion. On January 10, 1925, large sections of the building's concrete flooring had been removed then re-poured after a new staircase was put in place. On the eighth floor two workers were moving wheelbarrows across a ten-foot square of recently poured concrete when the floor beneath them collapsed.

> **T**ime after time since the inception of the company Rescue 1 was able to venture where no firefighters had ever been able to go and did so with amazing success.

The block of concrete, weighing a ton, crashed down, through each successive floor all the way to the basement. The two workers were trapped beneath the huge pile of rubble and many others were injured as FDNY units arrived and went to work.

Upon their arrival Rescue 1 was sent to the basement where the workers were trapped. Rescue men used jacks and hand tools to raise and move the huge blocks of concrete. Carefully each block was repositioned until they could pull the men from beneath the tons of rubble. Rescue then checked each floor for stability and made the area safe until engineers could asses the damage.

Time after time since the inception of the company Rescue 1 was able to venture where no firefighters had ever been able to go and did so with amazing success. Despite burns from acids and ammonia, the debilitating effects of heavy smoke and risking life and limb in building collapses and other emergencies the members of the company remained relatively healthy. This record would take a tragic turn on February 3, 1925 when smoke was seen coming from the cellar of 620 Fifth Avenue across the street from Saint Patrick's Cathedral, shortly after 3 p.m.

The fire, which originated in the cellar of one of the three interconnected buildings, extended quickly trapping many workers on the upper floors. The six story buildings were occupied by the Dobbs Hat Company, Bergdorf & Goodman Company, Loran Gowns, and a photography studio on the sixth floor of 616. Manhattan Box 857 would require three alarms as the fire raced up the rear of the structures and numerous people became trapped at the upper floor front windows.

Rescue 1 arrived, under the command of Acting Lieutenant William R. Fletcher and went to work. The husky, thirty-eight year-old former iron worker and father of three, had a grip like a vise. He'd joined the fire department in 1914. First Fletcher rescued a photographer trapped on the top floor of the building. Then he led a team into the smoke filled cellar to extinguish the fire. Several members, including Fletcher and John Conners, were rendered unconscious by the dense smoke. They were carried by their comrades back to the street where Doctor Archer had an aide station in the hallway of 628 Fifth Avenue.

As several spectacular ladder rescues were being performed a few doors away, Doctor Archer was reviving the overcome firemen. Fletcher regained consciousness and pleaded with the doctor to be allowed to return to his company. "I'm alright doctor," he said. But Archer could tell he had taken a very dangerous amount of smoke and had him rushed to Bellevue Hospital for further treatment. An hour later William Fletcher passed away. The cause of death was listed as smoke narcosis.

Fireman William R. Fletcher
Rescue Company No. 1
February 3, 1925
Manhattan Box 857

With the success of Rescue Company 1, the department brass decided it was time to double their capabilities by establishing a second rescue company in Brooklyn. As before, the call went out and volunteers submitted their names for consideration. The chief of department was again looking for a dynamic captain to lead the new unit. He didn't have to look too far. Captain Walter A. O'Leary of Ladder 6 was given the command. O'Leary joined the FDNY in 1909 and was one of the original members of Rescue 1 when it started in 1915.

Promoted to lieutenant in 1918 then to captain in 1922, O'Leary was assigned to Ladder 6 in Manhattan until word of the additional rescue unit hit the firehouses. The new captain then began to choose his crew. His lieutenant would be Peter F. Walsh of Rescue 1. Also joining them from Rescue 1's roster was Fireman John Kistenberger. Their transfers to the new company along with thirteen other firemen went into effect March 1, 1925.

A fire in the after-hold of the U.S. Navy destroyer USS *Coghlan*, was spreading faster than the crew could control and help from the FDNY was requested. It was the night of May 30, 1925 as the Manhattan fire units responded to the ship's location in the North River at 18th Street. An ensign was missing below decks and members of Rescue 1 donned smoke helmets and searched below for the missing man. Thick smoke was being produced by burning ropes, brushes and cleaning fluids and the flames were inching closer to stored torpedoes as the rescue men searched nearby. Five hose lines were stretched from shore based hydrants and the battle began. Rescue 1 was able to locate the unconscious sailor and carry him to the main deck where he was revived. The fire was extinguished and the weary firemen took up.

A man cleaning the College of the City of New York's chemical vault, sprinkled water on the stone floor, as he had done every day for years when suddenly flames sprang up around him and danced across the fifty-foot long and twenty-foot wide vault. As he ran from the vault he saw the fire closing in on the more than 5,000 jars, tubes and bottles containing several hundred varieties of chemicals. College chemists believe a leaking crock of sodium covered with kerosene spread a puddle across the floor that evaporated. The addition of water on the unprotected pure sodium ignited the flames at about 11 am, August 4, 1925.

The first fire companies to arrive could do little faced with a roaring furnace of chemicals. Deputy Chief Thomas Dougherty special called Rescue 1 to the location on Amsterdam Avenue at 138th Street. Rescue 1 arrived under the command of Lt. Thomas Kilbride, and conferred with the chemistry staff. The true danger quickly became apparent: besides the numerous chemicals, many that were water reactive, a large amount of ammonium nitrate was also stored inside. This highly explosive chemical compound was being threatened by the increasing temperatures around it.

Donning gas masks the rescue men moved towards the blazing vault. They tried applying several different fire extinguishing agents with no results. It was decided that water was the only remaining option. With the help of the units on scene hoses were stretched to the vault area and masked rescue men directed the streams from the vault doorway. At first the only effect seemed to be to lift the fire off the floor and make it burn on the surface of the rising pool of water.

As the pool of water deepened the chemicals were still erupting, and Lt. Kilbride decided that it was time to vent the vault. A team of firemen with mauls was sent to the sidewalk above the vault. They quickly pounded a hole through the concrete opening the roof of the vault to daylight. Inside the blazing chamber the lighter chemicals were burning out and the heavier were under the artificial lake formed by the hose stream run-off.

Despite receiving painful chemical burns where the rising water got above the tops of their boots, the rescue men held their position working the water streams into the super-heated vault. After two hours of dangerous work the fire was brought under control. Among the injured was Lt. Kilbride and the crew of Rescue 1: William Hutcheon, William Dorritie, Joseph Brown, Joseph Sullivan, John Milward and John Kaiser.

Different types of fires present different types of challenges. Ventilation is often difficult to accomplish especially in large fire-proof buildings with cellars and sub-cellars. Ship fires pose similar problems with limited available ventilation and limited access to locations within the ship.

One specific difficult type of fire: an under-pier fire, had all these dangers and difficulties mixed together. The piers were built upon a lattice-work of creosoted pilings that supported, quite often a concrete deck with multi-storied structures built on top. These fires were, and still are, very difficult to extinguish.

It was 5:21 in the afternoon when Manhattan Box 901 was transmitted for a fire at Pier 95 at the foot of West 55th Street on the North River. An employee of the Furness Bermuda Steamboat Line noticed the fire, in the sub-flooring underneath the concrete. He attempted to extinguish the fire himself and burned his hands. He then notified workers on a coal barge moored nearby and they also tried to extinguish the fire with no success. The FDNY was called.

Four fireboats and numerous land-based fire units descended on the pier. With the tide rising it was becoming more and more difficult to hit the body of fire underneath the blazing pier. A group of firemen climbed down onto floating wooden rafts. Laying flat they tried to direct their streams upwards as a strange greenish yellow smoke chugged from the creosoted pine timbers of the sub-flooring. Fireman after fireman fell to the toxic smoke.

Using a large drill members of Rescue 1 cut holes through the pier and cellar pipes were lowered into the 12-inch space below. Four alarms were transmitted and seventy-five firemen were knocked out battling this fire.

A crew of men were in the process of renovating an old four-story dwelling at 26 West 47th Street and converting the structure into offices on December 11, 1925. It was late afternoon and large sections of plaster and lathing were being removed and the resulting debris shoveled outside when a major collapse occurred. The two upper floors and attic dropped in a mass of timber, bricks and plaster dust. As the dust cloud cleared the crew realized workers were pinned beneath tons of beams and debris.

The first arriving units removed several lightly trapped workers to safety. Rescue 1 arrived and began to tunnel into the area where the two men were trapped. For several hours Captain Walter Lamb and Firemen Bela Varga and Cornell Garety carefully worked their way to the pinned men. They cleared away enough debris to allow a priest quick access to administer the Last Rites should things go badly. Doctor Archer joined them providing medical help and then fed liquids to the trapped men to keep up their strength.

As the sky darkened to evening an electrical engineer from a building around the corner rigged up a mast with lighting to make the rescue work safer within the tottering structure. As the last beams were moved away and the crushing weight was cleared the men were gently pulled free and quickly placed on oxygen and carried to a waiting ambulance.

For their life saving efforts under very dangerous conditions the three rescue men were placed on the Roll of Merit with Class II awards.

A speeding touring car being pursued by police became airborne and then collided head-on with a taxi cab in front of the Hotel Alamac on West 71st Street on January 24, 1926. With his friend clinging to the radiator hood, the drunk driver raced wildly through the upper Westside streets leaving a trail of damaged vehicles in his wake. The collision was so severe and the wreckage so twisted that Rescue 1 was special called from Spring Street. Using jacks, pry bars and other tools it took twenty minutes for the rescue men to disentangle the vehicles.

> **The collision was so severe and the wreckage so twisted that Rescue 1 was special called from Spring Street. Using jacks, pry bars and other tools it took twenty minutes for the rescue men to disentangle the vehicles.**

It was like deja vu for Manhattan firemen on February 16, 1926, when Box 54 was transmitted at three in the morning. The fire was on the thirty-third floor of the new Equitable Building, located on the same plot as the original at 120 Broadway. (The original building was completely destroyed by a fire in 1912 that claimed the life of a Battalion Chief). The flames this morning apparently touched off by a plumber's torch in a shaftway, spread upwards to other floors. Rescue 1 joined four alarms worth of firemen and battled this tough blaze for three hours.

Rescue 1 responded to a huge furniture warehouse fire in Harlem on April 24, 1926. Box 1459 would go to five-alarms and required twenty-one engines, six ladders and the rescue company to battle the blaze inside the four-story warehouse at 168 E. 123rd Street. Thirty firemen were injured in the four-hour battle including Firemen Roggencamp and Kennedy of Rescue 1 who both suffered cuts from broken glass.

Several months later companies were operating at an upper-floor fire at 543 Broadway an eight-story loft building. It was August 8, 1926 and the fire was so advanced upon arrival that Chief Henry Helm ordered the water tower set up and operated. For a half hour the powerful stream was directed into the burning floor until the chief believed it was safe to enter. Helm sent Lt. Charles Marquardt and his crew from Hook & Ladder 9 along with Captain Lamb and his crew from Rescue 1 to the fire floor to assess the fire situation.

Both units reached the seventh floor and began to search when a backdraught suddenly occurred toppling firemen left and right. Lt. Marquardt became separated from his crew and was driven to the front windows by heavy fire. The officer was forced to climb out onto the window ledge to avoid the flames. Firemen inside scrambled trying to reach the trapped man. Scaling ladders were called for as conditions worsened. Marquardt dangled by his finger tips from the ledge and worked his toes into the crevice between the bricks holding himself away from the flames and above a seven story fall.

Inside Captain Lamb and his men made a makeshift ladder from furniture and the officer leaned out trying to help the lieutenant. A scaling ladder was set in place next to the officer and he climbed onto to it then was helped in on the floor below. Somehow during the rescue operation Lamb's make-shift ladder of furniture collapsed beneath him and the captain took a painful fall onto the floor. Lamb and Marquardt shook off their minor injuries and returned to the firefighting. The blaze was held to a second alarm.

Great clouds of smoke poured from the sub-cellar of 105-107 Duane Street near Broadway during the afternoon of August 27, 1926. Members of Rescue 1 cut through iron-grated doors to allow access to the hot, smoky fire. They also pulled two unconscious firemen from the thick smoke and placed them at the aid station with the thirty other firemen, including several from Rescue 1, who were suffering from the dense smoke.

More than a thousand persons at a Sunday night concert at the Winter Garden Theatre watched the show completely unaware that right outside their building a much larger crowd was watching Rescue 1 don their smoke helmets and disappeared into ammonia fumes filling theatre basement. It was September 26, 1926 when the rescue men searched for the valves to the large ammonia tanks. After twenty minutes the danger was resolved and the firemen took up. Inside the Winter Garden the show went on without a hitch.

The rescue was masked up again on October 1st, when they plunged into deadly nitric acid fumes spewing from a chemical laboratory on the fourth floor of 47 Fulton Street. The first arriving units suffered greatly until the rescue wagon arrived. Seventeen firemen were overcome by the toxic fumes, many were dragged out by their comrades a few by helmeted rescue men. Under the cover of a hose stream rescue men entered the laboratory and removed the leaking carboy and removed it to the street.

An unusual special call for the company occured on the evening of December 20, 1926. The Central Theatre, Broadway and Forty-seventh Street, was to be the site of a movie premier featuring the film: *Fire Brigade*. Earlier in the evening, before the movie was to be shown, workers were erecting an electrical sign on top of the theatre's marquee. During this operation a large section of the two-ton marquee collapsed, and despite the efforts of the sign workers it could not be removed.

Chief Kenlon, a guest at the premier, telephoned the quarters of Rescue 1 and requested they respond. Working with Ladder 4, the rescue men used torches to cut away the collapsed section of the marquee as the Fire Department Band played nearby. The danger was cleared and the audience filled the theatre.

The firemen did not get to watch the film: an exciting depiction of the working day of a fireman, produced by Louis B. Mayer and Irving Thalberg. The movie was a hit and Chief Kenlon in his remarks stated "It was one of the finest films ever produced." Mayer and Thalberg also donated 25% of the movie receipts to the FDNY Fire College.

In January, 1927, New York City was feeling the chilling effects of the winter; it was the coldest January 27th in fifty-six years. The thermometer said the temperature was in the teens, and except for the unfortunate few with no home to go to, the streets of the city were deserted. As the day wore on, the mercury dropped even further.

At eight o'clock that blustery night, a patrolman walking his beat saw smoke coming from the third floor of 144 Goerck Street and summoned the fire department. Goerck Street was located under the Williamsburg Bridge and ran from East Houston Street to Grand Street. The transmission of Manhattan Box 416 sent Engines 11, 15, 25 and 28, Ladder Companies 11 and 18, the Third and Fourth Battalions along with two fireboats, the *William L. Strong* (Engine 66) from Grand Street and *Seth Low* (Engine 232) from Noble Street in Brooklyn.

The companies arrived to an advanced fire condition in the seven-story loft building. A number of explosions accelerated the fire and hastened its spread upward. Thick smoke and flames poured from the windows as lines from the first due engines protected people fleeing from nearby tenements. It was then decided to set up for an exterior attack. Second and third alarms were struck. This brought an additional ten engines, two ladder companies, a water tower, Rescue 1, and the fireboat *New Yorker* (Engine 77) from the foot of Beekman Street. Also responding were the chiefs of the Second Battalion, the Nineteenth Battalion (Marine Battalion) and First Division.

After about an hour it appeared the fire was knocked down enough to allow companies to enter the structure for the last stages of the battle and then for overhauling. In front of the building Assistant Chief Smoky Joe Martin and Deputy Chief Henry Helm discussed the possibility of releasing units as companies started moving in. Members of Engine 77, under the command of Lt. Alexander Gray, and Engine 9, led by Lt. Edward Smith entered the fire area with hand lines.

Smith later stated, "There were five men with me, when we heard a crash above us, followed by a crash after crash as the debris hit the overhead floors, broke through and descended. Then the fourth floor broke above our heads… crashed down upon us. The third floor broke beneath our feet and we tumbled beneath the accumulated debris of the overhead floors."

Fireman Klein of Engine 9 was about to step off the ladder into the building when the collapse threw him from the ladder saving him from tons of rubble. A huge, debris filled hole, from the seventh floor to the basement, now imprisoned the men of at least two companies. At the sound of the collapse, firemen engaged at other places stopped what they were doing and rallied for instructions. Entry through the front entrance proved impossible due to debris from the collapse.

As fallen portable ladders were being re-raised, Lt. Smith crawled from the debris and appeared at a second floor window, helmet-less, with blood streaming down his face and his clothes in tatters. He gave a weak wave and fell from sight. Moments later he was being removed from the building by brother firemen. Then Lt. Gray appeared and was also quickly removed to safety. Firemen began digging, searching for their trapped brothers as flames among the ruins began to intensify. The fire would have to be controlled without jeopardizing the imprisoned men. Leading the dangerous work was Lt. Thomas Kilbride and his crew from Rescue 1: Firemen Bela Varga, William Hutcheon, John Milward, James Walsh, Charles Kennedy, Edward Cronin, Peter Doyle and John Mayr.

Shortly after the digging began, Fireman Anzelone of Engine 9 was uncovered; first a hand, then a shoulder, then his head. Anzelone told his rescuers that he was afraid he was badly hurt and was going to die. A priest was sent for at Saint Rose of Lima Church just across the street from the fire.

Father McCarthy was in the rectory's tub enjoying a warm bath, when suddenly there was a banging at the front door. A few moments later a grim faced fireman stood framed in the doorway. The priest found himself being hurried from his warm quarters and into the sub-freezing night. The reverend, in his robe and slippers, was picked up by the burley fireman and carried across the rivers of ice-water that filled the street, then up and across the crumbled ruins to the point of the rescue operations.

The priest crawled on hands and knees through the charred and twisted remains of the collapsed building to Anzelone and administered the Last Rites. Before Father McCarthy left his side he asked if there was anything he wanted. A shivering Anzelone said he was cold and wondered if he could have some whisky. The priest returned to the street and went to Chief of Department Kenlon who had assumed command. Through clattering teeth and blue lips, McCarthy explained the wishes of the imprisoned man to the ice-covered chief. Honorary Chief Robert Mainzer, who stood nearby, was given the nod by Kenlon. Mainzer retraced the path the priest had taken through the collapsed areas of the fire building to the trapped man's side. He talked and shared a few sips from his flask with the injured man as firemen worked around them.

> The fire was now completely extinguished, and the only battle remaining for the firemen was with the ice and frozen rubble. A groan was heard, and a new spirit removed the fatigue from the weary rescuers.

At about eleven o'clock, after hours of careful digging, Anzelone was freed. Shortly thereafter Fireman Gallagher from Engine 77 was found and removed, unconscious. He was rushed to Gouveners Hospital where he joined Anzelone. The fire was now completely extinguished, and the only battle remaining for the firemen was with the ice and frozen rubble. A groan was heard, and a new spirit removed the fatigue from the weary rescuers. They renewed their work with the strength of fresh men. Fireman Egan from Engine 9 was found, and after a careful tunneling operation, he was rescued. As they removed Egan they heard Fireman Sweeney of Engine 77, who had been trapped beneath the other man. He too was carefully freed, and they both were removed to the hospital. Firemen Edward Fox and John Grane both of Engine 77 were later found dead among the timbers.

Hope in finding other firefighters still alive dwindled as the night dragged on. Many of the companies were placed back in service. Kilbride and Rescue 1, worked on beneath spotlights, using pry bars, hand saws, jacks and a block and tackle to remove timbers and other debris. At 6:20 a.m., Fireman Hesline of Engine 9 was found in an upright position, still holding the nozzle. All work was stopped and a priest was called for. Every firefighter on the scene stood quietly, helmet off, head bowed as the dead man received the Last Rites. The ritual completed, the exhausted firemen gently dug him out of the rubble and carried him from the fire building. The last of their brothers had been found.

It was later determined that the collapse was caused by a build-up of ice on the building and the weight of the tons of water soaked stock on the upper floors.

In what was probably the largest awarding of departmental recognition for a single operation before or since, the Board of Merit placed the names of all the men of Rescue 1, Engines 11, 15, 17, 25, 55 and Ladders 6, 9, 10, 11 18 and 20 on the Roll of Merit. A total of 112 members were awarded Class II's.

A dozen boys were playing at a construction site, the Sixth Avenue subway extension near Prince Street, on the evening of August 2, 1927. Without warning the walls of the excavation gave way burying four boys beneath tons of dirt. Rescue 1 responded and bounded into the dirt pile, the shear walls of the cut looming over them. Quickly but carefully they began digging out the trapped children. Two boys were buried up to their eyes, while the other two could not be seen at all.

After a few minutes of careful work the first two boys were freed and all efforts were then concentrated on the other two. Above on the street, crowds of frantic parents and excited neighbors moved in fearing their children were among those trapped. Even after the remaining two were pulled alive from the dirt the search continued just in case. Finally the search was called off after it was confirmed all the children were accounted for.

Despite their gas masks and smoke helmets, the men of Rescue 1 considered themselves "smoke-eaters". Like the rest of the department, the majority of their firefighting was done without breathing protection. A case in point was September 22, 1927 when a fire was discovered at 108 Duane Street next door the Ladder Company 1's quarters. It was 7:30 p.m. when the first of three alarms was transmitted for Box 139 for a fire in the five-story building housing the Hamilton Rubber Company and the Eureka Shoe Company.

The fire started on the second floor and the smoke became so thick that the lights in City Hall Park, five blocks away were almost blotted out. Fumes from burning celluloid used to cover the heels on women's shoes seriously affected many firemen. This fire generated one of the largest casualty lists from celluloid fumes in the department's history: with one hundred and twenty-five firemen overcome or affected by the dense smoke. The firehouses of Engine 7 (a double company) and Ladder 1 were transformed into a temporary hospital.

When the blaze was extinguished, Kilbride and the company returned to their Spring Street firehouse. Kilbride and Fireman Joseph Fullam who'd both taken a tremendous pounding at the fire and were having difficulty breathing, Doctor Archer was sent for. Fullam was given time off but remained in quarters. Kilbride was taken to St. Vincent's Hospital in serious condition suffering from "smoke poisoning." Kilbride would return to full-duty in a few days.

An engineer and his helper working on the refrigeration plant in the cellar of the Ambassador Hotel's annex on Park Avenue at 52nd Street, were overcome by fumes. It was 2 in the morning October 22, 1927 when Rescue 1 was called to the scene. Firemen Daugherty and Rogan donned smoke helmets and entered the toxic atmosphere. They located the unconscious men and dragged them to the street where other rescue men began to revive them with pulmotors. The smoke helmeted rescue

Rescue men working at a chemical leak. Often their clothing was left in tatters by the caustic smoke and chemical clouds they encountered.

men returned to the cellar and worked for forty-five minutes to stop the leak and disperse the fumes.

In the Spring of 1928 Rescue Company 1 and Rescue Company 2 were called to the FDNY drill yard in the rear of the training school on East 68th Street in Manhattan to conduct tests on new gas masks being considered by the department. One of the masks being tried was made by the Mine Safety Appliance Company (MSA) and the representative of that company was a familiar figure in the FDNY rescue community: Alfred Kinsella who was an original member of Rescue 1 in 1915. He retired from the FDNY with the rank of captain.

Many chief officers were on hand at the test and watched with interest as the smoke house was filled with rubber, sulphur and various other types of pungent smoke. Several members of the rescue companies used the American Atmos Company's mask (the mask currently in use by FDNY rescue units) while others donned the MSA "Burrell" masks.

Rescue 1 operated at this tenement fire at 55 Spring Street on March 3, 1927. A New York City police officer was killed, while attempting a rescue at this fire.

The Burrell mask is a filter type type containing a canister filled with chemicals for absorbing or rendering harmless all poisons, gases, smoke and fumes and for converting carbon monoxide into harmless carbon dioxide. It was also equipped with a tell-tail dial showing the amount of service the canister has been subjected to and indicates when a new canister should replace the one in use.

The test lasted a half-hour and the men wearing the Burrell mask remained in the smoke house as long as the Atmos wearers. Three times during the trial the test light in the regulation mine lamp went out, indicating the absence of oxygen in the air. The chief in charge of the test made no official comment to the media present citing he had to make a formal report to the chief of department first. Al Kinsella stated however he was very happy with the tests.

A series of subway excavation accidents kept Rescue 1 busy in the Spring of 1928. Fifteen men were buried seventy-five feet underground when the overhead dirt and rock fell on them as they worked digging the new Fort Washington subway at 174th Street and Broadway on April 18th. Rescue 1 responded and helped local companies remove the trapped men who were at the end of a long underground passage beyond where the steel superstructure and cement flooring had been installed. Two of the workers were killed but the remaining men were removed alive. Firemen also had to deal with forty sticks of dynamite buried along with the workers.

The following month, on May 25th, a 100-foot section of pavement on Saint Nicholas Avenue between 147th and 148th Streets suddenly collapsed into the new subway cut below. A woman rode down with the debris into the hole as workers below dodged the falling concrete. She was quickly removed unharmed. Rescue 1 and teams of firemen then dug in the area for a child believed to be missing and possibly under the collapse. Happily he was found safe and sound some time later.

On June 18, 1928, the FDNY celebrated Medal Day on the steps of City Hall. Captain Walter L. Lamb of Rescue Company 1 was awarded the Stephenson Medal for maintaining the best disciplined and most highly efficient company in the department for the year 1927. Lamb joined the FDNY in 1913 and later transferred to Rescue 1 where he worked until he was promoted lieutenant. Lamb had also received six citations for bravery in his carreer.

Captain Walter Lamb

The work being done by Rescue 1 saving the lives of numerous people and helping prevent the loss of thousands of dollars of property, captured the imagination of the media and the public. A headline article in the *New York Times* July 17, 1928 read:

FIREMEN REVIVE 3 KITTENS
SAVE THOUSANDS OF DOLLARS WORTH
OF CHEESE IN AMMONIA BLOW-OUT

The story related the response of Rescue 1 to the basement of the Kraft-Phenix Company plant on North Moore Street where a pressure gasket in an ammonia compressor blew out filling the basement with fumes that seeped upwards into the first floor. Quick work by the smoke helmeted rescue men diverted the fumes up an elevator shaft while the leak was controlled. These actions saved thousands of dollars of cheese stored in the basement. The firemen also revived three unconscious kittens found in the basement. Several minutes of vigorous artificial resuscitation and the kittens were soon back on the job as the cheese company's mascots.

Another story appearing two days later described how the FDNY would be sending 20 firemen to represent the department in the International Congress of Fire Brigades in Turin, Italy in September. Among those chosen to compete was Fireman Thomas K. Larkin of Rescue 1.

During 1928, The New York City Police Department detailed members of their emergency squads to the FDNY Rescue Companies 1 and 2, for thirty days "for the purpose of familiarizing themselves with the use and operation of tools, appliances etc., of the Rescue Companies, and creating greater cooperation between the Rescue Companies… and the Emergency Squads of the Police Department."

The morning of June 10, 1928 a young man working at the Manhattan Desk Company at 56 Thomas Street got his legs caught between the elevator and the walls of the shaft. Ladder Company 1 arrived and seeing that special tools would be needed called in Rescue 1. They were able to chip away three-feet of tile and mortar, enough to slip the youth clear.

The company again responded to a series of serious ammonia situations in July 1928. The first incident was on the afternoon of the 6th. Inside the Astor Theatre at 1531 Broadway, a valve burst and two men were overcome by the fumes from the leaking ammonia. Rescue 1 arrived and using their smoke helmets were able to control the leak. Six days later they were called to the cellar of a yeast company on East Ninth Street. With Lt. Hogan in charge they donned smoke helmets and worked for forty-five minutes to locate the burst gasket.

It was a few minutes after 10 pm on July 29, 1928 when two elevated subway trains collided on the Sixth Avenue Elevated Line. One car ran into the other telescoping the cars and trapping the motorman. The collision also threw the wheels of the two cars off the tracks and caused the short circuit of the third rail and a small fire. One of the passengers on the subway at the time was an off-duty fireman who called the dispatcher and requested the box to be transmitted and special calls for Rescue 1 and Searchlight 1.

Under the powerful spotlights of the Searchlight unit, Rescue 1 cut away steel and wood to allow the fires beneath the cars to be extinguished. A number of seriously injured people required medical attention including one man who's leg had to be amputated. Rescue 1 using torches and hand tools worked with ambulance doctors disentangling those trapped in the twisted wreckage.

On a cold, blustery January 6, 1929 Manhattan fire companies rolled out the door at 1:20 in the afternoon for a reported fire in a five-story building at 368 Broadway. Flames on the third floor were extending rapidly up the inner staircase. Working on the fifth floor was a young deaf mute man who tried to exit but was driven to the windows by the expanding fire and smoke condition. Arriving on the scene Fireman Walter Hazrick of Engine 7, who was driving the chief noticed the young man trapped above and had an aerial ladder placed at the window.

Fireman Hazrick hurried up the ladder into the cloud of smoke as gale force winds tore at his fire coat and whipped the flames below into a frenzy. Quick on his heels were two other firemen: Harry Schnall of Ladder 8 and William Dorritie of Rescue 1. The young man was located in the swirling smoke but before they could move out onto the ladder fire broke out the windows below them cutting off their escape. The three firemen and their charge were now trapped with fire below and in front and behind them.

Realizing the position they were in the water tower was hastily erected and water directed into the window below them to control the auto exposure. Hazrick tied a rope onto the young man before climbing out onto the still steaming aerial ladder. Schnall and Dorritie helped the young man climb out the window and make his way onto the ladder. Carefully with the wind buffeting their every step the young man was guided to the ground as the other two firemen returned to the ladder and then the ground.

For their heroic actions the three firemen were placed on the Roll of Merit. A Class I with the Crimmins and Department Medals went to Walter Hazrick. Class II awards went to Harry Schnall and William Dorritie.

A three-and-a-half ton bundle of eight steel girders were dropped from the twenty-second floor of the new 24-story Western Union Building at West Broadway and Thomas Streets, during construction on April 20, 1929. The falling steel tore through scaffolding on the eighth and second floors carrying four workers to their sudden death. At least a dozen others were injured and fire units quickly responded to the scene. With damaged equipment dangling above their heads Rescue 1 moved in and removed several injured workers. When the hazard above was contained they continued cutting and lifting debris until all those underneath were pulled clear.

A major ammonia leak occurred on the afternoon of June 29, 1929 at the Community Ice Company plant on Stebbins Avenue in the Bronx. First arriving cops and firemen had great difficulty helping the two hundred people fleeing from neighboring tenements as the choking fumes filled the streets. Conditions were becoming so severe that several persons three blocks away from the building were partially overcome and needed medical attention.

Rescue 1 was special called and made the 14-mile run from Spring Street in 21 minutes. Upon their arrival they donned their smoke helmets and plunged into the toxic atmosphere. They located the shut offs controlling the ammonia feed, and repaired the leak.

Another emergency that just seemed to get worse and worse happened on November 11, 1929. It was late afternoon at the subway excavation on Fourteenth Street just east of Eighth Avenue, when a dynamite driven boulder tore through a water main. Water flooded the cut and began to undermine the superstructure surrounding it. Crowds of people pressed in the watch the swirling waters. Despite warnings from workers, a small group crowded onto a fifty-foot section of planking and sidewalk that bridged the work area to watch the activity below. Several minutes later the entire sidewalk area collapsed from the building line carrying four people down with it. They fell into the muddy water with tumbling beams, scaffolding, concrete and debris falling on top of them.

Ten fire companies responded including Rescue 1. Rescue men moved in and began cutting away timbers making their way to those trapped. Working in the rising water it became clear that some of the falling timbers had also broken a nearby sewer line as raw sewage entered the cut.

Police lines were moved back two hundred feet from the collapsed area as the weight of the crowds threatened further damage. As the rescue work continued another large section of planking and sidewalk fell nearby. With all the civilians removed Rescue 1 continued the dangerous back breaking work of searching for possible workers trapped beneath the water logged rubble. When a true head count was made, and all workers were accounted for, the work was called off. Among the four of the trapped civilians rescued was a 77 year-old woman who was taken, in serious condition, to a nearby hospital with a fractured skull.

A most unusual airplane crash occurred on November 21, 1929 when a blue and yellow biplane carrying the pilot and a passenger lost power over the upper Westside and crashed into the new YMCA building at 2 West 64th Street just west of Central Park. Rescue 1 and other FDNY units responded to the scene. The pilot was killed in the crash, but the passenger, who was a lion tamer by trade, was able to parachute to safety and landed on a nearby roof. The plane struck the YMCA building then fell onto a setback of the building next door. Rescue 1 cut the pilot from the wreckage.

The National Board of Underwriters issued a report of the effectiveness of the New York City Fire Department. This report issued in October 1929, based on a survey and investigation conducted during the year. Every aspect of the department, including manning, number and location of units, apparatus, tools, hose, water supply, response, fire alarm system, etc., were evaluated, rated, and recommendations were made. The evaluation committee was so impressed with the accomplishments and operations of the rescue companies that they recommended establishment of additional rescue capabilities. They said this service should extend to "the Bronx, Flatbush, Long Island City, Jamaica, and other areas." This recommendation led to the establishment of Rescue 3 in the Bronx and Rescue 4 midway between Long Island City and Jamaica in Queens on June 1, 1931, and Rescue 5 in Staten Island during 1948.

> The evaluation committee was so impressed with the accomplishments and operations of the rescue companies that they recommended establishment of additional rescue capabilities.

Lt. Kilbride wearing the battery operated telephone set that could be hard-wired to the smoke helmets. This allowed instant communications between the inside teams and the outside.

Chapter 3

The Thirties

Still reeling from the Wall Street Crash that began in October of 1929, the country and the city were plunged into what would become known as the Great Depression. New York City firemen were now working a two-platoon system. A platoon was on duty from 9 a.m. to 6 p.m. for two days. On the third day the platoon was on duty for 24 hours. On the fourth and fifth days the platoon is on duty from 6 p.m. to 9 a.m. On the sixth day the platoon is off 24 hours. This new chart could be suspended at any time in the event of a public emergency. Firemen are now "only" working 84 hours a week. Prosperity or depression the job of fighting fires was still the same: difficult, dirty and dangerous.

> Firemen are now "only" working 84 hours a week. Prosperity or depression the job of fighting fires was still the same: difficult, dirty and dangerous.

The morning of January 4, 1930 had Rescue 1 responding to a building collapse at 182 South Street, in the shadow of the Brooklyn Bridge. The four-story ramshackle brick building, used to store and bale waste paper stock, had suffered serious fires in October and December the year before. Condemned, the building was in the process of demolition when the building collapsed trapping four workers beneath piles of charred wood, beams and soaked waste paper.

After two hours of dangerous work, Rescue 1 removed several trapped men who were rushed to the hospital each with multiple injuries. The last man was found still alive, but pinned under a heavy printing press. It took another hour to extricate him; he later died in the hospital. In all, the lives of two workers were lost, but four men were rescued alive.

Beneath the concrete platform of Wall Street subway station, a small fire smoldered within a rubbish heap. It was 1:10 in the afternoon on January 28, 1930 when the movement of passing trains fanned the fire until the smoke condition had become so thick all train traffic in and out of the station was halted. Fire companies were unable to access the seat of the fire until Rescue 1 arrived and was asked to drill through the concrete platform. For twenty minutes, under the direction of Captain Lamb, holes were made through the eight-inches of concrete until an opening large enough for a fireman to pass through was completed. Firemen then descended with a hose and quickly extinguished the fire.

Captain Walter Lamb would end his long tenure in Rescue 1 when he was promoted to Battalion Chief on March 1, 1930. On the same day Captain Cornell M. Garety was transferred from Hook & Ladder 40 and given command of Rescue Company 1. Garety had been assigned to Rescue 1 as a fireman.

While battling a fire in a one-story structure in the rear of the four-story loft building at 862 Sixth Avenue near Fiftieth Street, several explosions of stored flammables rocked the building. It was just past 7 a.m., March 14, 1930 when the first explosion threw several firemen into a parked engine. Meanwhile up on the roof, chopping holes to vent the heavy smoke, was Lt. Kilbride and six men from Rescue 1. Moments later another explosion caused the roof to collapse carrying the entire crew of Rescue 1 crashing to the ground. Amazingly no one was killed, but Kilbride and Firemen William Hutcheon, James Walsh, Bela Varga, Peter Doyle, Edward Cronin and John Milward were all cut and severely bruised. They were tended to by doctors, but remained on-duty.

It was about 2 o'clock in the afternoon of June 20, 1930, when an old seven-story brick warehouse at 417 Washington Street suddenly crashed to the ground. Mounds of red brick, beams and rubble swept into the street. Fire companies rolled into the dust cloud with reports stating that as many as twenty people could be trapped within the ruins. Fireman Edward Cronin of Rescue 1 observed a man clinging to a rear window sill of the collapsed building, one of the only walls still standing. With the unstable structure in danger of further collapse, swift action needed to be taken. Gaining a position above the trapped man, Cronin was lowered over forty feet by rope from the adjoining building. Another rope was then passed down to Cronin. He lowered it to the victim and told the victim to secure himself. Cronin then held him in place from this precarious position, with danger of further collapse, until a ladder could be positioned. Cronin was awarded the Kenny and Department Medals for his part in the rescue.

Fireman Edward Cronin, Jr.

A chemical explosion rocked the upper floor of a five-story building on Prince Street at 5:29 p.m., on August 11, 1930. The blast knocked a huge section of the side wall and roof down onto the roof of a two-story commercial building next door. A large portion of this building, a printing company filled with workers, then collapsed under the impact of the bricks and heavy timbers that rained down on it.

Fireman Bela Varga

Rescue 1 arrived on scene and went into action. Fireman Bela Varga descended into the debris in search of victims. While digging through the rubble, he saw a woman's hair and began clearing debris around her. She was in a seated position, completely covered with bricks and other building materials. With parts of the building still falling around him, Varga removed his helmet and placed it on the woman's head as he continued digging. Despite being struck by a falling brick and receiving a painful head laceration, Varga continued until he freed her her from the rubble. The woman was carefully removed and given medical attention by Doctor Archer. Amazingly she'd only suffered an abrasion to her nose. Fireman Varga was awarded the Walter Scott and Department Medals for this rescue. Rescue 1 Firemen Charles Kennedy, Charles Roggencamp and Lawrence Fullam were also placed on the Roll of Merit for their heroic operations at this collapse. Each was awarded a Class III.

It was 4 in the morning when the automatic alarm sounded for 11 West 19th Street a 12-story loft building that ran through to West 20th Street. It was September 14, 1930 and the first arriving units stepped from their rigs into a pouring rain seeing smoke chugging from an eleventh floor window. A second alarm was transmitted as firemen made their way up to the fire floor. As the attack commenced three firemen became separated and lost in the heavy smoke. Two of the men fell unconscious as the other staggered to a window.

Seeing the trapped man, and knowing the extreme conditions on the fire floor, Chief Martin sent Rescue 1 upstairs with smoke helmets. Under the protection of two hose streams, rescue men were able to press forward into the terrible heat and smoke. They located the two unconscious men and dragged them clear of the fire area, then plunged back into the searing heat. They were able to pull the now semi-conscious fireman from the window ledge. The three were taken to the street and worked on with inhalators. They all responded to treatment.

For their heroic efforts during this operation, Rescue 1 Firemen William Dorritie, Henry Mulholland, Peter Doyle, Charles Kennedy, Edward Cronin and John Conners were all placed on the Roll of Merit with Class III awards.

The department purchased two identical Mack rescue trucks in 1931. These were Bulldog AP-10 chain driven models that were purchased for $9,250 each. They were similar to the

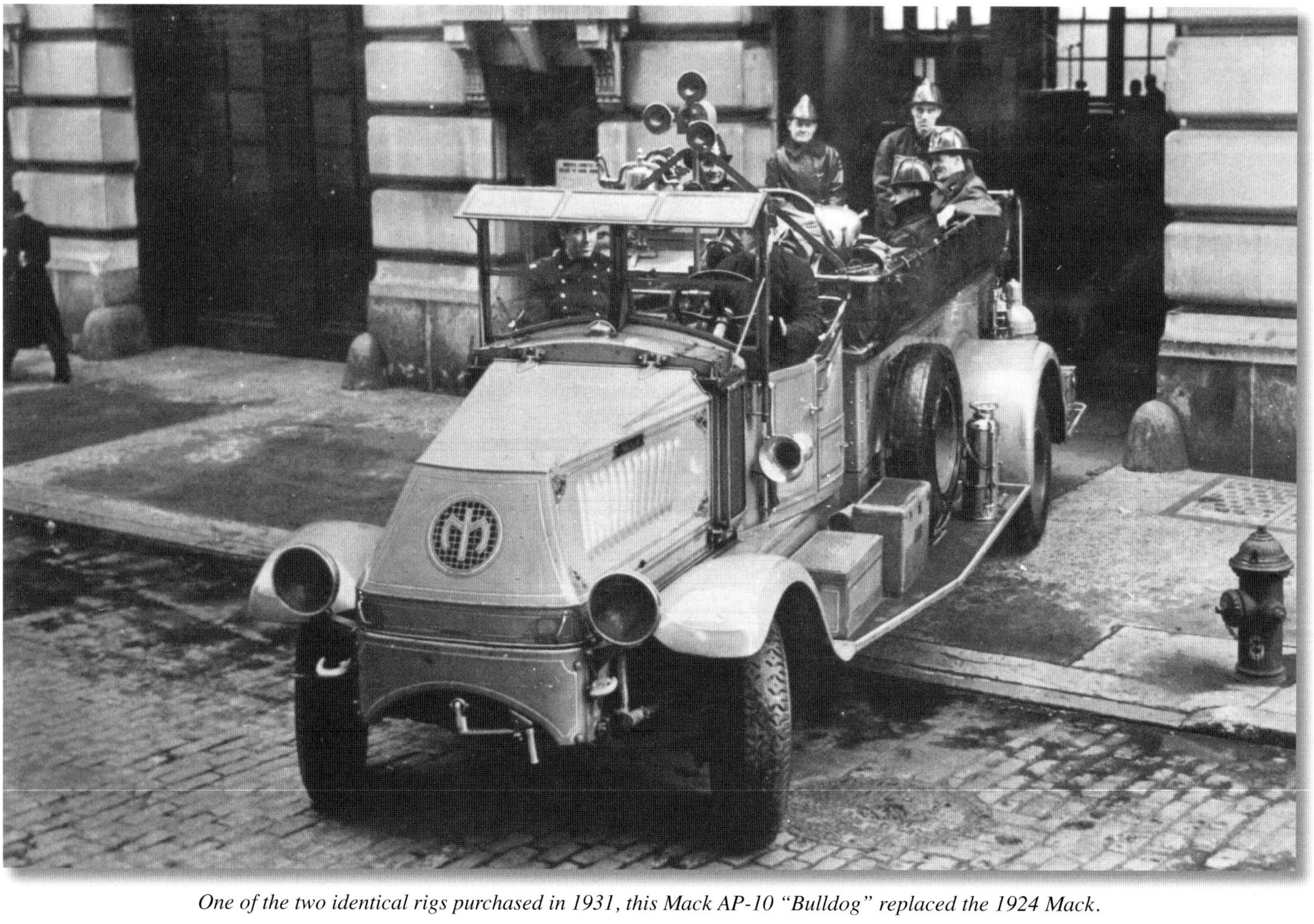

One of the two identical rigs purchased in 1931, this Mack AP-10 "Bulldog" replaced the 1924 Mack.

1924 rig in appearance, but were slightly longer and had lower bodies. They were assigned to Rescue Company 1 and Rescue Company 2. The one assigned to Rescue 1 was placed in service on March 19, 1931 with registration number 1009, and remained in service until 1940. It was then extensively upgraded by the addition of a roof over the entire rig with roll-down canvas sides to protect the members riding in the rear. It was then assigned to Rescue 3, where it remained in service until replaced with a new rig in 1953. It remained on the roster as a spare until January 31, 1955, when it was disposed of.

A fire was discovered burning in the plant of the Brooklyn Bridge Freezing and Cold Storage Company beneath the arch of the Brooklyn Bridge, at Frankfort, Vanderwater and Pearl Streets at 7:30 in the morning on April 30, 1931. The fire proved to be almost impossible to reach, due to the design of the building and the thick insulated walls. For hours firemen tried to reach the seat of the fire without luck. Rescue 1 loaded large pneumatic drills into the elevator and headed to the fire floor, with orders to penetrate the thick walls.

During their ascent the elevator became stalled, trapping Captain Cornell Garety, and Firemen Robert Tierney and Henry Mulholland in the smoke filled shaftway. Realizing their dangerous situation, Lt. Kilbride and the remaining members went to help them. It took five minutes for them to lower the car, but the smoke condition was so extreme that Garity, Mulholland and Tierney were all removed from the car unconscious. Lt. Kilbride was also overcome during their rescue.

The men were treated by Doctor Archer with Garity, Kilbride and Tierney all reviving quickly. A resuscitator was used to revive Mulholland. These men were then taken by ambulance to the quarters of Rescue 1. The remaining members of Rescue 1 went back to work drilling through the thick walls. This allowed nozzles and distributors to hit the fire directly.

With the continued success of Rescue 1 and Rescue 2, the fire department added two additional rescue companies to the FDNY roster on June 1, 1931. Rescue 3 was organized in the Bronx responding from the quarters of Hook & Ladder 17. On the new company's opening day roster were: Firemen Bela Varga, Lawrence Fullam and William Hutcheon transferred from Rescue 1. Also starting the same day was Rescue 4 in Queens stationed in the quarters of Engine 262 on Queens Boulevard. The officer in command of Rescue 4 was Lieutenant Thomas K. Larkin, a fireman in Rescue 1 from 1922 until his promotion to lieutenant and assignment to Hook & Ladder 10 on November 1, 1928. Larkin was later promoted to captain and would be given command of Rescue 3.

It was 4 o'clock in the afternoon on July 22, 1931. Workers were busy building the new five-story New York Telephone Company building on the block bounded by Walker, Church, and Lispenard Streets and Sixth Avenue. Cranes swung overhead moving materials to upper floors while the various trades went about their jobs. Suddenly a loud screeching and grinding sound knifed through the site. Heads turned to see cables snapping and tons of steel raining down. Unexpectedly, the crane itself then tore loose from its base on top of exposed structural steel girders and toppled over.

Firemen went to work moving the injured to safer locations, as the Rescue Company began lifting and shoring the jumble of fallen beams and girders entrapping several workers below. A man working in his office across Lispenard Street was also injured, when the boom of the collapsing derrick came crashing through the roof and front of his building. One worker was killed, thrown to his death as the steel gave way. Eight others were injured.

Seven workmen, part of a gang of twelve remodeling a three-story tenement at 327 E. 13th Street, were injured and narrowly escaped death as the building they were working in collapsed around them, on September 29, 1931. The crew had been on the job for only a few minutes that morning, when suddenly one of the walls began to sag. The men rushed for the street just as the walls and the rear part of the roof came tumbling down. As the cloud of dust settled, a quick headcount was taken. Men were missing. The fire department was called, and the first due units quickly rescued six workers suffering only slight injuries.

But, one worker was still missing beneath fallen debris. Fireman William Dorritie of Rescue 1 found a small opening and crawled into the pile of rubble in search of the trapped man. With a wall dangling dangerously over his head, Dorritie located the worker, unconscious and covered with bricks and debris. Carefully Dorritie began digging the man out by hand, stopping only to allow a doctor to examine and treat the injured man. After twenty minutes, the last pieces of debris were cleared away and the unconscious worker was gently pulled from the wreckage. For his heroic rescue Fireman William A. Dorritie was awarded the John H. Prentice Medal.

Fireman William A. Dorritie

Rescue 1 joined Manhattan companies in battling one of the largest pier fires in the department's history the morning of May 5, 1932. Five alarms would be needed, as almost 300 firemen were injured or overcome battling this difficult and smoky blaze at Pier 54, Fourteenth Street and the North River. The creosoted pilings beneath the 925-foot long pier gave off extremely noxious and thick smoke, and was nearly impossible to reach with hose streams. It was necessary to use breaking tools powered by air compressors to breach the heavy planking and one-inch thick concrete pier deck to reach the seat of the fire.

It was 10:39 on the evening of May 26, 1932, when Manhattan Box 549 was transmitted for a warehouse fire at 8 Gansevoort Street. Flames were pouring from the top floor windows and were already through the roof, as Engine 3 ascended the stairs with a hose line. The nozzle team tried valiantly to get water on the fire, but conditions were so intense chief officers ordered them to back down for their own safety. As the members pulled the hose line back, conditions on the fire floor had become extreme. Fearing for his men's safety, Captain William Heffernan remained to the last ensuring all his men were down.

The last man, Fireman George Cavanagh, stopped and looked back for his officer. Heffernan did not appear. He'd fallen unconscious in the suffocating heat and smoke. Cavanagh re-entered to cauldron of heat and smoke seeking his fallen captain. Somehow, without a mask, Cavanagh found his boss and began dragging Heffernan back towards the stairs. Before reaching safety, the captain became entangled in the hose line and as Cavanagh struggled to free him, he too collapsed unconscious, overcome by the dense smoke. Captain Cornell Garety of Rescue 1 entered the top floor and under extreme conditions was able to locate Captain Heffernan, and untangle him from the hose by removing his boots. He then dragged the fire officer back to the stairs, as members of Rescue 1 removed the unconscious Cavanagh.

The Board of Merit met and awarded a Class I and Department Medal to Captain Cornell Garety along with the James Gordon Bennett Medal as the most outstanding deed of valor for the year. Fireman Cavanagh also received a medal. Three other members of Rescue 1 were also honored for their life saving efforts at this fire. Firemen Charles Roggencamp, James E. Walsh and Dominico DiBenedetto were awarded Class III ratings. Also honored was Lt. George H. Friel a member of the Cambridge, Massachusetts Fire Department. Friel was attending the FDNY Fire College, and was temporarily assigned to Rescue 1. He responded and worked with them at this fire.

Captain Cornell Garety

Monday August 1, 1932 was a beautiful day in New York City. People strolled along the sun bathed streets, many in their shirt sleeves, enjoying the bright spring morning. In the Ritz Tower Hotel, a forty-one story apartment hotel on Park Avenue and 57th Street, people sat and chatted in the lobby before embarking on a day of sightseeing. The Doubleday-Doran Bookstore and the Kirkpatrick Jewelry Store, both within the hotel building structure, were doing a brisk business. The jewelry store's display attracted many curious window shoppers. Mid-morning pedestrians had just begun to pick up the quick pace of the city.

In a storeroom in the building's second sub-cellar, a building engineer noticed smoke issuing from a paint vault. The vault itself was nine feet by six feet and nine feet high; it was contained in a storeroom thirty feet by forty-five feet with twelve foot ceilings. The vault, not vented to the outside air, contained paints, kerosene, gasoline, turpentine, varnish remover and other flammables.

At first the engineer attempted to fight the fire with a house standpipe hose, but was driven back from the area by the dense smoke. He exited through the storeroom's only door, and quickly returned with the chief engineer. Conditions had become so bad at this point, they could get no further than the base of the stairs. Realizing they would be unable to fight the fire, they sent a man to call the fire department. This notification was received by the Manhattan Fire Dispatcher from a street alarm box (Box 918, Lexington Avenue and 57th Street) at 10:36 a.m.

Engines 26, 8, 65, 39 and Ladder Companies 2 and 16 responded along with two battalion chiefs and Acting Deputy Chief Roche. Upon their arrival, Engines 8 and 39 began to stretch a line down stairs into the cellar area. The smoke these companies encountered proved to be impenetrable. Again and again they tried to push in, but were unable to make any progress. Rescue Company 1 was special called for use of their masks.

Units on the scene continued their efforts to press to the seat of the fire. A ladder was placed down through a sidewalk hoist way to the sub-cellar; members of Ladder 2 descended to the base of the small shaft. Fireman William Pratt, detailed from Ladder 7 to Ladder 2 for the day, and Fireman Louis Hardina of Ladder 2 began forcing the sub-cellar door into the hoistway shaft. At the sidewalk level, Fireman William Kirkham of Engine 65 was feeding hose down to his company's nozzle team, Firemen Thomas Finn and James Greene.

On the interior staircase, companies were still taking quite a bit of smoke. Engines 39 and 8 followed Ladders 16 and 12, who searched for a way to reach the fire. Outside Rescue 1 had arrived and received a briefing from the chief. Members donned filter masks and smoke helmets then started into the building.

At the base of the sidewalk hoistway, the door to the sub-cellar was forced open. Almost immediately, a violent explosion shook the building. The tile partition of the paint locker crumbled and became airborne shrapnel. The sidewalk hoistway elevator track twisted and deformed, as two fifteen ton ammonia system machines ruptured. Firemen in the hallway just outside the storeroom were hurled violently to the floor, and covered with debris as flames roared over their heads. Battalion Chief John J. Ryan and Fireman Peter McGovern were near each other in the hallway; both were cut and burned. Ryan stated, "A sheet of flame passed over our heads and the walls and ceiling came tumbling down on us."

The lights went dark as all electrical power in the building was knocked out. The building's clocks stopped at 10:56 a.m. The dense smoke condition now became total blackness. Injured men groped, searching for their comrades. Stunned firemen, many with serious injuries, tried to lead each other out. Lt. Harnett and Fireman Finn at the base of the hoistway had been killed instantly, but other firemen, also injured, struggled trying to remove them to the street, hoping somehow to revive them.

Three minutes after the initial blast, a second more powerful explosion occurred. The jewelry store windows splintered, mixed with the gems on display and were scattered across the avenue. All the firemen, police officers and civilians in the immediate area were thrown to the ground. One fireman was thrown up through the hoistway shaft from the sub-cellar to the street.

Acting Deputy Chief Roche picked himself up, and transmitted a second alarm. Special calls were also placed for the department ambulance, and for six public ambulances. There were a few moments of stunned silence outside the fire building. Dazed firemen began to react as more of the injured made their way to the street. Injured firemen staggered outside, with those more seriously injured in their arms. Ropes were lowered down the shaftway, so the dead and injured could be hauled up.

Firemen, burned, cut and bleeding, blackened from the blast sat in the glass covered street. They tended to the wounded as best they could, until the ambulances and the second alarm units reached the scene. Arriving with the second alarm, fresh firemen renewed the attack on the fire, as men from Rescue 1 searched through the dark, smoke filled cellars for the injured and the dead. Assistant Chief Dougherty arrived and assumed command. The fire was extinguished without any further extension.

> A sad reality was again underscored: Alarms in even the most prestigious and expensive buildings in the city could mean sudden, violent death to firemen who answered them.

The cost to the department was extreme: eight men dead, eight seriously injured. Many other firemen, police officers and civilians were also injured, mostly cut by flying glass. The investigation of the explosions never reached a definite conclusion as to their cause. Steps were taken, however, to insure similar situations would not occur again. Automatic sprinklers and alarm systems to protect sub-surface areas were mandated.

A sad reality was again underscored: Alarms in even the most prestigious and expensive buildings in the city could mean sudden, violent death to firemen who answered them.

Shortly after 10 o'clock on the night of April 13, 1933, a fire broke out in a two-story meat packing plant on Brook Avenue in the Bronx. By midnight firemen were being knocked out left and right by the cold smoke inside the refrigerated areas.

Three different ways to breathe in smoke: filter mask, smoke helmet and hose mask.

Chief of Department John McElligott, former captain of Rescue 1 poses with rescue men at the Fire College in 1934. The rescue company demonstrated their special tools and equipment to the probationary firemen's class and the assembled media.

Rescue 1 members wearing smoke helmet and a "slightly altered" breathing apparatus.

Rescue 1 was special called to help Rescue 3 attempt to shut off the huge ammonia compressors inside the raging building. A wall was breached, and the rescue men made their way inside despite heavy smoke and thick ammonia fumes. The explosion was averted but several members of Rescue 3 and Rescue 1 were overcome or injured during the ardous operation.

It was half-past noon on July 30, 1933 when a raging cellar fire in a five-story building at 166 William Street severely tested the department. The fire conditions were so bad in the cellar that the attack was made from above. Rescue men and other firemen forced open a closed restaurant and hacked through thick pine floors, as others chopped through concrete sidewalks to allow distributers and cellar pipes to be put into operation.

The smoke was so thick that the Searchlight Unit was needed to illuminate the fire scene, despite the fact the it was daytime. Firemen battled the blaze for four hours before bringing the two-alarm fire under control. Twenty-three firemen were cut by flying glass or knocked unconscious by the heavy smoke.

On January 17, 1934 Rescue 1 put on a demonstration for the new class of eighty-six probationary firemen and the media at the Fire College on East Sixty-eighth Street in Manhattan. Newsreel and still cameras snapped away as Chief John McElligott, who'd organized the Rescue Company 1 nineteen years earlier, addressed the crowd. The day before the Chief had been sworn in by Mayor LaGuardia as Fire Commissioner, combining the two positions for the first time in the history of the paid department. McElligott explained to the new recruits that the rescue company, "began where the ordinary firemen left off."

The latest array of breathing equipment was demonstrated and explained. A smoky fire was ignited in the "smoke house" in the big yard behind the college. Captain Cornell Garety, donned a smoke helmet, and Firemen Robert Tierney and

Charles Kennedy donned canister filter masks and went into the smoke. Tierney pretended to be overcome and was carried out by the other two men and "revived" by other members of Rescue 1 who demonstrated the latest in artificial respiration.

Two other types of masks were also shown: The hose mask, which had 150-feet of wired hose through which air is manually pumped. The second, the phone mask which has 250-feet of wire that allows communications to the outside.

The Savannah liner *The City of Montgomery* carrying thirty-three passengers, ninety crewmen and tons of cargo raced towards New York City with a serious fire in her hold on March 6, 1934. The crew had been fighting the blaze for twenty-four hours, as the ship headed to Manhattan's North River. The ship berthed briefly at her regular pier at Charles Street, where passengers and the majority of the crew disembarked. The ship was then relocated, escorted by fireboats, to an open pier at Tenth Street that gave ample room for fireboats and land units to operate.

The hold was flooded with steam in an attempt to extinguish the fire. The gases and flames were too much for the system and firefighters then tried to move in and fight the blaze. For several hours company after company endeavored to get close enough to darken down the fire with little success. The hatches were opened and flames leapt into the sky. Finally, members of Rescue 1 donned smoke helmets and pushed a hose line into the blazing compartment. When the fire darkened a bit, engines were able to move in and finally knock the flames down. The fire was declared under control at 10 p.m.

One of the smokiest fires in the history of the FDNY occurred on Easter Saturday April 20, 1935. At one minute past noon Brooklyn Box 482 was transmitted for a fire in a 60 x 160, five-story warehouse of the New York Dock Company. The building, part of a 3000 foot-long row of continuous warehouses along the East River waterfront, was filled with tons of rubber and tarpaper. Due to the extremely thick impenetrable smoke, Rescue 2 was special called ten minutes into the fire.

The smoke from the burning rubber was so thick and permeating that it filled the ventilating system of the I.R.T. Subway and stopped train traffic between Brooklyn and Manhattan, trapping hundreds of passengers in the under river tunnel. Clouds of thick noxious smoke also filled the Wall Street station sending scores of people reeling into the streets gasping for air.

> **T**he smoke from the burning rubber was so thick and permeating that it filled the ventilating system of the I.R.T. Subway and stopped train traffic between Brooklyn and Manhattan, trapping hundreds of passengers in the under river tunnel. Clouds of thick noxious smoke also filled the Wall Street station sending scores of people reeling into the streets gasping for air.

Facing page top photo: At 1:15 on the afternoon of April 20, 1935, companies responded to Brooklyn Box 482 encountering what would become one of the most difficult fires in the department's history. At far right rescue company members are seen gearing up.

Facing page bottom photo: Rescue 1 worked together with Rescue 2 making several attempts to reach the seat of the fire. It would take 5-alarms, two "Master Stations" (like a borough call within the same borough) and several days to extinguish.

Rescue Company 1 was special called and joined forces with Rescue 2. Using masks and smoke helmets, the rescue companies vented the iron shutters. Under extreme conditions, rescue men then pressed into the blazing warehouse trying to get a foam hand line into position to hit the rubber fueled flames. Finally, the tremendous heat and numerous backdrafts forced the rescue men from the building. Fire chiefs had to switch to a completely defensive operation. The attack then became an exterior battle. For the next several days more than 10-million gallons of water were poured into the blazing structure. Five alarms, two Master Stations (requests for manpower only) were required. More than one thousand people (mostly firemen) needed treatment for smoke injuries.

It was ten minutes until noon, May 29, 1935 when Rescue 1 was dispatched to an explosion at First Avenue and 21st Street. An unemployed man trying to salvage some junk brass apparently set off a gas explosion that destroyed the four story building and wrecked two adjacent structures. The demolished building was in the shadow of a large twelve-story tank of the Consolidated Gas Company, one of the largest in the world. The blast also damaged a number of buildings in the neighborhood known as "The Gas House District."

The explosion was caused by accumulated gases mixing in the basement of the building from old tanks abandoned there. The man had been banging on several tanks ripping away copper and brass parts for salvage, when the blast occurred. Rescue 1 and local fire companies searched the building for any trapped or injured people and removed a woman by ladder, from an office near the blast.

On November 23, 1935 Madison Square Garden was the site of the first FDNY fund raising exhibition known as "The Midnight Alarm." *The New York Times* description of the first performance read in part:

Garden Audience of 12,000 Cheers First Exhibition of Firefighters as They Attack Synthetic Tenement Conflagration To Perform Rescues of Pajama-clad Victims

A smokeless blaze threatening a rickety five-story tenement with a saloon on the first floor drew an imposing turnout of fire apparatus… Broad-shouldered smoke-eaters with axes and hooded rescue men resembling deep sea divers plunged into the menaced building and did an excellent job of putting out the fire without water.

Two shows, one in the afternoon and the second later that evening, raised money for the purchase of a new FDNY department ambulance. One of the members of the show committee was Fireman William Dorritie of Rescue Company 1.

Just before 5 p.m. June 3, 1936, a workman soldering the cover onto a box containing motion picture film ignited a fire in the basement of a five-story building at 218 West 42nd Street. The burning celluloid film gave off noxious fumes that drove twenty persons from the building. First due units were unable to penetrate the fume laced smoke, so Rescue 1 was special called. Captain Garety and his crew donned masks and plunged into the blazing basement with a hose line and extinguished the fire.

On August 13, 1936, a southbound Third Avenue elevated four-car passenger train smashed into the rear of slowly moving five-car work train ahead of it at 10:10 p.m. The accident took place at 74th Street, shattering the wooden el cars and sending debris down onto Third Avenue. The damaged cars balanced dangerously on the elevated tracks. Rescue 1 responded and assisted in removing over fifty injured passengers. The rescue men then spent more than two hours using torches and hand tools to free the dead motorman trapped in the lead car.

More than a dozen occupants of a twelve-story loft building at 625 Broadway and seven firemen were treated for varying degrees of gas poisoning on the evening of September 3, 1936 following a fire on the seventh floor. The fire was started when a leaking drum containing a solution of chloride of potash, chloride of copper, an aluminum powder and clay used in heating pads, spontaneously combusted. The resulting fumes and smoke soared upwards through the building. Arriving on the second alarm, members of Rescue 1 donned gas masks and extinguished the blaze.

A very serious fire tore through two tenements at 137 & 139 Suffolk Street a little after 3 in the morning on March 3, 1937. Four alarms were needed to extinguish this fast moving and deadly fire. Six civilians were killed and as the newspapers put: "there were so many rescues that an exact count could not be arrived at."

Firemen were also menaced by falling bricks, broken glass and other debris as the roofs of both buildings caved in. Three members of Rescue 1 were treated for lacerations including Lt. Henry Mulholland.

On January 1, 1938, Captain Cornell Garety was promoted to Battalion Chief and Captain George F. Hughes was assigned to Rescue 1 as the new company commander. Three months later, with the advent of a three-platoon system, another lieutenant spot opened and Lt. Richard J. Donovan transferred from Rescue 2. (Donovan was the first member of Rescue 2 to be awarded a medal for valor, and at the time the only FDNY member to receive two medals for separate rescues in the same year when he was awarded the Brooklyn Citizen's Medal and the Kenny Medal in 1935. He was also awarded a Department Medal for valor in 1937.)

Eleven firemen were also placed on the Rescue 1 roster at this time to fill the positions needed with the new three-platoon system.

Flames broke out in the two-story Liberty Boarding Stable at 238 Cherry Street on the Lower East Side of Manhattan on April 3, 1938. One hundred and thirty-one horses were trapped in the blazing structure, as firemen began battling the blaze. As companies struggled to reach the seat of the fire the building began to collapse trapping several members. Rescue 1 began digging out their pinned comrades. They were able to save a member of the fire patrol, but sadly, Lt. Thomas Meehan of Engine 9 was killed.

All the horses except nine also perished in the blaze. One by one, the remaining horses were lifted from the building with a crane.

A boiler explosion inside the Pilsner Brewing Company on West 128th Street caused a major fire and collapse on March 4, 1938. Three workers were killed. Rescue companies made extensive searches in the rubble for any further victims. (Connecticut Firemen's Historical Society)

Members of Rescue 1 carry out injured firemen trapped in a collapse during a 3-alarm fire at 238 Cherry Street on April 3, 1938. One fire officer was killed and several firemen and members of the Fire Patrol were injured.

A very stubborn and difficult to reach fire was fought by the FDNY on June 26, 1938, during the construction of the Queens Midtown Tunnel. The well advanced fire was found blazing among timbers and packing equipment within the pressurized section of the tunnel. First arriving companies and sand hogs were not able to get through to the fire, due to the system of airlocks in place within the tunnel structure.

Dr. Archer and the tunnel physician conferred with chief officers and examined a number of firemen and officers, before the members were subject to the pressure of the tunnel and the extreme fire conditions on the other side of the locks. Five men were selected to pass through the air locks and attack the fire: Deputy Chief William Taubert, Battalion Chief John Herold, and three members of Rescue 1, Lt. Robert Tierney, Firemen Edward Lyons and James Ferguson.

They linked arms and entered the airlock. On their first attempt to enter they were driven back by the extreme conditions. It was then decided to lower the pressure of the air inside the tunnel, and allow the river seepage to knock down the fire. It took several hours and many calculations by engineers to accomplish this tactic. The fire was eventually brought under control after twelve hours.

A three-alarm fire tore through a bakery at 468 Cherry Street at 2 in the afternoon of August 21, 1938. Rescue 1 responded and worked at this extremely hot and smoky fire. It took two hours and twenty-three companies to stop the fire from spreading to a nearby paper plant and chemical factory. One member of Rescue 1 was slightly burned during the operation.

Seven firemen were seriously injured by gas poisoning and nine others required treatment, after they were overcome battling a cellar fire at 250 W. 57th Street in Manhattan on February 2, 1939. The alarm came in at 11 p.m., and units were quickly on scene. Engine 54 and Ladder 4, were faced with a serious fire condition in the cellar that had impinged on the gas lines causing a leak of both illuminating gas and methylene chloride from a large refrigerator. Braving the fumes, heat, and smoke the companies under the command of Battalion Chief Cornell Garety, pressed forward attempting to get to the seat of the fire. Conditions became so severe the firemen were forced from the cellar, with members dropping unconscious on their way outside.

Rescue 1 arrived and quickly donned helmets and gas masks helping several overcome members outside. Just as the rescue men were moving in with a hose line, an explosion rocked the cellar. Undaunted, they continued forward and were able to extinguish the fire.

In 1939 the FDNY placed in service a completely new style of rescue truck. Built the year before by Ward LaFrance, the vehicle was completely enclosed and modernistic in design for the time. It was powered by a 6-cylinder 150 horse power engine. It was 31-feet long, 8-1/2 feet wide, and 11-feet high. It was equipped with a two-way radio tuned to the Telegraph Headquarters (dispatcher's office) and also featured a public address system. The vehicle had a four-door crew cab, a futuristic slanted roof design, and skirts over the rear wheels. Most equipment was carried in the rear of the rig, although there were several small compartments accessible from the exterior. An A-frame crane with a 5-ton capacity was fitted to the rear of the unit and operated by means of a power take-off in the transmission. The vehicle carried registration number 39890. The cost of the new truck was $18,500.

It would be dubbed "the moving van" because of its appearance; chauffeurs of the unit found it bulky and unwieldy to manage in the heavy Manhattan traffic. This rig would be

During this era, the rescue chauffeur stayed back at the rig to provide special tools or to set up resuscitators and pulmotors to aid smoke victims. Here Rescue 1 men assist Doctor Archer treat overcome firemen. (Weegee)

During 1939 the department took delivery of a completely new style of rescue truck. The vehicle had a four-door crew cab and futuristic slanted roof design. This Ward LaFrance rig also featured an A-frame crane in the rear.

wrecked twice before being disposed of. It is interesting to note that the lettering of this rig was unusual. All rescue apparatus purchased before this rig and those afterwards were lettered for the respective rescue company assigned, but this rig was delivered lettered for "Rescue Squad No. 1." The only other rescue rigs to carry "squad" in their lettering were two Mack Bulldogs that were rebuilt by the shops during 1939 and 1940.

This new rig carried: two types of self contained oxygen masks, (the Draeger and the M.S.A.), a Hose Mask with 150-feet of hose and a manually operated blower, and All-service filter masks. Also carried were: sets of waders, rubber coats, rubber gloves and rubber hoods for entering heavy gases and poisons. A large Oxy-acetylene cutting set and a smaller portable Kerotest cutting set with asbestos blankets. A smoke ejector unit, with two 10-foot flexible hose lengths 11-inches in diameter powered by a 2-cylinder Homelight generator. An electric saw, complete set of elevator keys, combustible gas indicator, hydraulic jacks from 5 to 30 tons, screw jacks from 5 to 18 tons, a fog nozzle, and an M.S.A. Fire-Fiter Asbestos Uniform. Electric tongs, 400 pounds of foam powder with generator and hopper, inhalators and first aid kits.

Rescue 1 helped resuscitate a number of firemen overcome at a very smoky fire in Times Square on June 6, 1939. The afternoon building fire was fought behind two large billboards at the southwest corner of Seventh Avenue and 42nd Street. As Rescue 1 was arriving at the two-alarm fire, unconscious firemen were being pulled from the building and placed on the sidewalk. Under the direction of Doctor Archer, rescue men went to work with inhalators and revived the unconscious firemen.

Chapter 4

The Forties

Clouds of war were gathering over Europe and the Japanese Empire was rattling its saber across the Pacific. In New York City the FDNY was entering its seventy-fifth year of professional fire service protecting a growing population of seven and a half million people. The fire department consisted of 10,531 men answering forty thousand alarms. In 1940 there would be 28,413 fires of which 148 were multiple alarms. Three members of the FDNY travelled to England working with the London Fire Brigade and other British fire departments during what would become known as "The London Blitz." An intense period starting on September 7, 1940, and continuing for the next 57 days when London was bombed either during the night or the day. American fire departments, especially the FDNY, wanted to be prepared if the war visited our shores.

About 7:30 on the morning of February 25, 1940 a fire broke out on the sixth floor of the loft building at 256 West 23rd Street. With flames piercing the roof a third alarm was transmitted. Six members of Ladder 24 were operating on the roof of the seven-story building, when a chemical explosion below suddenly extended the fire beneath them. Within seconds they became cut off by flames. Rescue Company 1, under the command of Lt. Richard Donovan, saw the situation and hurried up an aerial ladder to an adjoining four-story building carrying a thirty-five foot extension ladder with them. From this adjacent roof they were able to raise the portable ladder to the roof of the fire building so the trapped men could descend.

On April 30, 1940 Rescue 1 responded to the entrapment of an elevator operator at 12 West Third Street. The man's leg was trapped between the platform and the sidewall of a sidewalk lift. Deputy Chief James Tubridy was overseeing the operation, when the lift tilted and both the chief and Lieutenant Henry Mulholland of Rescue 1 fell thirty-feet to the bottom of the shaft. The rescue officer landed on the chief, who received a fractured femur and internal injuries. The rescue officer was only slightly injured. The injured chief was rushed to the hospital and the rescue work continued until the trapped man was freed. Sadly, Deputy Chief James Tubridy died three months later from his injuries.

Eighty-six firemen and three refrigeration engineers were overcome by smoke, while the department battled a two-alarm "flameless fire" in the cellar of the New York Cold Storage Company plant at 46 Tenth Avenue near Fourteenth Street on May 19, 1940. The fire was located inside a series of master refrigerators protected by twenty-inches of insulation. High levels of carbon monoxide and ammonia gas laced the acrid dense clouds of smoke knocking out wave after wave of firefighters. The first alarm came in at 1:27 in the afternoon sending companies to the block-long three-story building. A second alarm was quickly transmitted.

As the thick smoke intensified and the number of men being overcome increased, Rescue 2 was special called to the scene. Both rescue companies were very busy dragging out unconscious firemen and searching for the seat of the fire. Finally after twelve long hours, the source of the smoke was located and the tiring work of chopping away the insulation would begin. First the five feet of accumulated water had to be pumped out. Eventually, the exhausted rescue men were able to extinguish the deep-seated fire.

On September 3, 1940, Rescue 1 responded to 211 West 22nd Street, there they found a man on a ledge of a fourth floor window threatening to commit suicide. Fireman Charles Sadera was lowered by roof rope from above. When the man on the ledge saw the firefighter swinging towards him, he jumped into the building and into the waiting arms of the police. This action was above and beyond the call of duty because the would-be jumper was also waving a revolver and a knife at anyone who came near. Fireman Sadera was awarded the Thomas Crimmins and Department Medals.

> When the man on the ledge saw the firefighter swinging towards him, he jumped into the building and into the waiting arms of the police. This action was above and beyond the call of duty because the would-be jumper was also waving a revolver and a knife at anyone who came near.

Fireman Charles Sadera

Captain Hughes and members of Rescue 1 display various breathing apparatus. The captain is cranking air into the hose-masks at left. Two filter masks are next, then the smoke helmet.

Fifty firemen required treatment for smoke and gas poisoning, while battling a fire in the Wholesale Electric Motor Company at 530-36 Canal Street. It was 1 o'clock on the afternoon of January 22, 1941 when Box 305 was transmitted for a fire in a six-story loft building. The first arriving unit, Engine 27, began stretching a line up the stairs toward the fire floor, when the entire company fell unconscious between the third and fourth floors. Second due Engine 24 carried out their unconscious comrades, as the fire intensified on the fourth floor above.

Out on the street a second alarm had been transmitted, and Doctor Archer set up an aid station on the sidewalk. It was determined that fire was burning among oil, excelsior and insulating materials and was producing at least four kinds of dangerous gases, one being phosgene. Members of Rescue 1 set up inhalators and broke out the newest tool in their arsenal of specialized equipment – "the poison bag." When attached to an inhalator it provided a chemical that in many cases gave relief quickly.

With the war raging in Europe the FDNY geared up in case things came our way. The Department Orders on September 19, 1941 detailed two members of Rescue 1, Firemen E. J. Barbour and C. Baden to the Fire College for instruction in a new course: Incendiary, Explosive & War Gas Control. It was a four day course.

After the attack on Pearl Harbor on December 7, 1941 the United States entered World War II on both fronts. In New York City Mayor LaGuardia, who was also the head of national civil defense, took steps to ensure that both the fire and police departments weren't caught in a manpower shortage by issuing an order that prevented members of these departments from voluntarily enlisting or being drafted into the armed forces. Many members of the fire department disagreed with this policy, and Fireman Henry "Hank" Williams of Rescue 1 managed to cir-

One of the last smoke helmet photographs. It shows them in action at a fire on May 19, 1940.

During World War II, Mayor LaGuardia was also the head of national Civil Defense. Numerous disaster drills were conducted in anticipation of air raids.

cumvent the rules by joining the Marine Corps Reserves, then having himself activated three days later. Upon his activation, Williams initiated a lawsuit to have LaGuardia's order overturned. The case went all the way to the New York State Court of Appeals where it was decided in Williams favor. This would enable numerous civil servants to go on active duty.

Members of the department, including several from Rescue 1, were granted leaves to join the military. Timothy J. Sullivan left Rescue 1 to pilot carrier-based Navy fighter planes throughout the Pacific. John A. Stanek and Ed Barbour, Jr., both served in the Army. FDNY Fireman Victor A. Miozzi (later a member of Rescue 1) became a member of Navy Underwater Demolition Team #12. These "frogmen" were the first warriors in a branch of the service that would later become Naval Special Warfare and the SEAL teams. Vic and his teammates battled their way across the Pacific, island hopping just in front of the Marines. They rolled out of rubber boats in the dead of night, swimming ashore to clear obstacles along the invasion sites, made maps and helped determine if heavy equipment could be sustained by the sand. For his heroism as a member of UDT 12, Victor Miozzi was awarded the Silver Star and Bronze Star for valor.

Because of his strong swimming background, Hank Williams, who was an alternate member of the 1936 U.S. Olympic Swim Team, was assigned to a specialized training unit where he trained Marines in amphibious operations. Sergeant Williams, accompanied by Major Jones, were to attend a special meeting and lecture at the Office of Strategic Services Base where "top secret" underwater breathing apparatus would be discussed. When the lecturer failed to show, Williams and Jones inspected the top-secret equipment which was covered by a canvas tarp at the pool's edge. When Williams uncovered it, he stated that it was German equipment and that he was quite familiar with it. When questioned how he could be familiar with this secret equipment, he pointed to the painted-over plate that read "Draeger" and explained he had regularly used this equipment at Rescue 1 prior to his activation. The Major was so impressed with Williams knowledge of the "top-secret" gear that he directed Williams to give the lecture. As the training stint came to an end the officers asked Williams if wanted to join their unit. This is how Rescue 1 Fireman Hank Williams became a member of the 2nd Raider Battalion, "Carlson's Raiders," and battled from island to island across the South Pacific.

The home-front would prove to be nearly as dangerous in many ways to the firefighters of New York City, as it was to our brave troops abroad.

On January 9, 1942, an early morning fire destroyed Municipal Pier 83 and two buildings at 43rd Street and the North River (Hudson). The five alarm fire taxed the department's resources as 44 pieces of apparatus and three fire boats were needed to extinguish the fire. This was the third major blaze along the waterfront that winter. At first it was believed to be sabotage, but was later proven to be accidental.

On the morning of February 9, 1942, everyone in the city was discussing that day's newspaper stories. General MacArthur and his men were battling an overwhelming Japanese force on the Philippine peninsula of Bataan. There were also reports of the sinking of yet another ship off the Atlantic coast. The U-Boats had taken 15 allied ships since January 14th. The war was becoming very real... and very near.

At Pier 88, the foot of West 48th Street on the North River, over 2,700 men, sailors, coast guardsmen, and numerous workers were on board the *Normandie*, the French cruise ship hastily being converted into a troop transport and soon to be re-named the U.S.S. *Lafayette*. The ship, her faded civilian colors now covered with grey camouflage paint, hummed with activity. It was about 2:35 in the afternoon when sparks from a cutting operation ignited a pile of life preservers. What happened next was best described by the NFPA report, "... the early stages of the fire has elements of Hollywood slapstick comedy."

An accidental fire onboard the S.S. Normandie *broke out on February 9, 1942. This fire went to five-alarms (Box 55-783) taking the life of one worker. The ship capsized the following morning. It later became the site of the U.S. Navy hard-hat diving school, as the ship was refloated and restored to service.*

The workers attempted to beat out the flames bare-handed; extinguishers failed to work, and a pail of water was spilled before it reached the fire. In desperation they began to throw the burning bales around, spreading the flames. A hose was connected to the standpipe; water was started, but despite all efforts the fire raged uncontrolled.

Due to another series of errors, the alarm to the fire department was delayed for between 10 to 15 minutes. At 2:49 p.m., Box 852 was transmitted, sending four engines, two ladders, one fireboat and two battalion chiefs to the scene. Battalion 9 quickly transmitted a 75 signal (all hands working) at 3:00 p.m., then transmitted a second alarm a minute later. The fire swept across the upper decks of the ship, as hand-lines were dragged into place. The standpipe connections were unusable due to incompatible threads, and hoses had to be stretched from the pumpers in the street, down the pier, then up the gangways to the various decks. Sailors were invaluable in the fire fighting efforts, helping stretch and man the lines as they were operated.

Fire fighters, sailors and construction workers joined forces in rescuing those trapped below decks. Assistant Chief John McCarthy arrived, assumed command, and transmitted a third alarm. Communications from the ship to those on the shore was proving difficult, and naval ingenuity again prevailed. Sailors were placed with the chief on the ship. Using semaphore signals, they could now communicate with the chief on the shore. They called for increased water pressures on the attack lines, and directed additional hose-line placement as needed. Other important information was also relayed via flags, during the course of the fire. With the flames out of control, a fourth alarm was placed at 3:12 p.m.

> **C**hief of Department Patrick Walsh said he would rather risk the loss of the ship than the possible destruction of the adjacent piers leaving a strong chance of a large un-contained, spreading fire situation.

As many as 40 hand-lines were now being operated, most of these onboard the ship, but several were being directed from other vantage points such as the roof of the pier building. Thousands of gallons of water were pouring into the blazing ship. One of the few naval officers actually familiar with the ship, Captain Clayton Simmons USN, began to express his fears to navy and fire officials at the scene. The ship's list was becoming more pronounced, and he feared the ship might capsize. He offered to scuttle the ship where she was, but navy officials refused. They wanted the fire department to stop pouring water into the ship.

Chief of Department Patrick Walsh said he would rather risk the loss of the ship than the possible destruction of the adjacent piers leaving a strong chance of a large un-contained, spreading fire situation. They were at an impasse, but not for long. The fire department was in charge and the safety of the city would not be gambled for a single ship.

As fire fighting continued, actions were taken to try and control the accumulating water. The navy made two attempts to reach the engine room through the smoke and heat filled ship but this proved to be impossible, and the effort was abandoned.

The fire department then began to relieve the water condition on their own. Members of Rescue 1 were lowered down the port side of the ship in bosuns' chairs, and using torches, attempted to cut holes through the steel plating to allow the water to run out. Only a few small holes could be made on this side of the ship, as the escaping water put out the torches' flame. The rescue men were then lowered on the starboard (pier) side of the ship, and a large hole was cut above the water line. Engine Company 44 was pulled up close to the ship, and used hard suction in an attempt to pump water from the lower portions of the ship. It was an inventive idea, but it did little to help the situation and was soon discontinued.

Fire fighting continued. At about 6:30 p.m., though the *Normandie* was still burning, the fire was placed "under control". More than four million gallons of water had been used to subdue the flames. Operations on board the ship continued, with many hand-lines still fighting pockets of fire as the fireboats backed off into the ice-filled river.

At 12:22 a.m., the ship had listed to 15 degrees, and it was decided to abandon ship. All personnel from both the navy and fire department left the ship, and the chief ordered hose-lines cut with axes, as it was too dangerous to attempt their retrieval. With no one onboard, the ship capsized the next day.

Sixty-eight days later the FDNY responded to Pier 88; the *Normandie* was on fire again. It was 6:10 in the evening on April 18, 1942, when great clouds of smoke were seen pouring from the ship almost obscuring the craft. Three alarms were quickly transmitted bringing 22 pieces of fire apparatus to the scene. Again, the FDNY was faced with a major problem: the ship was laying at a 45-degree angle on her port side, and all access to the burning sections of the ship were below the water line.

Rescue 1 moved across gangways to the upturned starboard side of the ship, and began cutting through the thick hull with acetylene torches. This difficult and very dangerous operation was made even harder by the dense clouds of smoke covering the entire pier area. For three hours rescue men cut away at the ship, until openings large enough could be made. Special spray nozzles were then directed into the blazing ship bringing the fire under control.

For their efforts under extreme conditions the following members of Rescue 1 were placed on the Roll of Merit: Lt. Patrick Green was awarded a Class III. Firemen William Anthony, Joseph Donohue, Herman Maier, John Stanek, Timothy J. Sullivan and James E. Walsh received Class A awards.

An electrical problem in a manhole in Greenwich Village, just after noon on June 20, 1942, ended in a five-alarm blaze that virtually wrecked the block bounded by Washington, Clarkson, Greenwich and Leroy Streets. Several buildings had electrical overloads that started fires within the structures. Rescue 1 was sent to the cellar of 591 Washington Street, the Great Atlantic Paper warehouse, a seven-story loft building. Captain George Hughes pulled a switch cutting all electricity to the building. Members began checking the cellar ceiling which was showing fresh signs of burning. Fireman Hugh Early was using a hook near a steam riser pipe, when he touched the pipe causing an electrical arch. Early received a jolting shock and the rescue men realized the building was still energized.

The team of rescue firemen hurried to the second floor, and found that the fire had indeed reached that floor and was extending above with amazing speed. This was communicated to the chief and a second, third and fourth alarms were transmitted in rapid succession, as the paper warehouse filled with flames as did several other nearby buildings.

A few minutes later a fifth alarm was transmitted, as flames roared high above the roof of the loft building. Water tower streams and numerous hand lines poured water into the doomed structure. A tearing crunching sound was heard, as the north wall of the building collapsed crushing Hook & Ladder 5 and damaging Engine 13. In all over 50 firemen were overcome by the heavy smoke conditions, most were treated at the scene.

Captain George F. Hughes was promoted to battalion chief on July 1, 1942. Taking his place as company commander of Rescue 1 was Captain Raymond T. Millner.

It was just after 8 o'clock on the morning of August 7, 1942, when the first of two incidents involving the release of tear gas on the Eighth Avenue subway. The first happened on a southbound Washington Heights Express and effected passengers in three cars. Rescue 1 responded and searched the cars while wearing masks. Fragments of the tear gas capsules were found and air samples were taken. Fire and Police chemical experts joined by the FBI investigated the incidents, but could not determine if it was a prank or an act of sabotage.

At 9:30 p.m. on July 18, 1943, Rescue 1 and Engine 30 roared out of the firehouse at 278 Spring Street and came to a quick stop outside the building. Twenty firemen then hooked up hose lines, donned masks and hurried back into the smoke filled firehouse. As the remainder of the first alarm units arrived a crowd of people had gathered and watched what they thought was some type of demonstration. Actually the thick smoke was being generated by a fire in the firehouse store room. Crates of composite shoe soles taken for analysis after a stubborn fire a few days before, filled the firehouse and the neighborhood with dense acrid smoke. The fire was under control in less than an hour.

> **M**embers of Rescue 1 donned smoke helmets and masks to operate hand lines, then helped at the first aid station as more than 100 firemen were overcome by the toxic smoke.

On August 12, 1943, Rescue 1, along with the other rescue companies, received two portable radio pack sets. These were the first portable radios issued to firefighting units. These large radio sets greatly increased fire ground effectiveness. The radio sets were 13-1/2 pounds, could work for sixty to one hundred hours, and had a range of two to three miles. The radio sets were worn like backpacks, and were developed and built by firemen in the FDNY radio laboratory.

Another new innovation was the creation of the FDNY Fire, Gas & Chemical Laboratory and its mobile version, a chemical laboratory on wheels: Field Unit No. 1. This new unit and its apparatus were placed in service in the quarters of Engine 33, Rescue 1's original home on Great Jones Street. Besides the specially designed and built mobile lab, a research laboratory and technical library was installed in the firehouse. One of the first members detailed to the new unit was Fireman Milton Brodey of Rescue 1.

A mutual aid request from the city of Hoboken, New Jersey on August 11, 1944, sent thirteen engines, four ladder companies and Rescue 1 through the Holland Tunnel responding to a raging multi-storied pier fire, where six civilians were killed and fifty more were injured. The FDNY sent a third alarm assignment to join forces with the entire Hoboken Fire Department, as the fire spread from pier to pier, each loaded with extremely dangerous cargo and munitions bound for the war in Europe. Members of Rescue 1 donned smoke helmets and masks to operate hand lines, then helped at the first aid station as more than 100 firemen were overcome by the toxic smoke.

A forty-year-old wooden BMT trolley car lost its brakes, as it crossed the steep down-hill grade of the Brooklyn Bridge and slammed into a pole 200-feet from Park Row. It was 6:05 on the evening of March 9, 1945 when Rescue 1 and other FDNY units responded to the crash. The impact sheared the trolley's body from the under carriage, and it landed sideways across the tracks. Fifty-four of the one hundred passengers, most of the workers from the Brooklyn Navy Yard, were injured. Rescue 1 helped extricate the trapped passengers, and cut the wires to the trolley when the power to the tracks was confirmed shut-off.

Captain Millner and "Boots" testing the new portable radios designed by FDNY firemen.

A rescue fireman climbs a scaling ladder with the new lightweight radio set. It only weighed 13.5 pounds but had a range of more than two miles.

On March 18, 1945 Rescue 1 was again testing new equipment. Rescue 1 was now under the command of Captain Patrick Green, who had served as a lieutenant in Rescue 1 before transferring to Rescue 3. Green and the captains of the other three rescue companies joined acting Chief of Department Frank Murphy and Doctor Archer at the Spring Street quarters of Rescue 1 and Engine 30, to test new breathing devices.

Rescue men donned various respirators, compressed air, compressed oxygen and oxygen regenerating gear, and began chopping heavy railroad ties with 8-pound axes (to simulate true work conditions). A gas mask used by the Navy was rejected as too bulky and unable to supply enough volume. Samples of compressed air and compressed oxygen masks were ordered for sixty day trials under actual fire conditions. One of these was a self contained breathing apparatus made by Scott Aviation. At the completion of the trail period, Captain Green and the other rescue company commanders fought a long and hard battle to get the New York City Fire Department to approve and accept this mask. His perseverance paid off. In today's modern fire service this basic piece of equipment is taken for granted. Fighting modern era fires without using masks is inconceivable.

On May 7, 1945 the war in Europe was finally over with the unconditional surrender of Germany. The battle in the Pacific however carried on. But the war, and its far reaching effects, played out danger and destruction high above the streets of Manhattan, on Saturday morning July 28, 1945.

On the 86th floor of the Empire State Building, the world's tallest structure, fifty to sixty people were trying to get a view of the city from the fog obscured observatory deck. Shortly before 10 a.m. a twin engine U.S. Army B-25 bomber on its way from Boston to Newark went off course, due to the bad visibility. It came out of the fog at a fifteen degree angle, flying directly into the north side of the Empire State Building. A thunderous crash was heard throughout Midtown. The streets and neighboring structures were soon showered with glass and debris. The Empire State Building, made of ten million Indiana limestone and granite bricks, shuddered.

Upon impact the planes wings sheared off, as the engines and fuselage ripped a hole eighteen feet wide and twenty feet high in the outer wall of the 78th and 79th floors a point 915-feet above the street. The bombers gasoline tanks exploded, sending flames up to the 86th floor observation deck. One of the plane's engines hurtled across the 78th floor crashing through the south wall, and plunging through the roof of a 13-story loft building.

Rivers of flaming gasoline poured through the 78th and 79th floors, setting fire to everything combustible. Burning fuel ran down the elevator shafts, stairwells and hallways. Street fire alarm Box 681 was pulled by a passing fire officer at 9:52 a.m. Arriving units were confronted with three separate serious fire situations: the point of impact, the pit of the elevator shaft below street level, and the thirteen-story loft building.

The largest and most difficult of the fire areas to be attacked was the blazing 79th floor. Seventeen engine companies, four ladder companies and members of Rescue 1 operated fifteen standpipe lines to battle and extinguish this large area of fire.

Other members of Rescue 1 went to the blazing elevator pit, in hopes of reaching people trapped in fallen elevator cars. They were joined by seventeen-year-old uniformed Coast Guard hospital apprentice, Donald Maloney of Detroit who had just finished nine months of training. He procured medical supplies from a drug store, after seeing the plane strike the building.

The burley members of Rescue 1 breached a hole through the wall to reach a damaged car and boosted Maloney, the smallest of the group, through the opening. "Thank God the Navy's here!" The burned woman said, as Maloney entered the car and began treating her. Outside the rescue men continued enlarging the hole. A short time later she was removed and taken to a hospital. Maloney and members of Rescue 1 treated several other persons in the cellar, before making their way, with Maloney in tow, to the upper fire floors.

Twenty-three members of the department were singled out for valorous or meritorious acts at this fire, and the actions of the young Coast Guard medic received wide coverage in the city newspapers.

In 1946 Rescue 1 was special called to cope with a serious fire located in the cellar of a candy factory at 234 West 56th Street, Manhattan. Heavy smoke conditions prevailed in this five-story non-fireproof building. Companies responding on the first alarm were unable to make any headway; thirteen members of these units were overcome and were revived only through the use of inhalators. Access to the cellar was gained after locating and descending a narrow interior stairway. Members of Rescue 1 donned self-contained breathing apparatus groping through the blinding smoke, and advanced hose lines into the cellar. During the course of the operation, a large com-

Apparatus Specialized Tools and Equipment

- The refrigeration emergency kit consists of: shut-off keys, sulphur tapers, ammonia, rubber gloves, hoods and waders (for heavy concentrations of ammonia and hydrocyanic acid gas) special wrenches for household and commercial units in addition to many miscellaneous tools.

- A Portable Kerotest Acetylene Unit, that could be worn as a vest with pockets that contain necessary tools. (It was noted this unit could even be operated while the wearer was suspended on a roof-rope!)

- A foam hopper and a supply of foam powder.

- Electrical equipment including long insulated tongs for handling high tension cables.

- Portable radios (walkie-talkies) for rapid 2-way communications with a coverage of a two-mile radius.

- A third rail tester.

- Special equipment for heavy rescue work: blocks of various size, tow-chains, hoists, Z-irons (used in conjunction with jacks to lift subway cars and trolleys) various size jacks (the largest a 32-ton jack).

- An electric power saw.

- First aid equipment includes: inhalators, oxygen and carbogen supply (carbogen is a 7% CO2, 93% O2 mixture) there was also a small auxiliary inhalator attachment that could be used simultaneously with an inhalator or by itself. A 20-foot hose attachment could also be added. Special nasal catheters. The first aid compartment also carried specialized medicines and drugs to be used by doctors at emergency scenes.

- MSA All-Service mask (a canister mask), MSA Oxygen Breathing Apparatus (which carried its own oxygen supply).

- A Homelite 2-cylinder gasoline driven smoke ejector.

- The rig also was fitted with a small desk that featured a department radio, alarm assignment cards, subway and water main maps. Allowing the rescue rig to be used as a Field Headquarters (Command Post).

mercial gas meter exploded. It was necessary for the rescue men to remain in the cellar in order to keep combustible materials in the vicinity of the meter cooled down, until the street could be broken up exposing the valves controlling the flow of gas into the building.

On May 20, 1946, at 8:10 in the evening, Rescue 1 responded to 40 Wall Street. An aircraft lost in dense fog crashed into the 58th floor of the 70-story building. The U.S. Army C-45 Beechcraft airplane was a twin engine, all metal, low wing monoplane used for staff transport. The aircraft was carrying five onboard, the pilot and four passengers, one passenger a women's army corp officer. The plane, on it's way to Newark airport, became lost in the fog and crashed into the fifty-eighth floor of the 927-foot building sending a sheet of flame into the night sky. Parts of the aircraft, oil, debris and pieces of brick and mortar rained onto Pine Street below.

The impact site on the northeast corner of the building left a gapping hole twenty-feet across and ten feet high. Several fires were touched off in the crash building, and others in the neighborhood. The plane's fuselage hurtled across the floor leaving severely crumpled wreckage with the passengers and pilot inside. Rescue 1 had the difficult job of disentangling the twisted steel and removing the bodies of those killed.

Six members of Ladder Company 7 were overcome during a sub-cellar fire at 49 East 25th Street on May 29, 1946. Rescue 1 responded, and utilizing their newly assigned Scott Air-Paks, were able to conduct a search, quickly locate, and remove the overcome firemen from the dense smoke. No doubt, the use of these new masks was responsible for saving six lives at this fire.

During 1946, the 1939 Ward La France rescue truck sustained extensive damage in a vehicle accident. While the rig was being rebuilt, a 1940 Mack hose wagon (registration number 284) that was formerly assigned to Engine 30 was outfitted and operated as a rescue truck. Rescue 1 used this rig until the Ward La France was returned to service in 1947. The hose wagon remained as the rescue spare and saw city-wide service. The 1939 Ward La France was returned to service with new fenders, grille, headlights and bumper, as well as having the rear wheel skirts removed. It remained with Rescue 1 until 1948, when it was reassigned to Rescue 4. On July 31, 1954, while assigned to two separate alarms, Rescue 4 and Ladder 136 collided. This resulted in a fire and explosion that destroyed both rigs killing Fireman Joseph Dugan of Ladder 136 and Fireman Samuel Schiller of Engine 324, who was detailed to Ladder 136.

In December of 1946, Rescue 1 operated at two major fires where the fire buildings collapsed. The first fire was on Wednesday December 11th, in an abandoned icehouse at 489 West 183rd Street near Amsterdam Avenue. Manhattan Box 1753, came in at 5:45 p.m., for a fire on the roof of the icehouse. This fire started by "mischievous boys" and was extinguished by a first alarm assignment. The fire building, unoccupied for eight years and the former home of the Knickerbocker Ice Company, was adjacent to a six-story tenement where twenty-eight families lived. The icehouse, the same height as the tenement, had massive 36-inch brick walls, insulated with cork, supporting a heavy concrete roof on steel members.

The fire-weakened wall of the former Knickerbocker Ice Warehouse building collapsed onto the six-story tenement next-door killing 37 including a fireman on December 12, 1946. Numerous heroic rescues were made as companies pulled people from the icy rubble.

Later that night at 11:59, another alarm came in from the same alarm box for a fire in the same building. Apparently, this second fire had been burning for some time. Firemen were working for an hour, when the roof of the icehouse collapsed pushing out the sidewalls and taking several firemen down with it. The icehouse structure fell onto the tenement, collapsing that building and trapping numerous persons. Multiple alarms were transmitted, and Rescue 1 was special called. Together with Rescue 3 and five alarms worth of firemen, they began a long dangerous rescue and recovery operation.

It took several days to recover all those killed by the terrible collapse. One fireman and thirty-seven civilians were killed and dozens were injured, including three firemen hospitalized with serious injuries. The FDNY operated for more than sixty-five straight hours.

Then on New Year's Eve, 1946, Manhattan Box 396 was transmitted at 5:27 p.m., for a fire in a seven-story loft building at 749 Broadway, between Astor Place and Eighth Street. Three engines, two trucks, a water tower and Rescue 1 responded to the alarm. Two hours into the fire, now at three alarms, the building collapsed, carrying the roof and seven heavily stocked floors into the basement. More than a score of firemen were trapped and buried beneath tons of stock and structural parts now reduced to a massive pile of rubble and debris.

Rescue 1, under the command of Captain Patrick Green, began the dangerous task of locating and removing the trapped firefighters. For the next ten hours, some of the most skilled and daring rescue work ever performed in the FDNY was carried out. Three trapped firemen in accessible positions were quickly removed by breaking through the sidewalk to gain access to the cellar. However, four members were trapped in very deep and dangerous positions. The men were partially buried under tons of debris, at the base of the structure's north wall, with an avalanche of stock and disarranged structural parts hanging dangerously over them. It was decided the safest access was to breach the wall of the adjoining building.

Captain Patrick T. Green

Using pneumatic drills, a diamond shape opening was cut through the wall at a point directly opposite the trapped members. As the operation commenced Rescue 2 was special called. Once the opening was completed, nine torturous hours of delicate dangerous work began. Using almost every tool on the rig, from tin snips to hand saws, jacks, trench braces and block and tackle, the rescue men worked in nearly every position from flat on their backs to suspended upside down, one by one the trapped men were removed.

In the early morning hours the rescue men reached Captain John McGuire of Ladder 5 and Lieutenant Jeremiah Cronin of Water Tower 2. Both men were carefully dug clear and removed to nearby hospitals. The rescue work continued until the last two men, Acting Deputy Chief William Hogan and Fireman Michael Bennett of Ladder 5, were removed.

Sadly, Chief Hogan and Fireman Winfield Walsh of Ladder 9 died several days later as a result of their injuries.

For his leadership and valor at this collapse rescue operation Captain Patrick T. Green was awarded a Class I and was presented the Chief John J. McElligott and Department Medals.

Rescue 1 took up from this fire and move to their new home, the former quarters of Engine 20, located at 243 Lafayette Street. Engine 20 had been disbanded effective the same day, January 1, 1947. Rescue 1 would now occupy this firehouse rather than leave it vacant, and the adjacent area unprotected.

Another unusual piece of Rescue 1 lore started the very second the year 1947 began. The story goes that one of the deputy commissioners of the department wanted his nephew to be assigned to Rescue 1 directly from proby school. It was decided that two probies would be sent to the company, the commissioner's nephew and one other. The chief in charge of training was asked who is the best student in the class? This recommendation would be the second probationary fireman assigned. The Department Orders stated: Effective 12:01 hours January 1, 1947 Firemen Arthur L. Moran and Joseph W. Rooney (best student in the class) were assigned to Rescue Company 1.

It is also interesting to note at this time the FDNY was restoring some of the reduced hours firemen had lost when World War II started. Firemen were working between 56 hours and 67 hours a week, depending where they were assigned. The two platoon system was dropped in favor of a three-platoons working 8-hour shifts. (The two-platoon system, with reduced hours, would be re-instituted in 1948.) The reduced work hours and expanded vacation days meant more firemen. So the Probationary Firemen's School was in full swing.

Rooney and Moran reported to the company and went to work. Apparently Moran only stayed in the company for a short while, before transferring to Ladder 122. Rooney however remained in Rescue 1 and excelled. In 1947 Fireman 3rd Grade Joseph W. Rooney was placed on the Roll of Merit with a Class I, (and received a Department Medal for the Battery Tunnel fire) and Class A awards.

A third fire and collapse occurred on January 10, 1947, this time burying four firemen and a lieutenant. This fire was on the third floor of 131 John Street in Manhattan, a four-story loft building. The floor gave way dropping four members of Engine Companies 6 and 32 and tons of debris to the second floor. Several were rescued quickly and removed through windows and down ladders. However, Lt. Rice of Engine 6, was trapped under beams, machinery and rubble. Rescue 1 had to shore up the third floor before they could begin to tunnel to the trapped officer. With the threat of further collapse looming above, for the next eighty minutes Rescue 1 used: jacks, saws, blocks, wedges, and other special equipment to free all the trapped men.

With the end of the world war, the technological improvements and inventions driven by the war effort began to find its way to the rest of the nation. One vast improvement, the development of better breating apparatus, came from the air force to the fire department by way of the Scott Aviation Company. This company had developed high-altitude breathing gear for bomber crews. It was quickly adapted for fire fighting. For the rescuemen of New York City it arrived just in time.

Since 1915 the members of Rescue 1 (followed by the other rescue companies as they were organized) had been using the Draeger Smoke Helmet to enter highly contaminated atmospheres. The Draeger mask, however, was never approved by the Bureau of Mines (Founded in 1910 to prevent mine diasters and to enhance safety; they set breathing apparatus standards). The smoke helmets being used in 1947 were already fifteen years old, and parts were now almost impossible to find. Besides their heavy weight and numerous negative features the helmets had served well, but progress had arrived.

In 1940 the M.S.A. One-Hour Type breathing apparatus was placed in-service on all New York rescue companies. These units were lighter and better designed, but it was soon realized

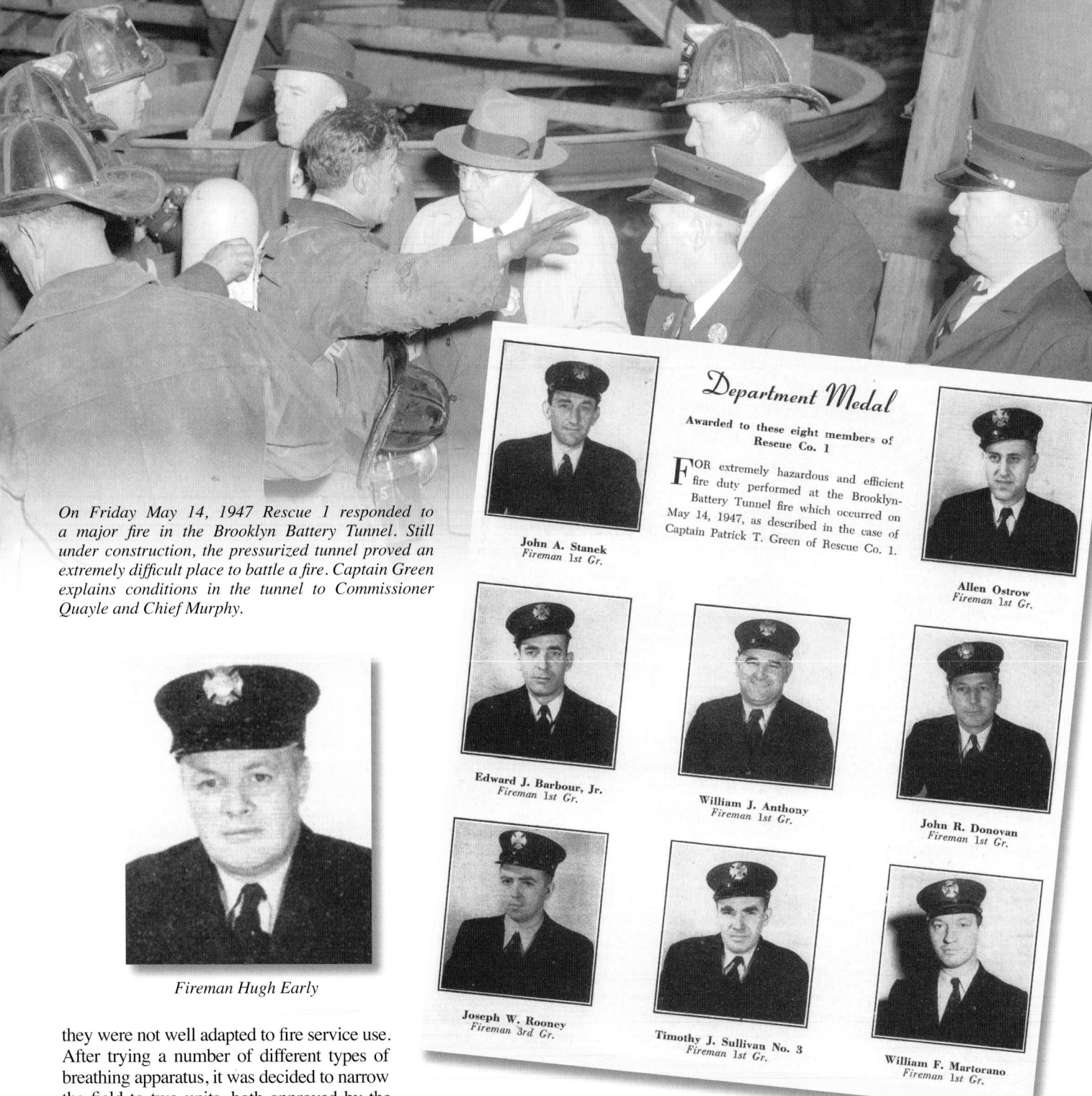

On Friday May 14, 1947 Rescue 1 responded to a major fire in the Brooklyn Battery Tunnel. Still under construction, the pressurized tunnel proved an extremely difficult place to battle a fire. Captain Green explains conditions in the tunnel to Commissioner Quayle and Chief Murphy.

Fireman Hugh Early

they were not well adapted to fire service use. After trying a number of different types of breathing apparatus, it was decided to narrow the field to two units, both approved by the Bueau of Mines: the Scott Air-Pak Mask (using compressed air) and the M.S.A. Demand Mask (using oxygen). These masks went through rigorous testing by the rescue companies, and were then used in real fires and emergency conditions. Two masks went to each rescue company to be used as regular equipment. (Whenever used however, the members were accompnied by other rescue men using our own masks to observe and assist if needed.

Both masks were lighter in weight, (18 lbs. less than the Draeger mask) both had "demand feed" (meaning air or oxygen was supplied as needed). They also provided better visibility and did not fog up. The trials and field testing continued.

A fire in an under-river tunnel under construction again occurred on May 14, 1947. This time the blaze was in the Brooklyn Battery Tunnel. It was 11:45 a.m. Forty-five sandhogs were busy working, when a fire broke out 150-feet below ground among the batteries of an electrically powered donkey engine used to haul carloads of dirt towards the tunnel entrance. The workers tried to extinguish the fire, but were driven from the tunnel by the fire and the noxious smoke.

The first arriving chiefs realized units would be unable to penetrate to the fire area, due to the dense smoke and the complications of working inside the pressurized tunnel. Rescue 1 was special called. Manhattan fire dispatchers phoned quarters and advised Capt. Green of the reported conditions. "A fire in an electric locomotive in the westbound tube of the partially constructed tunnel…severe smoke conditions prevailed…self contained breathing apparatus would be necessary…" The company rolled to the fire, and broke out the new Scott masks. In order to access the tube, the firemen would have to enter the main lock, or compression chamber, and have the pressure raised to almost twice atmospheric pressure.

Capt. Green and Firemen Edward Barbour and Timothy Sullivan entered the compression chamber with carbon dioxide extinguishers, and prepared for the increase of pressure. Suddenly the chamber filled with hot, acrid and thick smoke. The air being used to pressurize the chamber was being drawn from the fire area. Quickly masks were adjusted, a taste of what lay before them fresh in their mouths.

The chamber doors were opened to a blast of scorching heat and noxious smoke. Stationing a man at the door to prevent accidental closing, the rescue men ventured forward. They were forced to grope in complete darkness, through searing heat and thick smoke, to locate a metal ladder and climb down ten feet from the catwalk to the track level. After a difficult search, they located the fire. Batteries arranged in tiers aboard the locomotive were burning, and the rescue men attempted to control the fire with carbon dioxide extinguishers. The high underground pressure helped to eat up their air supply. After ten grueling minutes they were forced to return outside.

Green and his crew reported conditions as their cylinders were changed, and then re-entered the airlocks. Using smoke ejectors and foamite they again tried to extinguish the blaze. This tactic failed as well, and they returned using the same dangerous path they had taken in.

To completely decompress the tunnel would take more than an hour. As some of the pressure in the tunnel was reduced, Captain Green and his men plunged back into the tunnel searching for the tunnel's three-inch water main. The main was finally located, and an 1-1/2 inch hand line was stretched towards the locomotive. The line proved to be too short, but members were able to knock the fire down as a second small 1-inch hose was dragged close. With great difficulty they were able to extinguish the flames, and at 2:35 p.m. the fire was declared under control.

During the course of the operation, Captain Green had to pass through the compression locks five times. Rotating teams, the members endured tremendous punishment operating at this fire. The entire working platoon was placed on the Roll of Merit with Class I awards. Captain Green was presented the James Gordon Bennett and Department Medals, Fireman Hugh Early was presented the Bonner and Department Medals, and Firemen John A. Stanek, Allen Ostrow, Edward J. Barbour Jr., William J. Anthony, John R. Donovan, Joseph W. Rooney, Timothy J. Sullivan and William Martorano were presented Department Medals.

One of the most spectacular and costly pier fires to occur in the city took place on September 29, 1947. The 800-foot long Pier 57 on the North (Hudson) River on Eleventh Avenue and 16th Street was known as the Grace Line Pier. Eight alarms were transmitted for this blaze. Five alarms for Box 572, then a Borough call sending the third alarm assignment for Box 236- Broadway and Johnson Avenue in Brooklyn to the Manhattan fire.

Faced with a thick layer of concrete over the heavily creosoted planking pier structure, Rescue 1 operated pavement breakers in an attempt to open the pier deck. Thick clouds of noxious creosote laced smoke filled the pier and most of lower Manhattan. The tar like creosote also fueled the rapidly spreading fire beneath the pier. Finally conditions became so severe the department was forced to abandon the blazing pier. Two department compressor trucks were lost, when the pier collapsed into the river. Six fire boats worked three days to extinguish the fire.

It was the morning of November 28, 1947. Fireman Harold B. Andersen of Rescue 1 was off-duty, when he noticed smoke coming from a store at 84 Church Street in Brooklyn. It was 9:45 a.m., when Andersen ran into a nearby drug store telling the manager to notify the fire department. Fireman Andersen then hurried to the fire building, now fully involved on the first floor, and heard the shouts of persons trapped above. Answering their cries for help, Andersen made his way through heavy smoke to the top floor. There he found seven members of a family with no way out, except back through the heavy smoke filling the halls and stairs. At this time, the rear fire escape could not be used because of heavy fire venting out from below.

> Fireman Anderson made three separate trips through deteriorating conditions. He was able to remove all seven occupants, ranging in ages from nine-years-old to seventy-one years-old.

Fireman Andersen made three separate trips through deteriorating conditions. He was able to remove all seven occupants, ranging in ages from nine-years-old to seventy-one years-old. Upon the arrival of Brooklyn fire units, Fireman Andersen reported to the acting deputy chief who accepted his voluntary duty, and sent him to help raise ladders and stretch hose lines. For his bravery Andersen was awarded a Class A, and for his voluntary duty he was awarded another Class A.

Yet another fire building collapsed trapping members of the department on November 28, 1947. This five alarm fire was in 334 East 98th Street, a five-story former cigar factory that had been converted to an ice warehouse. At the time of the fire it

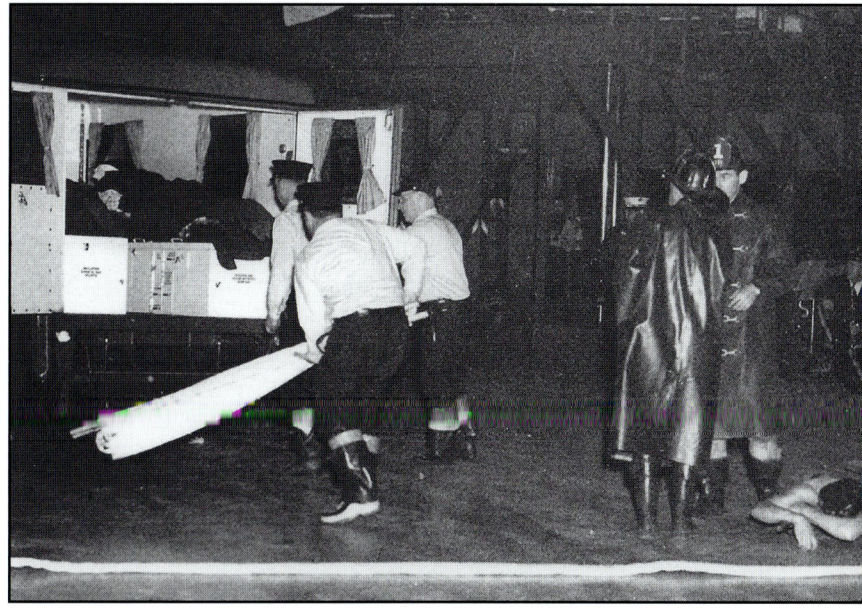

Madison Square Garden was the site of the thrill shows "Midnight Alarm." Staged in August of 1947, the proceeds went to the FDNY Welfare Fund. Rescues and firefighting techniques were demonstrated to the packed house. Rescue 1 and their rig, took part in every show.

was now a plumbing supply warehouse. The initial alarm came in at a little before 8 p.m. Members of Ladder Company 26 were on the roof of the fire building chopping holes and venting where they could. They worked their way around wooden crates filled with plumbing equipment stored on the roof. Suddenly, the building collapsed carrying a number of firemen with it. Rescue 1 began a quick survey of the collapse area, and determined the missing men were buried at the rear of the building's first floor. They were trapped beneath tons of debris hurled onto them when most of the roof and upper floors collapsed.

Rescue 1 went through the store of the Bel-Pen Auto Sales Company at 1891 First Avenue, to the west of the burning building, and through a small courtyard at the rear of the store to reach the warehouse's east wall. Behind this wall rescue men could hear the muffled shouts of the trapped men as they attacked the wall with pavement breakers, pneumatic drills and mauls. First, one fireman was pulled from the rubble and the breaching and digging continued. A half hour later a captain was removed, in very serious condition, and rushed to the hospital. On into the night the dangerous rescue work continued. In all, two members of Ladder 26, Firemen Howard Wynn and Jacob Bassman were killed by the collapse, Bassman dying the next day in the hospital. Three other members of the company were removed from the wreckage with serious injuries.

Three old wooden cars, used for refuse removal, were burning in the B.M.T. Subway tunnel under Centre Street, between Franklin and White Streets in Manhattan on March 6, 1948. Thick black smoke began pouring from the sidewalk ventilators. Box 163 was pulled at 11:57 a.m. Rescue 1 responded several minutes later, on the second alarm, and arrived to see flames shooting high into the air through the sidewalk gratings on the east side of Centre Street. The heat was so intense it warped and buckled the gratings. The smoke was so thick that, even though it was just past noon, the Searchlight Unit was special called to the scene.

Using mauls, crowbars and hooks, members of Rescue 1 removed the white-hot gratings on both sides of the street, then a 35-foot ladder was lowered through the opening to the bed of the railroad tracks below. Rescue 1 assisted the engine companies in stretching hand lines to the seat of the fire. The superheated concrete ceilings of the tunnel crumbled, when struck by the heavy volume of cold water.

On May 3, 1948, a new Mack rescue truck was received by Rescue Company 1, designed extensively from the input of members of the company. Because the 1939 Ward La France proved to be so impractical and inefficient in terms of equipment access, the department allowed the members of the unit to design their own rig. The result was registration number 75S2315, built by Approved Fire Apparatus on a Mack L model chassis at a cost of $26,600. The rig featured sixteen compartments on both sides of the walk-through body that were accessible from the outside. This provided for better space utilization and organization for the many special tools now carried by the unit, and allowed quicker retrieval of any specific tool. There were also seven interior compartments and a long bench seat inside the body accessible through rear doors. All members of the company could now ride inside with the rear doors closed, which was formerly impossible. The rig also contained a desk and guarded shelf space on both sides of the aisle. The new truck was five feet shorter and six inches narrower than the previous rig.

The new rig had a 16-foot extension hook ladder, two sets of linemen's spikes and harness, various sized trench jacks including a 30-ton hydraulic jack, and kits of CCL-4 bombs (carbon tetrachloride grenades used to extinguish fires by inhibiting the chemical chain reaction of the combustion process).

This unit remained with Rescue 1 until reassigned to Rescue 5 in 1959. It became a spare in 1962 and was used by Rescue 2 until 1967, although it was never officially assigned to that unit. It again served as a spare, until it was disposed of on November 16, 1971.

Rescue Company 5 went into service on May 16, 1948 in Richmond. The company shared quarters with Ladder 78 at 14 Brighton Avenue, New Brighton, Staten Island. That placed them very near the terminals, piers and warehouses, and the more densely populated business and residential areas of the borough. The company was manned by personnel of Hook

Members of Rescue 1 feverishly try to resuscitate a brother fireman in July of 1948, as a priest administers the Last Rites. Sadly, the fireman died.

& Ladder 78, who would operate as a rescue company when called (the ladder would be out of service).

A snapped elevator cable plunged an elevator car from the tenth floor with 25 passengers inside on March 31, 1948. The safety brakes stopped the dropping car between the second and third floors, where it remained jammed. As members of Ladder Company 3 removed three persons through a side panel of the elevator to an adjoining car, Rescue 1 accessed the the top of the car. First, rescue men removed the broken cable from the top of the car, then opened the emergency hatch and lowered a 16-foot ladder into the car. Two injured women, both with fractured ankles, were removed up through the emergency hatch using Stokes baskets.

Rescue 1 was special called to a fire in a transformer in a sub-station of the New York Transit System at 77 Murray Street, Manhattan on August 26, 1948. The transformer was handling 11,000 volts in its primary windings, and 400 volts in its secondary windings. In close proximity were four other transformers that were still operating. An attempt was made to extinguish the fire with CO_2 extinguishers applied through vent holes at the top. Suddenly, with a blinding flash and a loud boom, the entire substation was short-circuited. The plant was then de-energized, and fire fire subsequently extinguished with fog nozzles.

On the night of October 2, 1948, a tug and two barges it was towing were sunk after colliding with the freighter *Elizabeth J. Nichols* in the North River. Rescue 1 set up Homelite generators on the end of Pier 53, and placed floodlights out over the river to help detect any possible victims. The rescue officer and four members of the unit proceeded aboard a tug with inhalators, blankets, heating pads and stretchers, to the freighter anchored in mid-stream. Inhalator treatment and first aid were given to three survivors from the sunken tug, and after treatment from Doctor Archer, were taken to St. Vincent's Hospital.

Because of the swift outgoing tide, the current carried the wreckage of one of the barges to Pier 13, where it came to rest at the foot of Dey Street. This information was conveyed to Rescue 1 via department radio from the fireboat. Rescue 1 proceeded to that location. The cabin of the barge was above water, and rescue men were able to cut a hole through the roof using an electric saw. Lights were lowered inside and a thorough search was made. No additional victims were found.

On October 21, 1948 Rescue 1 was called to Broadway and Reade Streets for a major gas leak. A worker removing an old steam main, accidentally smashed a 6-inch gas main with a sledge hammer. The main carried gas at 6 to 7 pounds pressure. The break was about 10-inches long and 4-inches wide.

Members of Rescue 1 fashioned a temporary plug, by filling a burlap sack with sawdust and soaking it in water. Then wearing Scott masks, the rescue men jammed the bag into the break and sealed it by applying pressure with a trench jack. Finally, the company shut off all gas appliances in use in buildings on both sides of the street. Rescue 1 remained on the scene, until the gas company isolated the broken gas main.

The FDNY Annual Report for the year 1949 stated: Rescue Unit No. 1 developed three new devices during the year. One refills the compressed air cylinders used in masks, and also the oxygen cylinders in portable cutting equipment. This new invention also prepares the compound of oxygen and carbon dioxide known commercially as carbogen. (This new device provided a considerable savings to the department: Rescue 1 could now re-fill 12 inhalator cylinders for the cost of $1.56 instead of the former price of $36. Rescue 1 also provided carbogen to hook and ladder companies, fireboats and Rescue 5). Another new development provided spray treatment for burns, and is capable of treating 15 to 20 victims of severe and extensive burns simultaneously under the most sterile conditions. The third is a small, compact, single cylinder inhalator to provide treatment during transportation of stretcher cases, and for victims trapped in confined places where a standard inhalator could not be used.

It also stated that Rescue 1 responded to 663 alarms of fire and other emergencies from the Battery to 106th Street during the year. The mask equipment was used on 46 occasions, including: rescues, ventilating premises of dense smoke, irritant or noxious gases, locating and removing chemicals giving off lethal fumes, locating the seat of fires, advancing hose lines at difficult operations, controlling and shutting down leaks in commercial refrigerating plants and where pipes had been broken at fires, or because of mechanical difficulties.

They would use the inhalators 182 times for various forms of asphyxia induced by smoke narcosis, gas, submersion and oxygen deficiency.

The portable cutting equipment was used on 11 occasions, to cut through metal barred windows or other metal structural parts, to effect the rescue of persons trapped in buildings, elevators, train and automobile wrecks, building collapses, to cut through deck and hull plates of ships, structural parts of buildings and other obstructions to permit penetration of streams, ventilation, forcible entry, or to overcome other conditions that impeded operations.

The unit for generating large size foam streams was employed to control and extinguish fires in chemical and inflammable liquids and substances on 14 occasions.

But the biggest job of the year 1949 would come on May 13th, for an explosion and fire inside the mile-long Holland Tunnel. It was 8:48 a.m., when a 16-ton trailer truck loaded with 80 fifty-five gallon drums of the highly flammable carbon disulphide caught fire. The 48,536 pounds of deadly cargo, which should never have been in the tunnel, soon caught fire and filled the tube with deadly carbon disulphide fumes and thick smoke. A series of violent explosions occurred, spreading the flames to other vehicles. The first notice to the FDNY was a phone call to the Telegraph Bureau from the Holland Tunnel's New York Office at 9:13 a.m., stating that chemical fumes were escaping in the tunnel. A special call to Box 327 (West and Spring Streets) for Rescue 1 was transmitted immediately. Chief John Heaney of the Fifth Battalion and Rescue 1 arrived and quickly descended into the westbound tunnel. After traveling about 6,000-feet they crossed over to the eastbound tube to find that, "All Hell had broken loose!" A special call to Box 327 (West and Spring Streets) for Rescue 1 was transmitted immediately. Chief John Heaney of the Fifth Battalion and Rescue 1 arrived and quickly descended into the westbound tunnel. After traveling about 6,000-feet they crossed over to the eastbound tube to find that, "All Hell had broken loose!"

They were faced with ten trucks completely involved in fire, with intermittent explosions of the carbon disulphide drums. With each explosion a high ball of fire mushroomed against the ceiling of the tunnel. Blast after blast rocked the tubular structure, as smoke and toxic gases pumped from the blazing trucks. Extreme heat conditions and a heavy concentration of ammonia, chlorine and carbon disulphide fumes were present. The chief contacted tunnel personnel, via a phone, to their control room requesting the FDNY dispatchers be called and a full first-alarm assignment be transmitted.

Friday May 13, 1949 Rescue 1 works at a major fire in the Holland Tunnel. This photo shows the fire commissioner and chief officers conferring near the rescue truck. "Boots" the company mascot is observing from the side window.

Every young boy dreams of becoming a fireman, just as these three undoubtedly did. In fact, the boy on the left, Philip Mahaney grew up to be a fireman with Rescue 5. The boy in the middle is his twin brother, Patrick, who would become a captain in the FDNY. Both were Rescue 1 buffs as youngsters and watched as the 1948 Mack L backs into quarters.

Box 308 was sent out at 9:30 a.m., sending four engines, two trucks, the second due battalion chief and the First Division. Rescue 2 was special called at 9:32, with instructions to proceed through the Lincoln Tunnel and down through Jersey to the Jersey portal of the Holland Tunnel. At 10:12 Rescue 3, two police emergency squads, three public ambulances and the Bellevue Hospital Disaster Unit responded. Four minutes later the FDNY Department Ambulance with Doctor Archer was sent on the same route as Rescue 2. Department Ambulances 2 (Brooklyn) and Department Ambulance 3 (Manhattan) were ordered to the New York end of the tunnel. Rescue 4 was special called at 10:28. For the first time in department history four rescue companies were working together at the same operation. A second alarm and special calls for manpower were also sent.

The first alarm units utilized the tunnel's standpipe system to get lines into operation. Second alarm companies were used to supply an emergency means of water, in the event the standpipe system proved insufficient. The attack began. Ranking officers and firemen all knew this was going to be one of the toughest fires of their careers. The heat was intense, the explosions frequent, and smoke and fumes difficult to withstand. But not one man retreated or faltered.

For more than two hours the intense blaze was battled. Numerous firemen were quickly overcome by the chemical fumes, including the second due Battalion Chief Gunther Beake. He would later die as a result of the inhalation of these fumes. The heat was so intense that in some places the metal parts of the truck bodies were fused into one solid mass. Tiles and great slabs of reinforced concrete were torn in huge chunks from the walls and ceilings.

On June 22, 1949 Manhattan fire companies faced another extremely hot and smoky fire in the Metropolitan Opera House at Broadway and 40th Street. A smoldering fire in the third balcony erupted into roaring flames sending plumes of thick smoke chugging from roof top vents. The intense heat allowed the fire to burn through two floors of the balcony.

On August 18, 1949, portable walkie-talkie sets were issued to Rescue Companies 1, 2, 3 and 4.

A five-story building at 217 West 17th Street was the scene of a major fire on October 14, 1949. Fire companies were on the stairway backing out of the building when the floors collapsed; the men were saved because the stairs remained intact. However, the Fire Patrol was operating on the first floor at the time. Two members of Fire Patrol No. 3 were trapped and killed. Rescue 1 breached the walls from the adjoining buildings in an attempt to reach them, but because of the magnitude of the debris it took fifteen hours to recover the first man and over twenty-four to remove the second.

A special call 7-7-10-7332-1, received at 6:19 p.m., sent Rescue 1 to a train collision on the Long Island Rail Road right of way opposite 43rd Street and Dryer Avenue in Long Island City. There, under the command of Lieutenant Louis Werner, Rescue 1 worked to extricate the body of the trains motorman from the tangled steel wreckage.

Still suffering manpower shortages due to the war, in 1946, the 1,544 officers and 7,593 firemen of the FDNY were working 84-hour weeks for $3000. (With a cost of living bonus of $420) By the end of 1949, 1,733 officers and 8,780 firemen were working 45.8-hours a week for $4,150, a year. Vacation days increased from 21 to 30 days a year.

As the nineteen-forties came to a close, the way Rescue Company No. 1 was now operating was a preview of things to come for the entire New York City Fire Department. The rescue men drove to fires inside an enclosed cab. Eventually all FDNY apparatus would be totally enclosed. They were protected from smoke and fumes by wearing Scott air masks; this too would become the standard operating procedure for all firemen. In addition, they could communicate between the apparatus and the dispatchers. They could also communicate from inside the fire building to the chief outside by using their new walkie-talkies. It would take thirty more years for the FDNY to have a mask policy for all interior firefighting, and longer still to have portable radios for every member. The Rescue was again — leading the way.

Chapter 5

The Fifties

The new decade saw "The Cold War" heating up and an "Iron Curtain" dropping down. An era of air raid drills and bomb shelters was just beginning, as the world collectively held its breath. Remembering the devastation England faced during "The Blitz", the toll fire bombs and nuclear weapons took on major cities during the war, the FDNY prepared for the possibility of war reaching our shores. It would be a daunting task, but they geared up none the less. The department duplicated all the equipment carried by Rescue 1, so that a spare apparatus could be called into service as an additional rescue unit, in the event of an air attack on the city.

On the afternoon of March 18, 1950 fire companies responded to 287 West Tenth Street for a fire in a building occupied by the Whitehead Metal Products. First due units were faced with escaping sulphur fumes. Acting Battalion Chief Peter McMahon would not allow firemen without masks to enter the noxious clouds of smoke. First he special called Rescue 1, then Rescue 2 to battle the fire. The two rescue companies donned masks and pushed hose lines into the blazing building. It required an hour of hot, dangerous work to extinguish the fire.

The company was asked to perform a delicate operation on October 27th, when they were called to 201 West 87th Street for a boy pinned between an elevator car and the shaft wall. A team of rescue men placed ropes around the boy's torso to keep him from falling, as a second team of rescue men applied cable clamps to the keep the car from moving. Then an electric gun saw was used to cut away sections of the car's roof releasing the lad.

For the second time in department history four rescue companies would operate at the same incident, this time in Queens. It was 6:30 p.m., Thanksgiving Eve, November 22, 1950 when the FDNY responded to Metropolitan Avenue and 125th Street. A Long Island Rail Road commuter train filled with passengers slammed into the rear of another filled commuter train stopped on the tracks with a brake problem. Responding fire companies had a major rescue operation on their hands as more than 400 persons were injured, trapped in the wreckage or killed.

Four FDNY rescue companies worked at this tragic LIRR train crash November 24, 1950. The rear end collision happened at Metropolitan Avenue and 125th Street in Queens.

On board the train that was struck was off-duty Lieutenant Thomas Langford of Rescue 1. Langford, who'd been seated in a car two removed from the ill-fated car, was shaken up but not seriously injured. He immediately climbed up into the telescoped cars. Langford found a number of injured, and was able to remove them handing them down to other passengers at track side. He also applied tourniquets to two persons who were bleeding severely. Upon arrival of the first FDNY units, Lt. Langford continued working and eventually teamed up with Rescue 1 and worked with them.

The rescue companies used jacks, both hydraulic and mechanical, blocks, wedges, cutting torches, asbestos blankets, Halligans and other hand tools to raise the upper most car which had straddled the other trapping victims in between. The companies had to work quickly, but with great caution to avoid toppling the upper car onto themselves and those they were extricating. Rescue men crawled through the twisted wreckage, locating, treating and removing the passengers from the crumpled cars.

> Scores of lives were saved, as the rescue companies toiled for eleven long hours.

Scores of lives were saved, as the rescue companies toiled for eleven long hours. Sadly, 78 persons lost their lives. But many of the 363 injured were still alive, due to the exceptional bravery and professional skill of the FDNY rescue firemen.

Two days later, November 24th, Rescue 1 was called to the Pennsylvania Railroad yard at West 38th Street between Tenth and Eleventh Avenues in Manhattan for a worker trapped in a collapsed trench. The man was working in the trench being dug for a new sewer line when a forty-foot concrete wall, made unstable by the excavation, toppled over pushing earth into the ditch burying him up to his shoulders in dirt and debris. Under the command of Lieutenant James Ferguson, Rescue 1 shored up the wall, and the sides of the trench near the imprisoned man with jacks. Then the careful work of digging the man out by hand began. When the last of the clay, dirt and debris was cleared the injured man was removed from the trench and taken to the hospital.

The following day, November 25th, a major storm passed close to the city driving hurricane force wind gusts across Manhattan and the other boroughs. Gusts of up to 94 miles-per-hour were recorded reeking havoc on the five boroughs. At the height of tremendous winds, Rescue 1 responded to Mulberry Street where two workers were trapped on a swinging scaffold on the south side of Old St. Patrick's Cathedral. A rescue man was lowered by roof rope to calm the frantic men, as the remainder of the company manually lowered the scaffold safely to the ground.

Later that day, the company was called to a 32-story building at 82 Beaver Street where a cornice, torn loose by the gale, was in danger of crashing to the street. Six rescue men went onto the roof with safety ropes tied about them, and lashed the cornice down.

A train wreck and fire inside Pennsylvania Railroad Tunnel No. 2, beneath the East River on March 5, 1951, required both Rescue Companies 1 and 4 due to the extreme smoke and heat conditions. Rescue 4, wearing masks and carrying tools and extinguishers, entered the emergency exit shaft at 54th Avenue and Second Street, Queens. About 1,000-feet west of 50th Avenue they came upon the blazing wreck. A diesel-electric locomotive had telescoped into the rear of a pullman sleeper. The rescue men split up to battle the fire and search for injured or trapped people.

Rescue companies utilized their special tools to extricate people from the telescoped wreckage in the train crash on November 24, 1950.

With the growing concern of possible nuclear air raid attacks, the national and local Civil Defense agencies geared up their efforts. In this early 1951 photo of a realistic drill near Bellevue Hospital, members of Rescue 1 "dig out" victims as a nurse gives first aid. Note the Gieger Counter operator in the rear.

Meanwhile, Rescue 1 had entered the tunnel through a ventilation shaft at 33rd Street and First Avenue, Manhattan. They approached the wreck, which was one and quarter miles to the east. As the search for victims was completed, the members of Rescue 1 were forced to don masks before they could use their tools and extinguishers to help fight the fire.

With the fire extinguished, the rescue companies proceeded to the Queens yards placing masks on the engineer and brakeman of another locomotive that was used to remove the wreckage from the tunnel. Members of the two companies guided the locomotive by walking the catwalk and communicating conditions ahead, as the train moved through the smoke filled tunnel to the wreck. Two trips were required to remove the wreckage.

Once again the streets of lower Manhattan were filling with thick black smoke from a cellar fire. On May 6, 1951, firemen struggled to get water on a fire at 159 Duane Street. The five-story loft building housed the Tyler Rubber Company. Its cellar was filled with rubber boots, sneakers and other stored rubber goods. The extreme heat and thick smoke made the fire unapproachable, so Rescue 1 was ordered to cut holes through the first floor. Using a six-inch rotary cutter powered by a portable generator, the rescue men bored through the concrete to allow cellar pipes and other appliances to get water on the fire.

Two smoke ejectors were then placed at either end of the cellar, where one forced air in and the other pulled air out of the smoke filled cellar. Members of Rescue 1 donned masks, searched for hot spots and possible victims, before overhauling began.

It was just past noon on December 3, 1951 when Rescue 1 responded to what seemed an ordinary fire aboard the S.S. *American Miller*, berthed at Pier 60, North River. The fire had possession of part of Hold #5 and involved general cargo. The use of hand lines quickly brought the fire under control. Overhauling had just started when the strong odor of burning sulphur was detected. Despite the use of smoke ejectors, the sulphur gas was generating faster than the smoke ejectors could remove it. It quickly became impossible for anyone to remain in the hold without a mask.

At this point, members of Rescue 1 donned masks and entered the hold to remove cargo. While laboring with this removal they came across 150 steel drums, each containing 250 pounds of sodium hydro-sulphide, a chemical that burns spontaneously in the presence of heat or moisture, or both. A number of these drums were burning. Many were ruptured and gas was escaping. The rescue men were off-loading the dangerous drums, when several exploded knocking the firemen off their feet, and splattering them with the hot caustic chemicals. To avert other explosions, holes were punched in the remaining drums to release pressure. The burning drums, now red hot, were rigged and hoisted quickly to the main deck then dumped overboard. The prompt, courageous and tireless efforts of the members of Rescue 1 averted a serious fire loss and many injuries.

A spectacular five alarm fire tore through a five-story brick department store warehouse on East 13th Street at Fifth Avenue in Manhattan on the night of March 20, 1952. During the difficult battle eight firemen were overcome by the dense smoke as the top floor and cockloft of the large building blazed furiously. Fireman Taras Kinasewitz of Rescue 1 was singled out for his efforts at this fire. In a report from the deputy chief of the Second Division to the chief of department it stated: Fireman Kinasewitz displayed exceptional ability, stamina and courage while operating at this fire. In spite of a heavy and smoky fire involving the entire premises Fireman Kinasewitz labored long and hard in an effort to confine and extinguish the fire. The chief further recommended that Kinasewitz be considered for the "Fireman of the Month Award" in recognition of - "the terrific punishment and fatigue that he subjected himself to in performing duty at this fire."

With the FDNY still facing fire after smoky fire filled with toxic and at times deadly gases, the field testing of acceptable breathing apparatus continued. On April 22, 1952 a department spokesman told the media that 89 more masks would be purchased, but that training firefighters on how to use the new gear would take time.

This announcement just happened to follow a fire in Manhattan on the tenth floor of the Graybar Building at 420 Lexington Avenue. This small but smoky fire in a storage booth could not be extinguished by the first alarm units. Special called Rescue 1 donned air masks and plunged into the choking smoke and extinguished the fire.

Several months later, on September 26, 1952, members of the rescue companies gathered. This time in the quarters of Rescue 4 in Queens to again test air masks. At this time the FDNY had 200 masks of various types in service throughout the job. It was hoped this testing would determine a single mask the department would purchase.

With department medical officers standing by and the department ambulance parked out front, the cellar of the firehouse was filled with fumes from twenty pounds of sulphur dioxide and a quart of anhydrous ammonia. Twelve of the rescue men donned Scott masks, while the other twelve were outfitted with the MSA demand type air apparatus. The men began chopping railroad ties with heavy axes to simulate working conditions. After ten minutes of hard work, they all trotted up to the third floor exchanging types of masks. They then went through the performance a second time.

The Scott masks were chosen.

A special call brought Rescue 1 to Box 535, the corner of West and 12th Streets, at 7:24 a.m., on August 29, 1952. A truck had crashed into a pillar trapping the driver. Rescue 1 arrived, and under the command of Lieutenant Joseph W. Ryan, (detailed from Ladder 20 at the time) used an assortment of tools to carefully extricate the entangled man.

An unusual request for help on February 6, 1953, resulted in a response outside the city. Shortly before noon, Rescue 1, along with Engine Companies 6 and 10, and Ladder Company 15, boarded the fireboat *Firefighter* sailing over twenty miles out of the harbor to the *Ambrose* Lightship. There they met the Chilean freighter *Aconcagua* inbound from Hamburg, Germany. A fire was blazing in Hold #2. The fireboat escorted the burning ship to a remote location in Gravesend Bay in Brooklyn, where the ship dropped anchor.

Wearing masks, the members of Rescue 1 and the other companies stretched hose lines into the hold and began battling the fire. The burning cargo consisted of aluminum powder, a half ton of nitro-cellulose film in cans, hemp, rope, mail, sisal and jute. It took two hours for the fire to be brought under control.

In April of 1954 the FDNY received 190 new portable "walkie-talkie" radios. Up to this time the department had ten in service, issued to rescue companies and marine units. With the additional radios now being given in pairs to battalion and division chiefs, the department hoped to have much better local communications at fires. The year before, two mobile units: called Field Communications Units, were placed in service. These new units would become central contact headquarters at major fires and emergencies. These vans were equipped with two-way radios and also carried extra portable radios. With the broadening use of radios, the eighty-four year-old Bureau of Fire Alarm Telegraph was renamed the Bureau of Fire Communications.

A major fire at 166 Smith Street in Brooklyn was battled on April 13, 1954. The time of the fire was 10:45 p.m. Con-

Utilizing the new Scott Airpaks, members of Rescue 1 prepare to enter this cellar fire in 1952.

ditions became so bad that thirty families had to be removed from neighboring apartments, due to the threat of extension. Without warning the six-story building collapsed, pulling two firemen down with the tumbling debris. One fireman was located quickly and removed; the other was buried under six floors of charred, twisted rubble. Special called to the scene Rescue 1 joined Rescue 2, already working feverishly to reach the trapped fireman pinned under a twenty-foot pile-high pile in the cellar. With fire raging above them, and water cascading down and filling the cellar, the members of Rescues 1 and 2 shored and tunneled their way into the cellar. The work continued into the night and the next morning. At 4 a.m., the fireman was reached and removed in surprisingly good shape.

Rescue Company 1 responded to a fire in a building being demolished at 81 Ann Street in Manhattan on June 8, 1954. A fire lieutenant, overcome by heat exhaustion and smoke, had to be removed from the roof of the fire building. Some of the stairs of the partially demolished building had already been dismantled. This presented a challenge to the rescue men, who had to remove the semi-conscious officer to the street. An inhalator and a blanket were taken to the roof, where the lieutenant was placed on a pallet used to remove materials from the building. Accompanied by two members of Rescue 1, who continually administered oxygen, the pallet was lowered to the street by a crane in place to do demolition work. The officer was then carried across the street to Beekman Downtown Hospital.

An underground fire in a sewer under construction at 27th Street and 20th Avenue in Astoria Queens, on December 28, 1954, trapped three sandhogs. The blaze was started when a worker using an acetylene torch ignited wooden shoring in the tunnel. The burning timbers cut-off the escape route of three sandhogs, who were now trapped 880-feet from the only exit. Rescue Companies 1 and 2 were special called to the scene and joined forces with Rescue 4. The masked rescue men were lowered into a 90-feet shaft and had to wait ten minutes in a pressure chamber, before they ventured out into the thick hot smoke.

Members of the the three rescue companies worked under extreme conditions searching the smoke filled tunnel for over four city blocks, to locate and extinguish the fire and locate and remove the trapped workers. Crawling on hands and knees, they reached the workers. One sandhog had to be carried while the other two were led out. The exhausted group of rescuers and those they had rescued had to wait to be decompressed, before being raised back up the 90-foot shaft to the street.

This team of rescue men were later honored by the Board of Merit with Class I awards: Deputy Chief Edward O'Conner, Lt. Temme of Rescue 2, Firemen Hugh Early and Charles Sadera of Rescue 1 and Fireman Gerus of Rescue 4. They also all received medals.

As an interesting medal mishap, apparently the Board of Merit somehow misplaced Fireman Charles Sadera's write-up when assigning medals for the year. With a Class I award he should have gotten a department medal and a citizen's medal. When the mistake was noticed all the named citizen's medal were already announced, so the Board of Merit decided to present Sadera the Stephenson Medal. This medal was traditionally presented to a captain for maintaining the best disciplined and most highly efficient company in the department for the year. This was the first and only time the Stephenson Medal was presented for valor.

During 1954, the O'Brien Rotary Cutter was introduced. This tool was capable of making a cut through heavy pier decking, heavy wood flooring, and other wood structures. It was electric powered and permitted the positioning of distributors into inaccessible areas. Rescue 1 would use this tool at numerous pier, cellar and cockloft fires.

A fire had started in the third floor stairway of a five-story rear tenement at 62 Pitt Street on April 30, 1955. The fire spread quickly to the fourth and fifth floors and to the roof. A man was reported trapped on the fourth floor, in the rear. Since aerial ladders were blocked out by the front building and long ladders could not be brought through the front building, Lieutenant Joseph W. Ryan and Fireman John R. Donovan of Rescue 1 brought scaling ladders and a roof rope through to a second floor ledge opposite the burning rear building.

They climbed the scaling ladders to the fourth floor and entered. Searching under extremely difficult conditions, they located the badly burned, unconscious man. Upon returning to the window, with the aid of other firemen, Ryan and Donovan lowered the man with the roof rope to the second floor roof. He was then removed for medical treatment.

Lt. Joseph W. Ryan *Fireman John R. Donovan*

For this rescue both men were placed on the Roll of Merit with Class I awards. Lt. Ryan received the Commerce & Industry and Department Medals, while Fireman Donovan received the Crimmins and Department Medals.

It was 2:48 on the afternoon of May 9, 1955 when Rescue 1 responded to a reported collapse at the site of a building under construction at Columbus Circle. The New York Coliseum was a new convention center being erected by the Triborough Bridge and Tunnel Authority. Workers were pouring concrete from eight buggies (used to cart the wet cement) into two-story high forms in what would become the main exhibition hall. The weight of the poured cement and the loaded buggies standing by to spill their loads overloaded the bracing. This caused the failure of the formwork. Suddenly, 10,000 square-feet of wooden forms, miles of rebar and pipes, tons of wet concrete and a number of workers crashed 22-feet to the street level below.

Arriving units found fifty workers injured, one seriously and a cement worker missing. Rescue 1 plunged into the wet concrete. They began working with torches and other tools searching for the missing man. As the wet concrete began to cure, one-thousand pounds of sugar was rushed to the scene which firemen poured across the wet cement to slow its hardening. The search, under the direction of Lieutenant Louis Werner of Rescue 1, went on into the night. An extensive area was cleared and searched. The officer directed cutting of selected rebar and pipes by his men and supervised the removal of tons of debris by workers using a derrick.

The missing man was located and his body was removed at 8:30 a.m., May 11th. This hazardous operation was conducted over many hours without a single injury to the rescue men.

A few seconds after lifting off from the Port Authority's rooftop heliport at 111 Eighth Avenue, a helicopter crashed back onto the roof. The motor and cockpit of the aircraft were

A five-alarm fire engulfed the Wanamaker Building on July 14, 1956.

hanging precariously over the parapet, fourteen stories above the ground and in danger of falling onto the streets below. It was July 13, 1955 and Rescue 1 was special called to the location to help stabilize the dangerous scene. Using block and tackle, the company secured the craft and removed the wreckage.

Another unusual response occurred on September 2, 1955 when Rescue 1 was called to 19 West 21st Street where a thirty-seven year-old man, an employee of Expert Doll & Toy Company, was threatening to commit suicide by jumping from the eleventh floor window ledge. For an hour and a half, all efforts to coax the man back in had failed. A plan was developed, and Fireman Edward J. Barbour, Jr. was laced up in a bowline-on-a bight and waited at the twelfth floor window above. At the eleventh floor window firemen kept the man's attention and moved into position inside. When everyone was ready the deputy chief in the street below signaled and Barbour swung down pinning the man against the building. The firemen inside reached out, grabbing the man. Within seconds he was pulled inside to safety. For his swift and heroic actions Barbour was presented the Third Alarm Association and Department Medals.

Twenty days later Rescue 1 was called to 200 Lafayette Street. Here a man was perched atop a six-foot high metal chimney attached to a seven-foot high bulkhead at the edge of the building, seven-stories above the street. The man's position was one hundred feet above the street and fifty feet above the adjacent roof top. Upon reaching the roof, Lieutenant Louis Werner of Rescue 1 observed the location, actions and posture of the man on the chimney. He also noticed another civilian, a fellow employee of the man, standing on the bulkhead roof. Lt. Werner knew swift action would have to be taken.

He ordered a member of Rescue 1 to be placed in a bowline-on-a bight to secure the fireman, if he had to move in close to the roof's edge. Werner then climbed on to the bulkhead roof opposite the civilian, who was pleading with his friend not to jump. The man turned towards Lt. Werner and continued his loud threats. As the man turned, his friend started to move in. Simultaneously Lt. Werner moved in, and forcibly restrained the violently struggling man on the roof of the bulkhead. The man was then taken in hand by members of Rescue 1, placed in a Stokes basket, strapped in tightly and then taken to a nearby hospital for observation.

During the late 1950's Rescue 1 operated at some very difficult and unusual fires. Among these was the Wanamaker Building fire on July 14, 1956. The old Wanamaker Store consisted of two five-story buildings dating from 1876. Together they covered the entire block from Broadway, through Ninth and Tenth Streets to Fourth Avenue. They were joined by a tunnel and an arched bridge. It was 5:45 when Manhattan fire dispatchers transmitted Box 447, for a fire in the northern or older of the two buildings. First alarm units, including Rescue 1, arrived to find heavy smoke on the first floor with no visible fire. It quickly became obvious that the building, under demolition at the time, had a fire in the cellar or sub-cellar.

The fire, originating near the elevator shafts, was soon spreading with amazing speed throughout the huge structure. As the intensity of the fire grew, so did the number of alarms. Just over an hour after the initial alarm, five-alarms had been transmitted.

The smoke condition was so severe that masks had to be worn. Rescue 2 was special called from Brooklyn. Rescue 1 had taken up a position in the cellar of the adjoining building, manning hose lines and trying to halt the extending fire from

Fireman Edward J. Barbour, Jr.

Wanamaker Building Fire on July 14, 1956.

May 18, 1957, Rescue 1 works at tenement collapse at 137 Pitt Street. The three-story tenement collapsed, killing an elderly woman.

reaching the second structure. For many hours, masked rescue men operated fog nozzles and solid streams in this vital location, and were able to hold the raging flames in check.

Over two-hundred firefighters were overcome or injured battling this blaze. At one point, a subway train beneath the building was trapped by water run-off, which undermined the tracks and flooded the tunnel. Over 400 people onboard the train were safely removed. The fire was fought for two days by more than 800 firemen.

The first mechanical resuscitator in the department was assigned to Rescue 1 on October 1, 1956. It quickly proved its worth, saving two lives in the first three months it was carried.

Just after 9:00 a.m., on August 29, 1957, a northbound el train rounded the curve and smashed into a train stopped at the Zerega Avenue Station in the Bronx, causing the train to jackknife across three tracks and pinning the motorman in the cab. The first arriving units initiated evacuation and special called Rescue Companies 3 and 1. The rescue companies cut away as much wreckage as possible, using torches, jacks, saws, and other tools. After several hours work, the victim was free except for one foot, but his condition was deteriorating. A team of doctors on the scene decided it would be necessary to amputate the foot to save the motorman's life. The rescue companies set up generators, portable lighting, and administered oxygen while the doctors worked. The victim was finally freed after three hours. Less than a month later, a similar wreck occurred at Broadway and 230th Street, killing the motorman.

A fierce, smoky fire was battled in downtown Manhattan on Valentine's Day, February 14, 1958. Frigid cold and nine inches of snow made the fire in the Elkins Paper & Twine Company's one hundred-year-old six-story loft building extremely difficult to fight. The first five floors were supported by cast-iron columns, while above the six floor and roof were timber supports. The building was stocked with paper in 800-pound rolls, twine and other materials. There was also twine making material within the building.

At 6:30 p.m., seven employees at work on the ground floor heard breaking glass, then saw fire reflected in the windows of the building across the street. They quickly telephoned an alarm, as simultaneously, Box 334, at Wooster and Prince Street was pulled by a passer-by. Ladder 20 and Engine 13 responded from their quarters on Mercer Street, only two blocks away. Fire Patrol 2 also had a quick run from their quarters on West Third Street. Ladder 20 sent in a second alarm, as they placed the aerial to the roof. Members of the Fire Patrol entered the building and began to throw covers over valuables on the third floor.

Members of Ladder 20 climbed the aerial and began chopping holes in the roof to vent the thick smoke. Lines were stretched to the fire area, and Patrol 1 reinforced Patrol 2 on the third floor.

Approximately 12 minutes after the arrival of the fire units, the building collapsed without warning. The men on the roof scrambled for the safety of an adjoining building. As the roof dropped away, the captain of the ladder company hung from a window ledge until he could be pulled to safety. A quick roll call revealed two of his men were missing.

At 6:36 p.m., a third alarm was transmitted. Special calls for the department ambulance, (The 33-foot long Ambulance 1, placed in service on Medal Day 1949, was built on a bus chassis, and could operate as a mobile hospital with medical work being done on several patients at the same time) chaplains, medical officers and Fire Communications 1 were also placed. The additional alarms brought more than 200 firemen to the scene. Icy conditions became so severe that the thawing apparatus was called to the scene.

The flames were brought under control by 8 p.m., and the work of digging and clearing rubble in search of those trapped began in earnest. A heavy smoke condition enshrouded the three story pile of smoldering debris. Rescue 2 and 3 were brought to the scene, and with Rescue 1 and other firemen, dug under the glare of spotlights as others kept watch on the weakened walls above. They worked at a fevered pitch hoping to somehow find their brothers alive beneath the pile. At about 11 p.m., the bodies of Firemen Blumenthal and Schmid of Ladder 20 were found. The search for the missing members of Fire Patrol continued.

The news of the collapse spread quickly, and off-duty firemen began to arrive at the scene and volunteer their services. Ice continued to build, hampering the already dangerous work. FDNY and Con Ed compressors, powered tools used by rescue men to break up huge pieces of masonry.

On Saturday morning a wrecking crane was positioned to remove the front wall, that was a continual threat to fall on the working firemen. Rescue worked stopped until the wall was cleared. Then despite the 4-degree temperature, the three rescue companies and hundreds of on and off-duty firemen pushed back into the frozen, charred building remains. The bodies of Fire Patrolmen Devine and Tracy were recovered Monday night February 17. Sergeant McGee and Fire Patrolman Brusati were located and removed the following day.

Their is no reward that can repay a man for risking his life. Certainly no one who worked to recover a lost brother would even think about recognition. But due to the nature and severity of this operation, the department took the appropriate action. Department Orders No. 118 and 193 of 1958, published the findings of the Board of Merit as it related to department operations at the Wooster Street collapse. For heroic action involving unusual personal risk, 32 members assigned or detailed to Rescue Company 1 received Class III awards. For responding off-duty and operating at the collapse, the orders published more than 26 pages, listing more than 900 off-duty fire officers and firemen from across the city, each of whom was awarded a Voluntary Duty Class "A." (For a complete listing of Rescue 1 awards see the appendix)

Members of Rescue 1 worked for two days in near zero weather to recover the four fire patrolmen and two firemen killed in the Wooster Street collapse Valentine's Day 1958.

A five-alarm explosion and fire at 623 Broadway took the lives of 24 people on March 19, 1958.

A little over a month later, on March 19, 1958, Rescue 1 responded to a five alarm fire at Manhattan Box 55-341, 623 Broadway. The ancient five-story loft building that ran through to Mercer Street, near Houston Street, was the home of the Monarch Company, a garment factory. It was 3:55 p.m., when a textile-drying oven located on the third floor exploded. Flames from the gas explosion roared overhead and across the rows of wooden work tables, sending workers on that floor running for the fire exits. The workers on the floor above were not as fortunate. There, nearly forty people were forced towards the windows at the front and rear of the building, as flames poured up the stairs from below.

The first and second due ladders, Ladder Companies 20 and 9, made many spectacular rescues over their aerial ladders. Members of Rescue 1 made several rescues from the inside, as the conditions on the fourth floor were forcing some workers to jump. In all 24 people were killed and many others were injured. Captain John F. O'Hagan and Fireman John F. O'Rourke of Rescue 1, were placed on the Roll of Merit with Class III awards and Fireman Harold B. Anderson received a Class "A."

On April 15th a fire broke out on the second floor of the Museum of Modern Art during renovation work. One man lost his life, three others were injured and twenty-eight firemen were overcome battling the smoky blaze. Several persons were saved over aerial ladders, and a number of others were rescued by breaching a wall between the fire building and the adjacent structure on the fifth floor. Fireman Joseph M. Duffy of Rescue 1 received a Class III for his heroic actions at this fire. Several paintings, including two large paintings by Claude Monet from his famed "Water Lilies" series, were destroyed in the fire.

When selecting new members of the company, the captains of Rescue 1 were always on the look out for men with unique abilities. Being a good fireman was of course first on the list, but having special talents and abilities made for a better candidate. In 1958 Captain John O'Hagan brought a young fireman to the company, who certainly had a unique and specialized ability. Thomas Bonamo, was appointed to the FDNY in 1954, and was assigned to Engine Company 31. As a teenager Bonamo met the underwater pioneer Jacques-Yves Cousteau, after a lecture he'd given about his new invention – the aqua lung. Bonamo asked about the availability of this underwater diving gear, then purchased the equipment.

Several years later he joined the department and word spread of his unique ability. Not only was he a strong swimmer, but he could dive underwater for a prolonged amount of time. This captured the imagination of department officials faced with simple water emergencies like drownings, and complicated emergencies such as vehicles in the water. On September 15, 1958 the phone in Fireman Bonamo's home rang. His wife answered the phone and was surprised to learn it was the fire commissioner calling. Bonamo was requested to take his personal SCUBA gear and go to the St. George Terminal to meet the fireboat. The marine unit then rushed him to Newark Bay, where a commuter train filled with people had plunged into the water.

Rescue 1 members remove one of the twenty-four victims who died in the five-alarm fire on March 19, 1958.

Fireman Bonamo suited up and made numerous dives into the submerged train pulling out a victim with each trip. Among those he pulled from the depths was former New York Yankees all-star second baseman George "Snuffy" Stirnweiss.

Rescue 1 was dispatched to an unusual fire in the roof of the Hampshire House Hotel on July 22, 1958. The fire in the thirty-eight story structure, located at 150 Central Park South, had been burning for some time. While perched on scaffolds, the members of Rescue 1 operated electric pavement breakers to breach the concrete roof from the outside to allow extinguishment of the fire. The extreme height and pitch of the roof made this operation very hazardous.

Brooklyn Box 201, vicinity of Wythe and North First Street Williamsburg, was transmitted on August 11, 1959, when a delivery truck off-loaded 1,000 gallons of nitric acid into the wrong tank inside the Radio Receptor Company building at 240 Wythe Avenue. The product should have been pumped into an empty tank. Instead it was delivered into a tank already containing several thousand gallons of muriatic (hydrochloric) acid. A violent reaction ensued, producing a layer of suffocating gas that filled the cellar, then spilled out. Hugging the ground and held down by the humid weather, the gas spread across the neighborhood. FDNY units and Rescue 2 arrived. Sixty-five people were dazed by the fumes and required treatment. Hundreds of others had to be evacuated. Rescue Companies 1 and 4 were special called. The three rescue companies used over 100 cylinders of air as they mitigated the fumes, plugged a leak, searched the building for victims and placed smoke ejectors. More than 100 firemen and civilians were affected by the fumes.

Twenty-five firemen were treated for heat exhaustion and smoke inhalation during a two-alarm fire in a six-story loft building at 270 Canal Street, between Broadway and Lafayette Street. August 27, 1959 was a hot humid day, and the smoky fire proved difficult to extinguish. The fire began in the basement of a retail store and extended to the first and second floors before it was brought under control. Rescue 1 provided first aid and treated a number of firemen with inhalators and oxygen tanks.

A building collapse at Third Avenue and 15th Street on September 15, 1958, trapped four workmen. Rescue 1 was special called, and the workers were quickly dug out.

A new apparatus was assigned to Rescue 1 on May 4, 1959. The new rig was similar in style to the 1948 Mack but was slightly larger, again reflecting the increase in specialized tools and equipment continually assigned to the unit over the years. This truck was built by Gerstenslager on a B model Mack chassis and carried registration number 1334. It was replaced in 1971 but remained on the roster as a spare until disposed of on September 17, 1979. It is interesting to note that the Boston Fire Department purchased an almost identical twin to this unit from Gerstenslager in 1964. This rig differed only in minor details, such as mirrors, warning devices, and color scheme from the FDNY rig.

On November 16, 1959, Rescue 1 was special called to Staten Island Box 756 for a fire at 155 Richmond Avenue. Five alarms had been transmitted for a fire involving eight stores. A collapse trapped three members of Rescue Company 5 beneath the fallen debris. Using jacks and hand tools, two of the men were removed alive from the rubble, but the third, Fireman Edward Campbell, died as a result of the collapse.

As the nineteen-fifties came to a close the members of Rescue 1 were wondering what the new decade would bring. The sixties would prove to be as tough as any prior decade... if not worse.

A new rig was assigned to Rescue 1 on May 4, 1959. It was built by Gerstenslager on a B model Mack chassis.

Chapter 6

The Sixties

The nineteen-sixties began with a young war hero becoming president, a new leader in a time he described as "a decade of hope and fear, in an age of both knowledge and ignorance." Several months after he took office he pledged "...to achieving the goal, before this decade is out, of landing a man on the moon and returning him safely to earth." Lofty ideas and goals that would eventually create or improve many products, including technology and equipment used to help fight fires. But before these ideas could be realized, the young president would be killed and the very nation itself become a battleground of civil rights and civil disorder. Major cities would burn, including New York. It would be a long, hot decade.

Lt. Frank Yuskevich

While a six-story brick loft building located at 236 Eldridge Street was being demolished on January 6, 1960, a 30,000 gallon water tank pulled out of its roof supports plunging through the building carrying most of the structural and supporting beams with it, leaving the remaining walls very unstable. It was 11:28 a.m., when Box 10-407-1 was transmitted.

Upon arrival, Rescue 1 found a worker barely visible and pinned under tons of debris. The area was so tight and poorly lit, that Lieutenant Frank Yuskevich was compelled to work alone, as he cut a path through the tangled wreckage. Using a power saw, pipe cutters, and other hand tools Yuskevich worked his way to the man. In spite of the hazards around him, Lt. Yuskevich used speed and efficiency. He succeeded in extricating the worker and removing him from the unstable pile. For his actions Lt. Frank Yuskevich was awarded the William F. Conran Medal.

Railroad and subway fires provide a wide range of duty for Rescue 1. On April 13, 1960 rescue members wearing Scott masks fought a severe subway escalator fire in the Times Square station. They stretched and operated a hand line, and also set up smoke ejectors to help clear some of the dense smoke and heat trapped within the station.

This WNYF front cover photo shows three members of Rescue 1: Firemen Surdukowski, Bonamo (left) and Forsyth (right) operating from the tips of two aerial ladders at this furniture warehouse fire. Three-alarms (33-1095) were transmitted on February 4, 1960.

83

On April 25, 1960 Rescue 1 was moved to the quarters of Engine 65 at 33 West 43rd Street in Manhattan.

With the hazards of Manhattan constantly changing, it was decided to move Rescue Company 1 to midtown. On April 25, 1960 the company moved into the quarters of Engine 65 at 33 West 43rd Street. Sharing these quarters would allow the company to be more centrally located within their response district, and provide quicker responses to the garment district, the numerous theaters, restaurants and high-rise offices in midtown Manhattan.

With the hazards of Manhattan constantly changing, it was decided to move Rescue Company 1 to midtown. On April 25, 1960 the company moved into the quarters of Engine 65 at 33 West 43rd Street.

Seven firemen were injured when the roof of a blazing vacant tenement building at 104 Second Street near First Avenue collapsed. The first alarm was transmitted at 12:27 p.m., June 26, 1960. The arriving companies found a heavy smoke condition at the rear of the second floor of the large L-shaped building. Flames quickly extended to the third, fourth and fifth floors and the roof. Shortly after the second alarm was transmitted, 12:40 p.m., the ceiling, a skylight and part of the roof caved in on firemen battling the flames on the fifth floor. Among those injured and taken to the hospital was Fireman Victor Miozzi of Rescue 1. Miozzi was treated at Bellevue Hospital for second-degree burns of the neck and hands, and was later released.

While operating at a fire in a twelve-story loft building at 109 West 38th Street near Sixth Avenue, nitrous oxide fumes seeped through the masks or otherwise affected twenty fireman, as they battled a flash fire in celluloid film on July 15, 1960. The violent fire occurred among the stored films, causing the discharge of so many sprinkler heads that water pressure within the building dropped to the point that the sprinklers were

Lt. Yuskevich and members of Rescue 1 remove injured fireman to ambulance on July 15, 1960. This second alarm fire was on the 12th floor of 109 West 38th Street.

ineffective. Members of Rescue 1, wearing Scott masks, were forced to climb twelve stories to reach the fire area. The fire burned out the entire twelfth floor.

Fire companies battled an escalating blaze at Manhattan Box 199, on November 18, 1960, for a fire in a five-story loft building at 463-67 Broadway at Grand Street. A second alarm brought an additional four engines, a ladder company and Rescue 1 to the scene of this rapidly spreading fire. The flames quickly extended to the adjoining buildings, and a series of additional alarms were sounded. In the basement of the original fire building, 463 Broadway, an officer and four firemen were stretching a hose line down a chute into the sub-cellar. Within moments they became disoriented, then overcome in the heavy smoke. Two of the men, under extreme conditions, were pulled out of the cellar by men on a second hose line, but they were driven out by the heat and smoke. When it was learned three men were still missing, Rescue 1 was sent to the cellar and began to search. Under punishing conditions, with extreme heat and thick smoke, Rescue 1 pressed forward. Despite localized collapses they continued searching. The three firefighters were found floating in waist deep water in the sub-cellar. Sadly, the three men: Lt. John McDermott, Fr. Francis Sammon and Fr. John Costner were dead.

This fire also spread into the two adjacent buildings, both fully involved and touched off a blaze in another five-story loft building on Grand Street. These fires would required two alarms and two borough calls before the flames were out.

During December of 1960 the FDNY responded to two of the most complicated and challenging fire operations in the history of the department. Rescue 1 was special called to both fires and despite the years of experience each rescue man had, none would ever forget these difficult, dangerous and tragic fires.

A mixture of snow and rain was falling on the city the morning of December 16, 1960. Visibility in the skies above New York was poor, with an estimated ceiling of only 600-feet. A United Airlines four-engine DC-8 jet was heading to Idlewild Airport (now John F. Kennedy International Airport), with 84 people on board. Another plane, a TWA four-engine Super Constellation, was bound for LaGuardia Airport with 44 people on board. The two planes were supposed to be "stacked" at different altitudes as they approached the New York area.

It was about 10:34 a.m., when these two planes collided over Staten Island's south shore. The flaming TWA Super Constellation crashed into Miller Field, the little-used Army Air field on Staten Island. Three sections of the plane narrowly missed the homes of nearby New Dorp.

The second plane, struggling to remain airborne, roared on for ten more miles before it began plummeting toward one of the most densely populated sections of the city, Brooklyn's Park Slope. Just before it hit the ground, the jet's wing clipped an apartment building, leaving the wing jutting out of the roof. It then dove into a corner building, shearing its tail section, which travelled into the intersection of Sterling Place and Seventh Avenue. Numerous other parts of the plane smashed into a nearby church, a garage and a row of brownstone buildings, causing fires within the structures.

Arriving FDNY companies were faced with jet fuel fed fires raging in ten brownstones, a five-story brick apartment building filled with fire and in danger of collapse, the Pillar of Fire Church on fire, and the intersection and nearby streets filled with wreckage. Five alarms and a borough call were transmitted bringing fifty fire companies to the scene. Rescue 1 was special called on the second alarm, and raced to the scene. As they approached the blaze, the dispatcher crackled across the rig radio: "Rescue 1 be advised, there are eleven buildings on fire!"

As they approached the blaze, the dispatcher crackled across the rig radio: "Rescue 1 be advised, there are eleven buildings on fire!"

The company was ordered to stretch lines upon their arrival. Under the command of Lt. William McMahon, Firemen Thomas Bonamo, Herbert Peterson and Philip Prial turned right from Seventh Avenue onto Sterling Place, crawling and dragging a hose through the snow past the blazing remains of the Pillar of Fire Church. Across the strewn rubble, something caught their eye and the firemen quickly moved in that direction. There, in a snowbank, lay eleven-year-old Steven Baltz, the only surviving passenger of the crashed airplane. The boy was in extremely critical condition,

Rescue 1 was special called within minutes of the initial alarm, when this passenger jet crashed into a crowded Brooklyn neighborhood on December 16, 1960. The crash simultaneously set fire to eleven buildings.

and carefully placed into a Stokes basket by the members of Rescue 1. He was hurried back towards Seventh Avenue and handed over to medical personnel. The rescue men continued searching and moving in with their hoses. They located a section of the plane, difficult to make out through the heavy smoke, and found the body of a man in uniform, possibly a member of the flight crew. Due his condition, they were unable to recover his body. At one point, one of their lines burst and several men got soaked trying to control the leak with a Cooper hose jacket. They would spend the rest of day working in the cold weather wearing soaking wet uniforms.

Rescue 1 then joined three other rescue companies working in the wreckage, as hundreds of firemen battled the fires around them. It took over a week to recover the 134 bodies in Brooklyn and the 44 bodies in Staten Island. Five alarms had brought fifty-six apparatus manned by 200 firefighters to the scene. They were joined by almost two hundred off-duty members who'd responded on their own.

Just three days later, while companies were still operating at the crash site, a new dark column of smoke became visible over Brooklyn, pinpointing another historic FDNY response.

The New York Naval Ship Yard was bustling with activity on December 19, 1960. The huge aircraft carrier, the U.S.S. *Constellation* (at the time of the fire, one of the largest ships ever built), was in the final stages of fitting-out. The ship was more than 1000 feet long and 250 feet across at its widest point. The finished ship would displace 60,000 tons of water. Above the hangar deck were nine levels, with seven levels below, containing more than 1200 compartments.

Because construction was still being completed, the steel ship had a tremendous amount of wood below decks. Onboard the carrier were 3200 workers, with most of them working below decks. There was no Navy fire crew assigned to the ship; it was protected by the Navy Yard's fire department of 15 men, manning two pumpers and a ladder truck.

Five-alarms and a Borough call were needed for a major fire onboard the USS Constellation *in the Brooklyn Navy Yard on December 19, 1960. Fifty workers were killed, but determined firemen rescued thousands. The injured workers and firemen were lowered from the flight deck of the blazing ship by cranes.*

At about 10:20 a.m., a dumpster truck working on the hangar deck pushed a heavy trash bin into a steel plate, which bent upward shearing off the plug of a 500-gallon tank of JP-5 fuel (fuel used to power emergency generators and other equipment). Gallons of the highly flammable liquid poured out onto the hangar deck. Some of the fuel raced down a bomb elevator to where a welder was at work. Unknowingly, his torch ignited the fire. Hose lines were put into operation and CO_2 was discharged with no effect. The fire spread rapidly as the flaming fuel ignited the forest of wooden scaffolding and other cumbustibles on the deck.

The FDNY received their first notice of the fire at 10:30 a.m., when a special building box (a building fire alarm box connected directly to FDNY dispatchers) at Building 213, Kent Avenue and Clymer Street was pulled. Within the next 37 minutes, five alarms were sounded for the fire.

Arriving units were faced with a well-advanced fire situation in a structure the equivalent of five city blocks long, a block wide, and 14 stories high. Shortly after the fire started, the lighting failed plunging the entire vessel into total darkness. Deep within the maze of black compartments were hundreds of workers cut off from any avenue of escape with acrid, dense smoke and flames closing in.

As FDNY ladders were placed to every opening on the ship, a quick size up revealed: fire was in complete control of a large section of the hangar deck, forward and amidships (in or near the middle of the ship). Flames had also extended to galley decks (01, 02, 03 decks), immediately above the hangar deck and flight deck. Two hundred and fifty workers were rescued over ladders and a quick thinking crane operator swung a large platform onto the carrier deck lifting workers to safety.

Meanwhile a difficult and dramatic series of rescues were started inside the blazing ship, as members of the rescue, squad and ladder companies equipped with Scott masks made their way below decks. This was the beginning of one of the most difficult and daring rescue operations in the history of firefighting. The crane platform was transformed by firemen into a makeshift ambulance, as injured and unconscious workers and firemen were lowered for medical attention on shore.

The Mask Service Unit responded to the scene with 25 demand-type masks, 115 extra cylinders, 30 gas masks, and 50 extra canisters. Fifty cylinders were refilled on scene. In all, 220 masks were on the scene used by members of five ladder companies, six squads, four rescue companies and 35 engine companies. The firefighting force on hand was 580 members, plus an additional 100 off-duty members volunteering their services.

Upon the arrival of Rescue Company 1, Lieutenant William J. McMahon was ordered to make a search for trapped workers caught below the hangar deck. At this time the only access to the port side of the ship was through the hangar deck (Deck 1) in which the fire was raging. Two members of the company, Firemen Thomas Bonamo and Timothy Costello were lowered by rope from the flight deck to the smoke filled hangar deck, as other members of Rescue 1 sought another access to the decks below.

Lt. William McMahon

With a clear access point found, the company regrouped, and Lieutenant McMahon led them through intense heat and smoke. With their lives further endangered by heavy planking which was falling from the ceiling, they succeeded in crossing the hangar deck safely, and made their way below to Deck 2, where an estimated 100 workers were believed trapped.

Here, working in teams connected by life lines, Lt. McMahon and Firemen Thomas Bonamo and Timothy Costello, threaded their way through a maze of compartments and passageways. In their first search, 22 workmen were located and moved to safety. Following this, two men were found on Deck 3, who were having such difficulty breathing that Lt. McMahon shared his air supply with them, until they were removed. Still later, a large number of workmen were found in the bow, in the chain locker. Some of these men were unconscious and were immediately removed, by make-shift stretchers ingeniously constructed from debris found in the area. Shackles connecting the anchor and chains were parted, then the chains were lowered clearing the opening in the bow. Many workers escaped to aerial ladders placed at this location.

The fire was battled for twelve hours. Fifty workers were killed and 385 were injured. Many members of the FDNY, especially members of the rescue companies, showed courage and leadership beyond measure.

As the official report stated: Lieutenant McMahon was always at the forefront of the operations, utilizing his special training to the utmost advantage in attempting to rescue the victims..." Lieutenant William J. McMahon was awarded the Thomas E. Crimmins Medal for his actions at this fire. Firemen Thomas W. Bonamo, Jr., and Timothy P. Costello were also awarded Class II's. Firemen Alfred W. Hankin, George Planding, John C. Farragher, Casimir S. Surdukowski and Frank L. Caltabellotta were also cited for their heroic actions.

During 1960, the members of all the rescue companies were trained in the new techniques of mouth-to-mouth resuscitation and cardio-pulmonary massage. These procedures would prove invaluable, saving many lives. Eventually, all members of the department would receive this training.

Rescue 1's Lt. McMahon, provides oxygen as one of the rescued workers is hurried to an ambulance.

One workman was killed and two others were injured when tons of debris bricks collapsed at a construction site on Broadway across from City Hall Park. The bricks, part of an old foundation wall being shored, fell into an excavation for a new twenty-story office building. The collapsed occurred at 11 a.m., on July 28, 1961. Rescue 1 arrived, began digging, and were able to quickly remove two injured workers. Faced with a worker still missing and a large area to search, Rescue 2 was special called and joined Rescue 1. After two hours, rescue men located the dead man. Digging by hand and shoring up debris to prevent further collapse, the man was removed thirty minutes later.

The Times Tower, the twenty-five story building famous for the glittering New Year's Eve ball that dropped each year at midnight signifying the start of the new year, was the scene of a fifth-alarm on November 21, 1961. Two firefighters from Ladder 24 were killed by the heavy smoke on the eighteenth floor, while conducting a search for victims. The fire was in a sub-cellar area five stories below ground, as intense heat and smoke spread throughout the building via air ducts. Rescue 1 took part in the very punishing search and extinguishment operation. Firemen Joseph Reres and John McBride were both transported to the hospital and treated for smoke inhalation and exhaustion.

Queens Box 9876, Jamaica Avenue and 162nd Street, was transmitted at 10:42 a.m., on Wednesday May 5, 1962, for a fire in the basement of the Bond's Clothing Store. Companies were faced with a serious fire, and quickly evacuated employees and customers from the smoke-filled store. As members attempted to make access down the stairs to the basement, a powerful backdraft occurred hurling some members through the plate glass display windows and toppled others, scattering them across the floors. A second alarm was transmitted followed by a third alarm two minutes later. Fourth and fifth alarms were sent in, as firemen were quickly being overcome by the choking, deep yellow and black smoke.

At 11:50 Rescue 1 and Rescue 2 were special called. Using pneumatic drills, jack hammers, and mauls they breached the store's masonry walls, allowing deeper penetration of the hose streams to control the fire. All companies were heavily engaged, and rapidly becoming exhausted and overcome by the extreme heat and smoke conditions. Faced with this serious situation, Chief of Department George David requested an additional third alarm to the fire (A Simultaneous Call). The fire was finally placed under control at 2:20 p.m.

Violent explosions fed by gasoline, fuel oil and solvents greeted responding FDNY units on May 10, 1962, as they responded to a five-alarm fire at the Oil Company plant in Mill Basin, South Brooklyn. It was 3:56 p.m., when the first alarm was transmitted. In a short time flames were reaching 100 feet into the sky, as the fire was spreading to the surrounding structures. With a limited number of hydrants available, firemen were hard pressed to halt the spreading wall of flames. A call for all the available foam in the department brought Rescue 1 to the fire. For three hours the fire raged, as five-alarms and then a borough call were transmitted. Foam trucks from the Naval Air Station at Floyd Bennett Field and the Brooklyn Army Base joined the seventy pieces of fire apparatus at this spectacular blaze.

The second member of Rescue 1 would die in the line-of-duty on July 12, 1962. Fireman John C. Farragher was helping battle a fire in a five-story loft building at 390 Broadway between White and Walker Streets that was occupied by several textile companies. Fire was raging on the top three floors, when the roof suddenly collapsed killing Fireman Farragher. It would take four alarms to extinguish this difficult fire. Once the fire was knocked down eighty firemen, including the exhausted members of Rescue 1, began to search through the smoldering rubble for their missing brother. Farragher's body was not found until the next morning. Fireman John C. Farragher, the father of three children, was posthumously awarded a Department Medal.

Rescue 1 members administering CPR to downed fireman pulled from a blazing hallway, inside the Mayflower Hotel on Central Park West. This two-alarm fire (22-946) occurred on December 27, 1961. Sadly, the fireman died.

Fireman John C. Farragher
Rescue Company 1
July 12, 1962
Manhattan Box 164

Ep 2.03 DuPont Show Of The Week: FIRE RESCUE
30Sep1962
NBC Sun (rebroadcast 21Jul63)
written by Jack Fuller, directed by Fred Freed, narrator Walter Matthau

Synopsis 1:
This episode presents a documentary about the Rescue Company One of the New York Fire Department, a small corps of firefighters whose training and skills have equipped them for the most challenging assignments. The program follows the firefighters as they answer calls to multiple alarm fires, resuscitation calls and other emergencies day and night. Incidents include the death of firefighter John Farragher in a fire in the city's Hell's Hundred Acres section and a nine-alarm fire in a clothing store in Queens. The show focuses on Lt. William McMahon as he leads his men. There are scenes at the company's quarters on West 43rd Street

Synopsis 2:
For three months, cameras recorded New York City's Fire Rescue Company One in action and at the firehouse. There was a nine-alarmer in Queens; a fire in a Manhattan novelty store; a tough mopping up job in a fire-gutted building; the rescue of an 80 year-old woman trapped during a blaze; first aid to a girl who collapsed on the street; the rescue of other firemen overcome by smoke in a burning tenement; and a tragic loft fire in which one man in the squad lost his life. Off-camera narrator: Walter Matthau.

A five-alarm fire onboard the Argentine cargo-passenger ship the *Rio Jachal*, moored at Pier 25, North Moore and West Streets Manhattan, severely taxed the resources of the department on September 28, 1962. The 900-foot-long ship was described as a wood frame floating hotel within a steel shell. The fire was reported at 10 p.m., then after five alarms were transmitted, a Borough Call was transmitted at 1 a.m. This sent a third alarm assignment from a Brooklyn box to the fire. Rescue 1 took part in the difficult initial searches of the blazing ship. Twenty-nine firemen were injured or overcome battling the blaze.

Lt. McMahon and Rescue 1 members during filming of DuPont Show of the Week.

On Sunday, September 30, 1962, NBC Television's DuPont Show of the Week would broadcast the documentary "Fire Rescue" to an estimated forty million viewers. For three months NBC cameramen filmed members of Rescue 1 performing firefighting, first aid and rescue duties, then edited their film into this action-packed presentation. The show's narrator was Walter Matthau (the New York born actor famous for his role as Oscar Madison first on Broadway and later in the film "The Odd Couple). Unfortunately this documentary became even more dramatic than originally intended. It was during the filming of "Fire Rescue" that Fireman John C. Farragher was killed, showing the true dangers firefighters faced.

Firefighters, by their very nature, are willing to spring into action whenever it becomes necessary. Their exploits both on and off-duty attest to this on-going commitment. Actions that added to this legacy of valor occurred at 4:50 p.m., October 1, 1962, when the cries of a child screaming that his mother was in the water echoed across the Staten Island Ferry. Moments before, the distraught woman had thrown three of her children into the water. Then jumped in herself in an apparent suicide attempt. On the ferry at the time were four off-duty FDNY members, including Fireman William Curran of Rescue 1.

Responding to the child's cries, Fireman Curran saw the woman in the water some distance away, and began to lower a lifeboat. As he was doing so the boat's captain reversed engines. It was then that Curran saw two children floating face down in the churning water. Shouting a warning to the pilot house, he kicked off his shoes and dove into the turbulent waters at the stern of the ferry boat. He was joined in the water by another off duty fireman from Ladder 15. Fireman Curran rolled the lifeless girl over and began mouth to mouth resuscitation while treading water. The child quickly responded by gagging, coughing, and then resumed normal breathing.

Within seconds of the initial shouts for help, all four off-duty firemen had entered the swirling waters of New York Harbor. Their combined efforts saved the woman and two of her three children. The firemen held the water soaked victims afloat until a Coast Guard rescue boat arrived. The brave firemen were all placed on the Roll of Merit. For his courage, Fireman William Curran received the Thomas A. Kenny Medal.

It was the start of lunch hour in the New York Telephone Company building at 5030 Broadway at 213th Street. The basement cafeteria was filled with the tinkling noises of glasses and silverware, as one hundred employees began their lunch. It was Wednesday, October 3, 1962. At 12:07 in a room adjacent to the cafeteria, a one-ton lower pressure boiler suddenly exploded. The fifteen-foot long and six-foot in diameter boiler launched like a missile through a wall across the lunch room filled with unsuspecting women. It continued upwards through the ceiling, the flooring above, then continued on through another wall. The damaged sections crumbled, thick plate glass windows flew outwards, flames erupted in the boiler room, as a thick veil of smoke and dust settled over the basement room now filled with injured, dead or dying workers.

The Manhattan Fire Dispatchers answered the wave of frantic calls and sent units to the scene. Arriving companies filled the Manhattan fire radio frequency with descriptive calls for additional help. It was clear this was a major emergency.

Ten miles to the south of the explosion, six off-duty members of Rescue 1 were still in quarters after a late morning job. Lt. William McMahon, and Firemen Ronald McGhee, Paul Geidel, William Curran, Frank Caltabellotta and Walter Clarke heard the reports of the devastating blast on the fire radio. Instinctively they grabbed their fire gear to respond. The on-duty crew and apparatus of Rescue 1 were not in quarters. The rescue men knew that Engine 65 would not be assigned to an alarm that far north. With a split second decision, they all dashed for the sidewalk and hurried to the uptown subway.

Fireman William Curran

Reaching the chaotic scene, the officer reported in and volunteered the company's services. They were sent into the blackened smoke-filled basement of the damaged building to search for victims.

They worked for most of the afternoon, tending to the injured and helping to remove the dead. The sidewalks outside the building were covered with shattered glass, and injured or dead workers. It was a terrible toll. 21 people had been killed, nineteen of them women. Ninety five were injured, many seriously.

On December 1, 1962 Rescue 1 responded to Manhattan Box 789, where a man was dangling outside a building hanging from a window cleaning hook on the 15th floor. Fireman Paul E. Geidel and other members made their way to that floor and observed the window cleaner, a heavy-set man, was only loosely held by his safety belt, which had already slipped from his waist to his armpits. Realizing quick and decisive action was needed, Fireman Geidel had other members hold his feet while he was lowered headfirst to a position where he could attach a rope around the man. After tying the first rope around the man, a safety rope was put in place and both the victim and the rescuer were pulled up.

Rescue Company 1 responded to a fire at Box 822, at 11 a.m., on February 22, 1964. Upon arrival, heavy smoke was seen pouring from the fourth floor windows of 20 East 46th Street. People trapped on the floors above were at windows waving and calling for help. Fireman Paul E. Geidel and other members of Rescue 1, climbed to the fifth floor. Wearing a Scott Air Pac, Geidel began searching the maze-like hallway under a heavy smoke and high heat condition. In these dark and unfamiliar surroundings, Geidel located a building employee in a stalled elevator in duress and near panic. As he calmed the man, he heard others crying for help from an adjacent elevator car. Prying the door open, Fireman Geidel shared his air supply with the victim, then led him to the fire stairs and the safety of other FDNY members.

Returning through the heavy heat and smoke, he began forcing the second closed elevator door. With the assistance of a another fireman, he was able to open this door and find six prostrate occupants on the floor of the car. Fireman Geidel half dragged and half carried two men to the fire stairs, as additional firemen removed the other occupants. In the street Fireman Geidel used an inhalator on the victims, until they were taken to the hospital.

Yet another ship fire would challenge the capability and ingenuity of Rescue 1 and the FDNY on March 2, 1964. The vessel: *American Planter*, a C-2 freighter was 460-feet long and sixty-four feet at the beam. It was being loaded with general cargo being shipped to American Army personnel in Germany. The ship was moored at Pier 62, on the North River an open pier (no shed or building). Just before noon smoke was discovered in the No. 3 hold; the hatches were sealed, CO_2 was flooded into the hold, and the fire department was called.

With no standpipe system available, engines had to hand stretch and relay water from street hydrants. It was decided to continue flooding the hold with CO_2 and to stretch limited fire hoses below decks. One inch-and-a-half line was used to cool the engine room bulkhead, and two other inch-and-a-half lines were lowered into the hold. At 7 p.m., the hold cover was removed and masked firemen unloaded the cargo onto pallets, so the longshoremen could hoist them using a cargo boom.

Background photo: Building collapse on June 22, 1964 at 337-339 West 30th Street in Manhattan. Two buildings under going renovations collapsed trapping three workers. For seven hours Rescue 1 dug, tunneled, and shored removing two workers alive.

Inset photo: Overhead view of trapped worker freed by Rescue 1 on June 22, 1964.

Members of Rescue 1 worked with the Mask Service Unit, and adapted a special harnesses for the Scott masks that would provide a surface supplied air system without the heavy (20-pound) cylinder. The hoses were fed from a bank of air cylinders on the weather deck, and allowed four rescue men to work off one manifold for fifty-minutes at a time. (This is an early version of the air cart now used by all rescue and squad companies for confined space and other specialized situations).

One of the most punishing fires fought by Rescue 1 took place in the subway at 42nd Street and Vanderbilt Avenue on April 21, 1964. It was 4:56 a.m., when Box 789 at Park Avenue and East 42nd Street was transmitted. On arrival units could tell they had an advanced fire situation confronting them, as thick smoke and embers shot up through the subway ventilation grates along the sidewalks. Thick, black, super-heated smoke prevented a direct attack from the 42nd Street entrance and would compound an already difficult situation. In possible jeopardy were all passengers of both the City Subway System and the Grand Central Terminal, as well as all the people in the interconnecting arcades, corridors, mezzanines, stores, and stairways in the vicinity. An hour after the initial alarm, hose lines still had not reached the fire due to the extreme heat conditions. As streams moved in, it was noted that twenty-five steel support columns were warped from the 1200-degree temperatures and the street above had dropped ten-inches.

The blazing cars and wooden platforms were finally reached by firefighters advancing through a passageway that was slightly lower and at a right angle to the fire. This path afforded some protection from the extreme heat. The fire would require five alarms and a borough call to extinguish.

On June 22, 1964, Rescue 1 was special-called to a building collapse at 337-339 West 30th Street. Two, four-story brick buildings undergoing renovations had suddenly collapsed entombing three workers. Lieutenant Erwin J. Alexy and his crew had to work directly beneath a cracked and unstable brick wall that had once been a party wall between the two collapsed buildings. The under-footing was also treacherous, due to deep voids and unstable fallen debris. Lt. Alexy split his men into teams, to ensure they all would not be in the same place in the event of a secondary collapse. The first two workers were removed, but danger posed by the overhanging wall was too severe. All department personnel were pulled back, until a crane could remove part of the wall. Rescue 1 had worked for over four hours already tunneling and shoring under the collapsed portion of the building.

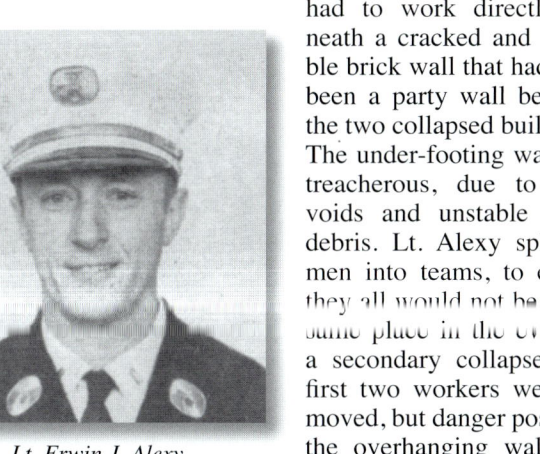

Lt. Erwin J. Alexy

The company returned to the collapse area and renewed their search. With other dangerous unstable walls still looming over them, they continued on until they finally reach the last trapped man. Sadly, he was dead. After seven-hours of difficult and dangerous work, the rescue men took up. For his courage, capability and leadership during this operation Lieutenant Erwin J. Alexy was awarded a Class II, and later the Delehanty Medal. Six members of Rescue 1 were also placed on the Roll of Merit with Class III awards.

On March 8, 1965, Rescue Company 1 celebrated it's Fiftieth Anniversary. In a *WNYF* article (1st Issue, 1965) Lieutenant Erwin Alexy traced the companies history from its inception in 1915. He also stated: "Today, the rescue companies are regularly assigned to first alarms and respond to "all-hands" or greater alarms in assigned areas. The compliment of a company is four officers and usually 28 firemen. As the manpower of Rescue 1 increased so did the workload. Rescue 1 now responds to an average of 1300 runs a year, compared to 86 in its first year of service… May the present and future members of this company always carry out their assigned tasks, no matter what the risks, in as grand and courageous a manner as those who preceded them did."

During the 1960's another major advance in the FDNY's firefighting tools arrived in the form of the Partner power saw. The members of Rescue 1 immediately saw the potential of this tool, even though it was never used at a working fire during its trial period. It was used constantly at drills, especially in vacant buildings. Captain Joseph Rooney wrote a very positive report urging the purchase of this tool. Shortly thereafter, these saws were accepted by the department, over some skepticism, and assigned only to the rescue companies. The saws were used to great advantage in roof ventilation and forcible entry.

Fireman Vic Miozzi of Rescue 1 carries a four-year-old girl to safety from blazing tenement fire at 302 West 51st Street in Manhattan. This fire took the life of another small child on April 18, 1965.

Seasoned ladder company firefighters were a bit annoyed by this new "rescue" tool. In Harlem, when Rescue 1 and the saw arrived on the roof, they and the saw were referred to as "instant holes," an accurate if somewhat unflattering nickname. Eventually, sound judgement would prevail and the saw would be given to all truck companies. While venting a roof today, rarely if ever, is an axe used to cut a hole. All FDNY ladder companies are assigned two power saws, while rescue companies have three in addition to chain saws.

The roof of a Brooklyn supermarket collapsed without warning, into a store filled with shoppers trapping thirty people in the rubble. It was 3:55 in the afternoon on May 19, 1965 when Box 2840 brought the FDNY to 6409 20th Avenue, in the Bensonhurst section. The converted theatre, now being used as a Key Food Store supermarket, was having work done on the roof when the collapse occurred. Special calls brought Rescue Companies 2 and 1 to the scene, along with the new FDNY tower ladder assigned to Ladder 1 in Manhattan.

Members of the rescue companies and other FDNY units work feverishly to remove all the trapped and injured persons from under the fallen roof. One person was removed from the rubble in serious condition, and rushed to a nearby hospital.

An evening of boxing drew a crowd of nearly 7,000 fans to Madison Square Garden on August 4, 1965. The Garden, the third indoor arena in New York City to hold the name and the first not located near Madison Square, was built in 1925 at Eighth Avenue between 49th and 50th Streets. The boxing card featured a number of bouts including the main event of Gabriel "Flash" Elorde from the Phillippines versus Frankie Narvaes, a local boy who was born in Puerto Rico. The winner of this fight was to then box for the world's lightweight championship. The battle was a close, bloody affair, with the enthusiastic crowd cheering each punch.

At the final bell the fighters were brought to the center of the ring and a split decision found the referee holding up Elorde's hand as a winner. The partisan crowd went wild. With cries of "Robbery!" and "Thieves!" the boxers returned to the dressing rooms, as the crowd turned into a mob.

Whiskey bottles were thrown, fire axes were used to chop up chairs, and hurl them into the ring. The security officers on hand had no control, as the crowd went into a frenzy. The arena's organ was toppled from its perch in the mezzanine, as the crowd moved its mayhem through the arena and out into the streets.

Along the way the fire alarm in the arena was pulled, and midtown companies including Rescue 1 rolled up to find hundreds of people rioting across Eighth Avenue. Several men crossed the street to the site of a building under demolition, and began to throw bricks into the crowd. One brick struck Rescue 1 Fireman Herb Peterson in the face. The fireman fell to the ground with facial fractures and several missing teeth. Led by Lt. William McMahon, swinging his rechargeable flashlight like a bludgeon, the rescue firemen swarmed into the crowd swinging their tools and hand lights too. They pulled their injured comrade to safety.

Peterson was rushed to Saint Clare's Hospital. The brick thrower was arrested by police and charged with felonious assault. For his heroic leadership Lt. McMahon would be known in Rescue 1 from that day on as – "Wheat light Willie!" The following day, the night tour crew visited the swollen Peterson in the hospital and brought him corn on the cob.

It was 5:28 p.m., on November 9, 1965, the lights went out- literally. A major power failure caused the lights to go out all across the region. "The Great Northeast Blackout" plunged New York City and every other community in a 80,000 square mile area into darkness. With no electricity in a large area of the United States and Canada: subway trains stopped dead where they were, elevators hung motionless inside their blackened shafts and hospitals lost power to vital medical equipment. Street lights and traffic signals went dark. All FDNY units were pressed into service providing whatever help they could. Rescue 1 worked throughout the night, almost continuously responding from one incident to another. Amazingly, the citizens of the city rose to the task. There were no riots, no looting and everyone seemed to be helping each other until power was restored.

A four-alarm blaze was battled in am 8-story fireproof building in lower Manhattan on July 8, 1966. The fire broke out around 11 a.m. Flames soon filled the cellar and extended up to the third floor of the Allied Envelope Company. Rescue 1 and the first alarm units were able to extinguish the fire on the first floor. Attempts to push into the cellar, even with masks, proved impossible due to the extreme heat being generated by the stored paper.

All companies were withdrawn. On a special mission Rescue 1 was then sent back in to the first floor. Using power tools they made small holes through the floor to define the fire area below. The department then broke out one of the newest fire fighting tools: High Expansion Foam. Using natural vent openings the foam was forced into the blazing cellar. It took 150 firemen six-hours to bring this hot, smoky fire under control.

It was very hot in New York City on July 12, 1966. The mercury reached 99-degrees and the city streets were sweltering. Inside a shed next to the Su Crest sugar warehouse on Richards Street in Brooklyn, a propane tank feeding a sugar loader suddenly exploded. It was 11 a.m. The already hot day would even get hotter for the members of the FDNY.

Rescue 1 was special called to this sugar warehouse fire in Brooklyn on July 12, 1966.

Members of Rescue 1 and Ladder 2 and Ladder 4 operating with foam at a stubborn midtown fire on August 31, 1966.

The fire quickly spread, fed by both the propane and the brown sugar it ignited. "Sugar is a vegetable fiber and burns with a fierce heat," Assistant Chief Charles McKeogh later explained to the media. Inside the warehouse temperatures were between 1,500 and 2,000 degrees. Brooklyn Box 1369 would go to a Borough-Call, the equivalent of 8-alarms. Among the companies sent to the scene was Rescue 1 from Manhattan.

To approach the blazing warehouse the company had to wade through deep streams of very hot sugar water, that had been heated to a molasses-like consistency. They were sent to the roof to attempt ventilation. On the roof conditions were very dangerous, hot-thick billowing smoke covered the roof and most of the Red Hook neighborhood. Rescue men carefully made their way to a point they thought they could vent with good effect. As the smoke cleared briefly, Fireman Thomas Bonamo, saw a fireboat only yards away from the pier based fire building.

"Wouldn't it be great to take the anchor and have the fireboat pull down the roof?" Lt. William McMahon looked at the young fireman, and thought he might have the start of an idea. He directed Bonamo to cut a hole up near the ridge pole, and called to the fireboat for a grappling hook attached to a cable. The hook was attached to some roof beams, made taut. Then the area was cleared for safety, as the boat increased tension. Suddenly, a large section of the roof and rear wall collapsed in one swift motion—the roof was vented.

Despite this ingenious effort it took more than 120 firemen and the Super Pumper, six-hours to extinguish this fire.

The first Unit Citation awarded to Rescue Company 1 was for their efforts at an extremely difficult and dangerous fire onboard the German liner S.S. *Hanseatic* while the ship was berthed at Pier 84 (foot of 47th Street) on the North River, in Manhattan on September 7, 1966. The five-alarm fire started in the ship's engine room and spread to the five decks above. Only 425 passengers were onboard the ship at the time of the fire (Box 817 was transmitted at 7:30 a.m.). The passengers and crew were quickly removed, as firefighters began their attack.

Flames had burned for some time undetected, but were now pouring out onto various passenger decks feeding on the fancy wood paneling and other flammables. Rescue 1 was assigned on the 7-5 signal (all hands working). They were ordered to stretch initial lines into the engine room, which was the seat of the fire. While in the engine room, a primary search for crew members was conducted. Then Rescue was asked to determine if the ships CO2 system had activated and to ascertain what, if any other extinguishing medium was available. Despite language barriers and directional signs written in German, the company was able to gain control of the ship's systems.

The rescue men then, using life-lines due to the severe conditions and zero visibility, carried out the tedious and hazardous job of sealing off the engine room area, shutting vents and air intakes, prior to their operating the CO2 system. These actions were conducted in the smoke filled labyrinth of passageways and below decks. With the help of several lines making a very aggressive attack, Rescue 1 was finally able to penetrate to the deepest fire areas. The heat was so intense that the steel decks and doors actually warped. After moving lines into the engine room, Rescue 1 re-opened dampers and air ducts to allow the delivery of 300 gallons of foam to the seat of the fire to extinguish the blaze that had caused $1 million in damages.

One of the twelve firefighters killed is solemnly carried from the scene.

Rescue 1 digging for firemen killed at the tragic 23rd Street collapse on October 17, 1966.

One of the most tragic events in the history of the department took place on October 17, 1966. A fire at Broadway and 23rd Street would escalate to five alarms. The building involved had been greatly altered over the years, and had also been interconnected with the structure behind it that faced out onto the next street. Without warning the first floor collapsed into the blazing cellar. Twelve firefighters, ranging in rank from a deputy chief to a probationary fireman, were tragically killed in this collapse. Thousands of off-duty firefighters responded to the scene to offer their services in the grim task of recovering their lost comrades. Many members of Rescue 1, both on and off-duty, worked throughout the night and into the next morning until the final body was carefully removed from the building.

> **M**any members of Rescue 1, both on and off duty, worked throughout the night and into the next morning until the final body was carefully removed from the building.

A few weeks after and a mile and a half north of the tragic 23rd Street collapse, another fire building would cave-in trapping seven firefighters inside. The fire, raging inside a clothing store, was first discovered when flames burst through a common wall into a bookstore that shared the first floor of 1169 Avenue of the Americas (Sixth Avenue). Manhattan fire companies rolled when Box 813 was transmitted at 9:11 p.m., on December 22, 1966, the height of the Christmas season. The four-story fire building located on the west side of the avenue near 45th Street was nearly 100 years-old, having been built in 1867.

Upon their arrival Rescue 1, under the command of Lt. Alexy, was ordered to the roof to provide ventilation. While opening the roof of the fire building and exposure #4, Chief of Department O'Hagan ordered Rescue 1 to the street of the fire building immediately. The members of Rescue 1 were then informed of a major collapse of the interior four stories of the building had occurred, and that seven members of the department were trapped in the debris.

Lt. Alexy directed debris removal and then a tunneling operation. Fireman Raymond M. Brown led the company's efforts. An official report read: "Fireman Brown did courageously dig, tunnel and shore for an hour and a half, and when a tunnel entrance was cleared he crawled into this void to provide additional shoring."

At one point the cry of "Get Out!" echoed across the collapse site. All members were pulled back when an unstable wall threatened to collapse. As soon as he was allowed, Fireman Brown returned re-entering the void and continued his work. Brown, Alexy and the members of Rescue 1 had made a tunnel 3-feet square and 50-feet deep to the point where the trapped men were pinned. One by one the following members were freed from the rubble: Fr. Thomas Johnson E54, Fr. James Costello E54, Fr. Robert Siddons E54, Fireman Anthony Santoro E54, Lt. Christian Heeg E54 and Fr. Francis Fagan L4.

Fireman Ray Brown had been working for two hours without relief and as the sixth fireman was freed it was realized the seventh, Fireman Harry Fay of Engine 54 was alive but trapped 50-feet further in. The job continued until Brown was able to clear a path to the pinned man and cut the final beams to free the trapped fireman.

What at first appeared to be another major tragedy for the department, turned out to be an amazing Christmas gift for the department and the trapped firemen's families. Each fireman stepped from this collapse, and walked away under their own power.

Fireman Raymond M. Brown

Assistant Chief Charles McKeogh told reporters "It certainly is the greatest miracle in the history of the department. It is still hard to believe those men are alive and uninjured."

Members of the department began calling it: "The Miracle on Sixth Avenue." For their heroic actions Fireman Raymond Brown was awarded the Trevor-Warren Medal, and Lt. Erwin Alexy was awarded the Delehanty Medal. Fireman Raymond Brown would eventually become Chief of Rescue Services before retiring.

"The Miracle on Sixth Avenue" Fireman Harry Foy, the last trapped man to be freed by Fr. Ray Brown of Rescue 1, walks away unharmed from a building fire and collapse on December 22, 1966.

Another off-duty member of Rescue 1, Fireman Alfred W. Hankin, would prove that valor is not a nine to five type of job for firemen. While on his way home from work on February 14, 1967, Hankin was standing on the southbound platform of the IRT 7th Avenue express at the 42nd Street station at the height of rush hour, when he saw a woman fall onto the northbound tracks across from him. Both the northbound and southbound platforms were crowded with people, yet no one went to help the woman.

Fireman Al Hankin unhesitatingly jumped onto the tracks knowing well the dangers he would face. Hankin had to cross over both sets of express tracks and two electrified third rails to reach her location. The brave fireman also realized the frequency of train passage in the busy station, with trains arriving as often as a minute apart. Reaching the fallen woman, Hankin heard the frantic screams of passengers on the platform who could see a train approaching the station.

Gauging the speed of the train and the time involved in lifting the woman, Hankin decided to shield the woman with his body, as he moved as quickly as possible toward the oncoming train waving his arms to attract the motorman's attention. His efforts proved successful as the train came to a screeching halt ten-feet from him. When the train was safely stopped Hankin, with the help of a transit police officer, lifted the injured woman onto the platform.

Firemen Ray Brown and Herb Peterson help injured chief at a Bronx fourth alarm. Box 44-3122 on Burnside Avenue on February 15, 1968.

The ten-story Morgan Post Office Annex covers an entire city-block at Ninth Avenue and 30th Street. On the night of December 15, 1967 a postal inspector saw smoke pouring up out of chutes from the cellar, and turned in a fire alarm. Box 676 was received at 9:07 p.m., for a fire inside the 200 x 800-foot structure that featured twenty-foot high ceilings. Built in 1935, the building had large wide-open areas that were pierced with numerous unprotected vertical openings, consisting of conveyor belts, spiral mail chutes, duct systems and flush floor openings. As the numerous employees evacuated the building, a second alarm and numerous special calls were transmitted to battle the large fire and contend with the horrible winter weather.

A biting wind resulted in a wind-chill factor of well below zero. Inside the building, the fire that had started in a sub-cellar had quickly spread upwards through the openings igniting among other things, twelve fully loaded railroad boxcars on the second floor, and numerous trucks parked inside the building. In all, eleven alarms were transmitted to control the fire. Rescue 1 assisted in searching and evacuating the building.

On the night of February 15, 1968, Rescue 1 responded to 202 East 42nd Street for a fire in the third floor apartment above a photographer's studio. Fire was venting from the front three windows of the building, as Fireman Paul Geidel worked his way up the front fire escape. He found a woman on the second floor fire escape landing screaming that her children were still inside and pointing to the third floor. Fireman Geidel took decisive action. Realizing no water was on the fire and that time was running out, Geidel donned his facepiece, broke out the middle window and dove under the venting flames. Working

One of the earliest known photos of the new power saws in action. Rescue 1 opens up the roof at 15 Mott Street in Chinatown. This two-alarm fire was fought on November 24, 1967.

Fireman Paul Geidel barely escapes the explosive flames in this dramatic attempt to rescue trapped children on February 15, 1968.

Rescue 1 Fireman Alfred Hankin and other members operating at a building collapse on December 4, 1968. Six workers were trapped inside the debris of the old Washington Street Market. Despite a driving rain, all the workers were rescued safely.

under extreme conditions, Geidel searched a small area before the uncontrolled flames burst across the room burning the fireman and forcing him back onto the fire escape. As the first shots of water knocked down the flames, Geidel reentered the building and found the children on a smoldering mattress. Sadly, they had been killed by the flames. Fireman Paul Geidel suffered burns of the head, hands and legs in this rescue attempt. He was treated at Bellevue Hospital.

The old Washington Street Market, a five-story red brick building, collapsed trapping six men on the morning of December 4, 1968. Rescue 1 raced to the site on the northeast corner of West and Duane Streets. The building was under demolition when the collapse occurred. The first two men were quickly removed from the surface rubble. Rescue men freed a third man, after a half-hour of careful digging and debris removal. Rescue 1 then started a tunneling operation to reach two other workers located in the huge debris pile. Despite a driving rain, the careful work continued. As these two workers were being removed, another man was located and he too was dug free.

A state of emergency was declared in New York City as a result of the riots that followed the assassination of Martin Luther King Jr., between April 5th and 12th, 1969. FDNY units, including Rescue 1 worked at numerous fires ignited as a result of this civil unrest. Pre-established emergency command procedures were put into operation. Command posts and staging areas within or close to anticipated trouble spots within the city were formed. All available apparatus were pressed into service to provide maximum firefighting capability. Alarms were dispatched, and companies responded in convoys to provide a measure of safety for the firefighting forces. The city and the fire department were gearing up for a period of fire duty never faced by firefighters except in war time.

A state of emergency was declared in New York City as a result of the riots that followed the assassination of Martin Luther King Jr., between April 5th and 12th, 1969. FDNY units, including Rescue 1 worked at numerous fires ignited as a result of this civil unrest.

Engine Company 65 and Rescue 1 arrived almost simultaneously at 595 Fifth Avenue on February 25, 1969. Here fire was blowing out several windows on the third floor of a five story office building. Numerous people were crying for help from the windows above. Lieutenant Baldwin split his company. Two men helped to stretch a hose line up the stairs, two others raced to vent the roof, as two rescue men strapped on their Scott masks and hurried towards the blazing third floor.

Fireman Martin J. Cunniff reached the door to the blazing foyer area only to find it wedged shut by victims on the other side. Pushing the door with all his might, he was able to move it just enough so he could squeeze through the small opening. Fireman Cunniff found himself in a small hallway, with fire rolling over head from the heavy body of fire in the occupancy. Looking right at the pile of people before him, he realized there was no time to wait for a line.

Even with the waves of extreme heat pressing down, Fireman Cunniff was able to push one victim through the tight door opening to other members. Keeping low to avoid the flames above, Cunniff began to move the second victim as the door wedged closed. Fireman Cunniff was now cut-off with fire raging around him. As a charged hose was pulled into position, Fireman Bessman of Rescue 1 and Fireman Moore of Ladder 4 forced the door open, then completely removed it from its hinges. Fireman Cunniff had not moved from his position, undeterred by the tremendous heat. As soon as the opening was made he began to physically lift, pull, and push the victims out into the waiting hands of other firefighters.

Front cover of WNYF showing rescue men removing one of nine killed at 595 Fifth Avenue.

Fireman Martin Cunniff and incinerated helmet after a series of punishing rescues made on February 25, 1969. Cunniff received 2nd and 3rd-degree burns to his face, neck and ears. He also received a Class I for his heroism.

Fireman Bessman and Driscoll carrying a victim of the February 25, 1969 fire. Both men joined Fr. Cunniff on the Roll of Merit for their heroic actions at this fire.

With a hose stream now directed overhead, Cunniff continued his valiant work, as he handed out person after person from the scalding foyer. Seven people were pulled from this blazing inferno. Cunniff received second degree burns to his face, neck and ears yet he continued tending to those he'd rescued. He helped carry them down stairs and worked with a resuscitator until the last victim was placed in an ambulance. Nine people were killed at this fire, most in an elevator on the third floor. For his heroic actions Fireman Martin J. Cunniff was awarded the Brummer Medal.

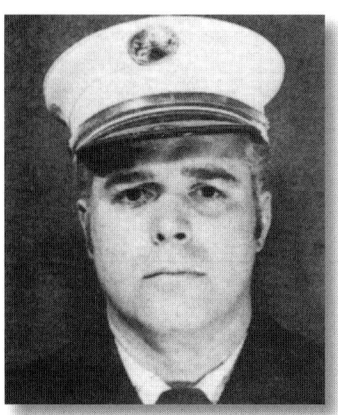

Fireman Martin J. Cunniff

VICTOR A. MIOZZI

Sincere, modest, determined – these words aptly describe Victor A. Miozzi, who, on June 30th, completed twenty years of active service with the Fire Department of the City of New York.

Vic joined the department in 1942, but left after six weeks to join the United States Navy. He was in the Pacific theatre for three years, and served as a frogman in the Demolition Unit. His record with the Navy earned him the Silver Star, Bronze Star, and the Presidential Citation. On his return to civilian life, Vic once more joined the fire department, namely Engine Company 247 in Brooklyn. After being with this company for six years, Vic was transferred to Rescue Company One, and has been with the company ever since.

Not only is Vic dedicated to his rescue work, but his devotion to people is a 24-hour job in itself, as many of those who come into contact with him will attest. He has sacrificed personal interest far beyond reasonable limits and human expectation, even for those who are little more than strangers to him.

We are proud that he is one of us.

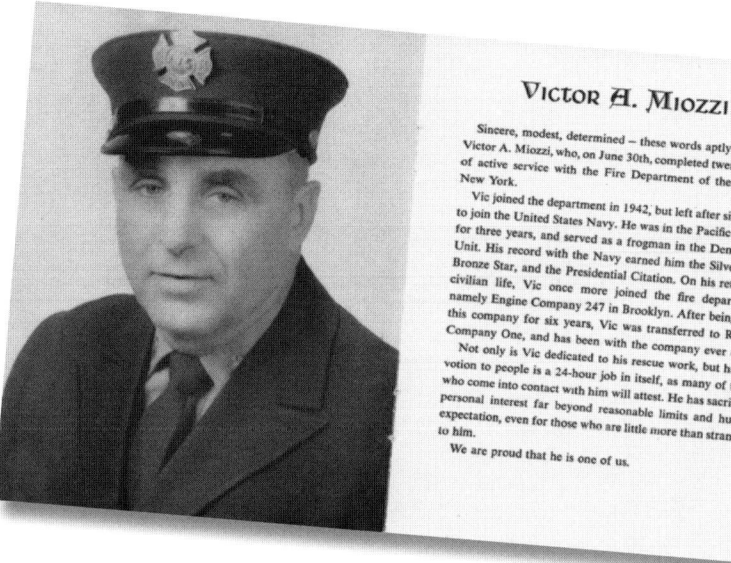

It was October 18, 1969, when a fire broke out in the Hotel Edison at 228 West 47th Street in Manhattan. Box 831 was transmitted for a fire on the 12th floor. Upon arrival, a serious panic and life hazard existed as two guests were perched on 12th floor window ledges with bedsheets draped from the windows. One guest room was completely involved in fire, extending to the adjoining room and hallway. Rescue 1 members heard a call on the handie-talkie requesting a resuscitator on the 11th floor. Reaching this location, the company was then directed by the 7th Battalion to search the fire floor. Despite the intense heat and dense smoke in the rooms and hallway, and conditions that were deteriorating rapidly, Rescue 1 was able to remove numerous occupants from the fire floor.

Approximately twelve civilians received first aid and nine were removed to the hospital. Deputy Chief Conklin in his report stated: "The operations of Rescue 1 at this fire were an important factor in preventing the loss of life of any occupant, and reducing the number of occupants affected by heat and smoke. I therefore recommend the award of a Unit Citation to Rescue 1 for their outstanding work at this fire." His report listed the names of the following members: Lt. William Will, and Firemen James Dowling, John Harney, Joseph Bryant, James Dunscomb (E21) and John Mauser (L16). This was the second Unit Citation awarded to the company.

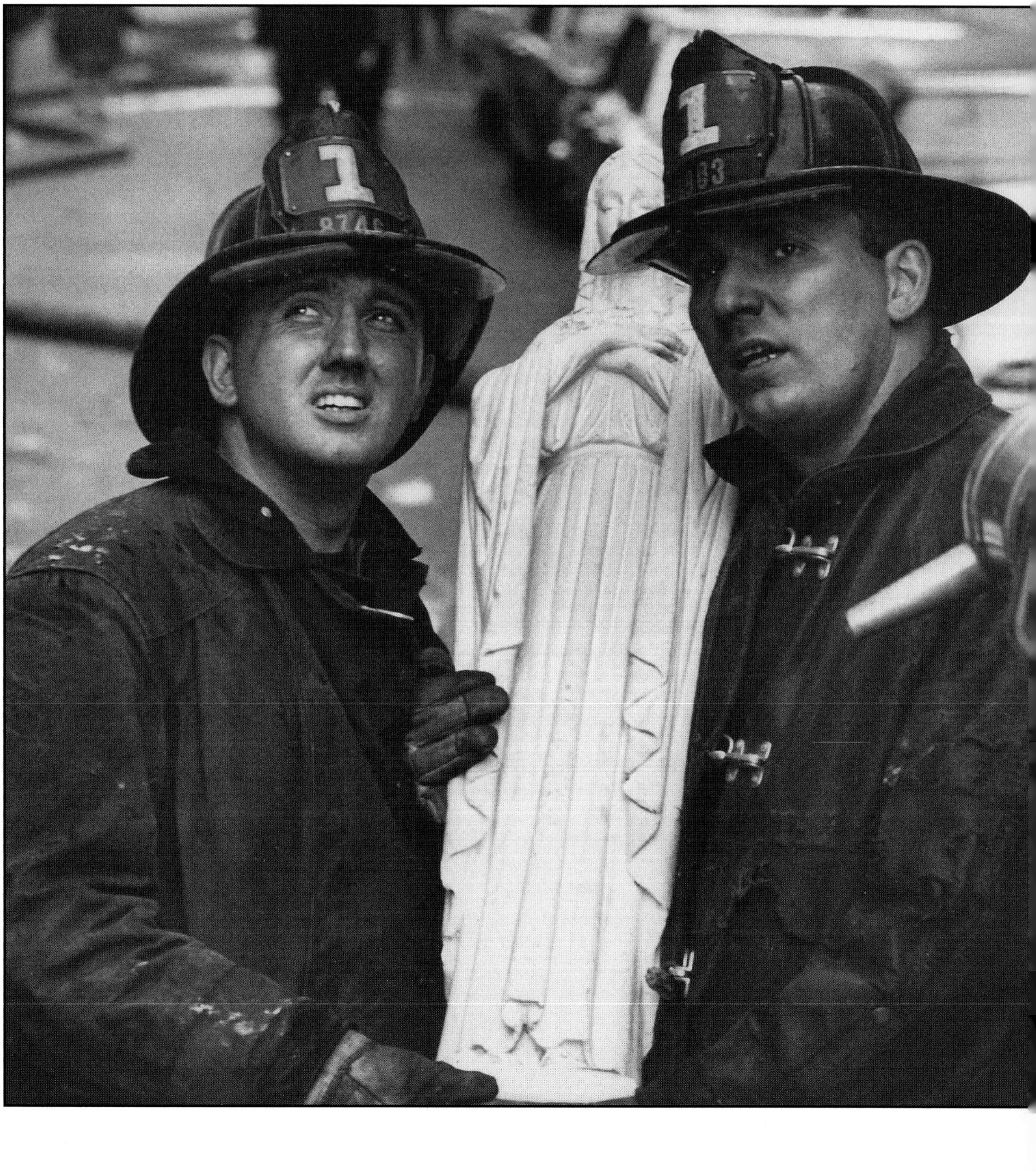

Firemen Bessman and McGann look back at the blazing Holy Cross parish recreation center after removing a Sacred Heart statue. The 3-alarm blaze at 321 West 43rd Street was battled on March 23, 1969.

Chapter 7

The Seventies

The nineteen-seventies would be a decade of fiscal difficulties, urban decay, political and social unrest, and fire-duty. Tremendous amounts of fire-duty. Fires had risen from 61,644 in 1961 to 127,249 in 1970. Civilian deaths had risen from 166 in 1961 to 310 in 1970. The heavy fire-duty that had begun several years before would continue. For the FDNY and the members of Rescue Company 1 these would be known as "The War Years."

A new danger was added on March 6, 1970, two members of the Weathermen, a group of radicals who had begun a string of bombings the year before, were constructing bombs in the basement of 18 West 11th Street in Greenwich Village. The bomb makers were surrounded by shelves filled with sticks of dynamite, alarm clocks used for timers, batteries, wires, blasting caps, and completed bombs filled with roofing nails and explosives.

Suddenly, a tremendous roar was heard. One of the bomb makers had made a wrong move and the device detonated, causing all the other explosives to explode. Most of the building collapsed immediately in a cloud of smoke and dust. The alarm was received and as FDNY units rolled in, two more blasts followed as gas mains burst into flames. Rescue 1 helped search the rubble and determine the stability of the devastated building and those adjacent to it. For the next several days Rescue 1 worked the site, searching the rubble.

It was 6:52 on the morning of March 8, 1970 (being Rescue 1's fifty-fifth anniversary) when they were special called to Box 512 for an emergency at 135 Charles Street, the location of the NYPD 5th Precinct. Lieutenant Thomas P. Baldwin and the on-duty rescue men were surprised to see a male victim lying sideways, impaled on five pointed spikes that topped a ten-foot fence surrounding the exterior airshaft of the building.

The man who had been in police custody attempted to escape by jumping out a window, only to land on the sharp pointed fence top. The spikes were one-inch square and had penetrated to a depth of fifteen inches. The spikes had penetrated his lung, stomach and pelvis. Two one-half inch ropes and a roof rope, held by members of Ladder 5 from an adjacent garage roof, were supporting the man. Two wooden planks (NYPD saw horses used for crowd control) had also

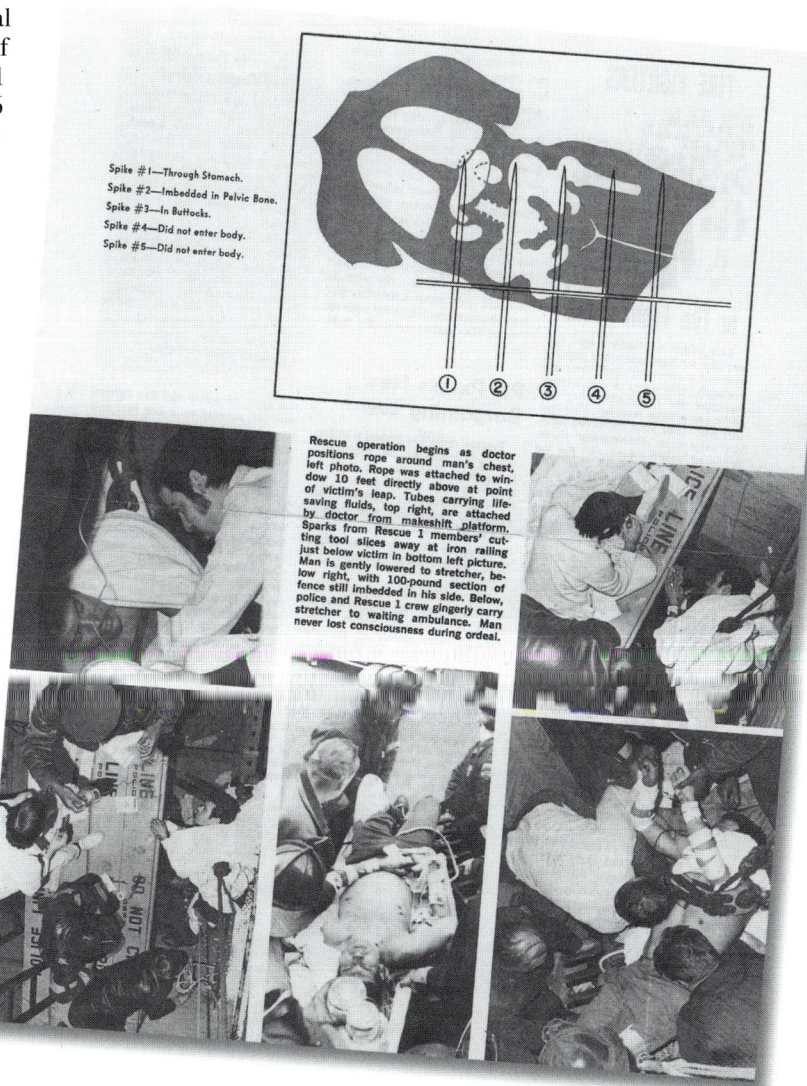

been placed to help support him. It was decided that Rescue 1 would make a series of cuts using an oxyacetylene torch to free the victim with the spikes still in him. The upper cuts were made by Fireman Frank Fehling, who then lowered the torch to Fireman John Driscoll who made the final cuts. This operation took less than 15-minutes.

103

The victim was transported to Saint Vincent's Hospital, with several members of Rescue 1 riding in the ambulance supporting him and the weight of the fence. The remaining members of the company finished taking up the tools and equipment used, and were directed by the dispatcher to respond to the hospital to further assist. Rescue men used a Sawzall (frequently replacing worn blades) to cut the crossbar holding the spikes together. The rescue men also assisted the hospital staff in lifting, turning, and supporting the victim during examination. They accompanied the victim down the hallways to the elevator leading to the operating room.

At 9:15 a.m., they packed up their tools and went in service. Returning to quarters, Lt. Baldwin and the night crew were relieved by the day crew. The company was then sent by the dispatcher back to the site of the explosion in Greenwich Village (West 11th Street) to search for possible victims in the rubble. At 10 a.m., Rescue 1, under the command of Lieutenant James Leddy of Division 3 (Leddy had previously been a fireman in Rescue 1) was told by D.A.C. Matthews that he and his crew: Firemen Max Segal, William Riley, Donald Wilday, Edward Tuite and Michael Walsh would be conducting this search "Unless something special came up." Shortly afterwards something special did: Saint Vincent's Hospital requested Rescue 1 to return.

The Rescue 1 crew that "operated" in St. Vincent's Hospital on March 8, 1970. From left: Max Segal, William Riley, Don Wilday, Jim Leddy, Ed Tuite and Mike Walsh.

They were directed to the 9th floor operating room where they were met by a team of surgeons. They explained to the rescue men that they had been working on the victim for more than an hour, and that the pickets were so deeply embedded into his pelvic bone nothing they tried could free them. The members of Rescue 1 scrubbed up and donned surgical gowns, before joining the doctors in the operating room. After sterilizing their tools they readied themselves for the operation. DAC Matthews arrived, conferred with the doctors, and gave Rescue the go ahead. With the possibility of fire, members of Engine 27 stood by with portable extinguishers and a house line just outside the door. Under the direction of surgeons, the rescue men cut each of the three spikes, and removed them from the injured victim. The man survived his ordeal.

As the men climbed onto the rig they could hear Lt. Leddy call the dispatcher:

"Rescue 1 to Manhattan-K"
Dispatcher: "Rescue 1-K"
"Rescue 1 from St. Vincent's Hospital,
reporting a successful 'operation' -10-8"
Dispatcher: "Rescue 1, 10-4"

As a sad epitaph to this story, it was later learned the man, after a period of convalescence, had returned to his home in Central America and was killed in a automobile accident.

The Hotel Edison, a twenty-three story fireproof hotel located at 228 West 47th Street, was the site of a top floor fire on March 24, 1970. FDNY units responding to Manhattan Box 811 at 7:52 a.m., were confronted with flames pouring out the windows and two male civilians hanging outside the adjacent windows screaming for help. Heat, flames, and heavy smoke filled the hallway behind them cutting off their escape route.

Ladder Company 4 arrived first due. Sizing up the situation quickly, Lieutenant McKee and Fireman John Cerato headed directly to the roof. Below them, one man was standing on the window ledge in a very dangerous position. He was straddling a window air conditioner with heavy smoke pushing out around him. Fireman Cerato was attached to the roof rope and lowered by Lt. McKee to the 22nd floor. Cerato reached the panic stricken man, and grasped him around the waist. Fireman Cerato quickly calmed the hysterical man assuring him that safety was moments away. Together they swung to the side of the window opening. By this time, Fireman Frank DeBellis of Rescue 1 was in position on the roof to offer assistance. A plan was devised and Cerato, using great strength, began to raise the victim high enough to allow DeBellis to reach him and pull him to the roof.

Fireman Cerato, at this point cut and bruised about the hands and neck from broken glass, with the aid of Lt. McKee and Fireman DeBellis, climbed back onto the roof. An immediate preparation was made to rescue the second man, but, by the spectacular efforts of other Ladder 4 and Rescue 1 members he was successfully reached through the interior hallway. For his actions Fireman John Cerato (later a member of Rescue 1) was awarded a medal.

As the members of the New York City Fire Department assembled at the Firemen's Monument at Riverside Drive and West 100th Street to observe the annual memorial day service, Manhattan Box 583 was transmitted downtown. Workers were busy renovating 512 West 19th Street, transforming an old ice house into a television studio. It was October 17, 1970 when a worker's torch apparently ignited a blaze within the building around 11 a.m. As part of the renovation a shaft was added to the building, unknown to responding firemen. Upon their arrival members of Rescue 1 were assigned various tasks with

This new rescue rig, built by the Providence Body Company on a Mack R chassis went into service on September 4, 1971.

Fireman Edward J. Tuite going to the roof with a saw to vent the smoke from the building. While cutting the roof gave way beneath him. He plunged one hundred feet to the base of the new shaft killing him instantly.

At the exact time of Tuite's death, Mayor John Lindsay, Fire Commissioner Robert O. Lowery, the chief officers of the department, and thousands of off-duty firemen were gathered at the Firemen's Memorial on Riverside Drive for the annual FDNY Memorial Services. This date was chosen to commemorate the fire four years earlier where twelve members lost their lives at the 23rd Street collapse. Fireman Edward J. Tuite, thirty-four years-old, was the father of an infant son.

Fireman Edward J. Tuite
Rescue Company 1
October 17, 1970
Manhattan Box 583

A violent explosion tore through a bar and grill on the first floor of 11 Park Row near City Hall at around 2 p.m., on December 11, 1970. The mangled three-story "L" shaped building was a sheet of flames, as the FDNY arrived at the scene. Debris was scattered across the street, and nearby windows had been shattered by the blast. Rescue 1 and teams of firemen worked to extinguish the blaze, then spent many hours combing the wreckage searching for victims of the blast. Ten people were killed and sixty were injured by the explosion and fire.

Three new rescue trucks were purchased in 1971. These were built by the Providence Body Company on Mack R model chassis. These rigs did not have walk-through bodies, but did have slightly larger bodies, and were equipped with rear winches. They were assigned to Rescue Companies 1, 3 and 4. Rescue 1 received registration number R611FC1032, shop number MR7102. Rescue 1 placed the rig in service on September 4, 1971. They would operate it until February 6, 1981, when it went to Rescue 4 for a month before becoming a spare. During 1987 this truck was converted into a collapse rescue unit assigned to Rescue 3 as a second piece.

rise buildings, the FDNY began testing different methods of combating the problems associated with these difficult fires. The Mayor's advisory committee on fire safety for high-rise buildings was formed in 1971. A study of fire safety and the physical science of combustion during actual fires was conducted by the FDNY. Under the direct command of Chief of Department John T. O'Hagan (former captain of Rescue 1) and Battalion Chief Joseph Rooney (who was also a captain of Rescue 1), a number of fires were set within a vacant 22-story office building at 30 Church Street. Tests included: stairway pressurization, stack effect, and the build up of various gases and temperatures. This study would go a long way to developing modern fire tactics in these buildings.

Another major problem facing firefighters during high-rise fires was window ventilation. Breaking the thick, fixed windows in tall buildings sent large, dangerous, and potentially deadly shards of glass falling onto the streets below, sometimes quite a distance from the fire building. To control this problem the FDNY began field testing new pressure-sensitive tape for use in these situations. Rescue Companies 1 and 2, along with ten ladder companies were issued two different

Left top: The first photo of Rescue 1 and a United States President was taken on October 23, 1970. The President's helicopter landed and was greeted by Firemen Curran, Walsh, Driscoll, President Nixon, Bessman, McGhee and B.C. Laufer. *Left bottom:* Photographs of the men of Rescue 1 and President Nixon hit the wire services and were seen in newspapers across the nation.

At one point during the blaze there were so many panic stricken people at the upper story windows, Rescue 1 was ordered to send a man down from the roof on a rope to keep the excited people from jumping. Fireman John Driscoll was lowered down to the 15th floor, where he crawled along the ledge making contact with the persons trapped at smoke filled windows. As hundreds of people watched from the steps of the museum across the street, Fireman Driscoll maintained his perilous perch until the people could be reached by firefighters inside the building. In all, a dozen residents and three firemen were taken to nearby hospitals. For his actions Fireman John Driscoll was placed on the Roll of Merit.

> At one point during the blaze there were so many panic stricken people at the upper story windows, Rescue 1 was ordered to send a man down from the roof on a rope to keep the excited people from jumping.

types of the pressure-sensitive film adhesive tapes. They were asked to review the existing methods, and to explore alternatives in ventilating or removing these fixed windows during fires and emergencies.

The sixteen story Stanhope Hotel had the fancy address of 995 Fifth Avenue. Across the street from the hotel was Central Park and the Metropolitan Museum of Art. It was just after 10:30 on the morning of October 14, 1971. Flames broke out in a basement kitchen sending thick, greasy, black smoke up through the ducts, elevator shafts and stairwells. Faced with dozens of tenants calling for help from all over the 180-unit hotel, a second alarm was transmitted.

This WNYF cover shows Fireman John Driscoll of Rescue 1 being lowered by rope to calm frantic occupants at the Stanhope Hotel on Fifth Avenue. This two-alarm fire was battled on October 14, 1971.

It was 4:17 in the afternoon on February 25, 1972, and the city was beginning another rush-hour. Thousands of commuters began descending on Grand Central Station for their train ride home, when flames broke out in the basement sporting goods store beneath the Commodore Hotel at Park Avenue and 42nd Street. The 26-story hotel was built above the terminal in 1919, and housed more than 500 guests at the time of the fire. Rescue 1 responded to Box 789, where they and the first alarm assignment faced a difficult and escalating fire situation. Heavy smoke filled the twenty-six story hotel, requiring the evacuation of the entire structure. Conditions became so severe and the search and rescue so complicated in the nearly 2000 rooms, that two additional rescue companies and numerous ladder companies were special called to help. Walls from adjoining cellar areas were breached to allow hose stream penetration to the deep-seated fire. The fire itself was battled for nearly eight hours and would expand to five-alarms, before being declared under control.

A cigarette was the apparent cause of a fire that roared through the Sloane House YMCA at 356 West 34th Street on March 22, 1972. It was 9:54 p.m., when the call was received for a fire in the 15-story building about a block away from Madison Square Garden. The "Y" was opened in 1930 and had been the temporary home for thousands of men newly arrived in New York City.

About 1000 guests were registered in the building when the fire broke out on the seventh floor, and quickly spread to the eighth floor. Arriving units, assigned to Box 712, were confronted with numerous people pleading for help from upper-floor windows. Many spectacular rescues were made, both from the tips of fully-extended aerial ladders and through the dense smoke and flames inside the building.

Reporting to the command post were Firemen James T. McCarthy and Bill Moclair of Rescue Company 1. They were directed to move an aerial ladder to the rear and assist people there. The duo ascertained the area of most danger in the building, and began their operation to assist those in the most jeopardy.

The ladder was raised toward a seventh-floor window. Because of its angle, the ladder was short of its objective. Quickly McCarthy climbed to the top rung, reached for the face of the building, and grabbed the windowsill. The victim then used McCarthy as a "human bridge" and climbed down the fireman to the top of the ladder.

The aerial was repositioned, and two more people were pulled from the blaze. As the exhausted duo stood on the turntable helping the last victim down, another victim showed. McCarthy duplicated his original feat, with Moclair guiding the civilian as he climbed down the fireman's back.

Rescue 1 members setting up torches for use on Dey Street in 1970.

NEW TOOL FREES ACCIDENT VICTIM

Device Being Tested by City Cuts Metal Quickly

In four minutes an injured woman was extricated from an automobile crushed in a collision on the Lower East Side last week when a Fire Department rescue squad used a new tool to pry off the vehicle's door. The portable power tool, weighing 50 pounds and resembling an oversize set of shears, can exert 10,000 pounds of pressure to expand or to slice heavy sheet metal quickly. Two weeks ago, the manufacturers, Hurst Performance Products, Inc. Of Warminster, PA., placed one of the instruments on consignment to the New York Fire Department. The tool was assigned to Rescue Squad No. 1 at 33 West 43rd Street and was put through a series of tests on the West Side waterfront, where some wrecked cars are stored.

At 4 P.M. Last Monday, the squad received an emergency call to an auto accident at Grand and Allen Streets. A car driven by Edward Gammandella of 181 Seaside Boulevard, Midland Beach, S.I., who was accompanied by his wife, Ellen, had been struck broadside on the passenger side. Mrs. Gammandella, who has a metal plate in her hip, could not be removed through the driver's door. Lieut. William Cooper and Firemen John Driscoll and Michael Maloney of the rescue squad set up a portable power unit, then applied the powerful steel jaws to the crushed door and pulled it away. Mrs. Gammandella was taken to Beth Israel Hospital for treatment.

In a similar situation, without the emergency power tool, the firemen said, they would have to use an acetylene torch to cut through the metal door.

"This equipment eliminates the danger of flying sparks or jets of flame," Lieutenant Cooper said, "We can move fast and get the trapped victim out fast."

In an experiment last week, the tool was used to split a 12-foot-long wooden beam that was 12 inches square.

Another demonstration showed that a collapsed steering column in a car could be pulled away from the driver's seat in less than 60 seconds.

The *New York Times* ran this story on June 4, 1972.

Four people died and thirty-six were injured by this fast-moving fire. For his outstanding operations on the aerial and his determined search and rescue efforts on the fire floor, Fireman James T. McCarthy was awarded the Trevor-Warren Medal.

Fireman James T. McCarthy

The Hurst tool, a revolutionary new rescue tool, that would quickly become known as "The Jaws of Life", was assigned to Rescue Company 1 on May 12, 1972. This tool was originally designed for auto extrication, but after intense and imaginative drilling it was soon realized it could possibly be useful at structural collapses, subway wrecks and many other types of emergencies.

Word of the amazing new tool spread through the department, and Rescue 1 began getting special called to difficult extrications throughout the city. Captain Anderson, in his evaluation of the tool, recommended its purchase for each of the rescue companies. Today all rescue, squad and ladder companies carry this versatile tool.

Engine Company 2, located at 530 West 43rd Street, was disbanded on November 25, 1972. That firehouse, built in 1874, had recently been renovated by the department. To maintain an FDNY presence in the neighborhood, on February 1, 1973 Rescue 1 left the quarters of Engine 65 and moved down the street to the former quarters of Engine 2. The company was now in their own quarters for the second time.

Rescue 1 moved to the former quarters of Engine 2 at 530 West 43rd Street on February 1, 1973

The kitchen sitting room of the new firehouse.

Fireman McCarthy realized there were additional people trapped on the floor and hauled himself through the window. As he started down the hall, he was pressed to the floor by hot smoke and gases. McCarthy was reaching his limits. He ducked into a room and grabbed a few breaths at the window before continuing his search. Working his way down a long corridor, he opened a window to help vent the smoke. He surprised to see a civilian straddling a chimney duct on the outside of the building. The fireman stayed with the man until an aerial ladder was positioned, and McCarthy was able to help the man climb from his perch.

Members drilling with "High Rise Tool" in 1973. This would allow a stream of water to be directed into the floor above.

A huge liquified natural gas storage tank, located in the Chelsea section of Staten Island was undergoing repairs, when an explosion tore through it shortly after 1 p.m., on February 10, 1973. The tank was a spectacular dome arching one hundred feet above the flat western shoreline. Two-foot thick concrete walls, concrete floor, and a concrete dome was designed to hold liquid to a depth of 61 feet across an interior diameter of 268 feet. When filled it would contain 600,000 barrels of powerful fuel. The tank was designed with a heavy reinforced concrete roof that was intended to collapse into the tank in the event of an explosion, thereby suppressing the explosion. The roof did exactly what it was designed to do. Unfortunately, the tank was not designed to have people inside of it and forty-one workers inside were buried under tons of concrete. Rescue Companies 1 and 2 were quickly called, and despite the fire in the insulation causing a heavy smoke condition, rescue operations were started. Eventually Rescue Companies 3 and 4 would also respond. Members were lowered into the tank via a platform attached to a crane. Pavement breakers, saws, and virtually every type of heavy tool carried by the rescue companies were used in an attempt to reach the trapped workers.

> This extremely frustrating operation was carried out under some of the most severe weather and cold temperature conditions ever encountered in the city.

When it was decided that the continuing efforts would change modes from rescue to recovery, a rotation system was set up where each rescue company, assisted by several ladder companies, would operate for several hours until relieved by another rescue company. This system continued around the clock for several weeks until the last body was recovered. This extremely frustrating operation was carried out under some of the most severe weather and cold temperature conditions ever encountered in the city.

Shortly before 1 a.m., on June 2, 1973, a collision occurred between the tanker *Esso Brussels* and the container ship *Sea Witch* resulting in an explosion and spectacular fire. The ships separated and became grounded in Gravesend Bay south of the Verrazano Bridge, resulting in two distinct operations. Fire operations continued for twenty-two days. Land units were shuttled to the burning ships by fireboats. The rescue companies took turns attempting to search below-deck areas of each ship. They recovered sixteen bodies.

A collapse of the University Hotel, better known as the Broadway Central Hotel, on August 3, 1973, killed four persons and trapped several others. Rescue 1 responded, tunneling and searching the debris. The companies were having a difficult time locating the trapped victims in the huge dangerous debris field. Temperatures were in the upper 90's making the dangerous work even harder. On August 5th Rescue 1 returned to the scene. Under extreme conditions they were able to locate and remove another victim. Operations continued for thirteen days.

Rescue 1 members: Lt. Geidel and Firemen Foote, Collins and McAllister remove one of the four persons killed in the collapse of the Broadway Central Hotel on August 3, 1973.

Rescue 1 at the scene of the Staten Island gas tank explosion and collapse in February 1973.

During September of 1973, a concrete core cutter was assigned to Rescue 1. This modified construction tool allowed an eight-inch diameter hole to be cut through concrete floors and walls. It was intended for use at high rise building fires where, because of the intense heat and fire conditions, a direct attack on the fire was not possible. Rescue 1 would cut a hole into the fire area, and an engine company would then use a hose stream to knock down the fire without taking a beating trying to advance under the punishing conditions encountered at these types of fires.

On January 17, 1974 Rescue 1 responded to a fire on the fourth floor of a tenement on West 48th Street in Manhattan. With reports of children in the apartment, Fireman John Driscoll crawled past the operating hose stream and began searching deep into the apartment. In the living room, he found two small children unconscious in a playpen and radioed his findings. Moments later Fireman Dan Killoran was at his side. They scooped up the children and hurried back past the fire to clear air on the floor below.

Despite applying artificial resuscitation and mouth to mouth breathing, the children could not be revived. For their heroic actions the rescue men were placed on the Roll of Merit with Class A awards.

It was just about 6 p.m., on January 17, 1974, when smoke began to fill the hallways of 810 Seventh Avenue, a fifty-story high-rise building. The all-hands fire started in the fifth floor reception lobby of the TTI Corporation, sending clouds of thick smoke up into the air-conditioning ducts and elevator shafts. Two window washers trapped on the fifth floor were removed by an aerial ladder as the remaining building occupants were removed through the interior. For their outstanding operations at this fire, Rescue Company 1 was awarded a Unit Citation.

At 6:58 a.m., on April 22, 1974, Manhattan Box 792 was transmitted for an explosion at 305 East 45th Street, a high-rise office building housing many delegations to the United Nations. Arriving units found an entire wall of the twenty-five story gone, with structural and explosion damage to several nearby buildings. Rescue 1 conducted difficult and dangerous searches inside the mangled building. The explosion was caused by a damaged gas main feeding the building. Seventy people were injured by the blast.

Firemen Peterson, Killoran, Bilboa, Noonan, Wilday and Bessman after a three-alarm fire at 666 Park Avenue. "Top of the Sixes" March 21, 1974.

Ronnie Foote drilling with the new "Core Cutter Tool" in January 1973. This tool allowed holes to be bored through poured concrete floors to allow stream application.

On June 6, 1974, a three-alarm fire was fought in a six-story tenement, with stores on the first floor. Bronx Box 2739 was transmitted at 6:54 p.m., and sent units to 862 Jennings Street, at the corner of Intervale Avenue. The fire was fought using hand lines on the interior and the stores, while deck guns covered the rescue of a civilian being removed down an aerial ladder. As the severity and amount of fire was realized, the attack switched to a defensive mode and lines were withdrawn.

After the fire was knocked down and conditions had stabilized, members moved back in to complete overhauling. The work continued until 8:08 p.m., when without warning a collapse occurred inside the building. Seven firemen working on the roof plunged six stories, and were buried in the debris. Two rescue companies, including Rescue 1, were special called to the scene. Despite extremely dangerous conditions, members worked without rest until the last man was dug free at 10:11 p.m. In all twenty firemen were hurt, eight of them seriously by the collapse and the rescue work that followed. For their efforts at this job, Rescue 1 was awarded a Unit Citation.

During August of 1974, another new tool was added to the arsenal of Rescue 1's equipment. The Superior Air Hammer, a compressed air power tool, intended for use in vehicle extrications, industrial accidents, and building collapse work.

On February 13, 1975, at 11:58 p.m., Manhattan Box 67 was sent out for a fire in "Tower A", the northern most of the two towers of the World Trade Center. The blaze apparently began in electrical wiring on the eleventh-floor and spread several floors. Rescue 1 responded at 12:10 a.m., with Lt. Martin Cunniff, and Firemen William Moclair, Henry Gonzalez, James Curran,

Firemen George Yeager and James Rogers on the back step after battling a fire in 1974.

Edward Noonan, Michael Walsh and Robert Burns. The company reported in to the command post and the First Division sent them up to the fire floor. There the company relieved two engine companies, and began an aggressive attack of the blazing 11th floor. Rescue then stretched a line down to the 10th floor, forced entry, and extinguished fire in the telephone wire room. They also forced entry to the telephone wire rooms on the 9th and 12th floors.

The Deputy Chief of the First Division recommended the company for a Unit Citation for their "aggressive attack on the fire floor…Then with excellent leadership and efficiency stretched a line down to the tenth floor… A unit that always gives their best."

Two weeks later, on February 27th, Rescue Company 1 was dispatched to one of the most difficult building fires the FDNY would ever face—the New York Telephone Company fire at Second Avenue and Thirteenth Street. The fire started in the sub-cellar cable vault in the twelve-story structure, and spread upwards in the building. Operations were hindered by heavy metal shutters and security windows, which limited ventilation, as well as the dense toxic smoke released by the burning polyvinyl chloride cable insulation. Five alarms and numerous special calls were transmitted, including the assignment of two additional rescue companies. Rescue 1 operated for almost twenty-four hours at this incident, assisting in ventilating the structure, searching the building, and searching for firefighters who had become lost in the maze-like sub-cellar.

> **"The Deputy Chief of the First Division recommended the company for a Unit Citation for their "aggressive attack on the fire floor…Then with excellent leadership and efficiency stretched a line down to the tenth floor… A unit that always gives their best."**

Rescue Firemen remove injured officer from second alarm fire (Box 22-906) on December 2, 1974.

To enhance the image of fire department members in dress uniform, the FDNY established a system of chest insignias to be worn by members who had performed meritorious acts. On June 3, 1975, members would wear Class I, II, III, A and B ribbons, and specially designed colored ribbons designating each of the citizens medals presented by the department. Later, unit citation ribbons were established. The rescue company unit citation ribbon consisted of the rescue company insignia (the Lyle gun) on a red, white and blue background. Up to this time members had worn small maltese cross badges (known as "bugs") on the sleeve of their uniforms to signify Class 1, 2 and 3 awards.

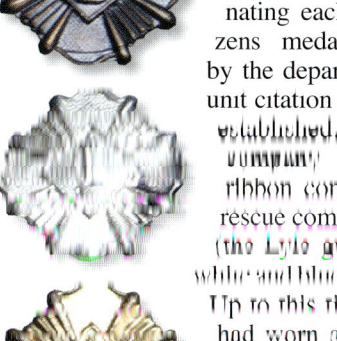

"Bugs" wore on uniform sleeves to signify Class Awards.

The Blue Angel Night Club, an upscale entertainment venue, was located in the fashionable East Side of Manhattan. On December 18, 1975, a night of enjoyment turned tragic as a fire broke out in the rear stage section of the club. Using pitchers of milk, employees of the night club initially attempted to fight the fire for 20 to 25 minutes, while as many as 50 patrons continued to party, unaware of any problem.

Battered Rescue 1 firefighters after the Grand Central Station fire on April 17, 1975.

Right: *Rescue men lower injured fireman from a midtown third alarm on November 16, 1975 are featured on this cover of WNYF.*

Another one of the twelve injured firemen is removed from Box 33-786. This difficult commercial fire in Times Square was battled for three hours.

Unbeknown to those attempting to fight the fire they believed to be limited to some insulation, flames were actually taking hold of the entire plenum (the open space between the ceiling and the floor above) over the club. Overhead, the heat build-up began to ignite other materials at the ceiling level. A dense toxic smoke quickly dropped down from the cockloft, filling the club as flames erupted around the stage. Patrons hurried from the club area, but many went to the coat check to retrieve their valuable fur coats. At about this time, a call was made to 911 reporting the fire. Rescue 1 and midtown FDNY companies raced to the East 54th Street address. Upon their arrival, they were faced with extremely hot smoke pushing out the front door of the packed club. The night club spread between two adjoining buildings that had been altered on the ground floor level.

President Gerald Ford with members of Rescue 1.

Outside, numerous patrons were in near hysterics reporting people trapped within the club. Several people still were attempting to re-enter to retrieve their furs. Lines were stretched and searches started, under extremely punishing conditions. With the situation worsening, second, third and forth alarms were transmitted.

Searches and line advancement proved to be extremely difficult and dangerous, because of the maze-like layout of the club. For three and a half hours, firemen battled the stubborn blaze, which also extended into four floors of apartments above. Sadly, seven people perished in the inferno.

A collapse during a supermarket fire on Atlantic Avenue in Brooklyn on January 7, 1976, trapped nine firefighters in the basement. Rescue 1 was special-called and raced to the scene. Upon arrival they reported to Deputy Chief Jacobs on the Clinton Street side of the building to attempt the rescue of members inside the building who had fallen into the cellar when the first floor collapsed. Under the command of Captain John O'Connor the members of Rescue 1: Firemen Robert Wilday, John McAllister, Dennis Dale, William Riley and William O'Keefe detailed from Ladder 4, immediately entered the building and followed a previously stretched hose line as a guide and probed fifty feet into the blazing collapsed structure. With the ever present danger of further collapse above and beneath them they continued until they found an injured member attempting to climb a portable ladder up from the cellar. This member was pulled to the first floor and dragged from the building. The ladder the member had climbed disappeared into the burning cellar. Members of Rescue 1 returned with a 25-foot wooden ladder and placed it into the hole. Fireman Robert Wilday descended the ladder and located another seriously injured fireman. Working as a team Rescue 1 pulled the injured firefighter to the first floor and dragged him from the building.

Members of Rescue 1 again plunged into the 100 x 100 fire building to continue searching for missing members. Fire at this time was spreading across the hole and the floor was collapsing into the cellar. The captain ordered the company out of the building. Members of Rescue 2 removed several firemen from a separate section of the blazing cellar. Eight of the nine trapped firemen were removed alive. Fireman Robert D. Wilday was awarded a Class A, and the members of Rescue 1 a Unit Citation for their work at this collapse.

Just after midnight on February 4, 1976 Rescue 1 was assigned to a fire at 311 West 94th Street on the Upper Westside of Manhattan. The six-story building was just east of Riverside Drive with front and rear apartments separated by the inner staircase. Upon Rescue's arrival the front fire escape was filled with tenants fleeing the fast moving fire. Rescue 1 under the command of Lt. Paul Geidel was sent to search the second floor, the area directly above the fire apartment.

Facing dense smoke and building heat the company made a quick search of the rear apartment, before being driven back by erupting flames. They called for a line and as water was being directed at the blazing second floor apartment they continued searching the upper floors. After searching the 3rd, 4th and 5th floors they reached the top floor and forced a door. Inside they found five young girls and three young men all unconscious. The company regrouped and dragged the lifeless victims across to the top floor front apartment, where conditions were relatively clear.

After radioing for help, members of Rescue 1 began CPR and mouth to mouth. Aided by other members the emergency care continued. Despite their best efforts, the young people could not be revived. In all ten people were killed in this terrible fire.

A strong wind was blowing on the afternoon of March 7, 1976, when a fire broke out inside an abandoned 200-foot wide pier at Bank and West Streets. Fanned by the winds, the blaze was soon out of control. Dark clouds of smoke pumped from Pier 48 across the unused elevated West Side Highway structure, filling the streets of Greenwich Village. Four-alarms were transmitted, as firemen were forced to move directly into the wind driven smoke and heat currents.

While companies were operating inside the structure, which had suffered previous fires, a collapse occurred and Fireman Edward Noonan of Rescue 1 was struck by a falling steel I-beam. Noonan suffered neck, back and hip injuries. The injured fireman was taken to the hospital, as the firefighting continued. In all, 100 firemen aided by four fireboats battled the blaze for hours. Twenty firemen were injured most minor except for the injuries sustained by Noonan. Sadly, as a result of this fire Fireman Edward S. Noonan was forced to retire on a disability in 1978.

It was 10:20 on the windy morning of December 9, 1976 when Rescue 1 responded to an "All-Hands" fire at Box 75-437, 104 Second Avenue an 8-story apartment house. Upon arrival Rescue was sent to the roof with their K-12 saw to vent the roof and possibly cut a trench. After cutting and pulling two large holes, the wind whipped flames on the top floor and cockloft were making conditions on the roof very dangerous. The six members of Rescue 1 working on the roof were under the command of Captain William Anderson, alongside them were six members of Ladder 6, a member of Ladder 18 and the Fourth Battalion. Also on the roof were two elderly women who had earlier taken refuge there.

Conditions were now becoming untenable, as the tarpaper on the roof ignited and a heavy volume of fire was venting across the front parapet from the top floor and the opened vent holes. Visibility was dropping quickly and the heat was building. It was time for the firefighters and the women to get off the roof. With the front cut-off by fire, the women were carefully helped down the rear fire escape to safety. The firefighters on the roof followed. The members of Rescue 1 then went to the 7th floor and assisted Engine 14 in advancing a line into the north side apartment, then completed a search. The company then reassembled on the 8th floor and helped advance two lines to extinguish the fires in the top floor apartments. The company then returned to the roof, and cut away parts of the roofing not yet collapsed. Captain Anderson and Firemen Dowling, Prial, Riley, Bryant and Kreuscher operated for three and a half hours under heavy fire and smoke conditions.

A special call at 6:15 p.m., February 21, 1977 brought Rescue 1 to 691 FDR Drive a 12-story apartment house were a ten-year old boy was trapped and injured on the roof of an elevator. Lt. Anthony Limberg, Firemen Christopher Glianna and John McAllister accessed the elevator's roof through the adjoining car. Glianna, an EMT, made a primary patient assessment, while Limberg and McAllister sized up extrication on the grease covered roof. Rescue Firemen Dennis Dale, James Dowling and Stephen Casani had assembled a cache of tools nearby including: the Hurst tool and a sawzall. Casani using the Hurst tool cutters made an initial cut on a double row of conduits below the victim. Despite assurances by building personnel that all power was shut off, sparks flew as the cuts were made. Without hesitation, the extrication continued.

A protective blanket was placed across the child as the cutting continued. The conduits were cleared away and brackets were bent freeing the small victim. Before he was moved further, a doctor administered an I.V. to compensate in case of internal injuries. The child was then very carefully lowered from the roof of the elevator through a breach in the wall made earlier by Firemen Dowling and Dale. The child was then taken to the hospital and x-rayed. He was later released with only minor injuries. The company received a Unit Citation for this extrication.

It was 5:43 in the morning on April 9, 1977 when Rescue 1 rolled on the initial alarm to 36 West 35th Street, an old seven-story non-fireproof hotel. Upon arrival heavy fire was in possession of the front rooms on the second floor and out into the public hallway. Fire had already auto exposed into a room above on the third floor, and a heavy heat and smoke condition was spreading throughout the building. Above, the windows were filling with people crying for help. The building was known to house many elderly tenants, and the ladder companies were heavily engaged removing tenants over portable ladders. Rescue 1 proceeded to the second floor and removed hallway doors to facilitate line advancement. The rescue men donned masks and searched the third floor. After completing this search the company moved to the fourth floor where they found two elderly men. They were removed to a safe area of refuge in the rear of the fourth floor.

Rescue 1 continued searching the floors above, then worked exposing hidden pockets of fire in partitions, walls and shafts. The fire eventually reached three alarms. Rescue 1 worked for nearly two and a half hours.

A tragic fire swept the Everard Baths, a gay bath house at 28 West 28th Street just off Fifth Avenue the morning of May 25, 1977. Rescue 1 arrived at the building, a 4-story, 50 x 100-foot former Turkish bath built in 1888. With fire on the third, and fourth floors, the roof and the rear, Lt. Anthony Limberg split the unit to cover more ground. Limberg and his forcible entry team went to the rear of the building where they vented the heavily charged top floors, and a second three man team went to the roof with the K-12 saw to vent there.

During venting operations, Rescue 1, member Fireman Robert Burns made a single slide from the roof of the fire building to the roof of an extension on the exposure #2 side (left side when facing the building) in an attempt to reach and rescue two victims trapped in the rear. The company also operated a 2 1/2 inch hose line on the fourth floor and performed primary searches under extreme conditions on the third and fourth floors. Various unidentified occupants were aided by the company during the initial firefighting. The incoming platoon relieved the night crew, and continued searching the collapsed sections of the building. Finally, the building was deemed too dangerous and Rescue 1 was ordered out by Chief O'Hagan. In all nine patrons were killed in this fire.

On June 17, 1977, Rescue 1 responded to a fire at 255 West 43rd Street, the 15-story Times Square Hotel. Upon arrival members of Rescue 1 could see two trapped occupants waving frantically from windows above only to be shrouded in thick billowing smoke. Battalion 9 directed Lt. Salvatore Russo and his men to concentrate their efforts on search and rescue on the fire floor five stories above. At the fifth floor the company was met with a wall of hot, thick smoke laced with the cries of many people trapped by the fire. Donning their masks the rescue men crawled out onto the blistering floor. Under severe conditions, Fireman Christopher Glianna of Rescue 1 made his way down the public hallway, forcing door after door, removing trapped people and leading them to safety. Despite near exhaustion, he continued searching knowing there was a dead end hallway ahead that had not been searched.

Crawling past a nozzle team waiting for water, he continued down the hall. Hearing weak voices calling from behind a locked door, unable to stand due to the tremendous heat built up overhead he forced the door by himself from the kneeling position. As Fireman Glianna pushed the door in it became apparent the victim, now unconscious, had fallen against the door, blocking it. Summoning his last ounces of strength, Glianna muscled the door inward and pulled the man into the hallway. Dragging the unconscious victim towards the stairs, Glianna's air mask became dislodged. With the fire closing in on him and the victim, he continued on despite the horrific smoke and heat conditions. Upon reaching safety, Glianna collapsed. Both he and the man he rescued were taken to the hospital. The remaining members of the company: Firemen Robert Burns, William Curran, Felix Mullen and George Symon (detailed from Ladder 4) also completed difficult searches, and were able rescue a number of trapped victims. Most of these people required oxygen and three were taken to hospitals.

For his outstanding act of valor, Fireman Christopher V. Glianna received the Captain Denis Lane Medal. Rescue Company 1 was also awarded a Unit Citation for their exceptional actions and teamwork at this, their third "all hands" of the tour.

It was the early morning hours of February 25, 1978. Rescue 1 already had worked three hours at a second alarm fire at Manhattan Box 904, that was transmitted at 1:10 a.m. Back in quarters long enough to clean the tools and change the cylinders on their masks, they were back out the door again heading to an "all hands" at Box 75-401, Ridge and Stanton Streets. On arrival the company, under the command of Lt. Paul Grassi (B-6), hurried to the command post. They advised Deputy Chief Blume that around the corner was another fire in an occupied building with no units yet on scene. The chief directed Rescue 1 to handle this fire and Box 412 was transmitted. This building, 415 Attorney Street, was a six-story tenement with fire visible on the third floor and civilians exiting the front door. Lt. Grassi split the company into teams, and Rescue 1 went to work. Firemen William Bessman and George Kreuscher obtained a portable ladder and ascended to the second floor (the fire escape ladder was inoperable). They then ascended to the third floor and entered the fire area. Making their way to a front apartment, they found four civilians (a man, a woman and two children). They removed them to the fire escape, then assisted them all safely to the ground.

Fireman Christopher V. Glianna

Meanwhile, Rescue Firemen Dennis Dale and John McAllister, without benefit of an engine company or hose line in position, ascended above the fire searching the fourth, fifth and sixth floors. They then went to the roof and vented the skylights, bulkhead and the top floor windows. Lt. Grassi and Fireman William Moclair entered the fire floor, and conducted a primary search on the third and fourth floor apartments. As the first line was being stretched, they helped Engine 14 advance the line into the fire apartment. They continued acting as the first due truck, providing ventilation and searches as the line moved in.

The company then regrouped. They completed all searches on the fire floor and above with negative results. Rescue then checked the cellar, shutting off the gas and electric. For their actions, operating alone and without the benefit of a hoseline, Rescue Company 1 was awarded a Unit Citation.

Rescue 1 rolled to a fire in the Hotel Rutledge on 30th Street on June 7, 1978. As they pulled into the block, a victim was seen trapped on a ninth floor window ledge and about to jump. Fireman James Rogers of Rescue 1 quickly made his way to the fire floor, by way of the rear fire escape. After assisting several occupants from the smoke filled fire floor, he pressed on searching for the trapped victim. With fire now in the public hall, Rogers crawled twenty feet down the hallway. Flames rolled over his head, driven by a hoseline moving in from the other end of the hall. Rogers forced the door, and moved into the room. After a punishing search, the room proved to be empty. The victim had evacuated himself.

Right: *The truss roof collapse forced rescue men to breach brick walls to reach the trapped men.*

The tragic Waldbuam's supermarket fire on August 2, 1978 took the lives of six firefighters.

After venting the windows another victim was seen at an adjacent window, burned and threatening to jump. Rogers plunged back into the blazing hallway, and kicked in the burning door of the next room. Crawling to the window with flames still over his head, Rogers reached up and pulled the man back into the room. Shielding the man with his body, Rogers retraced his path back under the flames and down the hallway to the safety of the stairs. For his heroic actions Fireman James D. Rogers was awarded the John H. Prentice Medal.

Mass tragedy struck the FDNY on August 2, 1970, when a truss roof collapsed in the early stages of a supermarket fire on Ocean Avenue in Brooklyn. It was nearing the morning change of tours when the alarm came in for Brooklyn Box 3300, the Waldbaum's Supermarket. It was 8:42 a.m. A second alarm was quickly transmitted, as fire companies began their battle. Nozzle and search teams moved into the first floor, as other teams climbed to the roof to provide ventilation to the blazing cockloft. Thirty-two minutes after arrival, the roof collapsed dropping twelve firemen into the blazing store, while several men clung to the parapet wall at the roof's edge. Immediately a rescue effort was started. The men trapped at the roof's edge were removed with aerial ladders, as firemen pushed their way into the burning store below.

Firemen James D. Rogers

Members of Rescue 1 had been glued to the department radio as the Brooklyn fire escalated. Just as the dispatcher came on with: "Rescue 1 respond to Brooklyn Box 44-3300, they were rolling out the door. Racing south, then through the Brooklyn-Battery Tunnel, they arrived at the fire. Special calls also brought Rescue Companies 3 and 4 to the scene. Several members had already been rescued, under extreme conditions, but the collapse hindered a thorough search.

Lt. James Curran was informed that ten firemen were missing inside the blazing store, and that Rescue 1 was to relieve Rescue 2 on a hose line. Following the hose into the hellish conditions, they found two exhausted members of Rescue 2. Firemen George Kreuscher, Michael Walsh and Robert Burns took the line and moved in further. A few minutes later, they were rejoined by the very men they'd come to relieve. Together they pressed forward.

From various directions rescue men breached solid brick walls, then plunged into the rubble strewn inferno searching for the trapped men. Off-duty members of Rescue 1 and other rescue companies moved in with those on-duty despite not having breathing equipment. Regardless of these superhuman efforts to reach the trapped members, six members would answer their last alarm.

John O'Rourke, Sal Russo, Ed Vomero, Bill Moclair, Ernie Andreacchi, Jess Bilboa, Steve Casani; Andrew Young, Abraham Beame, Hugh Carey, and President Jimmy Carter.

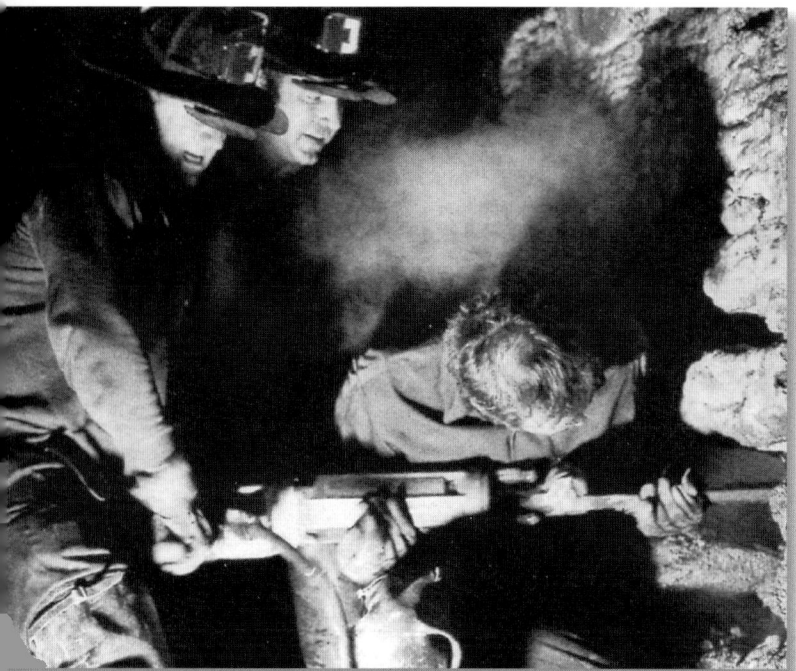

Members of Rescue 1 use a pavement breaker to breach a brick wall. This is one of the many specialized tools used to rescue people trapped in difficult locations.

During 1979 Rescue 1 was assigned the AmFire Water Drill. This tool utilized the water pressure in a hose line to cut through concrete, masonry, and many other materials.

During 1979, Rescue 1 was assigned an Amfire Water Drill. This combination tool utilized water pressure in a hose line to enable a hole to be cut through concrete, masonry, metal, lexan and wood. The water drill was designed to be operated by a single firefighter. Once the hole has been cut, a stream of water can be applied directly through the tool. This new tool operated at various water pressures between 100-200 psi.

At 4:08 p.m., June 14, 1979, Manhattan Box 714 was transmitted for a fire in Macy's Department Store. Due to the number of telephone calls, and the type of occupancy, the dispatcher sent Rescue 1 and and an additional ladder company along with the full first alarm assignment on the initial alarm. This proved to be a timely move, as many people would have to be evacuated from the huge building. Midtown companies made their way up and encountered a raging fire in the sporting goods section. Rescue 1's Lt. Anthony Limberg, Firemen George Kreuscher, William Riley, Norman Newkirk, Steve Casani and Dan Killoran were preparing to move in, when a "May Day" was declared. A member of Ladder 24 was missing on the fire floor.

The rescue men made several attempts to move into the blazing smoke-filled floor. The heat was so intense they could only penetrate ten feet or so before being driven back. The fire area, half the size of a football field, easily overwhelmed the single hose stream being pushed in by Engines 1 and 26. Water pressure was poor, due to the many sprinkler heads discharging. (In the immediate fire area, water to the sprinkler system was accidently left off after work was done. This allowed a major fire to develop).

Second, third and fourth alarms were transmitted. Eventually many hose lines were positioned at various vantage points around the fire and the flames darkened down. Sadly, the missing fireman was located during a secondary search. His body was carried reverently from the fire area by members of Rescue 1 and Ladder 24. They stopped briefly as Father Julian Deeken, the department beloved chaplain who lived in the rectory of Saint Francis of Assisi Church across the street from 24 Truck, prayed over the fallen fireman. The firemen then carried their brother from the fire building.

It was 1:35 on the afternoon of September 8, 1979 when Rescue 1 was directed to Box 812, Grand Central Station. Under the command of Captain Anthony Bruno (D-3), the company was sent to check the conditions in the Hotel Roosevelt, where they found a light smoke condition. The command post directed the company to the fire area, two levels below street level inside Grand Central Station. The company split into teams to determine the extent of the fire. Operating under difficult conditions, they searched a large complex area and numerous railroad cars. Heavy smoke now filled the huge station and all the associated tracks.

Rescue 1 located the string of burning railcars, and search inside for any trapped passengers. The train windows proved nearly impossible to vent and searches continued under extreme conditions. It was proving difficult to stretch lines from standpipes to the fire area due to obstructions, misaligned doors, and the narrow space between cars. The blaze was nestled within a string of railcars 1500-feet long and three tracks wide. A combination of vinyl, foam rubber, and the horse hair padding of upholstered seats gave off heavy noxious smoke.

Once the searches were complete, Rescue 1 relieved Engine 65 on a 2-1/2 inch hose and assisted in the final extinguishment. Despite the difficult conditions encountered, Rescue 1 once again displayed teamwork, coordination and initiative. The company was awarded a Unit Citation.

Chapter 8

The Eighties

The 1980's at first, seemed like a continuation of the previous decade's decline. Crime numbers were up, the numbers of homeless in the streets had dramatically increased, and a new epidemic was sweeping the city: crack cocaine. Fire duty in 1980 would continue on the dramatic track it had been on for more than a dozen years, as 3,303 serious fires were battled that year. The 289 fire deaths had only be surpassed twice in the sixties, and four times in the seventies. The day to day work of New York City firemen was still running at near historic levels. Then simultaneously in 1982, Wall Street began a small boom, which in turn fueled the real estate markets and property values slowly began to rise. The coming decade began to show promise.

During an all-hands fire at 545 West 49th Street on February 8, 1980, members of Rescue 1 would make separate rescues. It was 3:56 in the morning, when Rescue 1 rolled through the empty streets of the theatre district and pulled up to the blazing building. Fire and heavy smoke was showing out a fourth floor window, and a woman jumper was laying on the ground in the courtyard moaning "Save my babies." As Lt. Curran checked in with Battalion Chief William Grimes, a resident arrived shouting to follow him. Curran and Lt. Fred Daniels of Engine 54 went with the resident into what appeared to be a "H" type building, an appearance that would prove to be false. Upon reaching the fourth floor, they forced an apartment door. Reaching the window, they realized they were in the wrong building. The courtyard below was surrounded by three separate tenement buildings. The well meaning resident had taken them to this location to show them the victims, a window away in the adjoining building.

The man was trapped at a window, with flames jetting out over his head. Conditions around him were deteriorating so quickly, that moments before he had dropped a baby out the window, and into the arms of a fireman below. Above, Rescue 1's roofman and outside vent man were preparing a roof-rope rescue as Lieutenant Curran, sensing the victims time was running out, quickly tied a rope around his chest, straddled the window with one leg outside and leaned out stretching himself toward the trapped man. Stretching as far as he could across the five foot span, Curran pressed himself against the window frame. He instructed Lt. Daniels to hang onto him and the rope for dear life. Curran stretched out his arm, as the man plunged across the window sill and grasped the rescue officer's hand. Curran held fast, as the force of the jump and the man's weight nearly pulled both of them to the ground below. Holding the victim tightly, they swung back and forth a few agonizing seconds before Curran was able to pull the man up, and in the window.

Simultaneously, Rescue 1 Fireman John R. McAllister had raced up the stairs to the fourth floor of the fire building and entered a blazing apartment. Hearing cries for help ahead of him, McAllister donned his mask and crawled through a kitchen area with heavy flames rolling over his head. In the rear bedroom, McAllister found a semi-conscious man and dragged him back through the blazing kitchen, where both he and the victim received burns. Continuing to the hallway, McAllister met Rescue 1 Fireman Richard Martinsen and Lt. Joe D'Amico of Ladder 4 who were moving towards the apartment. McAllister was handing the victim off to them, when he heard more screams from the rear. McAllister attempted to re-enter the fire filled kitchen, but was driven back. As the screams continued, McAllister again tried to dive into the blazing room but was forcefully restrained by other firemen.

As Engine 54 began pushing in with the line, McAllister crawled next to the nozzleman assisting and directing him as best he could, as they moved through the kitchen and into the burning rear bedroom. As they advanced into this last room, Fireman McAllister fell from exhaustion landing several feet from the wife of the man he had rescued earlier. The woman was dead.

For his heroic actions Fireman John R. McAllister of Rescue Company 1 was awarded the Walter Scott Medal. He was joined on the steps of City Hall by Lt. James J. Curran who was presented the Albert S. Johnston Medal.

Fireman John R. McAllister

Lt. James J. Curran

Fires in high-rise buildings were becoming commonplace in New York City. One of the more difficult ones took place on June 23, 1980. On arrival at 299 Park Avenue, units found fire in possession of the northeast section of the 20th floor of this 42-story building. Rescue 1 was assigned to search the fire floor and above. On the 21st floor they found a cleaning lady and escorted her to safety. Back on the fire floor conditions were becoming extreme. Each of the members of Rescue 1 were running low on air, and additional cylinders were obtained. Firemen Bilboa and Glianna were each operating a hose line, by themselves. Despite the fact they were dangerously low on air, they remained in position taking tremendous punishment until each was relieved. Five alarms were transmitted with numerous units, including two additional rescue companies, special-called over the fifth alarm assignment.

The exhausted members of Rescue 1 made their way to the floor below the fire, for a brief rest and to change their cylinders, when a "May-Day!" crackled across the handie-talkies. The Rescue men quickly regrouped and plunged back onto the fire floor splitting into teams. Under very difficult conditions, they continued searching until the all clear was sounded. Rescue 1 then went to the lobby, where all the members were administered oxygen, transported to and treated at Roosevelt Hospital. For their efforts Rescue Company 1 was awarded a Unit Citation.

It was 2:41 in the morning on December 12, 1980, when Rescue 1 rolled out first due to 522 West 47th Street a five-story old law tenement. With heavy smoke at the front door and first floor windows, and numerous occupants visibly in peril above, some even threatening to jump, the company split into first due truck positions. Lt. Frank Miale (B-8) and his forcible entry team, Firemen Christopher Glianna and Barry Meade proceeded to the first floor right rear apartment. There fire was in complete control of the apartment, rolling out into the public hall ceiling towards the stairwell. The team expended a two and a half gallon water fire extinguisher in an attempt to close the apartment door, but were unable to due to the severe heat conditions. Lt. Miale rushed up the stairs to accomplish a quick search for victims in the hallway above, then forced the door to apartment 2E searching there. Moving to the third floor, the officer saw embers shooting up the stairwell and the heat building quickly; it was time to regroup.

As the first due engine stretched in, the forcible entry team attempted to enter apartments from the exterior. Fireman Dennis Horigan entered a second floor window, utilizing an old wooden ladder. He was able to calm a women threatening to jump. He held her at this location until a department ladder was positioned, and she was removed to safety. Glianna then climbed this same ladder, stepped across to the left window by standing on the ornamental coping above the first floor, and was able to physically restrain a man from jumping. At this time, Fireman Meade arrived with a FDNY 35-foot portable ladder which he extended alone.

After placing the rescue truck so as not to block the fire building, chauffeur Fireman Henry Gonzalez noticed an occupant holding a child out the window on the third floor. Gonzalez quickly helped Ladder 21 throw their aerial ladder to the third floor. He then climbed the ladder and removed the child, passing him down the ladder to Rescue Fireman Richard Martinsen. Gonzalez next took the mother and pulled her down past himself passing her to Martinsen, who escorted them to the street. After the ladder was repositioned, Gonzalez entered the fifth floor where he placed his mask over a women's face, until a tower ladder bucket was able to swing in and pick up the woman.

Simultaneously Lt. Miale and Fireman Meade re-entered the building via the public hallway, ascending to the fourth and fifth floors. Firemen Horigan and Glianna, after passing victims to a fireman on a portable ladder, searched the remainder of the second floor. The duo then advanced a hose line, stopping the extension of fire from the first floor. After, they were joined by Martinsen and searched the third floor.

For operating alone, under extremely dangerous conditions without the benefit of protective hose lines, and in a state of near exhaustion: Rescue Company 1 was awarded a Unit Citation. It should be noted the members of Rescue 1, had already operated at three previous "all-hands" for a total of 3 hours and 15 minutes of structural fire duty in the previous seven hours.

Three additional rescue apparatus were delivered as 1980 drew to a close. These units were purchased with funds from the 1979 fiscal year, and therefore were termed 1979 models by the department. The trucks were built by Pierce on Mack R model chassis. They were similar to the 1971 models, although slightly larger and higher, and having more diamond plate components in the body construction. These units replaced the 1971 rigs at Rescue Companies 1, 3 and 4. Registration number R611FC1061, shop number MR7902, was assigned to Rescue 1 during February, 1981. (The 1971 Mack MR7102 was then assigned to Rescue 4 for a month before becoming a spare. In 1987 this rig was converted into the first Collapse Rescue apparatus.)

> **F**or operating alone, under extremely dangerous conditions without the benefit of protective hose lines, and in a state of near exhaustion: Rescue Company 1 was awarded a Unit Citation.

Rescue 1's 1979 Mack/Pierce was placed in service in February 1981. (John Lee Gill)

People were trapped and yelling for help from the rear windows of a burning tenement at 23 West 31st Street, when Rescue 1 arrived on February 9, 1981. Fireman Norman L. Newkirk climbed to the top of a 25-foot extension ladder, calming the two frantic people just beyond his reach, while waiting for a scaling ladder to be brought to the rear.

When the scaling ladder arrived, Newkirk placed it into the window above, now pumping heavy smoke. He quickly climbed up the single-beamed ladder and over the window sill, into the heavily charged room. As thick smoke condition and high levels of heat were building around him, Newkirk had to move fast. Searching the immediate area, he found both victims, one unconscious on the floor. The rescue fireman scooped up the unconscious victim handing him out the window to another fireman. As the scaling ladder cleared, Fireman Newkirk climbed out directing the other civilian to follow. As they descended the slender ladder, Newkirk taught and encouraged the civilian step by step and carefully transferred them to the portable ladder.

Shortly after safely reaching the ground, the exhausted fireman looked up to see the window he'd just left explode with flames. For his heroism Fireman Norman L. Newkirk was awarded the American Legion Medal. This was most likely the last scaling ladder rescue made in the FDNY; the first being accomplished back in 1884.

Firefighter Norman L. Newkirk

On Friday afternoon July 3, 1981, an IRT Number 2 train slammed into the rear of another Number 2 train stopped because of signal problems, inside the Utica Avenue tunnel. The force of the 400-ton train drove the stopped train nine feet further down the tunnel, mangling the lead car on the second train and trapping the motorman in the wreckage. Upon receipt of the alarm, the FDNY fire alarm dispatchers assigned four rescue companies, including Rescue 1, on the first alarm. (This was the first time in department history four rescue companies were assigned on the initial alarm.) The rescue companies operated under difficult, humid conditions to extricate the motorman, who later died from his injuries. They were able to treat and evacuate the 135 injured passengers from the train and the tunnel.

Several days later, one of the most drawn-out pier fires in the city's history took place on July 8, 1981. The original alarm was transmitted at 3:39 p.m., for the 800-foot long Pier 58 located on the Hudson River at West 16th Street. Most of the fire was located beneath the pier deck, inaccessible to land units and fireboats. The burning creosote soaked wood sent thick, noxious clouds of smoke across Manhattan, plunging the streets into darkness. The department continued to battle the growing fire as night fell. Rescue 1, working in conjunction with other rescue companies, operated pneumatic hammers to open holes in the concrete covered pier deck. This allowed some water application into the building flames.

At one point it was feared the fire would extend around the land end and to the pier to the south, which was used as a city bus garage. To stop this extension, a trench cut was made by the rescue companies using pavement breakers and other heavy tools. This defensive operation was difficult and time consuming, but eventually worked. Five-alarms were transmitted. The fire was not placed under control until 5:19 p.m., on July 9th, over twenty-five hours after the initial alarm.

This arduous battle, and the problems encountered served as a catalyst for the formation of the FDNY's scuba teams, originally set up as in-water firefighting teams.

This difficult fire at Pier 58 in July 1981 directly led to the FDNY SCUBA program. (John Lee Gill)

It was just after 7:00 a.m., on Friday January 22, 1982, Rescue 1 was taking up from a restaurant fire on the Westside of Manhattan, when the department radio sent the company to a reported fire on the 15th floor of 305 East 41st Street, the Hotel Tudor. Upon arrival, the company could see smoke pouring from several windows on the 15th floor of the 200 x 200-foot, twenty-story building. Most alarming was a man clinging to a window frame surrounded by smoke. Reaching the lobby, they found the elevators unavailable. Without hesitation, the company led by Captain Brian E. O'Flaherty began to climbing stairs towards the fire floor. Stopping briefly on the floor below to get a layout, O'Flaherty leaned out the window below the trapped man. The captain shouted, "Hang on—we'll get to you!!"

Captain Brian E. O'Flaherty

Reaching the fire floor, O'Flaherty saw a dead-end hallway and realized the dangers entering it would entail. The captain split his team, sending men to the floor above to begin a rope rescue. With no line in place to protect him, O'Flaherty donned his mask, plunged into the dense smoke filled hallway, and crawled under heavy fire venting from the blazing apartment. Passing the flames, he continued on until he located the apartment door. Moving through this smoke filled apartment he made his way towards the window, and despite the searing heat stood up pulling the man back into the room.

Realizing he could not subject the man to the heat and smoke levels in the hallway, O'Flaherty closed the hallway door to provide some protection, as an engine company advanced a hose into the hallway from the other side of the fire apartment. O'Flaherty radioed his situation to the battalion chief, and waited until conditions improved enough to allow him to escort the man to safety.

For his life saving act of valor, Captain Brian E. O'Flaherty was awarded the Vincent J. Kane Medal.

A week later, on Friday January 29, 1982, Rescue 1 responded to a fire in the new skyscraper, the "Trump Towers". This building located at 725 Fifth Avenue was under construction and had just reached the 28th floor. A fire had started on the 27th floor and was building rapidly. Fueled by a veritable lumber yard of stored building materials and whipped by strong winds, the flames had trapped the operator of a sky crane. Upon their arrival Rescue 1, under the command of Lieutenant James J. Curran, was ordered to attempt to rescue the operator. Taking the exterior hoistway to the 20th floor, firemen continued on foot to the fire floor. There they were faced with fire blocking their way to the crane, and sections of construction collapsing around them.

Realizing it would take a coordinated effort, Rescue 1 teamed with Engine 23 and Ladder 16 to get a hose into position. As the line was pulled into position, Curran located a steel shaftway leading up four floors to the skycrane. He notified the others of his find and began to climb, but had to stop as the steel rungs burned through his fire gloves.

The Rescue 1 crew after the dramatic Trump Tower rescue, January 29, 1982.

When Engine 23 got water, Fireman Joseph Pierotti on the nozzle and Fireman Harry Weir backing him up, battled their way onto the floor and pushed towards the skycrane's access shaftway. With Lt. Owen Byrnes of Ladder 16, Lt. Curran, again attempted to climb the cherry-red ladder to no avail. As the nozzle team continued cooling the scalding steel cylinder, Curran and Byrnes donned their facepieces (with no tanks due to the tight size of the cylinder) then wrapped discarded cloth around their gloved hands, wrists, and forearms and climbed upwards. Three floors of fire surrounded them, while the nozzle team following them were cooling the red hot steel where they could. As the lieutenants reached the trapped operator (the son of a retired fireman) the nozzle team doused the glowing metal around them, knocking down what fire they could reach. Reaching the crane operator, the escape plan was quickly revised. They'd learned that they were sitting on a tank filled with 300 gallons of diesel fuel.

> On June 1, 1982 the term "Fireman" was changed to "Firefighter" in the New York City Fire Department.

Pierotti and Weir remained on the crane's superstructure, covering and cooling the officers and the operator as they entered the cylinder encased ladder and descended to safety. For their efforts three members of Engine 23: Lt. Owen Byrnes and Firemen Joseph Pierotti and Harry Weir were awarded medals for their outstanding and determined teamwork. Lieutenant James J. Curran of Rescue 1 was awarded the Brummer Medal.

On June 1, 1982 the term "Fireman" was changed to "Firefighter" in the New York City Fire Department.

Units of the Seventh Battalion and Rescue 1 responded to an advanced fire situation on March 13, 1983 at 4:30 in the morning. Flames were burning uncontrolled on the third and fourth floors, and through the roof of 229 Seventh Avenue, a converted loft building now redesigned into apartments. Upon arrival, Rescue 1 could see heavy fire out the windows on the top two floors of the four-story building. They were advised by Chief Downs there was heavy fire in the public hallways, and that people were trapped on the top floor. Lt. Gates, in command of Rescue 1, split the company into teams to try and rescue the trapped people from different access points. As an aerial ladder was placed at a top floor window, Firefighter William B. Bessman entered a tower ladder bucket that was raised to another top floor window.

Reaching the window, Bessman could see heavy fire venting from six windows to his right on the top floor, and three windows below on the third. Realizing time was of the essence, Bessman donned his mask and plunged into the thick hot smoke. Alone, Firefighter Bessman crawled towards the rear of the blazing building. Passing the hallway door, he could see fire pushing and lapping around its edges. With his exit now being threatened, he continued on until he was fifty feet deep into the burning building. Searching in the dense hot smoke, he found an unconscious man. Crawling backwards he dragged the man towards the front of the building. With fire conditions becoming extreme and fearing for Bessman's safety, a line was ordered up the aerial ladder to cover the top floor window if needed.

Nearing the window Bessman noticed the man was not breathing. Despite the punishing atmosphere, he pulled off his mask and administered four quick rescue breaths before handing him out the window to the firemen in the tower ladder bucket. Bessman scrambled out into the bucket and resumed rescue breathing, as the bucket was guided down to the street. The victim was handed off to ambulance personnel and rushed to the hospital. He would survive his ordeal.

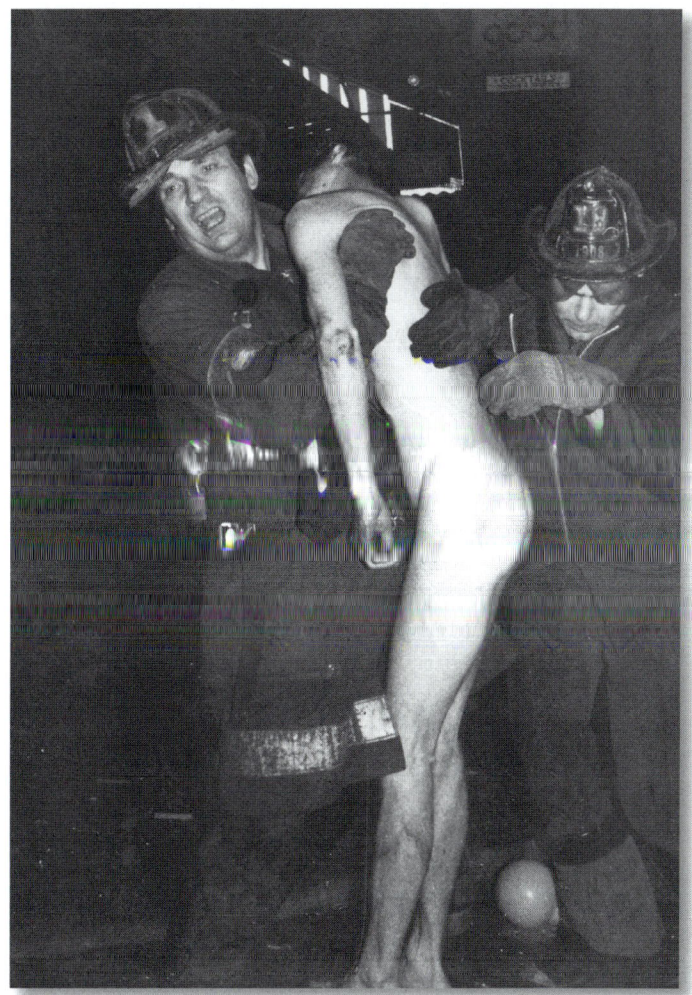

Firefighter Bessman carries the unconscious man he rescued March 13, 1983.

At this time, another report echoed across the radios stating another victim was trapped on the top floor. Bessman immediately returned to the top floor window, and again plunged into the thick smoke. He crawled to the rear room again, where he was met by other firemen who advised him the victim had just been found and removed. Bessman could finally relax his aggressive efforts.

For his act of valor Firefighter William B. Bessman was awarded the Hugh Bonner Medal.

The department, because of the geographic make-up of the city, has always been faced with water emergencies and pier fires. Although its members were ingenious and daring in their rescue work at such incidents, such as Fireman Thomas Bonamo's dives using personal SCUBA gear back in 1958, their operations and equipment were limited. Pier fires were still being fought in the old, time-consuming and laborious fashion of cutting holes in the pier deck from above, and lowering distributors to apply water underneath.

Firefighter William Bessman

On July 20, 1983 Department Order 97 officially designated Rescue Companies 1 & 2 as in-water firefighting teams.

Several other past water incidents forced the rescue companies to improvise equipment to attempt rescues. On March 4, 1963, a bus went out of control and crashed into the East River from Welfare Island. The initial dives at this incident were made by members of the rescue companies, utilizing improvised equipment consisting of primitive, rubber haz-mat suit and a Scott face mask connected to breathing air cylinders on shore by extension hoses. In January 1968, similar improvised equipment was used to rescue a youth from a submerged automobile in the harbor off Brooklyn.

Following the Pier 58 fire in 1981, both Rescue Companies 1 and 2 were developing in-water firefighting techniques and taking scuba training. In February 1982, Rescue 2 made a successful underwater rescue of a youth trapped in a submerged van. This was followed in November 1982, by another successful underwater rescue of a man trapped in a submerged vehicle by members of Rescues 1 and 2. These two rescues were the first of many successful water rescues that would be conducted by FDNY scuba teams. In fact, FDNY scuba teams were said to have the highest recovery rate of any rapid deployment underwater rescue team.

Because of the success of these in-water firefighting teams at pier fires as well as their numerous water-related rescues, the department initiated a formal training program for department scuba divers. Divers would take multiple courses and receive various scuba diving certifications. Finally, on July 20, 1983, Department Order No. 97 officially designated Rescue Companies 1 and 2 as in-water firefighting teams.

Photo of the some of the original Rescue 1 divers taken by Harvey Eisner for Firehouse Magazine *in 1983.*

Advanced dive training was completed by FDNY scuba team members in November 1983. During 1987, Rescue 5 would also be trained and designated for this function. The scuba program has proven to be very timely and efficient, with many members of these three units eventually becoming certified underwater search and rescue instructors.

It was 3:15 in the morning on Wednesday, August 10, 1983 when Rescue 1 rolled out to fire at 512 Seventh Avenue a 23-story, 150 x 150 commercial building. A serious fire was blazing in the cellar and subcellar of the huge structure. It was a classic domino effect that slipped Midtown Manhattan into chaos. At 1:30 a.m., a 68-year old, 12-inch water main burst underneath 30th Street and Seventh Avenue. Almost immediately, water flooded into a Con Ed substation, 40-feet below street level beneath the Navarro Building. At 3:15 a.m., Box 747 is transmitted as the electrical substation is blazing beneath the building. Rescue 1 and four alarms worth of FDNY units were faced with a major underground fire fueled by wires, insulation and 50,000 gallons of mineral oil used to cool the transformer. The fire was battled for hours before it was brought under control. The failure of the badly damaged substation plunged a 12 block area of Garment/Fashion District into a blackout. For three days, the area bounded by Sixth and Seventh Avenues from 42nd to 30th Streets was without power. For their outstanding efforts at battling this fire Rescue Company 1 was awarded a Unit Citation.

A new response policy for the rescue companies was established at the beginning of 1984. The rescue companies would now respond on the 10-75 signal, which is the indication of a working fire, rather than waiting for the entire first alarm assignment to be put to work before responding. In addition, the supervising dispatcher was given greater latitude in sending a rescue company on the initial alarm, when information received indicated that the rescue company's special tools or training would be advantageous.

On the afternoon of April 4, 1984, Rescue 1 was special called to a reported building collapse on Delancey Street in Manhattan. Two five-story buildings under renovation had collapsed, killing two workers with others reported trapped within the piles of rubble. Rescue 1 was ordered to assist police officers, who were attempting to extricate a victim from the cellar through a hole in the debris. Lieutenant James J. Curran ordered a sawzall be made ready and given to the police. He then offered to make available additional tools and requested entry into the collapse. The police refused any additional tools, and it did little to speed the officers in their job.

Lt. Curran made a quick survey of the exposures and saw exposure #2 was bulging toward the pile of debris, and that exposure #4 seemed fairly stable. Rescue 1 Firefighter Michael J. Fitzgerald advised him of another access to the cellar. They climbed down between two floor joists into the cellar and began a search for the victim. They also attempted to shut-off the utilities despite the huge volume of water cascading into the cellar from a ruptured 20-inch water main. Their search continued towards the rear of the building, where they were forced to wade through a sea of wet concrete with twisted and dislodged "I" beams hanging overhead.

Now 250-feet deep into the building, they climbed up to where a lone police officer was attempting to cut through the pile with Rescue 1's saw. The worker was pinned with his hand crushed beneath tons of rubble. Lieutenant Curran sized up the victims condition and called for the Hurst tool. Firefighter Richard Cody, Rescue 1's chauffeur, brought the tool to the scene, but was blocked by ESU personnel. He then found the void used by Curran and Fitzgerald and lugged the heavy tool and hand pump to their location. They were joined by Lt. James Rogers (a former Rescue 1 firefighter) and Firefighter John T. Kleehaas both of Rescue 2, who'd brought a second Hurst tool. Together the rescue men shored the immediate area, and using the tools extricated the pinned worker. They quickly carried the injured worker to the street, where he was taken by ambulance to Bellevue Hospital.

For their courage and team work the five rescue men would all receive medals. From Rescue 2: Lt. James D. Rogers, the Chief Joseph B. Martin Medal, and Firefighter John T. Kleehaas, the Police Honor Legion Medal. The members of Rescue Company 1 awarded for this rescue were: Lieutenant James J. Curran, the Columbian Association Medal. Firefighter Michael J. Fitzgerald, the Steuben Association Medal, and Firefighter Richard H. Cody, the Company Officers Association Medal.

Firefighter Michael J. Fitzgerald   *Firefighter Richard H. Cody*

A special call on Sunday night May 20, 1984 at 10 p.m., sent Rescue 1 to the North River at 14th Street. An automobile had plunged into the river. Donning their dive gear en route were: Firefighters George Kreuscher, Jack Boyle and Dick Martinsen. Kreuscher, the primary diver, entered the water and was directed into position on the surface by a member of FDNY Marine 2, who'd witnessed the accident. Getting the signal he was near the location, Kreuscher descended into the black water. Fifteen feet below the surface he located the car.

After procuring a marker float and a halligan, Kreuscher returned to the locked vehicle and marked its location. Despite exhaustive efforts the water pressure would not allow a single diver to force open the door. Kreuscher could feel the unconscious driver, but wearing all the bulky dive equipment, was unable to fit through the broken window. Surfacing he reported the situation, and within moments Boyle and Martinsen joined Kreuscher on the river bottom. The fresh team was led to the door and they muscled it open, rushing the man to the surface. Despite resuscitation efforts on shore the man died.

Hazardous Materials Company 1 (HazMat 1) was placed in service on October 15, 1984. The unit was quartered with Engine 288 in Maspeth Queens. The new, specially trained and equipped unit responded city-wide to handle most any kind of hazardous materials incident. Rescue 4 had received special training and had been handling haz mat jobs since 1981. Before this time each of the Rescue Companies, as they were established, were responding to and operating at hazardous material incidents within their respective response areas. Rescue 1 had been handling a wide array of hazardous materials including: ammonia leaks, chemical spills and fires and leaks of toxic gases since 1915.

It was 2:30 in the morning on November 3, 1984. Rescue Company 1 was wheeling through the empty streets of Manhattan heading across town to a reported fire on the fifth floor of 1264 Lexington Avenue. Driving the rescue rig was Firefighter John McAllister. Seated next to him was Lieutenant Joseph Dirks, an officer assigned to the 8th Battalion who frequently filled open groups in Rescue 1. The company was assigned to search the floors above the fire. Firefighters Richard Cody, John Boyle, Carl Feilmoser and James Corcoran joined Dirks and McAllister and climbed the interior stairs to the sixth floor. In doing so they all had to first pass the fire apartment, now fully involved in flames. The company then split into teams. Crouching low and staying near the outside wall of the staircase, they were able to reach the sixth floor landing. Conditions were extreme. Intense heat and heavy smoke were pumping up the stairwell from beneath them. Visibility was zero. Heat conditions were so intense they could not stand, as they forced entry into the apartment directly above the fire.

The first team forced the north apartment, 6N, and began a grueling search. The second team forced the south apartment, 6S. As soon as the door swung in, they heared fire crackling deep inside the flat. The two men began a search as their radios relayed the difficulties being encountered on the fire floor below them. With conditions deteriorating below and the heat level in the apartment increasing, Dirks and McAllister split up to cover more ground. Firefighter McAllister plunged into a bedroom to his right and searched, as Lt. Dirks continued down the apartment hallway in the direction of the extending fire. About 35-feet deep into the apartment, Dirks found a victim lying face down on the floor. With flames now filling the adjacent living room and extending towards the hallway, Dirks dragged the victim back towards the front door. He was joined by McAllister, and together they dragged the two-hundred pound victim down the apartment hallway, across the landing and into the opposite apartment.

Removal down the stairs was impossible, because of the extreme extending fire conditions. A tower ladder was called to remove the victim. While the bucket was being positioned, they administered CPR and rescue breathing. They continued to do so as they were lowered to the ground. The victim was then passed to EMS.

For their courage and tenacity Firefighter John R. McAllister was awarded the Chief Wesley Williams Medal and Lt. Joseph H. Dirks received the Bella Stiefel Medal. Rescue 1 was awarded a Unit Citation.

Twenty days later, Rescue 1 was responding to a gas leak when they where redirected to a reported fire at 166 West 72nd Street. Firefighter Thomas Baker was at the wheel, as the company arrived at the scene. It was just after 7 a.m., on November 23, 1984 and the first alarm companies were at work with smoke visible on the sixth floor. Lt. Curran and a team headed for the stairs, as Firefighter Baker and Hashagen prepared to ascend above via Ladder 25's aerial.

As the two members of Ladder 25, Firefighters Johnson and Yard were venting windows, a firefighter, Thomas Bala of Ladder 35, appeared at an adjacent window. Bala was surrounded by heavy pumping smoke, with quickly extending fire rolling overhead. Firefighters Baker and Hashagen had just been speaking with the chauffeur, Firefighter Bruce Newbery, (soon to be a member of Rescue 1), about the possible repositioning of the ladder, when the firefighter appeared. Members on the aerial ladder above were stretching out to reach the trapped firefighter, but the distance was too far to reach him safely. Firefighter Hashagen went for a portable ladder from the aerial's bed, as Baker ran to a tower ladder parked nearby and began setting it up for operation.

Within seconds conditions around Bala had become extreme. He was now straddling the window sill, with fire shooting out above his head six stories above 72nd Street. A huge crowd of spectators watched as a portable ladder was carried to the tip of the aerial and bridged across to Bala. He leaned out away from the fire raging over his head. Below him, Baker was ascending after single-handedly setting up the tower ladder. As members of Ladder 25 held the portable steady and Baker moved into position, the fire exploded behind Bala igniting his coat. Baker yelled to Bala to hold on, as he moved closer. With heavy fire above and around them, Baker reached across the gap pulling Bala into the bucket. Baker beat out the flaming coat and lowered the bucket towards the street.

Firefighter Thomas Bala was taken to the burn center where he was treated for first, second and third degree burns. For their valor Firefighters Yard and Johnson of Ladder 25 were awarded medals. Firefighter Thomas H. Baker Jr. would receive the Fire Marshal Benevolent Association Medal for his quick action and courage on the fateful morning.

Firefighter Thomas H. Baker, Jr.

Firefighters Thomas Baker and Thomas Bala meet in City Hall for the presentation of the Daily News Hero of the Month Award, December 1983.

A verbal alarm by off-duty members of Rescue 1 at 7:26 p.m., evolved into the largest single-building fire to strike New York City since 1967. This blaze, on January 23, 1985, broke out in the eight-story, 100 x 90-foot former piano factory building adjacent to company quarters on West 43rd Street. Rescue 1 arrived on the scene (after operating at another alarm) in the

At the height of the 10-alarm blaze hose streams were directed into the blazing building from every vantage point.

The 43rd Street side of the 10-alarm fire. (Harvey Eisner)

Hon. Battalion Chief John Gill took this amazing photo just as the wall collapsed onto Rescue 1's firehouse.

The original teleprinter message of the verbal alarm transmitted by members of Rescue 1 on January 23, 1985.

early stages of the fire. Despite the best efforts of the firefighters, the fire defied all efforts to contain it. With lightning speed the fire expanded to ten-alarms. The surrounding buildings were used as vantage points to direct multiple hose streams at the blaze.

Fearing the worst, members of Rescue 1, with the help of Firefighter Dan DeFranco, a union official and friend of the company, entered their threatened quarters and removed company records, gear, equipment and historic mementos from the first floor and office. As conditions worsened, the efforts were ended as the fire building's walls loomed over the firehouse threatening to fall at any moment. Fire was now venting out of more than eighty windows. Finally, the fire building collapsed. A huge section of the building's exposure 4-side brick wall plummeted through the roof of Rescue 1's quarters, virtually destroying it.

After a two hour and forty-two minute battle, Chief of Department John F. O'Rourke transmitted a probably will hold. A short while later, the Manhattan Fire Dispatcher asked the Field Communication Unit, if Rescue 1 was in service. After receiving an affirmative reply, the company was dispatched downtown for a man stuck in a machine. Upon completion of the assignment, the company rolled back to 43rd Street. There it finally sunk in…they were homeless.

Upon completion of the assignment, the company rolled back to 43rd Street. There it finally sunk in…they were homeless.

The next morning the damage to the firehouse could be clearly seen from above. (John Lee Gill)

Off-duty members of Rescue 2 join Rescue 1 as they dig through the firehouse rubble after the collapse.

From January 1985 until April 1989, Rescue 1 was stationed on West 38th Street with Engine 34 and Ladder 21.

Late in the morning, the company was stationed with Engine 23 on West 58th Street. Later that day, they moved to the quarters of Engine 34 and Ladder 21 at 440 West 38th Street where they would remain until their new quarters were built.

For many days afterwards, off-duty members of Rescue 1 worked their way through the rubble of their former firehouse recovering personal belongings and company tools and equipment. They were joined, at times, by members of other rescue companies and former members of Rescue 1. Despite the freezing weather, they helped with this time consuming operation. Former member Patrick Brown, brought his friend James Remar, the actor of "48 Hours" fame, and together spent many days working side by side with the members of Rescue 1 as the digging continued.

On the night of January 29, 1985, Rescue 1 responded to a wind-driven fire in a high rise multiple dwelling at 525 East 86th Street in Manhattan. The company conferred with Battalion Chief Petrocelli on the floor below the fire, before heading to the fire floor (sixth floor of the 20-story building). The company split with a two man team checking the layout of the floor below, and scouting for victims visible at windows above. One member was sent above to ventilate, the remaining members and the officer went to the fire floor. The company searched for and located the hose line, at the door of the fire apartment. Then proceeded under extreme conditions to press the attack into the wind driven flames. Despite the heavy fire, they were able to extinguish it and complete the searches. For their efforts the company was awarded a Unit Citation.

It was a bright and sunny afternoon on April 26, 1985. Rescue 1 was operating at a small fire in a high-rise building at Fifth Avenue and 53rd Street. A little over two miles away at the 34th Street heliport, a red and white Dauphin helicopter filled with passengers had just lifted off heading to JFK airport. Within moments a strange "clunk" was heard and the aircraft pitched left, lost power, and plunged into the East River. Moments later while stowing equipment in the rescue truck, Firefighter Norm Newkirk heard the Manhattan Fire Dispatcher announce a helicopter crash. Newkirk checked the company's availability with Lt. Curran. Two minutes later, the rig was rolling north with three rescue divers donning wet suits and SCUBA gear, in the rear of the bouncing rig.

Several civilians and police officers had entered the river helping the passengers and crew to shore, as Rescue 1 arrived. A small half-inch rope tethered the 40-foot long craft to a floating dock near the Water Club restaurant. The aircraft was upside down, and bobbing in the swift current. After securing himself with a tending rope, Rescue 1 Firefighter Paul Hashagen entered the water and swam to the helicopter. With reports of a passenger still inside the craft, Hashagen began a methodical search from the front to rear of the submerged aircraft. Moving among floating luggage and seat cushions, he located a passenger, in the last row of seats, upside-down, still belted in. Hashagen cut the seatbelt and swam the unconscious man to the surface.

Handing the man off, Hashagen paused briefly to catch his breath, as the rescue men and EMS worked on the unconscious passenger before rushing him across the street to Bellevue Hospital. Hashagen was joined in the water by Rescue 1 diver John Boyle, and together they completed a secondary search of the chopper and river bed below. Firefighter Paul F. Hashagen was awarded the Chief Tuttlemondo Medal. Rescue 1 was also awarded a Unit Citation.

It was just after noon, September 16, 1986. Rescue 1 was taking up from a small fire, when a dispatcher sent them to fill out a 10-75 signal at Box 1138, 483 Amsterdam Avenue, on the Upper Westside. As the company arrived, the entire fourth floor of the building was engulfed in flames. Firefighters Ronald Bucca and Thomas Reichel went into the adjoining tenement, on their way to the roof of the fire building. Facing a high heat condition from the blazing building next door, they suddenly heard a "Mayday!" crackle across their Handi-Talkie radios. A fire officer was trapped at a rear window, on the fifth floor of the fire building. Firefighter Bucca quickly made his way to the fire buildings rear fire escape, and started down the gooseneck ladder to help the trapped lieutenant.

Firefighter Paul F. Hashagen

Facing a high heat condition from the blazing building next door, they suddenly heard a "Mayday!" crackle across their Handi-Talkie radios.

Bucca reached the fifth floor fire escape landing and began an attack on the locked "scissor gates" that trapped the fire officer. Heavy smoke pumped from around the trapped man as Bucca, wearing his mask, began to pry with a Halligan tool. Leaning back to drive the tool into the window frame, Bucca slipped on broken glass, lost his footing and went over the edge of the railing. He fell past the fourth floor, the third floor, face up as he dropped. At the second floor level his air pack hit a metal conduit pipe that crossed the alley delivering electricity to the building. The impact flipped Bucca, and partially broke his fall. The former Green Beret paratrooper, landed hard on a pile of debris in the alley at the ground level.

Above, the trapped officer had broken free, climbed out onto the fire escape, and looked down. Below, the would-be rescuer was now lying in the alley, his boots at awkward angles, his body not moving. The officer transmitted another "Mayday!" This time for Firefighter Bucca.

Within minutes, members of Rescue 1 had Bucca immobilized, in a Stokes basket, and on his way to the Bellevue Hospital. There family, friends, off-duty rescue men and military friends descended on the hospital. Ronnie had suffered multiple contusions, a broken knee and had broken the first lumbar vertebra in his back.

Rescue 1 using pavement breaker inside burning restaurant, April 19, 1986.

Almost a year to the day, and after many hours of rigorous physical therapy, Firefighter Ronald Bucca, returned to the Division of Training and completely re-qualified as a FDNY full-duty firefighter. "The flying fireman" as he was called by some in the media, then walked through the doors of the firehouse and went back to work in Rescue 1.

It was just after 10 o'clock in the morning, when Rescue 1 arrived with first due units at 149 West 44th Street, a partially demolished vacant hotel, on September 30, 1986. Midtown firefighters became familiar with this building when the owner was caught illegally demolishing the structure without permits. They had also responded to other fires within the building, a dangerous refuge for some of the city's homeless. This morning, fire was blazing in the rear on three separate floors and extending quickly. With radio reports of water delays due to mechanical problems with a pumper, and with fire conditions worsening, a victim was seen on the roof. Firefighter Paul Hashagen took the interior stairs to the roof. There he met Lt. Tom Haring of Ladder 4, who had taken the same route moments before. They found the victim, actually two victims: twin brothers. The firefighters realized they could not re-enter the stairs. The only way off the roof was across a single beam, seven stories high and fifteen feet to a cantilevered aerial ladder.

With smoke pumping and swirling around them, Haring and Hashagen took the first brother across the beam to the aerial transferring him to the firefighter on the ladder. Firefighter Hashagen returned back across the beam to the roof, then started across the beam again, with the second brother. Approaching Haring, the second victim froze in fear. Then lunged at the officer. Haring held both the ladder and the victim, trying to maintain balance. Hashagen had to climb over the victim, and onto the aerial. Together they physically lifted the man up and onto the aerial ladder. Lt. Haring and Firefighter Hashagen were next to each other again at Medal Day. Firefighter Paul Hashagen was presented the Trevor-Warren and Police Honor Legion Medals for this rescue.

Rescue 1 members descending aerial after rescues were made at the partially demolished hotel, September 30, 1986.

> They found the victim, actually two victims: twin brothers. The firefighters realized they could not re-enter the stairs. The only way off the roof was across a single beam, seven stories high and fifteen feet to a cantilevered aerial ladder.

Firefighter John McClusky of Engine 54 took this shot of Rescue 1 saving the WNBC traffic helicopter pilot.

History has a habit of repeating itself. On October 22, 1986, the afternoon rush hour had just begun. While reporting live on the air, an WNBC traffic helicopter lost power and plunged into the Hudson River near the Intrepid Sea, Air and Space Museum at 45th Street and Twelfth Avenue. It was 4:44 p.m. One minute later Rescue 1 was rolling out of their quarters on West 38th Street with the on-duty crew and several off-duty members on board. Upon arrival, Firefighters Paul Hashagen and George Kreuscher finished donning SCUBA gear and entered the water. Hashagen swam to Rescue 1 Firefighter John Driscoll who'd jumped in the water, and located the very tip of one of the helicopters rotor blades underwater. Hashagen submerged and followed the blade down to the helicopter, now resting on the river bottom, in twenty-feet of water.

Hashagen located the pilot, William Pate, cut his seatbelt, and quickly surfaced with him, turning the unconscious victim over to rescue men Driscoll, Baker and Kreuscher. Hashagen returned to the submerged copter and located Jane Dornacker, the traffic reporter, and brought her to the surface. Joining the members already in the water Captain O'Flaherty, Lieutenant John Cerato and Firefighters John Theobald and Michael McLoughlin were busy performing mouth to mouth resuscitation and preparing the victims to be hauled to the street, while Hashagen completed a secondary underwater search.

> After a few minutes the tension was released as "He's breathing!" was shouted.

On the street, members of Engine 34 and 54, and Ladders 4 and 21 frantically worked on the two victims providing CPR and using resuscitators. After a few minutes the tension was released as "He's breathing!" was shouted. The efforts continued as both patients were rushed to nearby hospitals. Sadly, Jane Dornacker could not be revived. Her pilot would make a full recovery.

For his efforts at the WNBC helicopter crash Firefighter Paul F. Hashagen was awarded the Thomas E. Crimmins Medal. The members of Rescue Company 1 were not only awarded a unit citation, but would receive the first Burn Center Medal for outstanding company operations to ever be awarded. These members were:

Captain Brian O'Flaherty,
Lieutenant John Cerato,
Firefighters John Theobald,
Thomas Baker, John Driscoll,
George Kreuscher, Paul Hashagen
and Michael McLoughlin (L4)

Ground breaking ceremony on November 20, 1986.

Another landmark day for Rescue Company 1 was November 20, 1986. This cool, and slightly overcast day was actually a bright ray of sunshine for Captain Brian O'Flaherty and Lieutenant John Cerato, who both had been working tirelessly on a plan to re-build the company's quarters lost on January 23, 1985. This Thursday afternoon saw Fire Commissioner Joseph Spinatto, Chief of Department, Robert Butler, and union representatives Vincent Bollon and Nick Mancuso joining the officers and members of Rescue 1 at a ground breaking ceremony. Also in attendance was Firefighter Ron Bucca, who just two months before sustained a broken back while attempting to rescue a trapped fire officer. Bucca somehow managed to look sharp, despite a back and neck brace.

Two months later Rescue 1 was responding to yet another Hudson River dive job. The company was special called to Christopher Street at 10:22 p.m., on January 9, 1987, a bitterly cold night. Reports were that a man had fallen into the water off the Greenwich Village pier. Firefighter Norman L. Newkirk donned his gear and entered the 38 degree water, and began a search in the cold black waters. After covering the piling area, he initiated a crescent or half-moon search pattern (using the tender as a focal point the diver swims a 180-degree arc underwater, extending outward or inward after each pass).

With zero visibility and briefly becoming entangled in a submerged bicycle, Newkirk continued across the muddy bottom 30-feet below the surface and 50-feet from the dock. Here he contacted the victim's foot. Newkirk turned the man over, wrapped his arms around his chest, and inflated his vest bringing them both to the surface. At the surface, Newkirk was met by rescue man Ray Brown who helped swim the victim back to the ladder. The man was rushed to St. Vincent's Hospital where he died ten days later.

For his outstanding underwater rescue in frigid conditions, Firefighter Norman L. Newkirk was awarded the Susan Wagner Medal.

The winter of 1987 would prove to be filled with heroic actions by the members of Rescue 1 both on and off-duty. While traveling westbound on I-95 on his way home from his honeymoon, Firefighter Barry Meade came upon an accident scene on the side of the road. It was January 19th, 3:37 p.m. Only moments before, a van carrying a family of five, slid on some ice, hit a guard rail and plunged into the river. The van submerged into 12-feet of water about 30-feet from the shoreline of the East River located on the Guilford-Madison (Connecticut) Town Line. Despite freezing rain, air temperature of 20-degrees and a water temperature of 30-degrees, Meade pulled his car over, pulled rope from the trunk of his car, and sprang into action.

Meade, a certified rescue diver, entered the icy waters with a length of rope, and joined a man already in the water attempting to save an eight year old boy. Meade tied the rope around the child, and helped the other man return to the shore with the child. He then made several attempts to gain entry into the submerged vehicle in search of others still believed to be in the van. As fire units arrived, Meade called for tools to cut the roof open. With the effects of hypothermia setting in Meade reluctantly returned to shore and was take to the hospital for medical attention. In recognition of his heroic actions, Meade received a personal letter from President Ronald Reagan and his wife Nancy.

The following month Rescue 1 responded to an early morning fire at 405 West 40th Street, with Lieutenant Stephen J. Casani in charge. It was 2:24 a.m., on February 26, 1987 when a "10-75" was transmitted for Manhattan Box 765. Rescue 1 arrived with the first due units at the five-story multiple dwelling, where fire was showing out three windows on the second floor rear. The company went right to work. Casani and his forcible entry team went to the floor above to initiate searches. Every floor in the building was filled with heavy smoke, and conditions were becoming worse by the minute. Lt. Casani had his team continue searching the third floor, as he made his way to the fourth.

As the officer reached that level, his radio crackled with a report of a victim hanging out a rear window on the fourth floor. Casani quickly made his way down the hallway finding the door locked. With several shoulder slams, he burst through the door, and into the smoke filled apartment cluttered with personal belongings. Weaving his way through the maze of stuff, Casani found the 250-pound man semi-conscious near the window. Half carrying and dragging he pulled the large man down the hall, then down the stairs to a front apartment on the third-floor. Realizing the man was injured, Casani called for a tower ladder and passed the man out into the bucket, before returning to the fourth floor searches. The man was rushed to the hospital and treated for both smoke inhalation and a heart attack. He stayed twelve days in the hospital, before being released to a convalescent home.

> The company went right to work. Casani and his forcible entry team went to the floor above to initiate searches. Every floor in the building was filled with heavy smoke, and conditions were becoming worse by the minute.

Lt. Stephen Casani

For his extraordinary efforts at great personal risk Lieutenant Stephen J. Casani was awarded the Uniformed Fire Officers Association Medal.

In the spring of 1987, Rescue Company 1 received one of two new rigs purchased by the department. Massive by any standards, the truck had dual rear axles and was both longer and higher than any previous rescue apparatus. At the time, the new trucks were among the largest rescue trucks ever built for any department. They were built by Saulsbury on Mack MC chassis and had a far greater carrying capacity for tools and equipment. They were also equipped with a rear-mounted winch and portable A-frame crane. Purchased with funds from the 1985 fiscal budget, they were termed 1985 models by the department. The two rigs arrived with different lettering, the first time the department allowed the companies to design their own lettering. Rescue 1 was assigned shop number MR8501. This rig, incidentley, was over twice as long as the original 1914 Cadillac.

It was just after 4 on the afternoon of April 8, 1987 when Rescue 1 was special called to a building collapse in the Bronx. A gas explosion (the meter was later found to have three bullet holes in it) caused the collapse of a one-story grocery store and a four-story vacant tenement, trapping numerous people inside.

In the Spring of 1987 Rescue 1 received this Mack/Saulsbury rig. It was twice the length of the original apparatus.

Rescue 1 worked this Bronx explosion and collapse on April 8, 1987. (Harvey Eisner)

Rescue 1 responded with the entire day crew plus the officer and two firefighters scheduled to work that evening. Deputy Chief McBride sent Rescue 1 to the rear of the building to search the collapse area for trapped people. Lt. Ellson split the company into two teams: Ellson and Firefighters Henry Molle and Bruce Newbery entered the voids of the four-story building and began a search, while Firefighters Al Fuentes, Thomas Reichel and Don Sollecito entered the one-story building searching the voids and the basement. After completing both searches with negative results, Rescue 1 joined Rescue 3 providing additional shoring and bracing, then helped remove a 37-year-old man trapped in the rubble.

Firefighters Fuentes and Reichel entered the cellar to shore up beneath another victim found pinned in the debris. Molle and Newbery cut shoring to the needed size, then passed them to Fuentes and Reichel. During the operation Firefighter Fuentes calmed the trapped man explaining in Spanish what was being done to help him. This man was then carefully removed by rescue men from above.

Another victim, deceased, was located by Rescue 1. For the next hour this victim was dug out. Lt. Casani and Firefighters Thomas Baker and Barry Meade helped to extricate from above. Yet another victim was located, as this one was removed. For their professional efforts and teamwork performed under extremely dangerous conditions Rescue 1 was awarded a Unit Citation.

On June 8, 1987 Rescue 1 responded to a verbal alarm for a fire on the 9th floor of the Holland House, a 21-story welfare hotel at 351 West 42nd Street. Arriving first due, the company was met by a stream of fleeing occupants. The stairs were packed with excited people, mostly women and children. Lt. Ellson split the company into three teams: Firefighters Joseph Angelini, John Boyle and himself took the interior stairs, as

Rescue 1 removing injured victim from the rubble.

Firefighters Paul Hashagen, John Theobald, Michael Fitzgerald, and Carl Feilmoser took the elevator to the 7th floor. Hashagen and Theobald entered the fire floor, as Fitzgerald and Feilmoser hurried to the smoke filled floor above.

On the fire floor the two rescue men located the blazing apartment and tried to hold the flames back with a water extinguisher, as they controlled the fire spreading into the hallway over their heads by closing the apartment door. Handi-talkie reports from arriving units indicated a woman trapped at a 9th floor window screaming for help. Lt. Ellison and Firefighter Angelini forced the door, crawled in and found a woman and three children gasping for breath in the heavy smoke. They hurried them out to the rear stairs, and down to the street for first aid. The teamwork of the company averted a possible severe loss of life, by the rapid containment of the fire and the removal of the imperiled victims. Rescue 1 was awarded a Unit Citation.

Rescue 1 responded to a report of people in the water at West and 12th Streets on July 14, 1987 at 5:20 p.m. The company arrived at the pier, in the middle of a thunder storm, as surface victims were being removed from the river by first due units. With confirmed reports of a submerged victim, Rescue 1 prepared to conduct an underwater search and rescue operation. Lt. Casani located the point of operations sixty yards from the shoreline. Despite conflicting reports of the victims last known location, and a strong tide, the operation began as two members of Rescue 1, donned SCUBA gear and began their search. As their tanks became low on air, a team of back-up divers relieved them and continued the search. After fifty-five minutes of blackwater searching the victims was located and brought to the surface.

The Coney Island Creek in Brooklyn was the scene of a multiple drowning incident on July 26, 1987. Rescue Companies 2, 5 and 1 responded and entered the water to conduct searches. This was the first incident at which all three FDNY SCUBA units operated at the same time.

The time was 11 a.m., on November 11, 1987 when Rescue 1 responded to 177 Sullivan Street for a reported building collapse. Upon arrival, Lt. Ellson was informed by B.C. Turner that Ladder 9 had located an unknown number of victims buried and trapped, in the rear of the building. Ellson split the company into two teams: he and Firefighters Raymond Brown (son of former Rescue 1 Fireman and Lieutenant Raymond M. Brown), Don Sollecito and Joseph Pierotti assisted Ladder 9 in the rear, while Firefighters John McAllister and Henry Molle focused their searches in the front of the building. In the rear some debris was moved, and two victims were located and taken to EMS. This team then began a secondary search in the rear for any other victims.

While the search continued in the rear, Firefighter Molle located a 30-year-old woman trapped under a collapsed section of the third floor. Molle and McAllister, now joined by members of Rescue 3, began to shore up the surrounding sections. Finally, they were able to extricate the victim and hand her over for medical attention. Rescue 1 was awarded a Unit Citation for their efforts at this operation.

On December 28, 1987, Rescue 1 along with Rescue 2, responded to Staten Island to back up Rescue 5 at a prolonged SCUBA operation. A hard-hat commercial diver had become trapped under a concrete piling sixty-feet below the surface, at the site of the U.S. Navy home-port construction site. The involved and dangerous rescue took several hours to complete; the diver was removed safely. This was the deepest successful rescue dive ever made within the city.

In the early part of 1988, Rescue 1 was issued a Thermal Imaging Device. This electronic device was capable of discerning less than one degree of difference in temperature, and has become an extremely effective tool to search for victims in

Members of Rescue 1 removing a victim from a building collapse on Seventh Avenue in Manhattan on July 31, 1988. (Steve Spak)

building collapses. Other uses include searching for fire hidden in walls and ductwork, "seeing" through dense smoke conditions, and searching for victims in fires and similar situations. The new EEV thermal imaging device had been used by the U.S. Navy for shipboard firefighting.

The Rescue Liaison Unit was added to the FDNY in May of 1988. This unit acted as an inter-agency coordinator during rescue operations, and at joint operations between the FDNY and other city agencies. The unit was manned by three Rescue Captains who responded on all third alarms, SCUBA incidents, major emergencies, special operations and performed as the FDNY liaison at these incidents. They also helped coordinate the Rescue Companies, Haz-Mat and the Marine Division. Car 13-D, was staffed by a captain and firefighter 24 hours a day, that responded from Roosevelt Island. The original officers were: Captain Brian O'Flaherty Rescue 1, Captain Ray Downey Rescue 2, and two former members of Rescue 1, John Cerato and James Rogers (both of whom would later return to the company and serve as captain).

The last victim of the 31st Street collapse was removed alive nine hours later by Rescue 1.

Back in 1982, the Rescue Services unit was organized. It was staffed by an acting-battalion chief and a firefighter. Their mission was to provide assistance with tool and equipment purchases, training and administrative support, and other issues involving the Rescue Companies.

Another big step was made by the department when classes were held in the quarters of Rescue 5 on Staten Island to certify FDNY SCUBA instructors. Members of Rescue 1, 2 and 5 were chosen to participate in this two week class given by Walt Hendrik, a former US Navy SEAL. To facilitate their attendance at this course, the rescue members were allowed to make self mutuals to be paid back at the convenience of their local battalion. (Rescues were still assigned to battalions at this time.)

On October 24, 1988, a six-story building at 24 West 31st Street collapsed during repair work to a bearing wall. Rescue 1 responded. They were joined by Rescue Companies 3 and 4, Haz-Mat 1 and the Rescue Liaison Unit. Numerous victims were removed during the initial operations, then over nine-hours later, the rescue companies removed the last victim, a young woman, digging her out by hand.

Rescue 1 responded to Box 239 for a fire on the 6th floor of a 20-story multiple dwelling at 269 East Broadway on December 3, 1988. As the rig rolled to a stop, flames were seen blowing out a window on the 6th floor. As Rescue 1 members made their way towards the front entrance the fire disappeared, now blown inwards by a change in wind direction. Seconds later the handi-talkies came alive with "May-Day!" messages from the fire floor. Rescue hustled up the stairs towards the fire. The hallway above had become a blow torch burning and scattering the first due engine and trucks members.

Injured firefighters were tumbling down the crowded stairway. B.C. Rittmeyer advised Rescue 1 of the conditions above further stating that members were missing. The company was split into two teams: Lt. Ellson and Firefighters Hashagen and Angelini,

Group shot of off and on-duty members of Rescue 1 after operating at the 31st Street collapse, October 24, 1988.

and a second team of Firefighters Molle, Schmidt and Williams. Upon reaching the fire floor both teams encountered extreme heat and smoke; fire was blowing out of the fully involved apartment and flames were rolling across the hallway ceilings.

The search of the hallway began without the benefit of hoseline protection and within minutes the members found the captain of Engine 17 and helped him to the doorway. Crawling towards the fire apartment, Hashagen and Angelini located the hoseline and began an aggressive attack knocking the flames back into the fire apartment and regaining control of the hallway. With the hallway search completed, team two members moved in with the advancing hose to search the fire apartment. Despite the wind whipped flames and extreme heat, the members of Rescue 1 were able to extinguish the fire and finish the search of the fire apartment. For their team work under these extreme conditions the company was awarded a Unit Citation.

At the request of the Hoboken Fire Department, on April 2, 1989, Rescue Company 1 was special-called to Box 5001 to respond to Hoboken, New Jersey on mutual aid. Members of Rescue 1 were transported across the Hudson River by Marine 2 for the purpose of locating and searching a submerged auto. Two rescue divers, Firefighters Hank Molle and Neal Fredericksen, made primary and secondary searches of the submerged auto which proved to be negative. They then attached a cable to the underside of the vehicle, which was later pulled from the water. This was Rescue Company 1's first request on a mutual aid call for SCUBA operations.

The company moved into their new quarters on April 29, 1988.

First time a truck was backed into the new firehouse.

Rescue 1 Company Journal
Saturday, April 29, 1989

0900   RCD- Conducted R-1 members acc'td for Viz.
OD (9X6) Capt. O'Flaherty, FF Carroll, Driscoll, Killoran, Boyle, Hashagen
IC (6X9) Lt. Fischler, FF Carroll, Theobald, Burns, Driscoll, Geraghty
EE- Dept PAQ & Journal entries examined as per Regs.

Capt. Brian E. O'Flaherty

0900   Sp. This was the last roll call entry made in the quarters of Eng. 34/Lad. 21. Rescue 1 is moving today to the new quarters. We owe a special thanks to the officers and members of Eng. 34 & Lad. 21 for the hospitality extended to R-1 over the past 4 years. From this point onward the operation, administration, and records will again be recorded in this Company Journal.

0900   Sp. Capt. O'Flaherty records that the following members of Rescue 1 participated in moving all our equipment and furniture: 9X6 OD Platoon, Capt. O'Flaherty, Fr. Boyle, Carroll, Driscoll, Hashagen & Killoran. Off-duty Members: Lts. Casani, Ellison & Fischler, Fr's Angelini, Burns, Cody, Fredericksen, Geraghty, Harrell, Kreuscher, McAllister, Molle, Newbery, Riley, Schmidt, Theobald, Williams and also former members Brown, Bessman. Gentlemen thank you without your help this move would have been very long and drawn out.

1300   Capt. O'Flaherty records bringing Apparatus and members of R-1 over to new qtrs. (530 W. 43 St.) from here we will operate from this time forward.

On April 29, 1989, Rescue Company 1 moved to their new quarters on West 43rd Street. This building was constructed specifically for them, on the site of their old quarters destroyed by the 1985 fire. The entire original facade of the old building was incorporated into the new structure, as the rear wall of the new kitchen. With operations back on 43rd Street for the third time, yet another chapter was added to the company's history.

That morning Captain Brian O'Flaherty broke out the old Rescue 1 Company Journal. The last entry was Thursday, January 24, 1985 when Lt. John Cerato recorded the temporary suspension of the journal while R1 was quartered on 38th Street.

It was ten minutes to the nine o'clock start of the day tour on June 2, 1989 when Rescue 1 was dispatched to Manhattan Box 1506 for a building collapse at 135 West 128th Street, a four-story vacant tenement under renovation. Rescue 3 was on scene trying to reach a trapped worker buried beneath a major center collapse. The Rescue 3 officer via handi-talkie indicated immediate shoring was needed on the exposure #2 side of the first floor of this extremely unstable structure. Under the command of Lt. Jay Fischler, Rescue 1 sprang into action. Firefighters Edward Geraghty and George Kreuscher began skillfully placing trench jacks to several large timbers hanging precariously above the rescue operation. Firefighter Neal Fredericksen was assigned to operate with members of Rescue 3 to assist with the medical support of the trapped victim. While working in a confined area for a prolonged period of time, Fredericksen was able to administer oxygen and provide a primary and secondary patient survey.

Rescue chauffeur Daniel Killoran was able to position the rig, despite the apparatus jammed street, close enough to utilize the 15 KW onboard generator. Firefighter Thomas Baker was assigned to provide tools and power supplies to rescue members in the collapse zone. He set up much needed lighting and a tool staging area complete with: electric chain saws, sawzalls, torches, circular saws, and assorted hand tools.

Battalion 16 requested an assessment of the basement area below the collapse; Firefighters Killoran and John Carroll were assigned the task. They located and reported several potentially dangerous areas, then skillfully and carefully shored these areas. About halfway through the operation a secondary collapse occurred. Despite rumbling and a dust cloud, the strategically placed shoring minimized any shifting. Additional shoring was placed, as the trapped man was extricated. For their professionalism and teamwork, Rescue 1 was awarded a Unit Citation.

"Ten-seventy five Box 195!" echoed across the Manhattan fire radio prompting the dispatch of Rescue 1 at 1:01 a.m., September 3, 1989. Within minutes the rig was rolling to a blazing public hotel at 92 Bowery. The four-story building was filled with more than 200 cubicles, with open ceilings above. Heavy smoke and heat was pouring from all the windows of the third floor, cutting off the fire escape for any tenants above. Rescue 1 was assigned primary search of the floor above the fire (the fourth floor). Under the command of Lt. Casani, who realized the interior stairs might be compromised by fire, sent Firefighters Daniel Killoran, Henry Molle and Ron Bucca to the roof in an attempt to cover the fourth floor from that direction. Casani took Firefighters Thomas Baker and Ed Geraghty and headed up the interior stairs.

Entering the floor above, they found heavy smoke and heat. They soon realized they had numerous locked cubicles (with doors that open outwards) that had to be forced and searched. After forcing six door they found a semi-conscious man. He was dragged out and handed off to other firefighters. Meanwhile, the other team had descended down through extreme heat and smoke conditions and began their search from the Hester Street side of the building. This team also found an unconscious man and dragged him out. In addition, the company located several points of fire extension and called for a line before dropping down to the fire floor and helping the first due units complete the primary search.

Despite the heavy smoke, high heat and numerous locked doors the company operated quickly and was able to save the lives of at least two men. For their outstanding work at this second alarm they were awarded a Unit Citation.

The evening rush hour was reaching it's height on September 11, 1989 when just before 6:30 p.m., an accelerating commuter bus bound for New Jersey crashed into the brick wall entrance to the Lincoln Tunnel. Upon arrival Rescue 1 was faced with numerous injured passengers and two critically injured passengers pinned in the wreckage. Lt. Ellson split the company into two teams, one working inside the bus and the other working the outside. Inside, two passengers seated directly behind the bus driver's seat were seriously injured with their feet and legs entangled in a crushed section of the bus. Firefighter Hashagen called for tools and began immediate first aid. Firefighters Harrell and Driscoll set up two Hurst tools for immediate operations as the outside crew began to peel away the outer sections of the bus. Inside spreaders and cutters were used to clear away the twisted wreckage and expose the actual point of entrapment. For thirty minutes both teams carefully cut, pulled and cleared their way through the mangled steel until the first trapped passenger was removed. For the next fifteen minutes, using rams and air bags, the second victim was delicately freed.

On September 20, 1989, the FDNY responded to LaGuardia Airport when U.S. Air Flight 5050, a Boeing 737-400 jetliner, slid off the end of runway 13-31 after an aborted takeoff. The huge jet was filled with 57 passengers and a crew of six, when it's momentum carried it off the end of the runway snapping it into three pieces. The Rescue Liaison Unit, Captain John Cerato, immediately requested that all three of the FDNY scuba units respond. Rescues 1, 2 and 5 were added to the ticket that already included Rescue 3 and 4 as well as Haz-Mat 1 and a host of engine and ladder companies.

Rescue 1 Firefighter Carl Feilmoser, who was driving Captain Cerato that night, tied off one end of a lifeline on shore then entered the water and swam to the left wing and tied the rope off at the emergency exit. This would pinpoint the exit if the plane sank. Feilmoser and members of Rescue 3, 4 and Haz-Mat 1, then entered the partially submerged jetliner and began a dangerous extrication of trapped passengers. FDNY divers descended beneath the sinking tail section of the plane with a large steel sling, which was attached to Rescue 5's "A-frame". This action gave a small measure of safety to the members operating inside the aircraft.

Numerous persons were rescued from inside the aircraft and many others, including uniformed police officers who were swept away by the incoming tide, were pulled from the dark, cold, jet fuel covered waters around the crash site by members of Rescue 1 and 2 working from small boats. In all, five members would receive medals for their heroism including, Firefighter Carl B. Feilmoser of Rescue Company 1 who was awarded the Fireman David J. DeFranco Medal.

> The huge jet was filled with 57 passengers and a crew of six, when it's momentum carried it off the end of the runway snapping it into three pieces. The Rescue Liaison Unit, Captain John Cerato, immediately requested that all three of the FDNY scuba units respond. Rescues 1, 2 and 5 were added to the ticket that already included Rescue 3 and 4 as well as Haz-Mat 1 and a host of engine and ladder companies.

Chapter 9

The Nineties

The "nineteen-nineties" would be a decade of growth, technical training and of course fire duty for the members of Rescue Company 1 and the New York City Fire Department. In 1990, the FDNY became part of the Federal Emergency Management Agency's Urban Search and Rescue program. Members of the rescue companies made up the majority of the FDNY portion of New York City Task Force 1 (NYTF-1). One of 26 teams across the country, NYTF-1 could be deployed rapidly with a complete cache of tools, supplies, food and water, and be self-sufficient for up to seven days.

In February 1990, the FDNY organized the Special Operations Command (SOC) to address the administrative and training needs of the nine diversified units of the Department. Now under one command were: the Rescue Companies, the Marine Division, Hazardous Materials Unit, Squad 1, Rescue Liaison Unit, Mask Service Unit, Field Communications Unit, and the Decontamination Unit.

March 8, 1990 was a day of celebration for Rescue Company 1. It marked the company's 75th Anniversary. A party was held on board a ship moored on the Hudson River. Past and present members were joined by other firefighters, chief officers, and friends of the company. This author's first book: FIRE RESCUE, The History of FDNY Rescue Company 1 was given as gift to each of the current members of the company. The book, published by Jack Calderone's Fire Apparatus Journal Publications, was to be a small pamphlet to hand out at the anniversary party, but expanded into an eighty-eight page book filled with color and black & white photos thanks to Jack Calderone and Herb Eysser.

The Ansonia, a once elegant upper westside hotel located on Broadway between 73rd and 74th Streets, is an eighteen-story Beaux-Art style building that was built in 1899 and featured a mansard roof, elaborate cornices and round corner turrets. The building once a residential hotel, housed many famous people in its glory days including: Babe Ruth, composer Igor Stravinsky and Italian tenor Enrico Caruso.

Now a condo, the building featured a number of commercial establishments on the first floor along Broadway. One of these storefronts was operated by Croissant & Co., a bustling neighborhood coffeehouse. On March 12, 1990, the store was filled with customers and staff, when suddenly the ceiling collapsed, into the store. Four thousand pounds of concrete and plaster crashed down killing one customer standing at the counter. Ruptured water pipes broken overhead rained cold water down on top of the collapse area adding to the devastating scene below. FDNY units, including Rescue 1 under the command of Captain Brian O'Flaherty, responded to the scene with two additional members scheduled to work that evening. Rescue 1 chopped through a huge section of shattered glass and entered the water soaked rubble. The sheets of cascading water made the searches even more difficult and dangerous than usual.

A woman found buried up to her neck in debris was dug free, and taken from the building in a Stokes basket. The captain and two firefighters climbed over the counter and under a lean-to section of collapse debris, and removed two people trapped there. The searches continued, as FDNY members aided the injured and controlled the utilities. In all one woman was killed, and sixteen people were injured. For their efforts under these extreme conditions Rescue 1 was awarded a Unit Citation.

> Members of Rescue 1 assisted the injured to a place of safety, then helped the re-assembled nozzle teams. Two attack lines, inched their way into the wind driven inferno to extinguish. Four civilians and 34 firefighters were injured in the blaze.

A five-alarm fire broke out on the 51st floor of the Empire State Building on July 16, 1990 at 6:30 p.m. First due units were confronted by a heavy fire condition that vented into the hallway after a glass partition failed. Several members were injured, as flames blow torched down the hallway towards the fire tower. Members of Rescue 1 assisted the injured to a place of safety, then helped the re-assembled nozzle teams. Two attack lines, inched their way into the wind-driven inferno to extinguish the fire. Four civilians and 34 firefighters were injured in the blaze.

The following month a stubborn fire was battled in a three-story Con Ed substation at 237 Front Street in Manhattan. Rescue 1 and downtown units battled the flames for more than five hours. The August 13th fire caused a power outage that affected the entire downtown business district for many hours. The United States Coast Guard provided mutual aid, in the form of a unit carrying 150 pounds of dry chemical agent. The dry chemical was not used however. Thirty firefighters were injured during this long operation.

The next day, August 14, 1990, Con Ed was busy trying to get customers back on line. Some buildings never lost power due to back-up generators. One of those buildings was the New York Infirmary-Beekman Downtown Hospital. At about 3:30 p.m., the hospital's back-up generator died plunging the hospital into total darkness, and stopping all the emergency life saving equipment such as automatic ventilators and heart monitoring devices. The huge building also lost all of it's air conditioning, making a bad situation worse. The staff scrambled to the patients most in need, and began manual ventilation. The FDNY was called. Rescue 1 and other units raced to the scene.

Arriving quickly, Rescue 1's officer Lieutenant Jay Fischler split his team, to size up where power would be needed most, and to ready the rigs onboard generator to supply these most critical areas. Rescue firefighters were directed to various floors and units inside the hospital, and consulted the exhausted staff members who were hard at work manually bagging patients. A list was developed, and access points through front windows was established. Ropes were dropped, and electrical cables were pulled up and fastened in place. Power was started, and the most critical patient's equipment were the first to be attached. The most critical patient was back online approximately 4-minutes from the time Rescue 1 began to deploy their resources. A difficulty then arose, as rescue men realized the electricity they could provide was really designed to power large pavement breakers and other high wattage tools, and could not be easily branched out to supply the many small but vital units the hospital needed.

After a brief meeting, a team ran several blocks to a hardware store where they "commandeered" several dozen power strips, power splitters and small extension cords. They ran back to the hospital. Within a several minutes every important piece of equipment was powered up and in service by a bank of FDNY portable generators. Each power line was marked at both ends stating at each generator: where the power went, and in the hospital: which generator below fed power inside. This would avoid any confusion, if a problem developed on either end.

Rescue 1 and other FDNY units powering the ICU unit of Beekman Hospital on August 14, 1990.

This operation continued on into the night. Members were relieved on scene by the night tour. Another large portable generator was put into service to power the hospital, but that too ran into problems. The FDNY generators picked up the load again. Later that evening complete power was finally restored. Members of both tours working in Rescue 1 received Unit Citations for their life saving efforts. Not one of the many critical patient was lost during this challenging emergency.

In a letter to Fire Commissioner Carlos Rivers, the hospital's administrator and chief operating officer Lin H. Ho wrote:

"I must express my deepest gratitude to the heroes of the New York City Fire Department.

"On the afternoon of 8/4/90, the NYC fire fighters successfully prevented the loss of lives at our hospital when they pulled and hooked up portable generator lines from the Gold Street side of the hospital to the 3rd, 4th and 5th floors of the hospital where 25 of these critically ill patients were located.

"For everything that the firefighters gave our patients, I am forever indebted to them."

On May 13, 1991 Rescue 1 responded to 230 West 113th Street for a fire in a 6-story tenement. On their arrival, heavy smoke and fire was out three windows on the fourth floor. The company was ordered above the fire and search for trapped occupants and extension. With the fire building's stairs clogged with hoses and fleeing civilians, Lt. Ellson split the company with one team using the front fire escape to gain access (Ellson, and Firefighters Ed Mauro and John Moran) and the other (Firefighters Harvey Harrell, Gary Geidel and Bruce Newbery) to come across from the roof of the adjoining building.

The team crossing the roof immediately found an elderly woman, on the rear fire escape of the fire building and removed her to safety. She informed them that a handicapped man was trapped in a sixth floor apartment. They radioed this information. Lt. Ellson and FF Mauro entered the smoke filled apartment and located the leg-less man, placed a mask over his face and placed him on the fire escape. FF Gary Geidel removed his Scott mask and carried the 70-year old man "piggy-back" to the roof and safety.

While this rescue was in progress FF Harrell informed Lt. Ellson the other team was going to the assistance of a trapped firefighter on the fifth floor directly above the fire apartment. Harrell used an aerial ladder to enter the adjoining apartment where he met other firefighters trying to reach the trapped man. Rescue Firefighters John Moran and Bruce Newbery saw the trapped fireman from the street. Moran placed an aerial ladder to the window and Newbery hustled up to help the firefighter and other members out to safety. For their actions at this four-alarm fire Rescue 1 was awarded a Unit Citation.

On the following day, May 14th, one of the most spectacular fire rescues ever captured on film occurred high above the streets of Times Square. Box 837 was transmitted for a fire on the top floor of 737 Seventh Avenue at 48th Street in Manhattan. Rescue 1, under the command of Lieutenant Patrick Brown, arrived and found heavy smoke venting from the 12th floor of the commercial building. Excited civilians pointed to

Lt. Brown directs the lowering of FF Kevin Shea, who dangles high above Times Square on May 14, 1991.

The exhausted members of Rescue 1 meet the media after the amazing double rope rescue.

two men, trapped at windows on separate sides of the corner building. Battalion Chief John McDermott ordered Rescue 1 to effect the rescues.

On the roof the lifesaving rope was readied, as Lieutenant Brown climbed onto the parapet to communicate with one of the trapped men. Firefighter Patrick Barr of Ladder 43, detailed to Rescue 1 for the day, climbed over the parapet and waited while Firefighter Kevin Shea got into position to lower him. With nowhere to tie off and little time to improvise, Shea took turns of rope on the Atlas life belt and sat on the roof with his feet against the parapet.

As Barr was lowered, the weight on the rope began to lift Shea. Firefighters Bruce Newbery and Patrick O'Keefe moved in, physically holding Shea to the roof. Barr arrived at the window and took the man in his arms. They were carefully lowered to the 11th floor, where members of Ladders 21 and 35 cleared glass and pulled the men in the window, to the cheers of the growing crowd below. A quick wave of Barr's hand was seen to acknowledge the cheering.

The rope was untied and pulled back to the roof, and the operation shifted to the other side of the building. Since the rope had been subjected to the weight of two persons, Lieutenant Brown ordered the ends of the rope to be switched as the second evolution commenced. This time Shea was attached to the end of the rope. Firefighter Raymond McCormack of Ladder 24 would do the lowering with Newbery and O'Keefe holding

him down. Moments later Shea was dangling over the streets, as video cameras again filmed the action. The second man was plucked from his window and lowered with Shea to the floor below. The huge crowd again cheered the heroic acrobatics, as both men were pulled inside the building.

Below them the fire had reached three-alarms, but the men of Rescue 1 were not finished. A faint call of "Mayday" was heard on the Handie-Talkies. Firefighters Bruce Newbery and Patrick O'Keefe, already exhausted from the double roof rope rescues, plunged into the super heated top floor. Searching in zero visibility and a high heat condition, they located an exhausted firefighter attempting to drag and unconscious fire officer. Teaming up, they dragged the officer down the hall to the stairs and to safety. Only then could the company reorganize and help to extinguish the raging fire.

Kevin Shea

Television news shows across the nation and around the world showed the amazing rescue for the next several days. Several different angles of the rescues were filmed by amateur and professional photographers. These angles were then spliced together, increasing the dramatic effect. The rescues were also featured on prime time television reality shows. The following day, New York State Governor Mario Coumo, visited company quarters to congratulate the intrepid rescue men.

For their amazing display of heroism and teamwork the members of Rescue 1 received a Unit Citation. (This was Firefighter Bruce Newbery's second Unit Citation in two days). Firefighter Kevin Shea was awarded the Hugh Bonner Medal, and Patrick Barr was presented the Trevor-Warren Medal.

Rescue 1 responded to Manhattan Box 1493 on July 25, 1991 at 11:24 a.m., for a reported building collapse in an unoccupied 6-story tenement. Rescue 1 arrived at the scene, where

Rescue 3 had located and were reassuring a buried victim. Captain John Cerato of Rescue 1 was asked to survey the collapse area and to advise the chief. The captain found several issues that were addressed. It was then decided that Lt. Thomas Prin (Rescue 3) and one of his men would work beneath the lean-to collapse section, to shore and stabilize prior to any removal attempts. The remaining members of Rescues 1 and 3 would assist in this effort.

When this shoring was completed, they turned their efforts to removing a number of overhead secondary collapse dangers. This dangerous and time consuming job would finally allow the victim to be dug free and removed from the collapsed debris. Both rescue companies operated for five hours to save this trapped man.

It was 12:22 p.m., on August 28, 1991, when a speeding southbound IRT subway train derailed 100-yards north of the Union Square, 14th Street station. Under the command of Lieutenant James Corcoran, Rescue 1 made their way to the crash site, and immediately went to work extricating passengers from the tangled wreckage. The first subway car was sheared in half and more than 20 vertical steel support beams were displaced, as firefighters began their rescue operations. Numerous passengers were trapped in the sharp, twisted metal and many portable generators were set up to power lights and extrication tools. As the operation continued, levels of carbon monoxide began to climb making the delicate work even more dangerous. Firefighters Bruce Newbery, Kevin Shea, Joseph Angelini, Warren Forsyth and Richard Muldowney (detailed for the tour from Ladder 7) used nearly every tool on the truck during this extended operation.

Access to many of the trapped passengers was nearly impossible, and firefighter injury after injury began to take its toll on the rescuers. Lacerations, sprains and strains inflicted the firefighters who soldiered on despite the difficulties and dangers. Two rescue men, Lt. Corcoran and FF Kevin Shea were injured and ordered from the scene by EMS personnel. Lt. Corcoran's injuries were so severe he never returned to duty. FF Bruce Newbery was designated Acting Lieutenant in charge of Rescue 1 for the remainder of the operation.

After almost four hours of continuous rescue work, the last of the victims was removed. For their efforts at this major emergency the members of Rescue 1 were awarded a Unit Citation.

It was 4 in the morning, October 12, 1991, when Rescue 1 was assigned to a reported fire at 243 East 36th Street. The dispatcher was receiving numerous calls for a fire in a four-story occupied multiple dwelling near the entrance to the Queens Midtown Tunnel. Heavy fire had possession of the first floor and stairs of the building. With reports of people trapped, Rescue 1 was assigned to get above the fire and search. Firefighter Joseph Angelini saw a large tree blocking any possible portable ladder position, and party-wall balconies above that allowed access between adjoining buildings, but not from one floor to the next.

> Access to many of the trapped passengers was nearly impossible, and firefighter injury after injury began to take its toll on the rescuers. Lacerations, sprains and strains inflicted the firefighters who soldiered on despite the difficulties and dangers.

With heavy fire extending rapidly, Angelini and Firefighter Neal Fredericksen entered the adjoining building. They crawled around a party-wall balcony and entered the room directly above the raging fire. With conditions quickly deteriorating, Angelini made a move for the third floor. He dashed up the burning stairs and searched the public hall, then hurried to the top floor where he plunged into the front apartment. With flames still raging out of control and extending beneath him, he searched the apartment finding a 25-year-old woman unconscious in her bedroom. He placed his facepiece over the victim and called for help over the radio. He was joined by Firefighter Stan Sussina of Rescue 1, who helped Angelini remove the victim to the street. For his courage and perseverance Firefighter Joseph J. Angelini was awarded the Edith B. Goldman Medal.

FF Joseph Angelini

While returning to quarters after a run to the Eastside on December 5th, Rescue 1 was directed to respond to 251 West 42nd Street, near Times Square. The company arrived first due, and under the command of Lieutenant Patrick Brown, searched for and located an advanced fire blazing in the cellar of a book and video store. As Engine 65 stretched in, Rescue 1 helped bend the hose down the tight staircase. With flames pouring overhead, several attempts were made to advance through the tightly packed cellar towards the fire raging in the rear of the store. Conditions became so bad that the line was withdrawn, and companies were assigned to attempt to reach the seat of the fire from the exposure 4 side. Members of Rescue 1 went into the cellar of the adjacent building and began to breach the wall, as a hose line was pulled into position. Using pavement breakers they toiled for almost an hour piercing through two foundation walls, until they broke through and could get water on the fire.

At this point though, fire had extended dramatically in the original fire building. Deputy Chief Vincent Dunn pulled all companies from the exposures, and switched to a defensive attack. Fourteen exterior streams went into operation. Fifty-nine FDNY units operated, until the fire was under control at 2:25 p.m. Collapses on several floors of the fire building made overhaul impossible, and would require a rotating FDNY presence for the next four days.

Rescue 1 was special called to LaGuardia airport in Queens on the night of March 22, 1992. En route the members of Rescue 1 monitored both FDNY and NYPD radio frequencies. They knew they were heading to a confirmed airliner crash in the water with fire. Upon arrival, the rig was escorted to a position about 200 yards from the downed plane, USAir Flight 405. Large amounts of SCUBA and extrication equipment had to be carried through mud, over a hill, and down to the shoreline. Then ferried out to the aircraft. The operation would be made all the more difficult by the blustery snow and the icy currents of in Flushing Bay.

Firefighter Neal Fredericksen donned SCUBA gear and entered the water, and began an underwater search of the aft section of the plane. FF Gary Geidel acted as his above water tender and guide. After several minutes Fredericksen located two victims underwater, and they were removed to the shore in a small boat. Meanwhile, Firefighter Stan Sussina located another victim still seat belted and upside down. Fredericksen and

Four-alarm fire on West 42nd Street on December 5, 1991

Lt. Patrick Brown evacuates fire escape after difficult search of 200 E. 7th Street, Manhattan, January 16, 1992 (Pete O'Dea)

Geidel moved in to assist in the extrication. At this time Lt. Patrick Brown, Firefighters Joseph Angelini, and Thomas Baker were securing the aircraft with ropes, using portable ladders as bridges, and ferrying out extrication equipment in small boats.

The operation shifted, when the last surface victim was removed. Rescue 1 then split into teams— one concentrating on the aft passenger section, while the other team worked trying to gain access to the cockpit. Members utilized Hurst tools, air hammers, pneumatic drills and even Halligan tools trying to gain entry into the mangled wreckage. The conditions and weather became so severe that all members were ordered off the plane until low tide at dawn. Rescue 1 returned to the scene and assisted in operations, until relieved by Assistant Chief Fusco at 9 a.m. Sadly, of the fifty-one people onboard the plane when it crashed 27 were killed.

Manhattan Class 3- Box 865 (an automatic fire alarm system) was transmitted at 6:40 a.m., on March 29, 1992. Rescue 1 and other midtown units rolled to Mansfield Hall, a seven-story transient hotel at 226 West 50th Street, near the theatre district. Blow torch like flames were discovered auto-exposing upwards in an air shaft on the exposure 2 side (left) of the building. The wind whipped flames were extending into every floor in the large hotel. Numerous residents were trapped in the thick hot smoke. Rescue 1, under the command of Lt. Casani, reported to Al Turi the chief of the Ninth Battalion. They were assigned to the fire floor and the floors above. With heavy smoke filling the lobby, Lt. Casani sent Firefighters John Boyle and Dave Williams to the rear to check on fire conditions. Casani and the remaining members headed up the stairs. In the rear the rescue men could see numerous civilians on the rear fire escape, at windows and on a set back. They quickly radioed this information and grabbed a portable ladder from a nearby rig, and began removing people.

With the fire now blowing out many windows on the second floor in the rear "A" wing, Casani assigned Firefighter Eric Wiener to assist the engine (a four man engine) operating on the fire floor. Casani, Firefighters Ken Kaasmann, and Ed Mauro conducted a primary search of the "A" wing and assisted many people to the front fire escape. They then moved to the floor above, where Mauro found fire extending in the walls and floors. He called for a line. Lt. Casani sent Kaasmann to help Wiener with the line on the fire floor, then joined Mauro on the third floor to continue the primary search.

During this search a "May-Day!" was heard on the handi-talkies. Firefighter Boyle, now operating on the fourth floor, located a member cut-off by fire on the rear fire escape. Boyle was able to guide the member through heavy smoke and high heat to a position of safety. With the search of the third floor completed, Casani and Mauro began searching the fourth. Here they found fire extension in various rooms and a line was called for. Searches on the fifth and sixth floors revealed the same conditions. Firefighters Williams and Boyle then completed the seventh floors searches.

> **D**uring this search a "May-Day!" was heard on the handi-talkies.

Next, the company concentrated on assisting in the extinguishment of the fire on the various floors of the building. Members worked in high heat and dense smoke conditions, and also had to clear numerous pieces of 3/4-inch plywood covering doors.

Five alarms were transmitted bringing 40 companies to the scene. Members of Rescue 1 made a number of rescues, and helped battle the rapidly advancing fire. In all nineteen people were injured, thirteen of them firefighters. Each member of Rescue 1 expended at least two air cylinders during the operation. Four firefighters were transported to the Burn Center. For their determined efforts at this job, Rescue 1 was awarded a Unit Citation.

It was 6:50 on the morning of April 14, 1992, Rescue 1 could see smoke on the upper floors as they pulled in to Box 785. Heavy smoke was also visible in the rear at the 2nd and 3rd floor levels of this 12-story, 30 x 100 mixed occupancy, "L"-shaped building on the corner of 42nd Street and Eighth Avenue. Lt. Kevin Williams (SOC), recognizing the severe life hazard both in the multiple level 24-hour porn shop and the 24 occupied apartments above, split the company into teams. An outside team of Firefighters Paul Hashagen and Thomas Sullivan were directed to attempt vent, entry, and search from an aerial ladder, as the remaining members of the company entered the first floor from the 42nd Street side of the building.

About 25-feet into the store, it became obvious that alterations to the building had left an atrium-like large open space, that rose upwards past the second and third floors. Moving up an open stairs within this atrium, members of Rescue 1 encountered heavy fire extending unhindered due this renovation, and seriously exposing a number of floors simultaneously. Lt. Williams transmitted an "Urgent" message requesting a hand line to this location.

With a serious life hazard above, the company advanced upwards past fire. On the second floor they found an irregular layout of 25 cubicles. The inside team was split again, with Lt. Williams and FF Ken Kaasmann searching one part of the second floor, and Firefighters Harvey Harrell and Timothy Kelly searching the other. Meanwhile, the outside team had entered the third floor finding three panicked civilians. They were removed to the rear fire escape. Back on the second floor, Lt. Williams was happy with the progress of the searches. As the hose arrived at his position, he sent Harrell and Kelly to join the other two rescue firefighters on the third floor. He joined them several minutes later.

The regrouped company, then operated on the third floor. They located fire extension calling for another line to that location. The fire went to three alarms before it was declared under control.

Monday night, November 2, 1992 was rainy in New York City, the eve of election day. At 5:08 p.m., Box 1563 was transmitted for an explosion and fire at 2121 Madison Avenue at 135th Street in Harlem. A devastating gas explosion tore through the top floors of the twelve-story, red brick, multiple dwelling. The top three floors had blown completely away from the corner of the building, bombarding the ground below with bricks and shattered building parts. For a block, the trees were filled with clothing and household items sent airborne by the blast. Rescue 1, standing fast at a midtown box, was added to the assignment and quickly responded despite the rain slicked streets.

To reach the top floors, firefighters had to climb through stairways blocked with rubble and debris. Flashlights pierced the darkness, as searches began. Firefighter Paul Hashagen of Rescue 1 located a semi-conscious elderly woman, badly injured by the explosion. With no time to wait for a Stokes or stretcher, a piece of shelving was used as a backboard and the frail woman was carefully carried, with the help of a truck

President George Bush with men of Rescue 1.

member, to a safe hallway area. Hashagen was quickly joined by Firefighter Stan Sussina who using his own personal EMT kit, provided advanced first aid to the woman suffering bilateral fractures to both legs, as well as serious back and head trauma. Sussina was able to control her bleeding and stabilize her, as rescue Firefighters Lloyd Infanzon and Al Benjamin arrived with a Stokes basket. The woman was secured to the stretcher and carried twelve stories down to the street and into a waiting ambulance by Infanzon, Benjamin and several other firefighters.

The search of the top floor was continued by Rescue 1 Firefighters Henry Molle, Joseph Angelini, and Neal Fredericksen. With these searches completed, Lt. Williams redeployed the company, by sending Hashagen and Molle to the rig. They would assemble the tools and equipment needed to shore the dangerous sections of the blast area. Rescues 1 and 3 spent the next several hours completing a complex, difficult, and dangerous shoring operation. Various pieces of rescue equipment was called for. Each had to be carried by hand, up ten or more flights of stairs. Rescue 1 worked with Rescue 3 shoring the damaged sections, and completing the searches in the collapsed areas. Rescue 1 was relieved on scene by the incoming night tour: Captain Charles Kasper, Firefighters John Boyle, FF James Smith, and Ed Mauro. Rescue Company 1 was awarded a Unit Citation for their work at this explosion.

High-rise fires in both office buildings and multiple dwellings have become a fairly frequent event in New York City. With the vast majority of high-rise buildings located in Manhattan, and within the response area of Rescue 1, the company had become very experienced with these types of fires. It is not, therefore, unreasonable to assume that Rescue 1 has had more fire duty at high-rise fires than any other fire company in the world. From the Battery and Wall Street neighborhoods, to Midtown and both the upper east and west sides of the borough, high-rise building pierce the clouds. And, on occasion fill the sky with smoke and flames. It was true when the company was formed, and it is still true one hundred years later.

Another of these happened on November 23, 1992. Rescue 1 was special called to 90 John Street, an office building with a fire reported on the 21st floor. The company was on scene in five minutes, with Captain Charles Kasper in command. They reported to the First Battalion and were sent to assist in the VES (vent, entry and search) of the fire floor, and to investigate a report of a missing cleaning woman on the 22nd floor. The company took a fireman's service elevator to the 14th floor, then climbed the remaining flights of stairs.

The captain split the company into two teams with Firefighters Gary Geidel and Ken Kaasmann going to the 22nd floor to search for the missing woman, and the captain with Firefighters John Theobald and Ed Mauro proceeded to the point of attack, and assisted on operations there. Rescue chauffeur Dave Williams, who'd brought a resuscitator as well as his tools, was sent to the 18th floor to help overcome persons there. When the searches on 22 proved negative, Geidel and Kaasmann joined the captain on the fire floor.

Unable to make progress from the "A" stairs, Rescue 1 went to the "B" stairs, splitting again with half going clockwise and the other half searching counter clockwise. The main body of fire was located. A line was requested to the "B" stairs. Firefighter Williams searched the edges of the fire area and located extension. Until a line could be positioned, he used several extinguishers to slow the spreading flames. The company also conducted a difficult primary search without benefit of a charged hoseline in position. The maze-like layout demanded a rope search, as each of the offices were checked.

With the arrival of a 2-1/2 inch attack line, Rescue 1 moved in to help its advance. The line was operated with success, but had to shut down briefly to add lengths. This added to the considerable punishment the company had already taken. Rescue 1 operated for more than two hours at this fourth alarm, with each member changing cylinders several times without relief.

It was Super Bowl Sunday night, January 31, 1993, and most of America was watching the championship football game. In the quarters of Rescue 1 sat the on-duty platoon: Lieutenant Stephen Casani, Firefighters Bruce Newbery, Hank Molle, Kevin Shea, Ed Mauro, Lloyd Infanzon and a five man film crew from Germany, who were finishing a documentary about the company. At about 11 p.m., the housewatch computer alarm came to life. In a matter of seconds, midtown Manhattan fire companies were on their way to 280 Park Avenue. A 10-76 signal was transmitted by the first arriving unit. Responding units heard the report of a working fire in a high-rise office building crackle across the air. Then as they approached the scene, they could see it in the sky.

Fire was blowing out eight windows on the sixth floor. The battalion chief transmitted a second alarm and directed Rescue 1 to check the fire floor, then to search the floor above. Conditions on the seventh floor were so severe that the company had to use a search rope. Fire extension, auto-exposing through the floor was reported, and a hose line was urgently requested. (The concrete floor had buckled and fire was burning directly through from the floor below.) With these highly unusual and dangerous conditions, Lt. Casani left Firefighters Newbery and Molle at the seventh floor doorway to monitor conditions, while he and the remainder of the crew took the search ropes and went to check the eighth floor.

While checking conditions in the doorway, Molle and Newbery heard a "MayDay" transmitted on their Handie-Talkies. With conditions deteriorating, they took turns venturing out into the fire area. Newbery heard voices somewhere ahead and called back to Molle, who was by his side in seconds. Together they called out and followed the voices, using a wall as a guide. With their air supply dwindling, they crawled 70-feet deep into the 7th floor. Beneath them 6,000 square feet of uncontrolled fire was burning. Reaching the elevator lobby, they found two firefighters on the floor of an elevator sharing an air mask. Newbery placed his mask over one firefighters face, as Molle helped the other firefighter refasten his own mask.

FF Bruce H. Newbery *FF Henry G. Molle*

They took the firefighters and re-traced their path to the stairway. Newbery reported where the members were found and gave their condition. Newbery helped the men down to the 5th floor leaving them with FDNY members equipped with a resuscitator, before returning to Molle at the 7th floor doorway.

For their heroism under extreme conditions Firefighter Bruce H. Newbery was awarded the Lt. Robert R. Dolney Medal and Henry G. Molle was awarded the Thomas F. Dougherty Medal. The company was also given a Unit Citation.

Friday, February 26, 1993 was a cold day and light snow had dusted the city. At 12:18 p.m., a huge explosion tore through the parking garage beneath the Vista Hotel in the World Trade Center Complex in lower Manhattan. Within seconds the FDNY was in motion, as units raced towards the twin 110-story landmarks. First arriving units noticed damage to the large over-head doors, that opened to ramps leading down to lower levels parking areas. A gray smoke condition existed in the cellars and ramps. A 10-75 was transmitted.

First alarm companies moved in, still unaware of the actual nature of the explosion, believing it was electrical in nature. As companies began probing, they could hear voices crying out for help.

Rescue 1 arrived with Lt. John McAllister in command. They were directed to search the immediate area and report back. Firefighter Kevin Shea of Rescue 1 was making his way through the dense smoke heading towards a voice calling for help somewhere ahead of him. He continued crawling across some concrete rubble in hopes of finding the person, when suddenly, the section of concrete floor beneath him collapsed. Shea and the concrete flooring plunged more than thirty-feet into the super-heated blackness below.

Lt. McAllister and Firefighter Gary Geidel made their way carefully to the point where Shea had fallen, and tried to communicate with him. McAllister leaned over the edge straining to get some reception on his portable radio. Shea's situation was transmitted to Battalion Chief Rowkowski, who assumed command of the rescue effort. Shea described his location and injuries as best he could, while Rescue 1 worked with Squad 1 who were prepared to lower their officer into the hole.

The officer was lowered past the various levels of destruction, until he reached the floor. Others members were also making their way to Shea from different vantage points. Only as this dangerous rescue was being completed did the severity and size of the destruction begin to be revealed. Shea was loaded onto a Stokes basket, and carried from the cellar. Rescue after dangerous rescue was performed by FDNY firefighters and calls for help from both towers, now filled with smoke, were answered. A number of off-duty members of Rescue 1 responded to the scene, and using spare equipment from the truck went to work providing search and rescue throughout the building.

It was later learned a small band of terrorists, with ties to Al-Qaeda, built a 1,336 pound urea nitrate hydrogen gas enhanced bomb in New Jersey. Then drove to the World Trade Center underground parking lot. The lethal device was then detonated with a timer. The terrorists were later arrested and are now in prison.

Rescue 1's rig, the original command post of the 1993 bombing at the World Trade Center

The bombing of the World Trade Center, February 26, 1993 (featured on the cover of WNYF, on left) was the largest response, as of that date, in department history, the equivalent of 23-alarms.

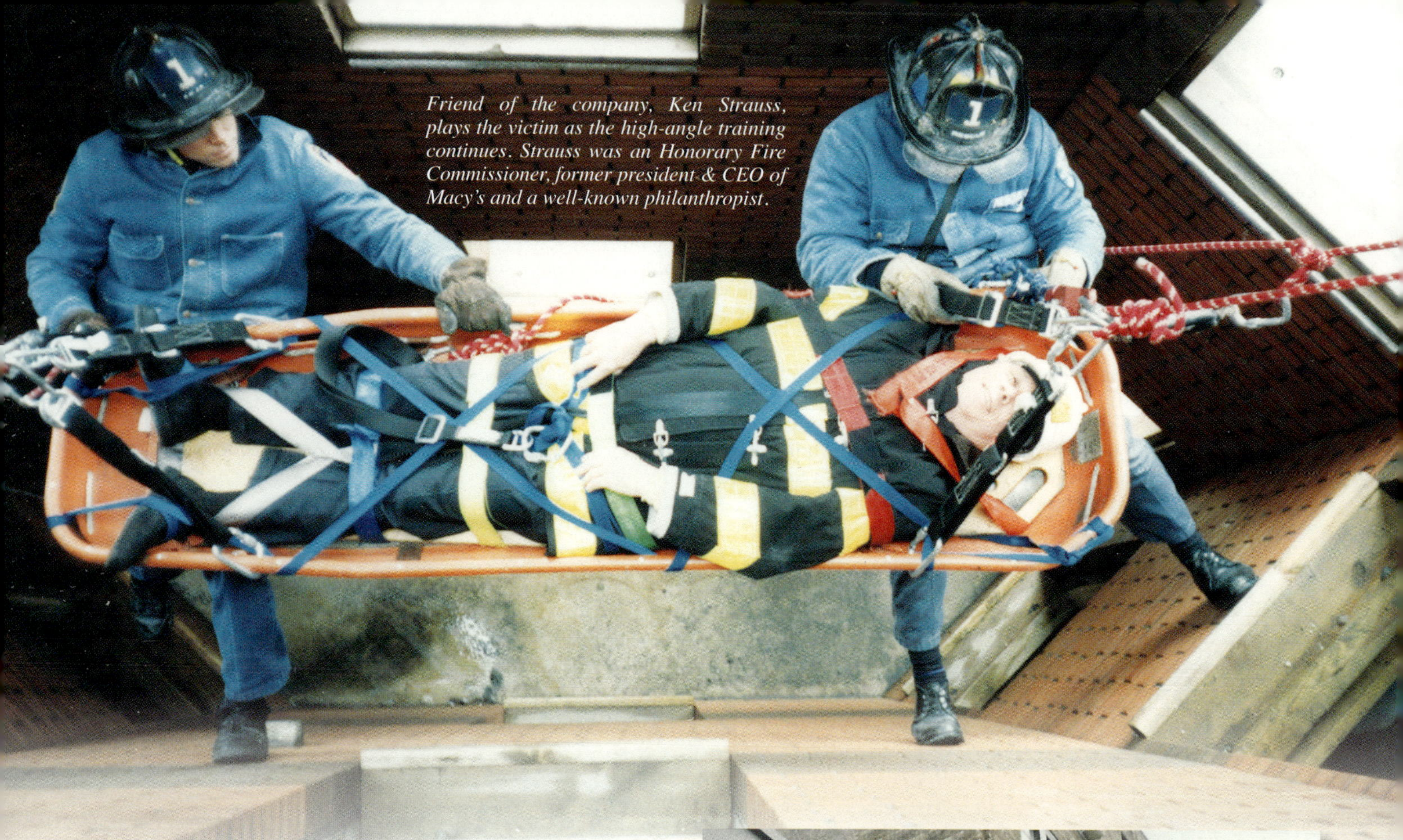

Friend of the company, Ken Strauss, plays the victim as the high-angle training continues. Strauss was an Honorary Fire Commissioner, former president & CEO of Macy's and a well-known philanthropist.

Up to this time the World Trade Center Bombing and the subsequent rescue operations was the largest movement of FDNY companies in its history. Within the first 24-hours of operations 135 FDNY companies and 775 uniformed members of the department were at the scene. After a long hospital stay and rehabilitation, Firefighter Kevin Shea returned to duty and was promoted to lieutenant.

As part of the company's on-going training the nationally recognized high angle rope training company, The ROCO Corporation, sent two instructors to provide 40-hour in-house training for each member of Rescue 1. The training commenced on April 25 through May 3, 1992 and certified all members: High Angle Rope Rescue I. The instructors returned again the following year on March 22 through 26 and brought the company up to High Angle Rope Rescue II.

On June 13, 1993 Rescue 1 was assigned to Manhattan Box 8200 for a fire at the Sanitation Pier at 57th Street in the Hudson River. Upon arrival, heavy smoke and fire was visible underneath the far end of the pier. The fire was quickly extending, and was burning under 100-feet of the 500-foot long pier. The fire was well entrenched beneath the pier, and inaccessible to any land units working above. Fireboats on scene also were unable to reach the seat of the fire from their positions. Members of Rescue 1 reported to Battalion Chief Al Turi offering their services as an in-water firefighting team. After a quick consultation with Deputy Chief Dunn, three members of Rescue 1: Firemen Paul Hashagen, Bruce Newbery and Harvey Harrell, donned SCUBA gear and entered the water with a 1-3/4 handline. While being tended from above by other rescue men, the trio began to systematically attack the fire from their position beneath the pier structure. A hose strap was placed around the nozzle, used to temporarily lash the hose in place, as the team leap-frogged from section to section. For an hour and a half they battled the fire, until the last of the flames were extinguished.

Rope work on the front of the firehouse.

In his endorsement of the unit citation report Deputy Chief Vincent Dunn wrote:

"I strongly recommend the unit citation be granted to the officer and firefighters of Rescue 1. I can not tell you how important their actions were. They single handedly extinguished the under pier fire after I had transmitted a 3rd alarm. They saved 50 sanitation trucks worth 25 million dollars, and kept a week of creosote smoke from flowing over midtown Manhattan. I have never seen an act more worthy of a unit citation in my entire career."

The chief's wishes were granted and the company was awarded a Unit Citation.

On Sunday July 4, 1993, Rescue 1 and midtown fire companies responded to one of the most unusual emergencies they would ever encounter. It was a hot summer afternoon, as units responded to the seven story apartment building at 410 West 53rd Street, between 9th and 10th Avenues. There they found a deflated 165 foot blimp draped across the roof and front of the building. The $4 million, nylon-skinned, helium filled airship, named "Bigfoot", bearing Pizza Hut logos, had been flying at an altitude of 800-feet, when the pilot lost control of the ship. The pilot and his co-pilot, injured in the crash, were first helped by building tenants who had been sunbathing on the roof. The injured were then treated by department members, and taken to a nearby hospital. Rescue 1 secured the limp dirigible, to prevent further damage to the building, until it could be removed.

On August 18, 1994 Rescue 1 responded to a reported ship fire on board the *Regal Empress* at Pier 88, on the Hudson River. Fire units arrived at the pier, only to find it empty. The ship soon became visible coming up the Hudson towards the pier. The companies waited, as the huge, white, 611-foot ship slowly slid up to the pier. There were no signs of smoke or fire, until a door was opened. The waiting FDNY crews could see rolling smoke and blackened water slopping out of the portal.

The fire broke out in the kitchen area of the main deck, while the ship was returning to New York. The crew tried their best to hold the flames until they reached port. The FDNY boarded the ship and went to work. Hose lines were stretched and searches began. Rescue 1, using the Paratech air hammer (a pneumatic impact tool with a chisel tip) opened a thick steel duct to stop fire extending inside. One thousand people calmly left the ship, while the fire was being fought; only eighteen passengers were injured. The fire would go to four-alarms, before being declared under control.

1966 Seventh Avenue is a 5-story tenement containing ten apartments. On August 22, 1993 at 7:27 in the morning, a fire broke out on the second floor and was soon blazing out of control. When Rescue 1 arrived, the chief ordered them to assist with the searches of the fire building. Captain Russell Vomero (SOC) split the company into two teams: Firefighters Dave Williams and Kevin Dowdell (detailed from Rescue 2 for the tour) went to the roof, the remainder of the company went up the interior stairs. With flames blowing out of a second floor apartment threatening the stairs and having no line in place, the company was unable to continue up to the third floor. Firefighter John Theobald made his way to the front windows of the adjoining apartment and asked the flame filled window be hit with a stream of water from the street. This knocked down the fire enough to allow Captain Vomero, Firefighters Paul Baldwin, and Al Benjamin to dash up the stairs. There, under extreme conditions, they began searching sections of the third floor.

Several persons had been removed by aerial ladders earlier, but the severity of the extending fire would not allow a complete primary search of the third floor. As lines were called for, Rescue 1 continued to the fourth floor where conditions were just as extreme. There was high heat, heavy smoke and extending fire with no lines in place. They could hear lines moving up the stairs from below, but it would still be several long minutes before the firefighters searching above would have any type of protection. Benjamin was sent below to help with the searches. As the lines moved in, and Vomero and Baldwin made the top floor, joining Dowdell on the primary search. During this search, a ladder company member appeared with a small child. Baldwin immediately headed in the direction they'd come from. Searching this apartment Baldwin found an unconscious, heavy-set woman. With the help of some ladder company members, the woman was moved to a safe area.

The battle continued, going to four-alarms. Rescue 1 worked for an hour and a half without stopping.

The Hotel Carter at 250 West 43rd Street was a very familiar address to the members of Rescue 1, and all the other midtown fire companies. The 24-story 100 x 100 fireproof building stood a half a block from Times Square. In 1976 it changed its name from "The Dixie Hotel" to the Hotel Carter, continuing its rather colorful and notorious history. By 1984 it was being used as a homeless shelter. By 1988 the building conditions were so bad the city moved the homeless. The hotel continued to have troubles. One such incident was a woman being thrown to her death from an upper story window in 1987.

On the afternoon of May 11, 1994, Rescue 1 responded to a report of a man impaled on a fence. On arrival Rescue 1, under the command of Lt. Kevin Williams (SOC), was directed to the sixteenth floor by hotel security. With a reported impalement, the forcible entry team, Firefighters Dennis Amodio and Michael Montesi carried a medical kit, resuscitator, cutting torch and fireproof blankets. They were directed to a room at the rear of the building, which had a very narrow three-foot wide balcony. The victim, who was an apparent suicide attempt and had fallen or jumped from above, was alive and conscious. He was impaled on two steel spikes, 160-feet above the ground. One spike, about 1/2-inch in diameter, was lodged in his back. The second, 1-inch spike, had pierced the victims midriff. The force of his landing had broken off a section of the fence, which was now hanging free over the balcony edge.

The damaged fence, the impaled victim, and a police officer standing on the edge of the balcony supporting the victim had to be tied off separately. Williams called Firefighters Thomas Baker, Paul Baldwin and John Theobald to bring ropes up. Baker and Baldwin proceeded to the 17th floor, tied off to substantial objects, and lowered life saving ropes to the cop and victim. Firefighter Theobald brought utility ropes to the 16th floor and secured the fence. All ropes were tightened, then FF Amodio began cutting the fence.

The victim, with the spikes still in place, was moved to the balcony where sections of the fence could be trimmed, before he could be secured on a long board. For their outstanding medical, high angle, and specialized tool rescue, the members of Rescue were awarded a Unit Citation.

The evening of June 5, 1994 would be a tour members of the on-duty platoon of Rescue 1 would never forget. At 6:20 p.m., Manhattan Box 151 was transmitted for a fire in a five-story commercial loft building at 79 Worth Street. Rescue 1 responded on the 10-75 and arriving quickly at the scene, with Firefighter Bruce Newbery at the wheel and Lt. Steve Casani in command.

As reports of rubbish fires on the upper floors filtered down via handi-talkie from the companies inside, Rescue 1 was told to take up. Minutes later conditions within the building changed, and the company responded back to the command post. Once again a rubbish fire was located inside, and Rescue 1 was told to "take up." Having a bad feeling about the way things were going, Casani told Newbery and the crew they were going 10-8 (available by radio) but would stay close by until the fire was under control.

Several minutes later excited radio reports advised that conditions had changed dramatically within the building: Companies were reporting a rapidly increasing heat and smoke condition. Once again Rescue 1 reported in. The company was sent to the cellar, where reports indicated things were becoming serious. FF Newbery brought along the company's thermal imaging camera, and was also wearing a new digital CO meter (carbon monoxide meter) on his turnout coat. As the company moved down towards the cellar, the CO meter reacted to the high levels of the poisonous gases building up within the building. Firefighter Newbery advised Casani, the other members of the company, and other firefighters working nearby.

As conditions worsened Rescue 1 Firefighter Neal Fredericksen began cutting the iron subcellar window shutters with a saw, to better ventilate the heavy smoke condition. (The cellar and subcellar of the building opened into a rear courtyard two stories below street level). Inside, Newbery's thermal imaging camera showed heavy fire trapped and moving within the subcellar's tin ceiling. As calls went out for ladder companies to join Rescue 1 in the subcellar to pull ceilings, a "May-Day" was transmitted for a missing officer believed to be lost in the cellar.

Leaving Newbery in the subcellar, Lt. Casani assembled his men and moved from the subcellar to the floor above to search for the missing officer. Newbery remained with an engine company and their line, in an attempt to extinguish some of the fire in that area.

While members of Rescue 1 were making an aggressive search of the cellar area, Lt. Casani stepped into a burned out section of flooring and fell forward, as the weakened floor collapsed beneath him. Struggling to maintain his footing, the officer seriously injured his knee, but was able to pull himself free and continue on. In the subcellar Newbery heard the muffled shouts of firefighters. They'd found the missing officer floating face down in eight-inches of blackwater, not in the cellar above—but right there in the subcellar. Newbery relayed the true location of the downed firefighter by radio, then helped the exhausted members of the engine drag the unconscious officer towards the rear windows Fredericksen had just cleared.

The limp, water soaked officer was handed out into the rear courtyard. Newbery and Fredericksen began first aid. With numerous companies working on the fire escapes above and the officer clearly not breathing, they shouted out for a resuscitator. Out of the darkness an Emerson modified resuscitator, in it's heavy carrying case, was dropped towards the courtyard below. Newbery seeing the oxygen set dropping, and fearing it would be damaged unless he could catch it, lunged forward. His efforts broke the fall of the box, but seriously injured the rescue man. Despite his injuries, Newbery moved in with the oxygen, and began administering to the downed brother.

A Stokes basket was lowered and members strapped the injured officer inside, then removed him through "Exposure Four" to the street, where he was raced to a nearby hospital.

The fire escalated to five alarms, before being placed under control at 9:15 p.m. This fire would be extremely costly to the FDNY: Seventeen firefighters were injured battling this arson fire. Forty-five days after he was found face down in the watery subcellar, Lt. George W. Lener of Ladder 6 would die of his injuries. Lt. Steve Casani would require surgery to repair his injured knee. Firefighter Bruce Newbery would also require major surgery on his damaged hip. Despite painful therapy, Newbery would never be able to return to full-duty. He was detailed to SOC and the Division of Training on light-duty, before retiring in 1999.

A telephone alarm was received on September 23, 1994 for a fire on the first floor of a six-story multiple dwelling. It was 8:21 in the evening, when Rescue 1 and other first alarm units descended on the the reported address. Arriving first, Rescue 1 transmitted a 10-75 signal at 8:24 p.m. Examination of the fire area proved the fire to be among food storage carts stored illegally, on the first floor of this tenement, behind a doorway covered with a roll-down gate. As members of Rescue 1 and Ladder 21 went above the fire to search for extension and evacuate civilians as needed, Engine 26 began to stretch a line to front entrance. Rescue 1 Firefighters David Williams and Henry Molle had forced the lock on the roll down gate leaving the gate partially closed, while the line was brought into position and charged.

Suddenly just as the door was about to be raised and water directed at the fire, a twenty pound propane cylinder exploded. A huge fire ball belched out from under the door, engulfing both Molle and Williams briefly. The rescue men scrambled to safety, as the hose stream opened up on the flames. The fire in the 12 x 35-foot room was quickly extinguished. Shocked firefighters found ten additional 20-pound propane tanks in the fire area.

As Dave Williams was taken to the hospital suffering first and second degree burns to his face, fire marshals investigated. Summonses were issued and the illegally stored cylinders were confiscated. After a brief hospital stay Williams returned to work driving the rescue rig. Interestingly a visiting firefighter, Masaru Ono from the Tokyo fire Department, caught the explosion on video and shared it with local media and the FDNY.

Monday morning, November 7, 1994 would get very, very busy for Rescue Company 1. The company rolled out to an all-hands in lower Manhattan, and then went 10-8. (Available by radio.) They were directed by the dispatcher to respond to a midtown alarm of bricks falling at a construction site. It was a very windy morning, as the big red Mack rescue truck responded up West Street towards the assignment. As they approached Jane Street, smoke could be seen coming from a vacant building on the corner. Lieutenant Steve Casani transmitted a 10-75, followed in moments by "All-hands with an extra truck—a tower ladder." Within seconds fire became visible on several floors being whipped into a frenzy by the 40 mile-per-hour winds.

At Casani's request the chauffeur, Firefighter Paul Hashagen transmitted a second alarm. With the usual first alarm companies at work downtown, Rescue 1 knew they would be alone for quite a while. Flames soon filled the building, and were blowing out every window. As two nearby exposures began igniting from the radiant heat, Lt. Casani returned to the rig radio transmitting a third then fourth alarms.

Rescue 1 transmitted all four-alarms as they operated alone at this wind whipped fire at West and Jane Streets. Manhattan Box 44-537, November 7, 1994.

The members of the company split into teams and headed to each of the exposed buildings. The most seriously exposed building was directly behind the fire building. A roof top garden, wooden picket fence and lawn furniture were just beginning to burn, when the rescue men located a garden hose and soaked the igniting flammables. People in this building and the other exposures were warned of the fire and began to evacuate, as the first sounds of incoming fire sirens could be heard.

Lines were stretched, hydrants taken, and tower ladders were set up as the fire reached it's height. A few minutes after the extending fire was halted on the exposure roof, the fire building collapsed, in a shower of sparks and flaming embers that spread across the surrounding buildings by the strong winds. Companies responded and worked several other small fires in the neighborhood started by the flying embers, until things finally calmed down. For their single-handed operation Rescue 1 was awarded a Unit Citation.

The company commander, Captain James D. Rogers died on December 20, 1994 after a brave battle with cancer. Due to the nature of the illness and the fact it was related to fire duty, the captain's loss was line-of-duty. The 53-year old Rogers had been cited for bravery 10-times in his 26-year career, and had a reputation for uncommon valor. James Rogers worked as a firefighter in Rescue 1, until he was promoted to Lieutenant. He was then assigned to Rescue 2, before being promoted to captain and returning to command Rescue 1.

Captain James D. Rogers
Rescue Company 1
December 20, 1994

On the morning of January 9, 1995 the day crew of Rescue 1 rolled out the door just eighteen minutes after the start of the tour, for a report of a seaplane down and in trouble in the East River at 23rd Street. This alarm proved to be non-founded. Six minutes later the company was re-directed to 320 Park Avenue near East 50th Street for a reported man down an elevator shaft. At that location, they found a worker had fallen ten to twelve feet into an open elevator shaft. He landed on several horizontal metal beams 10-feet below the lowest floor opening, but still 15 to 20-feet above the base of the shaft. Rescue 1 worked with members of Ladder 4 and Engine 54, treating and packaging the injured man.

Rescue 1 aiding victim in elevator shaft at 320 Park Avenue, January 9, 1995.

The man was placed on oxygen, immobilized with a cervical collar, then placed in an LSP Half-Back extrication/lifting harness. A diaper harness was placed around that. Using a high angle rope and mechanical advantage system, the patient was carefully lifted from the shaft, placed on a long board, and taken by EMS to a nearby hospital. Rescue 1, Ladder 4 and 54 Engine worked together for an hour and fifteen minutes to accomplish the rescue.

A large new law tenement on the East Village was the site of a fast moving four alarm fire on the morning of April 7, 1995. Manhattan Box 432 was transmitted at 7:23. Firefighters would see themselves pushed to the limit in a very short time. Rescue 1 was dispatched, due to numerous phone calls. They arrived to find find a building with fire on the fourth, fifth and sixth floors as well as the cockloft. Lt. Stephen Casani and his forcible entry team, Firefighters Henry Molle and Paul Baldwin, took the stairs towards the third floor, as Firefighters Al Benjamin and Joseph Sykes (detailed for the tour from Rescue 5) took an aerial ladder to the roof with a life saving rope (LSR) and a saw.

Reaching the third floor, Casani and his team found a battalion chief on the floor obviously injured. They helped him to his feet and placed him in the care of a firefighter, as they continued upwards. During their search they located extending fire racing in vertical voids in several locations, and called for lines. The rescue roof team was also reporting heavy fire extending through the cockloft. Upon the receipt of a "May-Day!", Casani ordered Molle and Baldwin to help get the second line into position in an attempt to hold the stairs, while he went above to investigate. At the half landing Casani looked out the window and saw, just above him, a firefighter out of air and hanging out of a sixth floor window. Casani radioed FF Boyle ordering him to the sixth floor, while he moved in to locate the trapped firefighter.

Then as Casani located and began removing the out of air firefighter, two others declared "May-Days!" A firefighter and an officer were cut-off and trapped at top floor windows on separate sides of the building. Members of Rescue 1 and Ladder 6 converged on the roof above the officer. Firefighter Al Benjamin began cutting away a chain link fence that blocked direct access above the officer. As Firefighters Henry Molle, Paul Baldwin, and Joseph Sykes began to ready a life saving rope evolution on the roof, Lt. Steve Casani and Firefighter John Boyle dove into the swirling top floor trying to reach the other trapped man from the inside.

With fire blazing in the cockloft beneath their feet and no place to tie-off the LSR, the members of Rescue 1 lowered Firefighter Joe Hodges of Ladder 6 towards the trapped man. As he inched his way down through dense swirling smoke outside, inside the blazing building Lt. Casani and FF Boyle crawled beneath a canopy of flames towards the other trapped firefighter. Firefighter John Boyle teamed up with Firefighter Michael Lopez of Ladder 18. Together they entered the rear apartment with a charged line fighting to gain control of the fire. Lopez broke off, leaving Boyle alone on the nozzle to hold back the roaring flames as he crawled ahead and located the missing firefighter, who he led back to safety while Boyle covered them.

Lt. Casani and Firefighter Boyle (both now out of air) again re-entered the sixth floor apartment, in an attempt to find yet another missing member. While in this apartment, both rescue men had to withdraw due to an extreme build up of heat. At this fire Rescue Company 1 directly contributed to the coordinated and swift rescue of three firefighters trapped by a rapidly spreading fire.

Lt. Casani and Firefighters Boyle and Baldwin were placed on the Roll of Merit for their actions at this fire.

A terrorist blast tore apart the Alfred P. Murrah Building in downtown Oklahoma City on April 19, 1995. As part of the FEMA Urban Search and Rescue response, New York Task Force-1 (NYTF-1) composed of members of the NYPD and FDNY, including members of Rescue 1, responded to the site. On the night of their arrival, Thursday April 20th, the team went to work immediately and continued on the night shift, relieving the team from Los Angeles. Each shift was 12-hours long, with two hours for preparation and two hours for cleanup. Eleven of FEMA's 27 US&R task forces worked in the building. NYTF-1 demobilized on Wednesday April 26th, and returned home. The team upheld the finest traditions of the rescue service, and was a major component of the operation.

It was 4:25 p.m., on May 22, 1995, when Rescue 1 was dispatched to the 20th Century Garage, a multi-level parking structure located at 318 East 48th Street. Moments before, inside the building, a parking attendant drove a car into a shaft, when the elevator door opened without the platform. The car and driver plunged four stories to the base of the shaft, pinning the driver in the mangled wreckage. The rescue men had to work in the cramped confined space at the base of the shaft, with the threat of fire, poor ventilation and poor lighting. Using the Hurst tool and several other rescue tools, the members of Rescue 1 stabilized the car, then carefully extricated the injured driver. The man suffered multiple arm and leg fractures, neck and back fractures and internal injuries. Rescue 1 was awarded a Unit Citation for this difficult and dangerous operation.

Rescue work is not all fires, crashes, and extrications. Sometimes it's just having the right tools, and the right personnel to do what has to be done. On September 18, 1995, Rescue 1 was called to Pier 61, at West 21st Street and the Hudson River for a boat sinking. The lightship "Frying Pan", now listed on both the New York State and Federal Registers of Historic Places, is one of 13 lightships remaining out of more than 100. Built in 1929, Lightship #115 "Frying Pan" guarded its namesake, Frying Pan Shoals, which is 30 miles off of Cape Fear, North Carolina, from 1930 to 1965. The ship was placed out of service and eventually made its way to New York.

Rescue 1 arrived at the pier under the command of covering officer Lt. DelMaestro to find the ship listing to the port at a 45-degree angle. The ship's captain was imploring the rescue men that "time was of the essence", as the ship was taking on water fast. He estimated within 15 to 20 minutes the "Frying Pan" would capsize. Lt. DelMaestro, Firefighters Joseph Angelini and Lloyd Intanzon boarded the ship, with Al Benjamin taking readings with the explosive meter. Outside, Firefighters Paul Hashagen and Ronald Morstadt brought the Stanley hydraulic generator into position and set it up as a pump.

With the inside team three decks down, hoses were set up and pumping began. For three hours Rescue 1 operated, until the water level lowered enough that the holes were plugged and the flooding was stopped. Rescue 1 had saved the ship from sinking.

Rescue 1 responded to a most unusual rescue call just after 2 p.m., on May 13, 1996. The location was the century-old Salvatore Spina Stables at 538 West 38th Street in Manhattan. The job was to free a handsom cab horse stuck in a hay and manure chute, on the second floor of the building. The horse, a thirteen year-old large white gelding, had gotten free from its stall and followed a thin trail of feed into a 5 x 8-foot area where nearly the entire floor funneled into a chute used to transfer manure down and hay up as needed. The animal was calmed by the rescue men as the equipment was positioned.

A high-point beam was positioned across a similar chute above and a Griphoist was attached to it. Rescue men then carefully attached two Atlas life belts together encircling the horse. A series of trial lifts were started to position the belts, now being used as slings, in the correct position. After several close attempts, the horse was finally lifted up and as the rescue men tried to lead the horse out of the area it panicked, slipped and slid back into the chute.

Extrication of victim from auto that drove into elevator shaft.

The horse was again calmed and examined for injuries before the operation was again commenced. This time the huge animal was lifted clear, and moved away from the chute. A veterinary doctor immediately examined the horse, and provided some minor medical attention. When asked the horse's name by the assembled media Battalion Chief Joseph Grasso replied simply, "Stupid."

The shocking news of a major airline crash just off the coast of Long Island echoed across the New York airwaves on July 17, 1996. TWA Flight 800 went down, approximately 12 miles south of the Moriches Inlet in Suffolk County. The FDNY sent rescue divers, special operations personnel and the fireboat *Kevin Kane*, (Marine 6) to the scene. Several members of Rescue Company 1 responded to the scene, as part of the dive rescue team. On the first day the FDNY dive team followed a police boat equipped with side-scanning sonar, and were ready to deploy if any large debris fields were located. They also helped with a surface search of the crash area, and collected several pieces of luggage and floating debris. The FDNY crew then worked with a team of U.S. Navy divers. The Navy UDT divers would lead the FDNY to GPS locations of interest. These areas were noted by the criss-crossing sonar boats performing grid searches. A UDT diver then went down and searched the oceans floor. If any passenger's remains were located, the FDNY divers would do the recovery. This plan of action went on for several days with FDNY divers entering the water several times. As the Navy brought more resources to the scene, they took a greater role and the FDNY dive team was demobilized.

Department Order No. 82 dated August 1, 1996 singled out the FDNY divers who responded and worked at the crash site. This list included from Rescue Company 1: Captain John Norman, FF Paul Hashagen, FF Neal Fredericksen, FF Clifford Stabner, and FF Timothy Kelly.

In the early morning hours of August 23, 1996, Rescue 1 was assigned to Box 733 transmitted at 3:06 a.m. At first locating the cause of the smoke condition in the area proved difficult for first due companies as they were sent to incorrect locations. Finally, the search led them to the former B. Altman Department Store, at Fifth Avenue and 36th Street, a 13-story 420 x 200 foot building that took up the entire square block. Smoke could be seen coming from the upper floors, and a 10-75 was transmitted at 3:40 a.m. Within three minutes it had become a second alarm. For the next ten hours firefighters would battle one of the hottest and smokiest fires they would ever encounter.

The fire originated in the stores fur vault, a large windowless room built of cinderblock and lined with cork insulation. The difficult battle required ventilating the extremely hot vault area, and locating the hot spots using Thermal Imaging Cameras. Another complication arose, when firefighters realized there was asbestos abatement in progress in the building. The fire would require five-alarms and numerous special calls to control. Twenty-five firefighters suffered heat exhaustion and ten were hospitalized. The fire was declared under control at 1:14 in the afternoon.

In 1996 two recently promoted captains, Terence Hatton (who later became captain of Rescue Company 1) and Philip Ruvolo (later the captain of Rescue 2), began working on a project that would standardized training within Special Operations. This project built on the concepts started earlier that decade, when the first Rescue School was initiated. They hand-picked members, who began writing curriculum and designing classes to be used for a new concept: The Technical Rescue School. In the fall of 1996, after months of hard work the FDNY Special Operations Command Technical Rescue School was established to continuously train the members of the command. In the school's mission statement it further stated: Prior to the formation of this school, members were trained through programs and classes developed to address specific needs. Other training was conducted by officers and members within the companies addressing the needs of that unit. This worked well for much of the history of these special units. The captains were able to hand pick members who had experience in firefighting, and had a special talent or skill that would enhance the units ability to function at major emergencies. Many of these individuals had worked as crane operators, riggers, welders, carpenters or other trades, before they became firefighters.

Today, because fire department candidates are much younger, and need college prerequisites, many of the new members do not have a trade background. Therefore, the pool of special skills has diminished. In addition, technology has also changed with new equipment and procedures to constantly keep up with.

To address these needs, Rescue School was formed to provide a comprehensive standardized training program for all members of these units. These programs include: Basic Rescue Technician Course, Confined Space, Collapse & Rescue Operations, Rigging, and High Angle Rope Rescue. Members are also familiarized with all aspects of underwater search and rescue, and vehicle extrication and disentanglement.

Due to the timely initiation of this training program, the Special Operations Commands: 5 Rescues, 7 Squads, 2 Tactical Support Units, Hazardous Materials Unit, the SOC Battalion and SOC Support Staff were able to meet or exceed newly enacted federal training standards. As stated in the mission statement: Our goal is to "Build on the Reputation, not rest on it".

Flames pouring from wind-driven fire at the Lionel Hampton fire January 7, 1997.

The year 1997 got off to a wild start, when Rescue 1 responded to a wind-driven blaze on the 28th floor of the 42-story high-rise multiple dwelling known as One Lincoln Plaza. It was 2:32 p.m., January 7th, when Box 969 was transmitted for a fire in the apartment of the famed musician Lionel Hampton. A high-intensity lamp had fallen over onto a bed igniting the blaze. Then as the tenants, Mr. Hampton included, evacuated the apartment door was inadvertently left open. Moments later the window failed. Flames suddenly roared down the hallway with blowtorch intensity.

Arriving units could see flames pouring out the 28th floor windows of the building located at 64th Street and Columbus Avenue. Conditions on the fire floor were extreme. Lines were connected to standpipes, flaps were pulled down, and collars pulled up as the first of the nozzle teams attempted to inch their way into the wall of flames.

The Ninth Battalion received reports that two women were seen trapped, at a smoke-filled window on the fire floor. The chief sent Rescue 1 to attempt to reach them. Lieutenant Dennis Mojica and Firefighters Stan Sussina, Patrick O'Keefe and Warren Forsyth made their way to the floor above the fire and located the apartment directly above the location of the trapped woman. Despite a multi lock door and the heavy smoke condition, they were soon in the apartment. Reports from the fire floor indicated conditions were getting worse by the minute. It was time to take action.

FF Stanley J. Sussina.

Firefighter Stan Sussina was attached to the life-saving rope, and climbed out the window. Firefighter Patrick O'Keefe carefully lowered him to the window below. Sussina entered the apartment finding conditions inside bad and becoming worse. The apartment door was extremely hot, and smoke was pumping in from all sides. The two women were in a panicked state. Sussina instructed the women to stay down low by some windows to get fresh air, as he gathered towels to stuff around the door in an attempt to hold back some of the smoke. This and the lowering of two air-packs helped calm the women.

Outside in the public hallway, nozzle teams were rotated as two 2-1/2 inch hose lines were pushed into the flames. It took the combined efforts of ten engine companies to reach the fire apartment, and knock the fire down. Five alarms had been transmitted to provide enough manpower to advance the hoses and search the large building.

For his daring rope work and for staying in a very dangerous position, Firefighter Stan J. Sussina was awarded the James Gordon Bennett and NYS Honorary Chiefs Association Medals. Rescue 1 was also awarded a Unit Citation.

Manhattan Box 619 was transmitted at 1:15 p.m., on June 27, 1997. Rescue 1 was assigned to the alarm, a reported boat crashed into a pier. Rescue 1 arrived at the Chelsea Pier first due. They were met by frantic civilians reporting that a ship had crashed into the pier. Captain Terry Hatton, Firefighters Dave Marmann and Fred Herrmann pressed through the surging crowd heading towards the western end of the pier. As the members neared, the magnitude of the crash became apparent. As the 190-foot cruise ship cruise ship pulled into the pier a problem with the transmission developed, and the vessel was unable to stop or slow itself. It burrowed in onto dry land, ripping a pedestrian gangway from the pier promenade, before crashing her bow through a brick building on the adjoining enclosed pier. Civilians on the pier and on the ship were yelling conflicting information to the rescue members, with regard to the number and severity of the injuries onboard the ship *Spirit of New York*. At the captain's request, rescue chauffeur Firefighter Paul Hashagen radioed the Manhattan fire dispatcher requesting they: "Fill out the box, and start out four EMS units with a supervisor." Gaining access to the ship from a port side gangway, Marmann and Herrmann began to triage patients.

With the ship's engines still racing at full speed ahead, and 500 passengers and crew still on board, the rescue men began treating the injured. Upon their arrival Captain Hatton requested the Ninth Battalion to transmit a 10-60 signal. Firefighters Joe Angelini and Michael Geidel arrived with SCUBA gear and floatation devices. They began a search for any passengers in the open water. After completing their searches, they joined the members on the ship, and began treating and transporting the injured passengers. Members of Rescue 1 transferred pa-

*Rescue Company 1 officers,
Lt. Dennis Mojica, Capt. Terence Hatton
and Lt. John Kiernan. (Dan Alfonso)*

tient care to other FDNY members, so they could clear the wreckage partially blocking the gangways. The passengers were calmly escorted from the ship, as EMS personnel took charge of the injured.

A secondary search commenced, as the ship's engines were shut down. The huge ship was then made secure, and FDNY units began to take up.

On the night of August 6, 1997, Rescue 1's Lieutenant Dennis Mojica was working the night tour in Rescue 2. At 3:36 a.m., the company responded to a reported building collapse at 3851 Flatlands Avenue, Brooklyn. Lt. Mojica and Firefighter Robert Galione were able to extricate a trapped man, despite the building shifting and collapsing around them. For their heroic rescue, they both received medals.

A most unusual technical rescue operation occurred on the afternoon of September 29, 1997, when Rescue 1 was called to the Queensboro Bridge. Box 937 was transmitted at 1:20 p.m., for an construction accident on the bridge. A private construction company, hired to repair the outer roadway of the bridge, were placing large sections of scaffold underneath the bridge to facilitate this work. As it was being secured, a loud crack was heard and the scaffold suddenly collapsed. The six workers on it at the time were left dangling on their safety ropes 135-feet above the East River. Arriving FDNY units and police made their way to the accident site and pulled the workers to safety.

One worker was seen dangling a distance away from the others. Rescue 1, under the command of Captain Phil Ruvolo (SOC), was sent to reach him. Firefighters Joe Angelini, Gerry Nevins and Paul Hashagen crawled out onto a small wooden walkway that extended beneath the the bridge, without guard rails or safety devices of any type. The rescue men crawled out 50-feet to reach the injured man, who had just been pulled in by his fellow workers. Before this first man could be packaged, one of his co-workers began complaining of injuries he'd sustained. This man was helped up, cleared from his harness, and then taken to the roadbed. Meanwhile, the more seriously injured man was given a quick medical assessment that showed signs of neck and back injuries. While still on the narrow walkway, a cervical collar was placed on the man. Next, he was carefully positioned on a longboard. The rescue men then methodically diamond lashed him into a Stokes basket, and when all was ready they delicately pulled him back down the unprotected walkway. This particular patient packaging and removal was done on the four-foot wide wooden walkway 135-feet above the river, without benefit of safety ropes. The remaining members of Rescue 1, Firefighters Steve Mockler and James Leavey, fashioned a high angle rope system that allowed the injured worker to be smoothly raised to the roadway above. Sadly one worker was killed by the initial collapse, the five others were taken to Bellevue Hospital. For their actions Rescue 1 was awarded a Unit Citation.

On January 19, 1998, the FDNY provided mutual aid to Jersey City, New Jersey. A landmark building, the State Theatre, collapsed onto the three-story building next door. The collapse injured at least 17 people, and required two alarms of Jersey City companies. A request to the FDNY sent Rescue 3 with the collapse rig, Battalion 9 and Battalion Chief Ray Downey of Special Operations. That evening, Rescue 1 was special called to relieve Rescue 3 at the scene. Both FDNY rescue companies were later honored with Unit Citations by the Jersey City Fire Department for their actions at the collapse operation.

Another unusual rescue job occurred on June 26, 1998 right in the middle of Times Square. Rescue 1 was called to number 4 Times Square at 9:39 a.m. The ticket read: EMS-TRAUMA: MAN JAMMED IN ELEVATOR SHAFT. Despite the heavier than usual traffic, Rescue 1 was on scene in three minutes. Rescue 1 was directed to an exterior construction elevator and told the emergency was on the 40th floor. With Lt. Stephen Spall (SOC) in charge, Firefighters Thomas Sullivan, Gary Geidel, and Michael Montesi entered the elevator. En route Montesi donned a Class-Three high angle rope rescue harness, so he would be ready to take action. Firefighters Dave Williams, rescue chauffeur, and John Schoff, detailed for the tour from Squad 41, remained with the rig to provide tools and maintain control of the elevator.

Lt. Dennis Mojica

Queensboro Bridge rescue crew, September 29, 1997.

Upon arrival at the 40th floor the victim, a 38 year-old construction worker, was visibly pinned between the elevator car and the shaft wall. His shoulders were pinned at the same level as the floor of the car; his face was 12-feet above the 40th floor level. The man was ashen gray in color, indicating oxygen deficiency. His body was acting like a wedge, jamming the elevator car. Both the platform and the elevator shaft were constructed of pipe scaffolding. Walls were cross braced, providing little to prevent a 40-story fall.

The platform was crowded with members of Ladder 4, and more than twenty-five construction workers trying to help their friend. Lt. Spall ordered all non-essential workers off the platform to alleviate both the falling and collapse hazards. He then ordered measures to secure the elevator from any movement up or down. FF Geidel was sent to the floor above, with ropes to secure the car at that level, and the victim if possible. FF Sullivan mounted the exterior scaffolding, and climbed to the victim securing himself with his personal harness. This access, while extremely perilous, provided rapid access. All other alternatives (like ladders or building a platform) would have taken considerable time.

Montesi passed Sullivan a sawzall, and while dangling on his personal harness, began making cuts. This operation was made more complicated, given the fact the victims face was less than 2-inches from the required cut. When the cut was completed, the victim was freed and the car remained stationary. Firefighters Sullivan and Geidel held the victim, then with Montesi, they manually lowered him to the platform. Montesi found no pulse. He immediately began CPR and ventilations assisted by a member of Ladder 4. After approximately 30-seconds a pulse was established. EMS arrived and assumed patient care, transporting him to the hospital. For their spectacular efforts, Rescue 1 was awarded a Unit Citation.

A verbal alarm for Manhattan Box 795 was transmitted at 8:25 a.m., on July 21, 1998, when a scaffolding collapsed at the Conde Nast Building construction site at Four Times Square. The new building had been under construction since 1996, and was listed as having 48-stories, with two additional floors for machinery rooms above. Erection of scaffolding (exterior construction elevators encased in netting) at the 49th and 50th floors was nearing completion that morning, when workers noticed the "tracks" that carry the elevator cars were beginning to buckle at the 19th floor. Workers cleared the area of pedestrians, just as the tracks tore away from the structure. Several sections fell to the street, or landed on a parking garage. The largest section crushed through the roof of the 12-story Woodstock Hotel across the street. This section penetrated the reinforced concrete roof of the hotel smashing into a top-floor room.

Rescue 1 arrived at the scene quickly and, directed by Battalion Chief Nardone, split into two teams. The first team went into the Woodstock Hotel to check the top floor impact site, while the second team went to the building under construction to check the stability of the scaffolding. When Special Operations Chief Ray Downey arrived, he conferred via radio with Lieutenant Michael Pena of Rescue 1 who was on the 19th floor of the Conde Nast building. Rescue 1 then began to lash the vertical legs of the scaffolding to substantial structural components on each floor. It was estimated that each floor of scaffolding weighed 8,000 pounds.

Due to the potential for further collapse the Woodstock Hotel was evacuated, while Rescue 1 continued stabilizing the scaffolding. This operation took nearly the entire first day. The FDNY commanders on scene realized the safe removal of the collapsed scaffolding, and the repair of the subsequent damage would be a very long and drawn out process. A rotation system was arranged for Special Operations companies, including Rescue 1. The FDNY maintained a 24-hour presence at the scene for 26 days until the scaffold removal was completed.

In September of 1998, FDNY Special Operations Command members, including members of Rescue 1, were activated as part of NYTF-1 by the mayor's office. The team was flown to the Dominican Republic recently devastated by Hurricane Georges. They were taken to an abandoned sports housing complex, called the Olympic Village, using this as their base of operations. Several team members were dropped by helicopter into remote areas, to provide medical attention to villagers cut-off from the outside world. Drugs were administered, first aid provided, and surgery performed.

Other teams spent many hours cutting trees to clear the roads for ambulances and military vehicles. Another team travelled to San Pedro de Macoris. Here they found the regional hospital. It was hard hit by the storm and left without a roof, power, or running water. After a hard days work beneath a broiling sun, the team members using ingenuity and make-shift tools, had re-fabricated the roof and restored power and water to the hospital. After eight days the team returned to New York.

Shortly before 10 a.m., on the morning of Wednesday December 23, 1998, Rescue 1 responded to a phone alarm reporting a fire on the 19th floor of 124 West 60th Street, a 51-story high rise multiple dwelling. Units arrived to see a heavy body of fire coming out the windows of the fire floor. First due units were stretching in on the fire floor, as Rescue 1 hopped in an elevator ascending towards the fire. Suddenly the wind shifted, driving the heat and flames down on the nozzle team. It was virtually the same fire situation and conditions that had taken the lives of three FDNY firefighters five days earlier, on Vandalia Avenue in Brooklyn.

The 19th floor hallway had become a 2,000-degree blast furnace, and the open door to the attack stairs a super-heated chimney. The nozzle team attempted to protect themselves with the stream as "May-days" were called, by burned members and officers separated from their men. In the elevator below, the members of Rescue 1 were startled as water cascaded down the shaft stopping the car. They quickly forced open the door and hit the stairs at a gallop.

On the half landing below the fire floor, Rescue 1 found injured and disoriented members and dazed officers trying to find their men. Captain Hatton split the company. An all out assault was started, as the scorching hall was searched for injured and missing firefighters. The door to the fire apartment, left open by fleeing occupants, was located 70-feet from the attack stairs. Under extreme conditions, the line was operated to maintain control of the hallway. As reports indicated all members were accounted for, Rescue 1 concentrated on attacking the fire, which they could see was significant. The fire apartment, which was later identified to belong to the actor Macaulay Culkin's mother adjoined his, in wrap-around fashion. They realized there was fire behind them as well as in front of them.

Four alarms were transmitted, before the fire could be controlled. Sadly, four people were killed in the attack stairs on the floors above the fire. Nineteen others, including nine firefighters were injured.

The day after Saint Patrick's Day, March 18, 1999, a serious problem developed in Midtown Manhattan. Box 786 was transmitted for One Times Square, for a reported fallen sign with injuries to people. The 22-story commercial building, famed as the site of the New Year's Eve ball drop, featured a large sign measuring 80 x 50-feet. It weighed more than 500-pounds, and became dislodged by high winds. Several people were injured by falling debris, that rained down on them even as fire apparatus arrived.

159

Three sides of the sign had pulled free, and the wind gusting above 40 mph was whipping the sign about dangerously. Battalion 9 sent Rescue 1 to the roof to evaluate the situation, as the injured were treated and the area below was cordoned-off. On the roof, Captain Terry Hatton conferred with licensed sign riggers, who determined the wind conditions made it too dangerous for them to work on the sign. The danger still existed, so a plan was formulated with Division 3 and Battalion 9.

Firefighter Gerard Nevins, outfitted with a Class-Three harness, spent nearly an hour straddling the parapet wall trying to gain control of the twisting sign. A powerful gust pulled the sign and a lighting fixture away from the wall. The fixture ripped from the building, crashing to the sidewalk with chunks of concrete. Hatton advised the chiefs he'd have to lower a member on rope to correct the condition manually.

FF Gerry Nevins

Nevins was attached to a high-angle rope system, and was lowered towards the dangling sign. He squeezed through a small space between the sign and the building, and began the tedious process of taking the sign apart. With dangerously sharp pieces moving around him, he worked his way to each level, cutting nylon straps and removing the aluminum backing, until he reached the bottom of the sign. With that danger cleared, he concentrated on the damaged electrical fixtures and lighting system.

Finally, after two-hours, all the overhead dangers were secured and Nevins was carefully pulled back up to the roof. For his great courage and determination, Firefighter Gerard T. Nevins was awarded the Thomas A. Kenny Medal.

It was a half hour before the start of the day tour on July 7, 1999, when FDNY units were dispatched to Stanton and Essex Streets on the Lower East Side of Manhattan. What they found on arrival would turn into a multiple alarm fire. First due units transmitted a 10-75 for a fire inside a two-story, 50 x 80-foot building at 163 Essex Street. It was an MTA (Metropolitan Transportation Authority) sub-station, that contained transformers and wiring to provide power to the third rail on the F, A and E lines of the subway system. These sub-stations receive voltages of up to 27,000 volts from Con Ed, then reduce and rectify the voltage for use by the subway trains. Another thing contained inside the cellar was a Con Ed transformer, that was not on the MTA plans of the building. This caused size-up problems, as the type of fire was being identified.

First due units were pulled back from their search of the cellar, due to high heat and "loud popping noises". The city had been in a major heat wave recently, with temperatures reaching more than 100-degrees, and high humidity. These factors contributed to a great strain on the power grid.

Two foam lines were stretched to the front of the building as Rescue 1, under the command of Captain Terry Hatton, entered the sub-station to search for the seat of the fire, using thermal imaging cameras. Members of the company had just emerged from a subway emergency exit in front of the fire building, where they located a stalled, occupied "F" train. This train was evacuated.

Acting Chief of Department Pete Ganci and fire commanders then received a reliable report about the transformer, and associated equipment in the cellar. It was decided to use high expansion foam to control the blaze. Rescue 1, re-entered the thick smoke to search for a two-piece metal plate on the first floor of the building, that was used as an equipment hatch. This hatch was found to be several hundred pounds and eight-inches thick. With the regular hoist used to raise the cover invisible somewhere overhead in the swirling dense smoke, Rescue 1 rigged their own device — the Griphoist. Using pry bars and the Griphoist, members of Rescue 1 aided by Squad 18 lifted the cover clear of the opening. A major foam attack was begun.

Members of Rescue 1 with President Bill Clinton.

It was now clear the cellar contained several, burning transformers that might contain PCB's. A full decontamination process began, as samples of run-off water were taken. Members of Rescue 1 were scrubbed down, and their gear confiscated. Once deconned, the members returned to quarters, replaced the missing gear and went back into service.

It was around 4 in the morning on July 25, 1999, when the company rolled out to a report of a person-in-the-water at the Hudson River and West 55th Street. Arriving at the pier, Lieutenant Michael Pena shone his flashlight across the choppy waters. About 500-feet from shore, he spotted a man being swept south by the current. The company's inflatable boat was quickly deployed, by Firefighters Joel Kanasky, Lloyd Intannone and Steven Modica. Lt. Pena, Firefighters Michael Montesi (in dive gear), and David Weiss scrambled onboard and pushed away into the river.

They motored towards the man; his head was still above water, but he was obviously struggling. They hoped it would remain a surface rescue, as they closed the distance. Montesi braced on the side of the boat, prepared to dive into the water as soon as they were close enough. A passing tug towing a barge, caused a wake that at times covered the man. As they neared, he began to sink beneath the waves. Everything changed in an instant—it was no longer a surface removal. It was an underwater rescue.

> As they neared, he began to sink beneath the waves. Everything changed in an instant—it was no longer a surface removal. It was an underwater rescue.

With no time to strap on an air tank, Montesi entered the blackwater. Montesi dove towards the last place he'd seen the man. Feeling something near his feet he grabbed for clothing, anything to get hold of. The man was nude and sinking. Montesi improvised, snatching the man's hair and pulling him upwards. As the body rose, he re-gripped the man around the torso, and moved towards the boat.

Pena and Weiss pulled the unconscious man into the boat. Then as Weiss tilted the man's head to open his airway, Pena helped Montesi onboard. The man regained consciousness and began to struggle. They restrained

FF Mike Montesi and Lt. Mike Pena hold drowning victim, as FF Dave Weiss pilots the boat to the pier on July 25, 1999.

Mike Montesi receives the 873rd Daily News *Hero of the Month, August 1999.*

him as they sped back to shore. The 29-year-old man was turned over to EMS personnel, and taken to St. Vincent's Hospital. He was released two days later. For his outstanding water rescue FF Michael Montesi was placed on the Roll of Merit with a Class B award. He was also presented the *New York Daily News* Hero of the Month award.

Hundreds of bricks rained down on West 57th Street in Manhattan, on October 12, 1999, as an aluminum scaffold with two workers aboard failed. The scaffold was pushed away from the building, toppling the two workers. They were hanging by their safety ropes 70-feet above the ground in front of 315 West 57th Street. Rescue 1 was assigned to Box 929 at 10:30 a.m., and was on scene in minutes. Captain Terry Hatton and his crew, Firefighters Kevin Kroth, Gerry Nevins, Joe Angelini, Thor Johannessen and David Weiss hurried to the eighth and ninth floors. There they found the two workers swaying back and forth, just beyond their reach. Rescue 1 quickly set up high angle rope systems, and began to pull the injured men inside one by one.

Meanwhile, behind and around the rescue men working on the ninth floor, a dispute between a police officer and a fire officer became physical. The police officer shoved the fire lieutenant, who toppled over furniture and onto the floor injuring his neck and back. Despite the chaos around them, Rescue 1 concentrated on the task at hand. They were able to safely remove both workers from their precarious perches. The workers and the injured fire officer were all taken to the hospital.

For their outstanding high angle teamwork, Rescue Company 1 was awarded a Unit Citation.

On November 6, 1999, at 7:22 p.m., Rescue Company 1 was assigned to Manhattan Box 579 for a reported person fallen into an airshaft, at 101 West 18th Street. Upon arrival, Lt. Michael Pena reported to Battalion Chief Belnavis. The chief had just been informed by Ladder 12 that a victim was in the shaft on the exposure 3 side (rear) of the building, approximately 20-feet down from the roof. The shaft was 5-stories in height, about 4-feet wide, and 40-feet long. After locking himself out, the victim tried entering his top floor apartment by sliding down a pipe to his window. Losing his grip, he fell 15 feet, and landed on some angle iron protruding into the shaft. There was no other window access to the shaft, and ladders could not be used. This would be a high-angle rope operation. The members of Rescue 1: Firefighters Kevin Kroth, Gary Geidel, William Henry, John Flatley, and Dave Williams hurried the bags of rope, harnesses, and other gear to the roof.

A main line and safety line were set up, as well as a 4 to 1 mechanical advantage system. Two different anchor points were used to insure safety. A rescue man was quickly lowered to the victim. After a quick medical assessment, the victim was placed in a seat harness. When all was ready, the victim and rescuer were hauled up to the roof parapet, and carefully helped onto the roof. The man was treated for minor injuries. Rescue 1 stowed their gear and went back into service.

It was 5:45 p.m. on November 21, 1999, when Rescue 1 was assigned to Box 1023 for a fire at 140 West 71st Street in Manhattan. Members of Rescue 1 were donning their gear in the back of the responding rig, when they heard Engine 40 transmit a "10-75!" They further stated the street was blocked by cars, and the hydrants near the building were not accessible. The rescue men knew delayed water could cause serious problems.

When Rescue arrived at the scene, they saw an extremely heavy fire condition on the fourth floor, extending to the fifth floor of the nine-story apartment house. Occupants were being helped down aerial ladders. Rescue 1 split into three teams: one team went to the fire floor, the second team to the floors above, and the third team went to the roof.

Entering the floor above the fire were Rescue 1 Firefighters Gerry Nevins and Patrick O'Keefe. They systematically forced locked doors, and searched fifteen apartments on the fifth and sixth floors. In apartment 6-F Nevins found three occupants, advising them to remain in place. One of them told Nevins about a woman in trouble on the eighth floor. Looking up the shaft window, Nevins could see heavy smoke pushing from the eighth floor window.

Nevins radioed his officer and headed for the eighth floor, while O'Keefe searched the seventh floor. The self closing stairwell doors had been blocked open on the fourth (fire floor) and the eighth floors, allowing a tremendous build up of heat and smoke throughout the eighth floor. Conditions were becoming extreme, as Nevins crawled down the hallway searching for the opened door. To add to this Firefighter Nevins' SCBA began "Vibralert", telling him his air supply was running low.

Pressing on Firefighter Nevins located the open door to apartment 8-B and began a search. He located two unconscious people, and radioed 10-45 to Battalion 11. He dragged the first victim to the living room, near the apartment entrance. Returning for the second victim, he found a third and again radioed the chief. While dragging the second victim to the door, he was joined by other firefighters, who helped remove the three victims. For his tenacious actions and bravery, Firefighter Gerard T. Nevins was awarded the William Friedberg Medal.

Chapter 10

The Millennium

For a while, it appeared that the year 2000 was truly going to be quite different than any other New Year. Many things had changed in the FDNY since the turn of the last century: the horses were gone, and the apparatus was bigger and more powerful than ever. All personnel on the fire ground could easily communicate by radio, and computers were located at the housewatch and in every FDNY apparatus. It was this modern technology, that many thought was going to become the problem. Millions of dollars were spent by the government and the private sector to solve a potential problem: Y2K, or "the Millennium Bug". Would the world's computers be able to see the number 2000 as a valid date? Would they follow automated commands? Would the lights stay on?

> Moments later computers would print out alarms and fire companies would respond — Just like last year — No problem — business as usual.

At midnight the ball dropped in Times Square, and the huge crowds cheered wildly as the the numbers "2000" flashed overhead. Moments later computers would print out alarms and fire companies would respond—Just like last year—No problem— business as usual.

March 7, 2000, Manhattan Box 175 was transmitted at 5:27 a.m. A 10-75 was given, as first due units were confronted by a heavy smoke condition in the narrow street obscuring the front of 81 Mott Street, a five-story building. The mixed occupancy building had stores on the basement, first floor and second floor levels, with apartments above. Conditions were so bad, that companies were having great difficulty advancing.

Fire was known to be on the second and third floors of the building. Lines were stretched to those locations. The command post received a report of a possible civilian trapped on the fourth floor. Rescue 1 was sent to search. The company used the rear fire escape to access the apartments on the fourth floor. They searched the exposure four side apartments, then regrouped and reentered to search the other apartments, under the protection of a hose line operated by Engine Company 4. The searches proved to be negative. This went to four-alarms before it was declared under control.

On the night of October 8, 2000, Rescue 1 responded to a high-rise building fire at 250 West 57th Street. Due to the size of the building, (half a city block) it was difficult to determine the correct entrance. The fire had gained tremendous headway prior to fire department arrival, and proved rather difficult to extinguish, requiring four-alarms to control. With companies bogged down due to the high heat and dense smoke, Captain Hatton and members of Rescue 1 crawled up to the operating nozzle teams on the ninth floor, to assess the situation.

Capt. Hatton, Firefighters Weiss and Benjamin preparing for presidential landing at the Downtown Heliport. (Dan Alfonso)

Capt. Hatton and crew take a break after battling a 4-alarm fire on October 8, 2000. (Dan Alfonso)

Firefighters Benjamin, O'Keefe, Nevins, Duddy, Hashagen and Capt. Hatton after working Box 44-0915 at 250 West 57th Street and Eighth Avenue, October 8, 2000. (Dan Alfonso)

Friend of the company, Chef Tom Hurley, brought some high-powered help from the French Culinary Institute to quarters in July of 2001 to help him cook dinner. (l. to r.) Capt. Hatton, Chefs Andre Soltner, Jaques Pepin, and Tom Hurley.

FF Mike Montesi operating jaws during FDNY demo at the Intrepid. (Dan Alfonso)

FF Gary Geidel cuts vehicle apart during the Intrepid demo. (Dan Alfonso)

Rescue 1 operated at this difficult 3-alarm fire in the Waterside Plaza on April 24, 2001.

Firefighters Gerry Nevins, Al Benjamin, Paul Hashagen, Patrick O'Keefe and Daniel Duddy operated on the fire floor attempting to identify the location and extent of the fire. Using a thermal imaging camera, Captain Hatton advised command that the amount of heat was far beyond the ability of the hose lines to extinguish. It was decided to hit the large volume of fire using an outside stream. All units backed off the fire floor. The fire area was hit using a ladder pipe and tower ladder. Then members of Rescue 1 under command of Captain Hatton, and Rescue 4, under the command of Captain Brian Hickey, manned two 2-1/2" hose lines and moved in to extinguish the remaining rooms of fire.

Rescue 1 had a slightly different response policy starting in the year 2000. The unit was no longer assigned to automatic alarms in midtown high-rise buildings. However, they were being dispatched to any report of a motor vehicle accident with people trapped within their response district. This change in response gave a boost to morale and also helped to make the company even more effective, as the statistics bear out: Runs 3016, Workers 1412, Occupied Structural Workers 421. Almost half the time the company rolled out the door they went to work.

In March the company operated at two separate major fires. On March 5, 2001, Rescue 1 worked at a three-alarm fire (Box 33-547) at 410 Tenth Avenue. Then on March 12th, they responded to a fifth-alarm fire (Box 55-805) on West 45th Street near Fifth Avenue.

A three-alarm fire tore through the Waterside Plaza apartment complex on the East River near 25th Street, just before 11:30 a.m., on April 24, 2001. The fire started on the 24th floor of 30 Waterside Plaza, a 37-story high-rise multiple dwelling. It became even more difficult and dangerous to battle, when the elevators failed to operate for the second wave of responding firefighters. Rescue 1 members and the remainder of the incoming troops were forced to climb the stairs to reach the fire floor, where they found a thick wall of hot black smoke. Conditions became extreme, as the fire auto-exposed to the floor above. Firefighters now had two floors of fire to fight.

Members of Rescue 1 searched and operated lines on both floors, changing cylinders and going back for more fire fighting. After the difficult blaze was extinguish, Captain Patrick Brown (a former member of Rescue 1) showed the assembled media the new thermal imaging device used to locate the fire through all the thick smoke. Rescue 1 had been using thermal imaging devices since the original EEV model was issued to them in early 1988. The success of this new tool prompted the purchase of the new Argus 2 for all ladder companies. This was one of that new tools first tests.

The FDNY Holy Name Society annually honors one of their own for the work they perform for the organization. The senior man of Rescue 1, Firefighter Joseph Angelini was named "Man of the Year" and was presented the award at their Mass and Breakfast on May 20, 2001. The award was given for his 40-years of dedication to the Holy Name Society: working the St. Patrick's Day parade, selling tickets to the Communion breakfast, collecting donations in the firehouse for the children at Christmas, and all the behind the scenes work he did each and every year. The event honoring the forty year veteran was held at Saint Patrick's Cathedral in midtown Manhattan. It was an honor well deserved.

September 11, 2001

The riding board for the September 10th night tour with the day crew added later. They are "Still Riding".

The weather forecast for the day was coming true: clear blue skies, low humidity, light winds, and a pleasant afternoon temperature in the mid-80's.

In the quarters of Rescue 1, the day tour was trickling into the kitchen. Coffee was brewing. Personal firefighting gear was being brought upstairs and placed near the rig. The white board with the September 10th night tour riding positions read: Boss–Lt. Mojica, Chauf–O'Keefe, Can–Nevins, Irons–Henry, Hook–Montesi, Roof–Weiss.

Upstairs in the office, Lt. Dennis Mojica and Capt. Terry Hatton were going over the day book and readying the manpower reports: the senior man Joe Angelini was detailed to SOC, while the junior man Brian Sweeney was just finishing the night tour on overtime at Squad 288. Several firefighters were on vacation, two firefighters were detailed for SCUBA training, and a few group changes were being made to equalize the openings, and spots were filled with company members on overtime. Captain Hatton was also preparing to interview a prospective new member this morning: Firefighter Jason Faso.

It was looking like just another day.

Amazing David Handschuh photo of Rescue 1 responding to Box 8087. (Daily News)

ERS - 1ST ALARM - ERS-
E010 E006 E004 L010 E024 L015 RS01 BC02
DC01

BOX 8087 - 2 WTC LOBBY CMD DESK
LIBERTY ST
INCIDENT# 103
FDID:
-0103
/11/01 0847

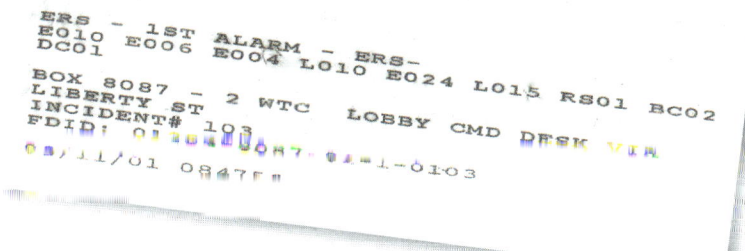

The original teleprinter ticket for Rescue 1's response to the WTC. They were on the road before it was finished printing.

8:46 a.m.

The scanners and department radios scattered around quarters all crackled with an urgent message from the First Battalion. Chief Pfeifer was requesting a third alarm for a plane that intentionally flew into Tower 1 of the World Trade Center. What firefighters didn't know was that the plane, a wide-body 767-200 with 10,000 gallons of fuel and 76 passengers and crew, had been hi-jacked by terrorists. The plane struck the north facade at 96th floor, leaving a gapping hole from the 93rd to the 99th floor.

Immediately both officers, the on-duty night crew, and the off-duty day crew clambered onto the rescue rig heading downtown. As the huge rescue truck roared south on West Street, the chauffeur slid over into on coming traffic to speed the response. A civilian car following behind mirrored this move settling in behind the responding truck. The driver, quite familiar with firefighters and their ways, was David Handschuh, a prize winning photographer with the *Daily News*. He smiled and waved at the rescue men gearing up in the rear of the rig. They waved back and continued dressing. Handschuh picked up his camera and snapped the shutter. His remarkable photograph shows Rescue 1 approaching the blazing World Trade Center. (Handschuh would continue photographing the unfolding story until he was caught as the towers collapsed. Amazingly, he was rescued by a firefighter and recovered.)

Captain Hatton had the rig parked under the north pedestrian bridge to protect the men, as they hustled to the fire building, and to shelter the rig from falling debris. With spare cylinders and tools, the members of Rescue 1 entered the lobby of Tower 1. Captain Hatton reported in to Chief Pfeifer at the fire command post. The rescue officer was given a brief size up of the situation as it was known: There could be as many as twenty floors on fire, there were reports of numerous civilians injured and burned on the upper floors, and all the elevators were out of service.

Stepping away from the command post, Captain Hatton saw his friend Tim Brown (firefighter in Rescue 3 and detailed as a supervisor of operations in OEM, Office of Emergency Management). The captain motioned him over. They hugged and Hatton kissed Tim's cheek saying, "I love you brother, it might be the last time I ever see you." They hugged again. Moments later Hatton, Mojica, O'Keefe, Nevins, Henry, Geidel, Montesi, Weiss and Marino entered the stairwell, and started their climb to the fire floor.

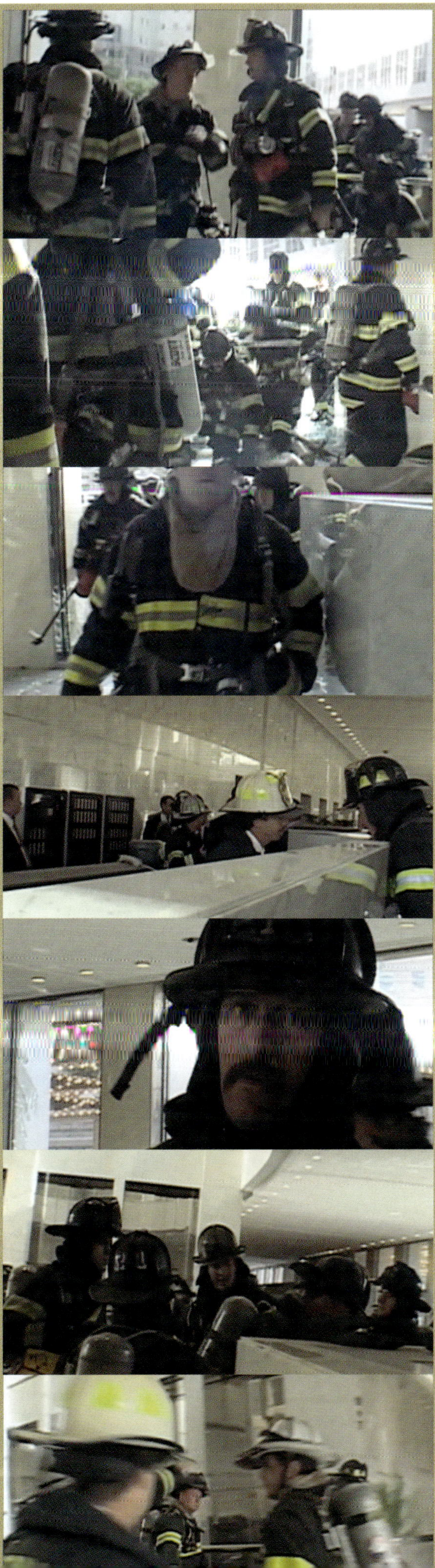

Left, top to bottom: 1. *Capt. Hatton speaks with Lt. Billy McGinn of Sq. 18 in WTC lobby.* ***2.*** *Rescue 1 men entering lobby through broken window.* ***3.*** *Rescue 1 men continue into lobby.* ***4.*** *Capt. Terry Hatton speaking with Chief Pfeifer at WTC Command Post.* ***5.*** *Firefighter David Weiss* ***6.*** *Hatton gives last minute instructions to his men.* ***7.*** *FF Patty O'Keefe heading for the stairs at the WTC. (All images courtesy of Goldfish Pictures)*

September 11, 2001

At 9:00 a.m. while en route, Chief of Department Peter Ganci upgraded the response to a fifth-alarm. This call would bring more than 200 personnel and 33 units to the scene.

As the members of Rescue 1 continued their ascent of the stairs in Tower 1, a second hi-jacked airliner, another 767-200 with 60 passengers and crew, and 9,100 gallons of fuel, intentionally crashed into the south tower at 9:02 a.m. The plane impacted the 81st floor leaving visible damage from the 77th to 85th floors. At 9:12 Chief Ganci called for a second fifth-alarm assignment for the south tower.

Every on-duty rescue firefighter from each of the five rescue companies, and every squad company (except Squad 61) were assigned to one of the two fifth alarms. Nearly the entire Special Operations Command was at, or heading to the scene.

Also responding to the fire scene was the company's senior man, Joseph Angelini. The forty-year veteran was on light-duty and detailed to Special Operations Command headquarters on Randall's Island. Joe jumped on the TAC unit heading to the towers with Rescue 3 firefighter, Ray Phillips. The company's newest member, Firefighter Brian Sweeney, was responding from Queens onboard Squad 288. They, like most of the FDNY, were all heading to the World Trade Center.

Chief Ganci orders a full recall of all off-duty FDNY personnel at 9:29 a.m.

Across the city, off-duty FDNY personnel were heading to their firehouses. Like their brethren, off-duty and retired members of Rescue 1 were responding to lower Manhattan.

Several former members of the company, who'd been promoted were also operating or responding to the scene including: Battalion Chiefs Brian O'Flaherty, Charles Kasper, Edward Geraghty and John Moran, Acting Battalion Chief Alfredo Fuentes (now commanding the Marine Companies), Captain Patrick Brown in command of Ladder 3, Lieutenants Harvey Harrell with Rescue 5, Raymond Brown Jr., in Ladder 113, and Fire Marshal Ronald Bucca.

9:59 a.m.
Tower 2 - The South Tower Collapsed

There were now three major operations occurring simultaneously: the continued rescue efforts going on in the north tower, operations inside the badly damaged Marriott Hotel, and the collapsed south tower and other associated damages. The command post had to relocate temporarily to the World Financial Center garage. Chief Ganci then ordered his staff to reestablish the command post north of the incident, while he initiated rescue operations at the south tower collapse.

Meanwhile, the members of Rescue 1 were still at work inside Tower 1. Where they were and what they were doing exactly is not known. However, NYPD ESU Officer Dave Norman (Chief John Norman's brother) was busy evacuating people, when he encountered David Weiss of Rescue 1 on the 31st Floor calling for medical gear. "There were four firemen having chest pains. They were on the floor. We administered oxygen and took vital signs." Norman advised Weiss the police department was evacuating the building. "Weiss said they were attempting to make a push higher…" Norman said. Following orders transmitted on the NYPD radio, Officer Norman evacuated the tower. David Weiss continued working.

On the streets below, off-duty members of the department were arriving and offering their services. Several members of Rescue 1 approached Battalion Chief Ray Downey and report in. He ordered them to stage a few blocks north and await further orders. This action saved their lives.

Hatton had the rig parked under the pedestrian bridge to protect his men. The front was destroyed by the collapse, but responding firefighters were still able to use the tools from the rig.

World Trade Center

Firefighter Joseph Angelini is carried from the site by Rescue 1.

Firefighter Patrick O'Keefe and Rescue 1 are lowered by crane.

September 11, 2001

10:29 a.m. Tower 1 - The North Tower Collapsed

The entire neighborhood around the World Trade Center site was now covered in a thick cloud of smoke, dust, and fluffy debris. It was difficult, almost impossible to breathe. Mountainous piles of twisted steel were strewn across the streets and other buildings. Numerous building fires added to the dense cloud. The FDNY department radio became eerily quiet for a brief time. Slowly, the injured and trapped began to call for help. In the dust cloud on West Street was Firefighter John Flatley of Rescue 1. He, with a group of off-duty Rescue 1 members, had raced to the scene from their homes on Long Island. Now he could just make out the muffled cries for help squawking from a department radio, and carefully made his way towards the sound. He found a man pinned in a mangled car, debris covering the vehicle and the man. Flatley began to clear the debris by hand.

The man was completely covered by the powdery dust; a huge gash was visible across the top of his head. At first the man was unresponsive. Flatley used the vehicle's department radio requesting help and tools, giving the best size-up he could under the circumstances. He again asked the man his name and this time he got an answer.

"Fuentes"

He'd found Acting Battalion Chief Alfredo Fuentes, a former member of Rescue 1 now in command of the FDNY marine units. Flatley was joined by Rescue 1 Firefighter Neal Fredericksen, who'd brought a pry bar. Together they began to extricate the injured officer. They were soon joined by two other Rescue 1 men, retired Firefighter Bruce Newbery and Firefighter Frank Fee, who'd driven into the city with Flatley. They were preparing to fashion a make-shift stretcher, when a member of the Marine Division arrived with a Stokes basket. They carefully lifted Fuentes into the basket, but were left with a dilemma. Which direction to go?

The marine firefighter said they should head to the water, so they did. They carried Fuentes across the girder filled street into the World Financial Center, and out of the cloud to the river's edge. There they found a small fireboat, and loaded the seriously injured Fuentes onboard. They watched for a moment, as he was rushed across the river towards medical help in a New Jersey hospital. The weary rescue men, then turned and headed back into the cloud – their day just beginning.

When the dust finally settled, the department was faced with numerous fires of all types, from large high-rise building fires to small vehicle fires, and the deep-seated fire that was just beginning to burn beneath the huge debris and collapse pile. Rescue attempts and searches continued. What began that morning would go on for many months. Firefighters and volunteers climbed high onto the pile, checking every crevasse, every void, looking for survivors. The sounds of PASS alarms echoed across the site. Rescue Company 1's rig, the 1996 HME/Saulsbury was located beneath the now collapsed walkway. Rescue 1 members and other FDNY members climbed into the truck, retrieving various pieces of rescue equipment and hand tools. After hours and hours of exhausting and extremely dangerous work, the sad realization sank in. It became evident that despite the officers and firefighters swarming across the acres of rubble, help from FEMA teams, mutual aid departments and all of the other volunteers, live rescues were becoming improbable. But still the work continued. The pile slowly began to give up clues— flashlights, tools and finally some firefighters.

Bands of fathers, former and current members of the department spent day after day looking for their missing sons. Lt. Paul Geidel, (retired member of Rescue 1) who along with his two sons spent hundreds of hours at the site, searching for Gary. Sadly despite the enormous time and effort spent at the site, not everyone recovered.

Lost that day from Rescue 1 were: Captain Terence S. Hatton, Lieutenant Dennis Mojica, Firefighter Joseph Angelini, Firefighter Gary Geidel, Firefighter Patrick O'Keefe, Firefighter Gerard T. Nevins, Firefighter Michael Montesi, Firefighter William Henry, Firefighter Kenneth J. Marino, Firefighter David M. Weiss, and Firefighter Brian E. Sweeney.

Former members of Rescue 1 lost that day: B.C. Charles Kasper, B.C. Edward Geraghty, B.C. John Moran, Capt. Patrick Brown, Lt. Harvey Harrell, and Fire Marshal Ronald Bucca.

Also lost that day were Chief of Department Peter Ganci, First Dep. Commissioner Feehan, and Chief of Special Operations Chief Raymond Downey, and numerous

9/11 memorial in the quarters of Rescue 1.

staff chiefs, officers and firefighters totaling 343 members of the FDNY. The PAPD lost 37 officers and the NYPD lost 23 officers. The civilian deaths brought the total to 2,606.

Several former members: B.C. Brian O'Flaherty, Acting B.C. Al Fuentes and Lt. Raymond Brown Jr., were seriously injured in the collapses. Thankfully, they all recovered.

The "Rescue Family" came together as never before. Current and past members and their families, along with many friends of the company, attended funerals and memorials for those lost. A growing memorial of flowers outside company quarters was lovingly tended by several neighbors. Firefighters from across the country and around the world came to New York City. Attending funerals and supporting the firefighters of the FDNY and their families.

The FDNY was able to reassemble itself and get back to work. Spare rigs replaced those damaged. New tools were ordered and placed on the rigs as soon as they arrived. Rescue 1 went back into service on September 21st. The company was on limited response. Special Operations Command, who'd been especially hard hit by the collapse, lost close to one-fifth of its members, this included six chief officers, 19 company officers and 70 firefighters. SOC began to reorganize the command. A plan was developed to utilize the remaining members still assigned to the units, by using a temporary three-group rotating chart system. At first the groups worked a schedule of 12 hours on and 24 off. This was quickly adjusted to 24 on and 48 off.

World Trade Center

Rescue Company 1
September 11, 2001
Manhattan Box 8087

Captain
Terence S. Hatton

Lieutenant
Dennis Mojica

Firefighter
Joseph J. Angelini, Sr.

Firefighter
Patrick J. O'Keefe

Firefighter
Gary P. Geidel

Firefighter
Michael G. Montesi

Firefighter
William L. Henry

Firefighter
David M. Weiss

Firefighter
Gerard T. Nevins

Firefighter
Kenneth J. Marino

Firefighter
Brian E. Sweeney

The Rescue Company 1
Post 9-11 Three Group Chart

Group A	Group B	Group C
Lt. Weisheit	Capt. O'Brien	Lt. Healy
FF Benjamin	FF Duddy	FF Kroth
FF Fee	FF Myslinski	FF Marmann
FF Hashagen	FF Smith	FF Tedeschi
FF Flatley	FF Johannessen	FF Bullock
FF Leavey		FF Kanasky

Lieutenant Michael Pena was assigned to work with Chief Norman at the WTC command post.

Special Operations Command units, rescues, and squad companies alternated assignments to the WTC site. At first, one rescue and one squad worked on a rotating basis of 9 a.m.-5 p.m., 5 p.m.-1 a.m., 1 a.m.-9 a.m. everyday. This was later adjusted to alternating companies, in early November. Now only one SOC unit, a rescue or squad would be assigned at a time.

On October 3, 2001, Rescue 1 resumed responding to 10-75 signals.

On October 24, 2001, a 160-foot-high scaffold being used to replace the cracked brick facade within the courtyard at 215 Park Avenue South collapsed, killing five workers. Responding to the incident were Lt. Steve Terilli detailed to the company from Battalion 18, Firefighters Glenn Bullock, Joel Kanasky, Todd Smith, Al Benjamin and Ed Myslinski. A total of fifteen workers were busy in the courtyard, when the collapse occurred. Rescue 1 lifted and cut sections of the scaffold piping, to free the injured and those killed. FF Bullock was injured during the operation, and placed on medical leave. For their outstanding company operations at this emergency they were awarded a Unit Citation.

On October 25th the company returned to their normal response assignments. During this time members of Rescue 1 were regularly working their assigned tour in the firehouse (including time at the WTC), then spending their off days either at the WTC site or teaching at the SOC Technical Rescue School. The school was running at full-speed, trying to fill the open spots in the various SOC unit rosters. The first new members to be detailed to Rescue 1 after 9-11 were Firefighters Stephen Katz and David Newbery. Dave's uncle, Bruce Newbery, was a former member of Rescue 1. They began working in the company after completing the first Rescue Tech class since the attacks. They were followed by Shawn Ashe, Cosmo DiOrio, and Michael Schunk.

Manhattan fire companies responded to a dangerous fire inside One New York Plaza on December 1, 2001. First arriving units found a smoke condition emanating from a large concrete encased mechanical room in the basement. Inside the room was a large-diameter "chiller" unit (a heat exchanger utilizing a cool water source, and a second medium such as a coolant or refrigerant. In this case titanium tubes were used, because the cool water source was water from NY Harbor.) This chiller unit was located on a raised steel platform approximately 15-feet above the basement floor level, and was in the process of being dismantled. Part of this operation included cutting away the upper section of the housing with a torch. Apparently, this torch ignited a large number of titanium rods inside the chiller.

First due companies stretched a line into position, but were standing fast as the chiefs considered their strategy. Rescue 1 arrived, just as a second line was being stretched. With little ventilation available, the First Battalion requested Rescue 1 to find a way to vent the area from above. Lt. John Weisheit split his company into two teams, leaving Firefighters Jack Flatley, Frank Fee and Paul Hashagen just outside the fire room incase they were needed. Lt. Weisheit then took Firefighters Thor Johannessen and Todd Smith to the street level to locate a ventilation point.

Just as Rescue 1 began to open a steel fan assembly above the fire area, spray from a hose in the cellar hit the chiller unit. Coming in contact with the burning titanium the water caused a significant explosion. In this room the entire first alarm assignment were knocked from their feet, and thrown into walls or across the floor. Just outside the room, the three members of Rescue 1 were tossed down the length of the hallway. In the street above, flames shot 50-feet into the air burning the members of Rescue 1 opening the fan assembly.

> In this room the entire first alarm assignment were knocked from their feet, and thrown into walls or across the floor. Just outside the room, the three members of Rescue 1 were tossed down the length of the hallway.

The inside team of Rescue 1 scrambled to their feet rushing into the explosion area, and helping several injured firefighters and officers from the blast. As the smoke cleared, a number of firefighters and officers were injured. Amazingly none seriously. The three members of Rescue 1 working on the street level were placed on medical leave.

On December 18, 2001 the Department Orders formally transferred Captain Fred LaFemina to Rescue 1, as the new company commander. Captain LaFemina had been detailed to the company since the 28th of September.

The ABC chart continued until December 24, 2001.

As part of the company's regular rotation to the WTC site, Rescue 1 arrived at the site at 9 a.m., December 25, 2001—Christmas morning.

One of the few rays of sunlight during the dismal days following the collapse of the Twin Towers was in early October; Captain Terry Hatton's wife, Beth, found out she was expecting a baby. Beth Petrone Hatton, Rudy Giuliani's long-time executive assistant, was working in City Hall only blocks away from the world Trade Center that fateful morning. She knew instinctively, her husband would be at the fire. Eight months later she would give birth to a beautiful baby girl, Terri Elizabeth Hatton.

Despite being out of regular service between September 11 and October 25, Rescue 1 still responded to 2592 alarms, with 1057 workers and 333 OSW (occupied structural workers) for the year 2001.

A direct phone call to the Manhattan fire dispatcher, on February 27, 2002 at 4:39 in the morning sent Rescue 1 to Box 857 for a reported man trapped in a shaft. As the company rolled out, Lt. John Weisheit instructed FF Todd Smith, designated at roll call as entry-man, to don a Class 3 harness, and the

RESCUE 1 DAY

December 31, 2001
Mayor Rudolph W. Giuliani
Signed an Official Proclamation
that read in part:

On the darkest day in our history - September 11, 2001- New York City firefighters showed the world the strength and resilience of free people. Faced with an unprovoked act of war, our firefighters raced to the front lines. The courage of New York's Bravest helped to rally a nation, while saving more than 25,000 lives in the largest most successful effort our country has ever seen; and "The New York City Fire Department gave 343 lives in defense of our liberty that day. Captain Terence Hatton, Lieutenant Dennis Mojica, and Firefighters Joseph Angelini, William Henry, Michael Montesi, Gerard Nevins, Patrick O'Keefe, Gary Geidel, Kenneth Marino, and Dave Weiss from special unit Rescue 1 located at 530 West 43rd Street; and…

As a way of expressing our eternal respect and love, I Rudolph W. Giuliani, Mayor of the New York of New York, offer the final proclamation of my administration in honor of our fallen heroes, and in recognition of their bravery and sacrifice, do hereby proclaim Monday, December 31, 2001 in the City of New York as "Rescue 1 Day!"

Rescue 1 went back into service with their former rig, the 1985 Mack.

Returning to quarters May 2002.

It looked as if FF Smith would have to be lowered head-first into the tight shaftway, and operate inverted the entire time. It was determined the trapped man was 200-feet below, and a safety line was quickly lowered to the man. He was able to attach it to himself. Weisheit decided to lower another rope to be used as a main/haul line, and attempt to pull the man up without sending anyone else into the tight confines of the shaftway. After several attempts, and difficulty in language communications, it was determined the trapped man had successfully attached the second rope (main line) to himself. With FF Smith (attached to a lowering system if anything went wrong) and Lt. Weisheit at the opening, the haul teams began to slowly and steadily pull the man up.

Members of Rescue 1 aiding a person hit by a subway train on May 15, 2002.

rigger and safety man to gather the necessary gear. When Rescue 1 pulled up to the 42-story 250 x 250 commercial building at 630 Fifth Avenue, part of the Rockefeller Center complex, they were met by the caller, the fire safety director, Dick Webb (retired FDNY member and medal recipient.) He advised them a man doing maintenance was trapped in an unknown location within a 4 x 4 smoke shaft. Rescue 1 proceeded to the elevator machinery room, the only known access point to the shaft.

Lt. Weisheit called into the shaft, making verbal contact with the man. However, they were faced with a language barrier, since the trapped man spoke little English. Weisheit could hear the man, but was unable to see him. It was clear this would be both a high angle and confined space rescue operation. The company was split into two teams: one team Firefighters Sean Cummins and Jason Faso were to operate the main line. The second team: Firefighters Frank Fee and William Butler (detailed from Ladder 6) would operate the haul line. Members of Ladder 4 assisted both teams, as a complicated series of rope systems were set up. Limited space inside the elevator machinery room made the tricky operation even more difficult

With limited space available, the mechanical advantage system being used to pull the man up had to re-set several times. After about 100-feet of hauling, the victim became visible and the operation continued until the man was pulled clear. He was then given a medical exam by FDNY personnel. This complicated technical operation was smoothly accomplished by a relatively small team.

Family and friends gather to dedicate the new truck.

One of the many pages of plans Capt. Hatton and his men worked on for the new rig.

Matthew Smith a prospective future rescue firefighter and the new rig with Captain Hatton's personal motto "Outstanding" featured on the front.

Airbus/FEMA had Hatton's dream truck built and delivered. The new rig went in service June 10, 2002.

The morning of April 11, 2002 was a clear pleasant day. West 43rd Street was closed to traffic due to an FDNY ceremony being held in the quarters of Rescue Company 1. The firehouse was filled with current members, retired members, and the families of those lost on September 11, 2001. Excitement filled the air as the new rescue truck was about to be dedicated.

This new truck, an Emergency One/Saulsbury, was custom built to Captain Terence Hatton's specifications. Hatton, his officers and men had spent countless hours designing every aspect of this new rig. It became necessary to move up the manufacturing time frame, when the company's 1996 rig was destroyed on September 11th. Donated by Airbus, a global aircraft manufacturer based in France, the new rig gleamed as firefighters, their families and the assembled media took their positions for the dedication.

Brief remarks were given by Battalion Chief Kenneth Hatton (Captain Terry Hatton's father), Battalion Chief Fred LaFemina, former Mayor Rudolph Giuliani, FEMA Director Joe Allbaugh and Airbus President and CEO Noel Forgeard. During his remarks Mr. Forgeard said while Airbus was the best at "designing large airplanes, we cannot take a bit of credit in designing this apparatus. Those honors belong to the men of Rescue 1, and Captain Terry Hatton and the ten good men who died with him on September 11."

In homage to Captain Hatton's personal motto: "OUTSTANDING" was written in gold leaf across the front of the truck.

It was 5:53 in the morning, on November 22, 2003 when Rescue 1 rolled on a reported "automobile in the water". The site was the Hudson River and 133rd Street: Manhattan Box 1542. Traffic was light. The Rescue rig made great time speeding north on the Henry Hudson Parkway. Lt. Tony Tarabocchia glanced back to see his two divers, Firefighters Cosmo DiOrio and Sean Cummins already dressed and ready in their dry suits and SCUBA gear, as the rig arrived at the scene. Engine 37 had interviewed a passenger who'd escaped, after the vehicle entered the water. The divers had a reliable witness, and a confirmed person in the submerged vehicle.

Firefighter Cosmo DiOrio was given the information, as he descended a portable ladder. He paused briefly to check his gear, then plunged into the cold, black waters of the Hudson River. As he was making his way to the bottom, approximately 30-feet deep, DiOrio was aware of the swift current pushing on him. Orienting himself towards the land-based tending line that dis-appeared inches from his face, he began a fan search pattern, carving half circles through the lightless water. On his second sweep he located the vehicle. By feel, he could tell it had turned 90-degrees, and moved thirty feet up river. The car was now facing the sea wall. DiOrio tried to open one of the doors, but it would not yield due to water pressure. He then used a spring-loaded center punch to shatter the windows.

As he was clearing the windows, DiOrio was keeping an on-going dialogue with Lt. Tarabocchia through the tending ropes hard wire communication system. Unable to open the doors, the diver would have to enter the submerged vehicle, a large SUV, to search for the trapped victim. This, his only option, was very risky. He was faced with zero visibility, limited access and egress, and a high chance of his entanglement or the tending line becoming snagged.

Despite these additional dangers, Firefighter Cosmo DiOrio immediately entered the vehicle and began a search. The driver, a heavy man, was located in the driver's seat. Realizing the victim had little time, DiOrio was able to pull him clear of the front seat. Moving with the victim within the tight confines of the auto his tending rope becoming snagged. DiOrio quickly disconnected the safety line, and attached it to the vehicle. This allowed him to maneuver with the victim through the broken window; he then re-attached the tending line and brought the man to the surface.

> The firehouse was filled with current members, retired members, and the families of those lost on September 11, 2001. Excitement filled the air as the new rescue truck was about to be dedicated.

FF Cosmo DiOrio

Rescue men join the "Fighting Swordsmen" of Strike Fighter Force 32, U.S. Navy, during the opening bell ceremony at the NY Stock Exchange, August 8, 2003. (NYSE)

The rescue was not over, as an exhausted DiOrio had to swim back through the moving water a distance of thirty feet to reach the ladder. Firefighter Cummins, also in the water, swam to help pull the large victim to shore. The unconscious man was lifted onto the shore and resuscitation efforts began in earnest. The man was rushed to St. Luke's Hospital, but later died from his injuries.

For this difficult and dangerous underwater rescue Firefighter Cosmo DiOrio was awarded the Firefighter David J. DeFranco Medal. This medal in honor of Firefighter David DeFranco of Rescue 2, is awarded for water related rescues.

A minute before 3 o'clock, on the afternoon of February 6, 2004, Rescue 1 responded to 64 West 35th Street in Manhattan for a reported elevator accident inside the 12-story commercial building. Upon arrival, Captain Robert Morris and his crew found that two men had fallen four-stories into an elevator shaft, with both men sustaining critical injuries. As FF Robert Rufh (roofman) raced to cut-off power to the elevator, Firefighters Frank Rush and Chris Mandeville climbed down from the floor above to the top of the car. Here they began treating and packaging the first injured man, who was suffering severe head trauma and multiple fractures including two broken legs. The first man was then removed from the top of the car and placed in the hands of EMS.

The second victim, not immediately visible, was crushed between the rear of the elevator car and the shaft wall five feet below the top of the car. Reaching and removing this victim would require skill and effort. Splitting his remaining crew into teams, Capt. Morris and FF Frank Rush worked on top of the car to release the trapped man, while FF Mandeville set up rail clamps and rigging slings to support the elevator car. This would prevent it moving during the delicate operation. Each of the 24 bolts of the rail clamps was torqued to 95 foot pounds to securely fasten the clamp to the guide rails. The elevator guide shoes could now be safely removed, and the elevator itself could be moved away from the trapped victim.

With the car stabilized and the victim supported, FF Jason Faso set up air-bags with a 3-inch wood block, and lowered them into position by rope, to move the car. The block was carefully placed near the victims head. The slow controlled inflation of the air-bags pushed the car 15-inches freeing the man. Capt. Morris could now see the severity of the conscious man's injuries: an open skull fracture, possible broken neck, open leg fracture, with an amputated foot that was severely bleeding.

The final part of the rescue involved cutting a 5 x 5 foot hole in the rear of the elevator car, to allow safe removal of the injured man. FF Cosmo DiOrio and FF Robert Rufh began cutting using the "Quik-Cut" air tool and a sawzall. Carefully, they cut the heavy gauge steel cab in very close proximity to the patient and the inflated air-bags. After assuring the car was fully supported, the captain ordered the final cuts of the structural steel members. The patient was placed on a backboard, packaged and removed from the elevator, and placed in the hands of EMS.

For their operation showing "proficiency and precision" Rescue 1 was awarded a Unit Citation.

It was a beautiful, warm, sunny day on May 13, 2005 and Rescue 1 was taking advantage of the pleasant conditions to do what they do frequently—drill. The Manhattan fire dispatcher alerted the company to respond to Box 1123, a SRO (single room occupancy) hotel at 80 Riverside Drive. With FF Frank Fee at the wheel, the rig rolled uptown. En route, the radio was alive with reports of heavy fire, the transmission of a second alarm, and fire on two floors and in the shaft. The company arrived at the fire and covered several different assignments for the chief. He then sent them to a report of a civilian hanging out the window on the left side of the structure.

Firefighter Francis (Frank) Fee, raced up the narrow stairs to the ninth floor and entered the public hallway. Extreme heat and dense smoke filled the hallway. Crawling towards the cries of help from apartment #7, FF Fee reached the fully involved apartment #8, its open door pouring heat and flames into the hall above him. With no time to wait for a line, he crawled under the fire and past the blazing room to the open door of apartment #7. Fee entered, closed the door behind him, and began searching for the trapped occupant. He found the 53-year-old man unconscious on the floor.

FF Francis G. Fee, Jr.

Venting a nearby window, Fee could see that the aerial ladder positioned outside could not reach his location. With no real alternative, Fee forced some air from his mask into the unconscious man's lungs, then took a deep breath himself. He began dragging the man back to the apartment door. In the hall he was met by Capt. Thomas Hughes of Ladder 16 and FF Patrick Barry of Rescue 1, who assisted in bringing the victim back past the fire to the stairwell. The man's condition was so severe he was transferred from St. Luke's Hospital to Jacobi Hospital for high exposure to CO treatment.

For his bravery and daring, Firefighter Francis G. Fee, Jr. was awarded the Emily Trevor/Mary B. Warren Medal.

On September 26, 2006 Rescue 1 was assigned to Manhattan Box 849 for an emergency at 825 Eighth Avenue. Upon arrival, the company was advised by Battalion Chief Joyce, of the Ninth Battalion, that two workers were dangling on ropes, due to a scaffold collapse on the 48th floor. At the site of the accident, Lt. Thomas Donnelly found the scaffold hanging almost vertically, with the workers hanging on their safety lines just below a setback. After a quick conference with the chief a high-angle rope rescue evolution was begun, with the assistance of Ladder Company 4.

Donnelly advised Rescue Firefighter Roderka that he'd be lowered to assist the workers, as Firefighters Faso, Mannion and Cioffi assembled and built the necessary rope systems, while FF Kanasky set up the safety belay line. With no anchors available in close proximity, a rope was stretched to a steel beam 100-feet away. With little room on the setback, the lowering operation and retrieval would be conducted from the hallway.

The company carefully lowered FF Roderka over a four-foot high railing on the 48th floor set-back, to a point alongside the workers. All three were now 850-feet above street level. The first worker was attached to the rescue retrieval system, and upon Donnelly's command, members of Ladder 4 began the hauling procedure. The worker was maneuvered around the parapet and onto the set-back. The system was then lowered and attached to the second worker, who was also lifted to safety. Both workers were medically evaluated by Ladder 4, as Rescue 1 retrieved FF Roderka.

With Roderka safely on the setback, the workers were packaged and taken to a service elevator. They were then turned over to EMS. This complicated rescue was smoothly and successfully conducted, despite close quarters and the fact it was 850-feet above the sidewalk below.

It was 8:15 in the morning when Manhattan Box 973 was transmitted for a reported building fire at 142 West 65th Street, a five-story multiple dwelling. Upon arrival the company was

During July 2005 this Mack/Ferrara Collapse Rescue 1 was assigned to Rescue 1 and stationed in the spare bay in the quarters of Ladder 25 on W. 77th Street.

directed by B.C. Williams of the Ninth Battalion, to assist in locating the fire in the basement. Lt. Tarabocchia split his crew sending FF Mandeville (irons) and FF Miranda (hook) to the floor above, while sending FF Owens to the roof. Lt. Tarabocchia and FF Bullock (can) went into the basement with Ladder 35. The company found a large body of fire in the extreme rear of the building, and under debilitating conditions a primary search was conducted before a charged line could be positioned. Once the fire was partially knocked down by Engine 54, Lt. Tarabocchia reported fire rapidly extending upwards through three pipe chases piercing the unprotected basement ceiling.

Firefighters Miranda and Mandeville made their way to the rear of the first floor and found a heavy smoke condition and fire in the walls. A line was called for. FF Miranda and FF Kroth headed to the second floor rear, while FF Mandeville waited for the line and operated with Engine 23.

On the second floor they forced open a rear apartment door and were confronted by a high heat condition and zero visibility. Groping towards the rear bedroom to vent, FF Kroth found fire extending upwards through the baseboards and called for a line. At this time, Deputy Chief McKavanagh (Division Three) summoned Rescue 1 to assist Ladder 4 in the removal of victims on the third floor rear fire escape. Tarabocchia moved towards the third floor through the interior, as Bullock went up the fire escape.

Conditions on the second floor had become so bad FF Kroth was forced from the blazing apartment. He took a position controlling the apartment door to protect the hallway from the extending flames, as FF Miranda moved towards the third floor to assist with what turned out to be two victims. As Tarabocchia reached the third floor, he could see Miranda and a member of Ladder 4 carrying an unconscious women to a safe area. Miranda then used his positive pressure SCBA to force some air into the unconscious woman.

FF Mandeville rejoined Kroth and with Engine 39 made an aggressive push into the fully involved second floor rear apartment. Tarabocchia found extending fire on the third floor and called for a line, as FF Bullock assisted with the second unconscious victim. During this rapidly extending fire, FF Owens helped vent the roof and top floor staying in his position incase a life saving rope removal became necessary.

For their outstanding teamwork and aggressive fire fighting at this three-alarm fire, Rescue 1 was awarded a Unit Citation.

A reported construction accident at 8:37 p.m. on July 24, 2007 sent Rescue 1 to Box 10 in the subway tunnel east of the State Street Station at Whitehall Street in lower Manhattan. On arrival, the company was advised by Battalion One of a construction worker pinned under a large earth type drilling machine being used in the tunnel. Ladder 15 was already in the tunnel with their trauma kit and a set of air-bags. Under the command of Lieutenant Thomas Donnelly, a team from Rescue 1 descended into the tunnel and began a quick size-up. A 20,000 ton earth drill had rolled to one side, completely pinning a worker from the neck down. The huge machine was leaning, completely unsupported. It was only held by several workers using pinch bars and brute strength. Donnelly called the second team to site with additional tools and equipment.

Rescue chauffeur FF Jason Faso and the team carried down stabilizing jacks, cribbing, and the Hurst tool set. As the gear was brought into position FF Glenn Bullock, an EMT, crawled under the drill to assess the victim's medical condition. He reported back that the victim had a possible fractured pelvis, fractured femur, and was pinned almost up to his neck.

Under the direction of Lt. Donnelly, a two-sided extrication operation began. Firefighters Jason Faso, Vincent McMahon, Carl Scheetz, and members of Ladder 15 operated on the unsupported side of the machine, attempting to stabilize it using a combination of air-bags, cribbing, and jacks. Lt. Donnelly, Firefighters Robert Roderka, and Glenn Bullock operated underneath the drill and used the air-bags and Hurst tool system near the victim. As Roderka used the Hurst tool to push some of the heavy steel off the victim, Bullock placed bottle jacks and cribbing alongside the victim.

After 25-minutes of extremely difficult and dangerous extrication work, and high levels of CO due to the operation of the gasoline powered Hurst tool motors running in the tunnel 250-feet past the station platform, Rescue 1 and Ladder 15 were able to free the trapped man. He was re-examined and placed in a Stokes basket and transported to street level, where he was transported to Bellevue Hospital. Dr. Rachel Pearl, the emergency room attending physician, credited the difficult rescue operation with saving the man's life. He suffered a fractured pelvis and fractured ankle, but due to the efforts of Rescue 1, he did not suffer any serious internal injuries.

For their outstanding efforts utilizing unusual rescue tactics, Rescue 1 and Ladder 15 were awarded Unit Citations.

It was a few minutes before three in the morning September 8, 2005, when the alert tones echoed across the apparatus floor in the quarters of Rescue 1. Box 1312 came in for a reported fire in a six-story multiple dwelling at 964 Amsterdam Avenue. As the rig rolled north, reports crackled across the Manhattan fire frequency, "receiving numerous phone calls…numerous people trapped!" Rescue 1 arrived at the box under the command of Lt. Antonio Tarabocchia, and reported in to the Eleventh Battalion. The chief directed the company to effect the rescue of a confirmed person trapped on the fifth floor. Above them heavy smoke was pumping from the top floor windows, as the lieutenant sent Firefighters Sean Cummins and Chris Mandeville to try and gain access to the victim from the front fire escape, as the rest of the company used the interior stairs.

On the fourth floor fire escape landing, Mandeville stopped briefly to help several civilians, as Cummins continued up. At the fifth floor window Cummins donned his facepiece and entered the smoke filled apartment. Searching as he crawled, he moved forward through the living room until finding a door to the bedroom. There in the thick smoke he found a 85-year-old female, conscious but unable to move. FF Cummins picked her up, and made his way back to the fire escape. Cummins was able to get her out the window and turned her over to other firefighters, who brought her down to the street.

Meanwhile on the floor below, FF Mandeville who'd just helped some people down, heard a muffled voice from inside the smoke-filled apartment. An elderly man appeared, and Mandeville helped him onto the fire escape. Due to a language problem, the firefighter could not find out if anyone else was in the apartment. He vented a nearby window and entered the smoky flat. Searching all the way to the front door, Mandeville found the door warped from the heat and forced it open. In the flaming hallway Mandeville heard a cry for help. He immediately forced the adjacent apartment door, and crawled into the heavy smoke and high heat. Halfway through the living room, he found a semi-conscious woman. Half-dragging half-carrying the woman towards the fire escape, he found the window blocked by a locked gate. In addition, two more women were huddled in a corner gasping for breath.

FF Mandeville forced the gate from the wall, opened the window, and passed the three women out the window to members of Ladder 22, who were on the fire escape. All the women were admitted to the hospital, one with respiratory burns. Mandeville continued working, as the fast moving fire was still extending inside the building. Above FF Cummins continued searching and battling the fire, now at four alarms. Sadly, one person lost their life at this fire, but due to the aggressive work of firefighters like Mandeville and Cummins many people were rescued.

For his courageous search without a charged line, Firefighter Christopher R. Mandeville was awarded the M.J. Delehanty Medal. Firefighter Sean G. Cummins, who also operated alone without a charged line, was awarded the Captain Denis W. Lane Medal.

FF Christopher R. Mandeville *FF Sean G. Cummins*

The following June when the medals were awarded, FF Sean Cummins could not attend the ceremony. As a U.S. Army Airborne Civil Affairs Sergeant, he'd been activated April of 2006, and began a tour of duty in Iraq. At the ceremony FF Cummins 11-year old son, Sean, played along with the members of the FDNY Emerald Society's Pipe and Drum Band. When FF Sean G. Cummins name was announced his wife Maureen, Sean, and his twin daughters, Hanna and Tara, accepted the award.

Rescue Company 1 responded to another construction accident, this one in a shaft that was part of the Water Tunnel Project. This project was the largest construction endeavor in New York City history, and one of the largest engineering projects in the history of the world. When completed, it would span 60-miles (through bedrock 450-800 feet below the surface) from upstate reservoirs to the city. The tunnel was being carved by the huge TBM (tunnel boring machine) also known as "The Mole". The Manhattan section of the tunnel was 8-1/2 miles. Running south along the far West Side for 3-1/2 miles to lower Manhattan, and north 2-1/2 miles to Central Park. The tunnel is accessed through riser shafts connecting the water tunnel to the surface. It was in one of these riser shafts the FDNY would be tested again.

It was a mild evening, December 1, 2005 when at 9:22 p.m., Engine 7 responded on an EMS run for an injured worker. Additional information stated a male had fallen down a shaft: this led to a confined space response, that included Rescue 1. As the size-up continued, it became clear the worker had not fallen, but was pinned against the shaft wall by a huge drilling machine. The shaft was really a 10 foot wide hole inside a 40-foot-wide hole. The entire shaft had been dug to about 110 feet, while the center hole extended all the way down to the water tunnel 600 feet below. Workers were operating on an eight-foot-wide "shelf" at the 110-foot level, when the accident occurred.

Rescue 1, under the command of Lieutenant Antonio Tarabocchia, arrived at the scene and conferred with the incident commander. It was decided a man-basket suspended by a crane would be used to access the victim. Ladder 1 extended their tower ladder basket over the shaft to serve as a highpoint. The rescue officer and Firefighters Frank Fee, Cosmo DiOrio and Ed Myslinski of Rescue 1, and FF Arsen Kasparian (a paramedic from Squad 18) were lowered to the accident site in a man-basket, as the members above began to assemble tools they believed they would need to accomplish an extrication. FF Rob Roderka set up a high-angle rope system, including a tool lowering line, that could be converted into a victim haul line in case it was needed.

As the officer and firefighters reached the victim's location, they saw the workers were already moving the drill by using the crane from above, not the preferred method. Lt. Tarabocchia and his team then made a patient assessment (the worker had suffered multiple leg fractures) and radioed the information to the command post. The injured man was immobilized, packaged, and lifted to the street using the the man-basket. The patient was turned over to EMS and removed to a hospital.

The morning of July 10, 2006 was the start of a beautiful warm summer day, until the thunderous sounds of a major explosion rocked the East Side of Manhattan at 8:40 a.m. Fire dispatchers were receiving numerous calls for an explosion and building collapse at the corner of Madison Avenue and East 62nd Street. Their heavy dispatch assignment included four engines, three trucks, Rescue 1, Squad 18, several specialized units assigned on major collapse incidents, and the rescue collapse vehicles.

First due units were faced with a large cloud of smoke and dust, as they turned onto 62nd Street from Madison Avenue. A "10-60" signal was transmitted, as responding companies were faced with: a fully collapsed building with heavy fire throughout the debris, reports of people possibly trapped in the collapsed building, major damages and unknown situations in all the adjacent buildings. Rescue 1 arrived, under the command of Lt. Thomas Donnelly, and went into the flaming debris to provide a primary search. Several dangerous minutes later, Rescue 4 arrived. The collapse area was divided as Rescue 1 began searching for viable voids in the rear, and Rescue 4 operated in the front.

> Several dangerous minutes later, Rescue 4 arrived. The collapse area was divided as Rescue 1 began searching for viable voids in the rear, and Rescue 4 operated in the front.

Companies operated under severe conditions at this third alarm, as the debris was checked for survivable voids. Members of Rescue 4 found a void in the front, and were able to locate and remove the building's owner (who had intentionally caused the explosion).

It was about 10:30 on the evening of July 20, 2006, Rescue 1 was out procuring the evening meal. The rescue rig was parked on Columbus Avenue near West 71st Street. Members were returning to the truck with food, when a taxi cab drove directly into the rear of the apparatus hitting two rescue firefighters. Injured in the collision were Firefighters Michael Schunk and John Walters. Schunk was thrown to the ground by the collision, while Walters was pinned between the vehicles. Walters was freed by other members of Rescue 1. Both were treated by their comrades until ambulances arrived.

The on-duty crew realized both rescue men were seriously injured. Walters was rushed to Bellevue Hospital with compound fractures of his crushed right leg. Schunk was taken to NY Presbyterian Hospital with a fractured right tibia. Five days after the crash, doctors were forced to amputate Walter's leg. Schunk also required surgery, to insert a rod into his broken leg. Both men were forced to retire on disability.

Firefighters John Walters and Michael Schunk who were seriously injured on July 19, 2006 when struck by a taxicab.

Tuesday morning, September 26, 2006 was a clear and windy day. Two window washers were working on a scaffold on the upper floors of 850 Eighth Avenue in Manhattan. The two men suddenly found themselves dangling by their manila safety lines, as the scaffold fell out from under them. Due to numerous phone calls, dispatchers sent out Box 849. Moments later Rescue 1 arrived. They were sent to the 48th floor, where Engine 54 and Ladder 4 had lowered lifesaving ropes (LSR) and anchored them as safety backups. Rescue 1 rigged their high-angle rope systems, and a rescue firefighter was lowered towards the two workers. One by one, both workers were safely lifted up by mechanical advantage systems to the 48th floor setback.

Later that morning, Rescue 1 was dispatched to Box 1056, where two workers were hanging in a shaft at 215 West 57th Street. One worker was at the fifth floor level, and the second at the seventh floor. Rescue 1 split into two teams, each with a complete set of high-angle rope equipment. Rope systems were set up inside residential apartments, and both workers were placed on FDNY safety rope.

Members of Rescue 1 and Ladder 25 moved the dangling scaffold clear of the workers, then pulled them up and into the apartment windows. Both workers were given medical assessments, placed in stokes baskets, and brought to EMS at the street level.

On October 11, 2006 at 2:43 p.m. Rescue 1 responded to Box 1031, a 40-story apartment building at 524 East 72nd Street, for a reported plane crash into a high-rise building. Upon arrival, Lt. Antonio Tarabocchia of Rescue 1 requested a helicopter to survey the exterior of the blazing building. The buildings numbering system cause some confusion. Although the apartments involved were considered on the 40th floor, they were actually only 30 stories above street level.

As engines aggressively moved in extinguishing fire, Rescue 1 joined Ladder 13 conducting the primary search on the fire floor (40th floor). The fire was knocked down, and all searches on the 40th floor proved negative. Reports then indicated heavy fire on the 41st floor. Rescue 1 joined Ladder 2 and began searching this floor. Members also assisted in the aggressive fire attack. The fire was placed under control at 4:34 p.m.

It was later determined the plane, a single-engine Cirrus SR20, was piloted by New York Yankees pitcher Cory Lidle. Both the pilot and his instructor were killed in the crash.

It was just before 7 a.m., on March 1, 2007, when the voice alarm pierced the still morning air in the firehouse on 43rd Street. The dispatcher sent the company out this cold winter's morning to a reported person in the water. As Firefighter Kevin Kroth maneuvered the big rescue truck through the streets heading for East River, two rescue divers were getting dressed in the back of the rig. Firefighters Cosmo DiOrio and Frederick Ill both donned dry suits and SCUBA gear and were ready to dive, as the truck pulled up to the reported location at 18th Street. Lieutenant Tarabocchia located the eyewitness and interviewed her. She could only give a general location where she saw a young man in a white, hooded sweatshirt in the water.

FF DiOrio plunged into the frigid water and began a search. DiOrio reported a strong current, zero visibility and considerable debris on the river bottom to his tender, FF Jason Faso. Then Faso relayed the info to the officer and the second diver. Tarabocchia had DiOrio surface as FF James Hodges (the tender) guided Frederick Ill to a point 50-feet straight out from the seawall. There FF Ill descended. Faced with the same obstacles, a strong current, black water and very cold conditions, Ill began his search pattern. Fanning back and forth across the bottom, his line became entangled in some rebar. Once cleared he continued the final leg of his search. At the edge of his vision he saw a hazy glow and swam towards it. He'd found the victim.

FF Ill wrapped his arms around the man and surfaced. Then, with the victim in tow, he swam to a ladder, placed by FDNY members, and the victim was hoisted up. EMS immediately began CPR on the drowning victim. Sadly, he could not be revived.

For his heroic underwater rescue Firefighter Frederick J. Ill, III was awarded the Brummer Medal.

Two days after the water rescue, the company rolled out for a reported elevator stuck in a blind shaftway. Manhattan Box 563 came in at 8:35 p.m., March 3, 2007 sending Rescue 1 to 111 Eighth Avenue, a 17-story building. The elevator was stuck at the sixth floor level, with the nearest access on the ninth floor. In the elevator car was a 25-year-old woman, who was panicking and hyperventilating. Lt. Anthony Tarabocchia suggested the use of the high-angle rope equipment to Chief Boyle of the Seventh Battalion, who then gave the go ahead. After assuring the power was turned off and a member of the department was stationed at the power source, Lt. Tarabocchia put his plan into action. Firefighter Frank Rush was lowered by rope (with a safety) to the stalled car to calm the woman, and to install two rail clamps to secure the car from any possible movement.

FF Frederick J. Ill, III

The mainline was retrieved, and tools and gear were lowered to Rush using this rope. Above, FF Jason Faso established a high point at the 9th floor level. The main line was passed through a pulley and attached to this high point. FF Carl Gelardi exposed a column in the hallway, which would act as an anchor point to change direction, as FF James Feeley added another pulley to change the direction of the haul, to a separate column in an office allowing a long unobstructed pull. FF Richard Miranda attached the 4 to 1 mechanical advantage system to the main line. The company could now easily and quickly haul from the stalled car to their position.

Back in the elevator car, FF Rush had opened the hatch to access the very frightened woman. He calmed and reassured her, as he fitted her into a Petzel seat harness, attaching the main line and a safety. A life saving line had been stretched to act as

Members prepare for a dive job on Manhattan's Westside. (Larry Shapiro)

a tag line. With the help of members from Ladder 12, FF Miranda began to haul on the 4 to 1, lifting the woman in a very controlled ascent. The woman was safely removed from the car and shaft, then examined by EMS personnel.

At 7:05 a.m. on the morning of May 17, 2007, Rescue 1 was assigned to Manhattan Box 864 for a woman who had fallen into a transformer vault in front of 150 West 51st Street. The 26 year-old woman was walking to work, when suddenly the sidewalk grate below gave way, plunging her more than 12-feet to the bottom of a Con Ed transformer vault. The injured woman was within inches of the 13,000 volt transformer. Upon arrival Lt. Thomas Donnelly made a quick size-up and communicated to the injured woman, telling her not to move. The injured woman was complaining of serious neck pain and tingling sensation throughout her body. Donnelly ordered meter readings taken in the space, as a tripod was set up above the hole.

Realizing the woman was within inches of the live buss bars, Donnelly and Firefighter Frank Rush donned FDNY electrical linemen's gloves and tested the vault with a TAC (FDNY approved electrical tester). The test proved positive, the buss bars were live and carrying 5,000 amps. Donnelly was attached to a safety rope, then lowered into the vault. Rush followed moments later.

The two rescue men had to work carefully in the restricted space, as they assessed her injuries and began to package her. She was immobilized and placed in a confined space stretcher. The packaged patient was then carefully lifted by a mechanical advantage system, operated by Rescue 1 members on the street. She was pulled clear of the vault and placed in the hands of medical personnel who took her to the hospital

This dangerous and highly technical rescue was performed with numerous obstacles, and live electric surrounding the victim and her rescuers. Lt. Thomas Donnelly and Firefighter Frank Rush were awarded Class A ratings.

At 8:10 a.m. on the morning of March 27, 2007, Rescue 1 responded to Box 973 for a fire in a 5-story tenement building, at 142 West 65th Street in Manhattan. Upon arrival, Battalion 9 ordered the company to help locate the fire in the basement of the building. Lt. Tarabocchia split the company, sending Firefighters Mandeville and Miranda to the floor above and Firefighter Owens to the roof. Tarabocchia then descended into the smoke-filled basement with FF Bullock, to assist Ladder 35 in locating the seat of the fire. Under difficult conditions, the fire was found deep in the rear of the basement and a line was called for. The fire was then partially knocked down by a hoseline operated by Engine 54.

Rescue 1 members reported heavy smoke and fire extending above the first floor, through three open pipe chases. FF Mandeville waited on the first floor to open the walls. When the line arrived, Firefighters Miranda and Kroth moved to the second floor. Kroth forced a second floor rear apartment and encountered extreme heat. Crawling deeper into the apartment, Kroth located extending fire and called for a line.

Division 3 then requested members of Rescue 1 to help Ladder 4 with the removal of an unconscious person, on a 3rd floor rear fire escape. The fire was now spreading so violently that Kroth was forced from the apartment. He held the door closed to protect the interior stairs, while FF Miranda hurried to the floor above to assist with what turned out to be two victims. Miranda dragged the second unconscious woman to an area of refuge, and used the positive pressure feature of his mask facepiece to force fresh air into the woman.

Mandeville joined Kroth, and together with Engine 39 made an aggressive attack on the raging fire in the rear apartment. Three alarms were transmitted for this quick moving and difficult fire. For their outstanding operations Rescue 1 was awarded a Unit Citation.

It was just before six on the evening of July 18, 2007, when the Manhattan fire radio boomed with excited reports of large explosion at 41st Street and Lexington Avenue. Rescue 1 responded, and with local ladder company units operating at another location, arrived first due. They were faced with a massive steam pipe explosion that was sending a shower of mud, steam and flying debris up in a huge column that reached higher than the nearby skyscrapers. Large chunks of roadway, dirt, and rock were raining down on the surrounding area. Rescue chauffeur, Firefighter Jason Faso, parked the rig on 42nd Street to avoid falling debris.

Lt. Tarabocchia and his crew Firefighters Sean Cummins Frederick Ill, Michael Cioffi, Jason Faso and Richard Miranda reported in to Battalion 9. They were ordered to search two city buses that had stopped within 10-feet of the crater. Dodging the falling missiles, they raced to the buses. Cioffi was sent to search automobiles stopped behind the buses; this search was negative. Inside the first bus they found the driver and an elderly man. Lt. Tarabocchia and FF Cummins placed their helmets onto the civilians, hurrying them from the blast site to an area of safety.

Meanwhile, the back door of the second bus was forced by FF Ill who found eight frightened passengers. FF Miranda picked up one woman, carrying her across ankle deep scalding water and into the safety of a nearby building. Back inside the bus, FF Ill was handing off passenger after passenger to FF Cioffi and members of Ladder 4, who hurried them to safety. While these rescues were going on, FF Faso monitored the condition of the ruptured pipe inside the crater. With the bus passengers safely removed, Rescue 1 then concentrated on moving 50 people trapped in the lobby of 370 Lexington Avenue. The quick thinking rescue men and members of Ladder 24 forced a locked roll down gate, enabling them to move the trapped people to safety on 40th Street.

Rescue 1 members then searched all the stores in the immediate area. They reported a tow truck hanging precariously into the crater. A nearby school bus was also found and searched. In addition, Rescue 1 members search the basement of 375 Lexington Avenue for possible damages done by the steam blast.

In all, the members of Rescue 1 under very dangerous conditions rescued 10 passengers from trapped buses and 50 people trapped in a building lobby. For their efficient and timely work the members of Rescue 1 were awarded a Unit Citation.

In January of 2008, former Rescue 1 firefighter and retired FDNY lieutenant George Kreuscher published a book called Fireman. This 212-page book chronicled his 31-year career with the New York City Fire Department and received great reviews. It also garnered the author some prestigious awards for his writing: WINNER – Writer's Digest International Self-published Book Contest First Place Non-fiction 2009, and WINNER New York Book Festival First Place Biography/Memoir 2008. George's writing ability is only matched by his fire floor and teaching prowess.

Saturday, March 15, 2008 at 2:22 in the afternoon a major emergency played out on the streets of Manhattan. Box 861 was transmitted for a reported construction accident: a crane collapse — with people trapped. At 300 East 51st Street at the corner of Second Avenue was a 200-foot, 250-ton tower crane that had broken away from a building under construction, and crashed into the top floors of a 23-story high-rise multiple dwelling across the street. A 10-60 signal (a major emergency: sending an additional 3-engines, 2-ladders, a FAST unit, 5-battalion chiefs, a deputy chief, two additional rescue companies, a squad and several other special units) was given. Units arriving on the Second Avenue side encountered a much worse problem at 50th Street; the boom and cab of the crane had broken from the tower and landed on the roof of a four-story brownstone, located at 305 East 50th Street, causing a pancake collapse of the entire structure.

Rescue 1, assigned to the initial box, made good time reaching the 50th Street scene with the first due units and immediately went to work. Lieutenant Thomas Donnelly split the company into 3-teams: Donnelly and FF Sean Cummins ascended to the top of the debris pile, where they located two victims pinned up to their waists. One person was seriously injured and the second obviously dead. Cummins began working on the injured person, while Donnelly called Firefighters Matt Beatty, Michael Scharr. Members of other companies moved in to assist with the trapped injured victim. As Donnelly and Cummins crawled deeper into the pile, they located a third victim. With debris still falling around them, Donnelly and Cummins used small entrenching shovels and a small hand-powered spreader to free this victim. He was placed in a Stokes basket and lowered down a portable ladder. Nearby, Team 3, (Rescue 1 Firefighters Glenn Bullock and Carl Gelardi) was conducting a recon of the collapse area looking for survivable voids, where victims might be located.

FF Bullock called to Donnelly. He'd made verbal contact with another victim (the fourth) towards the exposure 4-side wall of the brownstone on the East 51st Street side. Donnelly relayed the information by radio to Battalion 9, the operations chief. Realizing it was going to be a prolonged operation, Donnelly requested an air-cart, 200 feet of hose for the air tools, an air pack for the trapped victim, and a rescue Paramedic to attend to the victim's medical needs.

Under the supervision of Lt. Donnelly, Rescue 1 members Cummins and Bullock began a tunneling operation supported by Gelardi, Beatty, and Scharr. For two hours the rescue men worked inside the small tunnel, selectively removing debris. As the tunnel became narrower it was necessary for Firefighters Bullock and Cummins to rotate positions, with Donnelly maintaining his position to supervise this extremely dangerous operation. A search-cam was used to pinpoint the victim's location, then using small hand tools and battery operated tools, they continued tunneling until the victim was reached.

A rescue paramedic was lowered into the void to take vital signs and carefully monitor the patient. An I.V. was started to stabilize the patient and to minimize crush syndrome. With ALS care established, the paramedic was removed. The extrication continued until the patient was extricated, packaged, and removed. Rescue Company 1 operated for more than three hours and removed four victims, three viable at the time of their rescue. Rescue 1 worked under extremely dangerous and difficult conditions.

For this outstanding operation Rescue Company 1 was awarded a Unit Citation.

A 10-75 signal for Manhattan Box 418 sent Rescue 1 to a fire within a subway construction tunnel at Second Avenue and Houston Street, on April 29, 2009. Companies were having a difficult time finding the seat of an extremely smoky fire somewhere inside a 500-foot long tunnel. Members of Rescue 1, under the command of Captain Robert Morris, entered the blackened tunnel and began their search.

The smoldering fire was located behind a fence in a construction area of the subway tunnel. The members began to clear away the fence to allow extinguishment. During the operation the SCBA cylinders of several members were emptied. They tried to change out the cylinders where they were, rather than try to return down the 500-foot long tunnel. During this time, two members of Rescue 1 and several other members were overcome by the carbon monoxide laced smoke. (Estimates of the deadly gas was more than 2000 parts per million)

May-days were transmitted, and the unconscious firefighters were carried outside and rushed to nearby hospitals. Several of the members required a trip to the hyperbaric chamber, but all were able to return to full duty.

On December 31, 2009 Rescue 1 responded to a report of a person in the water at West 15th Street and the Hudson River. On arrival, they found a man clinging to a rotted piling that was part of a collapsed pier. The air temperature was 20°F and the water temperature was 38°F. Firefighter William Owens, designated as Diver #2 (surface rescue) for the tour, climbed over the numerous broken and rotted sections of the collapsed pier, and entered the frigid water.

Owens swam 100-feet to the stranded man, who was still clinging to the rotted piling. Realizing the man was suffering the debilitating effects of hypothermia and that he would not be able to help himself, Owens placed a floatation device about the man. Owens started back towards the pier head, towing the man and making sure his head remained above water. Several police officers joined Owens and the man in the water for the final leg of the cold wet journey.

The man was pulled from the water and wrapped in warm dry blankets. He taken by EMS to a nearby hospital. For his cold water rescue FF William Owens was placed on the Roll of Merit with a Class B award.

FF Matt Beatty and injured construction worker are removed from a 30-foot hole by crane at Amsterdam Avenue and 76th Street, Manhattan, September 22, 2007.

Chapter 11

The 2010s

The year 2010 marked 145 years since the paid department relieved the volunteers. The size and number of buildings and the population density of the city had grown tremendously since the horse-drawn days. But the basic job remained the same, get to the fire or emergency quickly and handle the problem safely and efficiently. Rescue Company 1 was about to start their 95th year in service. The company had grown from a small Cadillac touring car with smoke helmets and a small cache of tools, to a huge 26-foot long 2007 Pierce Arrow XT rescue truck filled with the latest high-tech rescue gear, SCUBA diving gear, and an inflatable boat strapped to the roof.

Members and former members of Rescue 1 mobilized, as part of the 80-man technical rescue team known as NYTF-1. (The New York City FEMA Task Force) The group responded to an earthquake that had rocked the Caribbean country of Haiti (located in the western smaller portion of the island of Hispaniola, in the Greater Antillean archipelago). The Dominican Republic occupies the eastern, larger portion of the island. NYTF-1 had travelled to the Dominican Republic after Hurricane Georges in September of 1998.

During their week long stay, they rescued six people trapped in collapsed structures. They also searched numerous other collapsed buildings, and provided aid to many other people devastated by the earthquake.

On February 24, 2010 Rescue 1 responded to Box 78 at 28 Cliff Street in lower Manhattan. Upon arrival a heavy smoke condition was seen in the 4-story old law tenement. The exact location of the fire within the building was unknown. First due companies were bogged down on the first floor of the building, unable to locate the stairs or a means to gain access to the floor below. Captain Morris split his company. One team, Firefighters Faso, Mandeville and Owens searched the first floor commercial occupancy (a bar), while the second team: Morris, FF Rush and FF Hodges located a small sidewalk hatch, approximately 24″ x 30″ with a narrow vertical ladder to the cellar. Morris and his team descended, clipping the search rope to the base of the ladder. With zero visibility, Morris used a thermal imaging device to navigate their way towards the rear of the cellar. With deteriorating conditions, BC Sarrocco (Battalion 1) ordered Engine 10 to stretch a protection line to the bottom of the ladder to cover Rescue 1, while they searched for fire.

Rescue men working at bench

Operating at collapsed trench rescue March 2, 2012.

Continuing forward under hanging wires, pipes, and other obstructions Morris found fire rolling across the ceiling some 100-feet from the entry point. He called for the line. FF Rush followed the search line back to the ladder, and led the nozzle team to the fire. Morris positioned the camera, so the nozzleman could view the fire and direct the stream more effectively. Then Captain Morris notified the chief, water was on the fire.

Next Rescue 1 made openings through a wall to allow the complete extinguishment of the large body of fire. In all, four separate engine companies operated this line. Each member of Rescue 1 used three cylinders of air battling this three-alarm fire. For their determination Rescue 1 was awarded a Unit Citation.

It was one minute to six on the evening of June 7, 2010, when Rescue 1 was directed to respond to Manhattan Box 619 for a reported fire at Pier 60 located at 12th Avenue and West 23rd Street. Upon arrival the department was faced with a serious fire condition engulfing a work platform, underneath the famed tourist attraction known as the Chelsea Piers. The fire was only accessible through a hatchway in the pier decking, that lead straight down to the water. Rescue 1 reported to Battalion 7, prepared to enter the water and commence under pier firefighting operations.

With the hatchway the only access, and the entire perimeter of the pier covered at the waterline, it had become a "confined space dive". The primary diver, FF John Bardak, was lowered through the opening into the water. He requested his tender be lowered to the water level, due to the acute angles that would be involved in searching for the seat of the fire. While tended by FF Sean Cummins (also in SCUBA gear), Bardak began his search. Despite a very heavy smoke condition he located the fire some 60 to 75-feet west of the opening. A ladder had been placed through the hatch, with FF Frank Rush taking up a position at the base acting as a safety diver.

Lieutenant Tom Donnelly also entered the water in a dry suit, to supervise this dangerous and very technical operation. Extinguishment would require moving a charged hose line through a veritable obstacle course beneath the pier. An 1-3/4" hose was dropped down to the in-water firefighting team, who'd donned SCUBA facepieces due to the thick smoke and building heat condition. The team of Bardak, Cummins, and Rush had to haul this attack line against moving water under the pier, from more than sixty feet to the point of operations. Above Firefighters Joel Kanasky and Al Benjamin fed the attack line and controlled the tending lines, as the in-water team moved in.

Due to the difficult nature of the operation and extreme smoke and heat conditions encountered, FF's Bardak, Rush, and Cummins took turns operating the nozzle, at the different and various angles needed. Each directed water through the lattice work of blazing creosoted pier beams and columns. When the fire was finally extinguished, the exhausted divers climbed the ladder, stripped off their dive gear, and went in-service. They were ready for their next job. For their efforts at this all-hands fire, Rescue 1 was awarded a Unit Citation.

On the morning of September 17, 2010 Rescue 1 members were in the Hudson River again, this time because of an alarm stating "people in the water." It was 6:37 when Rescue 1 raced to the foot of 12th Street, with Marine 1 confirming person in the water. Unfortunately, the fireboat was blocked by the pier and unable to reach him. FF Glenn Bullock in a dry suit, PFD, and harness hurried more than a block on foot, to a point where he observed the victim struggling to stay afloat. He was bouncing against pilings, driven by the current, and the wakes of passing vessels. Realizing time was of the essence, Bullock scaled a four foot fence, and prepared to be lowered 15-feet down into the water by Lt. John Tobin. Tobin took four turns of rope on his personal harness, and with no substantial object handy laid on his back and lowered Bullock.

Once in the water Bullock swam 25-feet to reach the man. Bullock was able to control and calm the frantic and nearly exhausted victim. Bullock then pulled him from beneath the pilings, and swam him back, against the current towards the embankment, where a ladder had been lowered into the water. Bullock lifted the victim onto the ladder, then proceeded up behind him until he was safely on the embankment. For his water rescue, FF Glenn Bullock was awarded a Class B by the Board of Merit.

One of the most difficult fires to fight is a church fire. At five minutes after noon on January 10, 2011, Rescue 1 was assigned to Manhattan Box 22-132, a working fire within Saint James Roman Catholic Church, at 20 James Street. Report indicated fire burning through the roof on the #2 side of the church, as FF Jason Faso wheeled the apparatus through the downtown traffic. Upon arrival Rescue 1 was requested to gain access to the church attic above the vaulted ceiling, to allow a line to extinguish fire at that location. Reaching the attic was tricky and dangerous. The members of the company had to climb a 30-foot, straight wooden ladder, then squeeze into a 14-inch space between the ladder and the organ. Captain Robert Morris had the men remove their SCBA's to facilitate their climb. One by one Firefighters Francis Rush, Al Benjamin, Sean Cummins and Captain Morris climbed the ladder, entering the attic space. A rope was then lowered, and they hauled up their SCBA's and tools.

They encountered a heavy smoke condition in the attic, but could not see any visible fire. Using the thermal imaging camera, they were able to locate fire 90-feet away from their location. Captain Morris advised the First Division: Rescue 1 had located the fire, and he believed they could cross over the exposed beams of the hanging ceiling. He requested an inch and three-quarter hose line, and a vent hole cut to attack the fire. The Rescue 1 outside team, Firefighters Jason Faso and Michael Cioffi made their way to the roof via aerial ladder. Faced with an icy, six-story high ornamental roof with a severe slope, Cioffi climbed to the peak and crawled across the ridge with a life saving rope. He tied the rope to a substantial object, then attached the rope to himself and FF Faso who'd joined him. Together they cut a 10- by 10 vent hole, despite the thick heavy-timber roof construction.

Inside the conditions were becoming severe, as dense smoke permeated the attic space making the dangerous crossing even more difficult. With heavy fire running up the trusses to the ridge Rescue 1, aided by Squad 18 members, advanced the hand-line and water was put on the fire. Due to the tight quarters of the attic, members were forced to remove their SCBAs and use a reduced profile maneuvers, in order to advance the hose.

> "If any unit was ever deserving of a Unit Citation for an outstanding operation, Rescue 1 at this fire certainly met the mark."

The members of Rescue Company 1, whose experience on this tour totaled 150 years, safely and efficiently extinguished a heavy body of fire in an attic with no regular means of access. They also managed to vent a steep, ice-covered roof. Both of these operations required great care, as a misstep could have serious consequences. As stated by the Manhattan Borough Commander, Assistant Chief James Esposito in his recommendation: "If any unit was ever deserving of a Unit Citation for an outstanding operation, Rescue 1 at this fire certainly met the mark."

Rescue 1 was awarded a Unit Citation and the Firefighter Thomas R. Elsasser Memorial Medal for their heroic actions at this fire.

This 2011 Ferrara rescue rig went in service March 7, 2012. (Ron Jeffers)

On March 22, 2012, Rescue Company 1 responded to a major building collapse at 3:27 p.m. The scene was a huge vacant warehouse under going demolition, at 608 West 130th Street. Rescue 1 arrived as the first due rescue company, where they found a total collapse of the structure with reports of several workers trapped within. Battalion 16 ordered the company to search the north side (Exposure 1). Under the direction of Captain Robert Morris, they began to search a void area under a lean-to type of collapse. A worker was located by sound and found to be completely entombed by a collapsed bearing wall. He was directly underneath a 20 x 6 foot section of 2-foot thick wall (approximately 15,000 pounds), which had broken off and was attached at either end.

Captain Morris, Firefighters Alfred Benjamin, John Bardak and FF Mike Sheppard (a member of Squad 41) began to work beneath this unstable wall. The shoring plan was devised to support the wall above the small void containing the worker. Using four Paratech struts the wall was stabilized, as the workers head was uncovered and medical assistance started. Oxygen was given to the worker, as the clearing of debris covering his legs and lower torso was accomplished.

The captain remained in communication with his chauffeur, FF Jason Faso, and the Rescue 1 outside-team, Firefighters Christopher Morgan and Thomas Cosgrove. These members and members of Squad 41 and Ladder 14 carried in, and set up the required tools and equipment as needed. As the clearing of the workers chest continued, it became clear his right arm and legs were "pinned". The arm was under a large slab of concrete weighing some 2,500 pounds, and could not be lifted, as it was supporting the slab overhead. They began to support the slab with more shoring, so they could breakout the section pinning the man's arm. The rescue men worked carefully with their tools, chipping away at the slab. Using a Sawzall, they were also able to cut the steel pipe that held the worker's legs fast. After an examination by Doctor Gonzales, the man was packaged on a long board and carried from the collapse area.

For their technical rescue, under very dangerous conditions, the members of Rescue 1 were awarded a Unit Citation.

On Saturday night May 12, 2012 around 8:20 p.m., a 15-year old boy, playing with some friends slipped, and fell into the East River at 102 Street in Manhattan. He immediately disappeared beneath the inky surface. The frantic children called 9-1-1. Moments later Rescue 1 was responding from quarters with rescue divers gearing up. Upon arrival rescue men hopped over two fences to reach the river. Captain Morris, and Battalion Chief John Donnelly interviewed witnesses and initiated an underwater search and rescue.

FF Brian Burik, wearing a drysuit and SCUBA gear, was lowered twelve feet down the seawall, into the black water. With FF Carl Scheetz acting as his tender, Burik began his search pattern despite a strong 2 to 3 knot current. Operating in zero visibility Burik concentrated on his search, feeling his way along the river's bottom. After several passes, Burik felt the child. They were about 25-feet north of where he'd fallen in. Burik asked his tender to begin pulling as he filled his buoyancy compensator and kicked his way to the surface.

Reaching the ladder Burik hoisted the child onto his shoulder. A piece of webbing quickly encircled the child and he was pulled up the sea wall. Resuscitation efforts began immediately and the child was rushed to the hospital. Sadly, the child could not be revived. For his difficult dive Firefighter Brian Burik was awarded a Class B.

Sunday morning June 10, 2012, Rescue 1 was rolling back towards quarters after an extrication run, when at 6:09 the dispatcher directed them to East 32nd Street and Lexington Avenue. The telephone circuits at the dispatch office lit like a Christmas tree, as numerous reports of a fire were received. Rescue responded, and due to their proximity to the alarm arrived as one of the first units.

The companies were faced with an advanced fire condition on the roof of a two-story commercial building, that was exposing the luxury high rise next door. Captain Morris split the company into three teams upon arrival. The heavy fire and extending flames would quickly alter this plan. As they entered the high rise, they were faced with numerous civilians self evacuating, and the building's doorman reporting that apartment 3H was on fire. Morris radioed his men to regroup inside 151 East 31 Street, also known as the Windsor Court. (The building occupies the entire square block, and has 709 apartments on 31 floors.)

Morris sent Firefighters John Bardak, Joel Kanasky and Tim Geraghty to the fourth floor, as he and Firefighters Frank Rush, and Kevin Kroth entered the third floor hallway. Moving down the 90-foot hallway, they encountered severe smoke and heat conditions, due to the open door of apartment 3H. Captain Morris transmitted an "Urgent" message requesting a hose line and informing the chief of the dangerous conditions within the high rise.

While Morris controlled the door to the fire apartment, Rush and Kroth forced apartment 3G, to search for extension and provide an area of refuge if needed. Rejoining the captain, the three rescue men entered 3H, without the benefit of a hose line, and were faced with a heavy body of fire, due to numerous failed windows. A door was ripped off it's hinges and used to cover the kitchen opening, temporarily holding back the extending flames. Using the door and a water extinguisher, this position was held allowing the other two men to search the apartment. The first door burned through, allowing the fire to again roll across the ceilings and extend though the apartment. Another door was located and torn free to re-seal the opening.

Meanwhile on the floor above, the second team also found extension and called for a hose line. Their search through the large apartment proved negative. Additional companies made their way to the third and fourth floors and were able to extinguish the fires, as the exterior roof fire was also knocked down. Two alarms were required to control this fast moving fire.

For locating the most critical area of fire extension and life hazard, operating alone without the benefit of hose line protection, and searching and controlling a rapidly extending fire, Rescue 1 was awarded a Unit Citation.

On July 5, 2012 the Rescue 1 riding list assigned FF Christopher Morgan as Diver #2. This dive position also requires the member to act as the Surface Rescue Swimmer. Rescue 1 responded to the East River, where a water rescue was in progress. On the far shore BC Hayde had spotted the victim, and was directing first due units to the correct position. A member of Ladder 16 and a police officer were in the water assisting the victim, but were being swept north by the strong river currents (estimated at 4-knots).

Rescue 1 operating at midtown scaffold collapse.

Members of Rescue 1 following an under-pier firefighting drill at Pier 54.

Rescue FF Morgan, wearing a drysuit, personal floatation device and tended to a safety rope entered the river and swam out. Reaching the victim he was able to quickly tie a rope around the man to halt his being swept away and to allow members on shore to pull him towards a ladder. Morgan helped the exhausted man climb the ladder to the waiting arms of EMS.

It was 9:45 on the morning of July 17, 2012 when Rescue 1 was dispatched to 355 East 76th Street in Manhattan, for an auto that plunged into an elevator shaft inside the six-story parking garage. Upon their arrival the members of Rescue 1 were directed to the second floor elevator landing, where they met members of Ladder 43 and Engine 44. The vehicle, which had fallen from the fifth floor, was hanging precariously upside down on top of the elevator car with the auto's front end up, and the back end broken through the top of the elevator. Rescue's officer Captain Lawrence Tompkins (SOC covering) and FF John Norman climbed onto the top front half of the elevator, joining two department members already at that location. These members pointed out the patient's location. In order to reach him, Capt. Tompkins and FF Norman had to climb outside the elevator car and into the shaft itself, then to the point where the vehicle had crashed through the elevator roof. They squeezed through this opening and reached a position where they could make contact with the patient.

Rescue Firefighters Thomas Cosgrove and Christopher Morgan climbed onto the elevator roof, and were able to secure the elevator car by placing clamps on the elevator rails. Rescue chauffeur Joel Kanasky, FF Michael Cioffi, and members of the first due units brought the necessary tools and equipment needed to stabilize the elevator and the automobile. Then the extrication equipment, patient packaging, and medical gear was assembled.

Rescue 1 was then joined by Rescue Company 4. These combined units set up Rescue 1's 32-ton grip hoists to secure the auto. FF Norman entered the vehicle and began patient care, as the front windshield was removed to provide better access. A battery powered Jaws was used to remove the side door, but could not break the hinges. The large cutter was passed down and used to cut the door free. With large structural beams blocking the easiest path of removal, the combined rescue teams used webbing, neck stabilization, and a long board. They were then able to delicately remove the patient from the vehicle.

As this was being accomplished, members of Squad 18 forced open a shaft way door that opened to the street. The patient was carefully lowered ten feet by the rescue teams to the squad men below, and finally to an ambulance.

This complicated and dangerous technical rescue employed two grip hoists, directional pulleys, the apparatus winch from Rescue 1, as well as numerous tools. The members of Rescue 1 were awarded a Unit Citation for their rescue work.

Since September 11, 2001, Rescue 1 has received kind words, letters and visits to quarters by firefighters and civilians from around the world. Well-wishers came from every walk of life. The company has also received numerous honors from the military including: flags flow in honor of our lost brothers, special patches worn into battle, and other memorabilia.

U.S. fighter pilot wearing Rescue 1 patch during a mission.

Our Rescue 1 patch goes supersonic thanks to this fighter pilot.

On the evening of October 29, 2012 the City of New York and the FDNY braced, as Hurricane Sandy made landfall in southern New Jersey battering the city and the northeast portion of the nation with heavy rain, strong winds and record storm surges. To provide additional coverage the Special Operations Command placed in service Rescue Company 6, an additional Squad company and six Swift Water Units (each team had an officer and five firefighters, all trained in swift water operations. They were equipped with two Zodiac rugedized inflatable boats, outboard engines, ropes, rigging equipment, a set of irons, CFR-D equipment and radios. Each member also had personalized water rescue equipment; the units responded using spare pumpers. SOC also had other specialized units to handle the emergency situations expected as the storm closed in. Several members of Rescue 1 were assigned to some of these temporary units.

Dear Crew of Rescue One Company,

The reason we are writing to you today, September 11th 2012 is to reinforce to you guys that the sacrifices you've made and courage you've shown during that fateful September Morning 11 years ago and every day since are not forgotten.

In 2003 I had the privilege of shadowing some of your crew members as part of our college Paramedic clinical rotations with FDNY. It blew me away how much you lost in an instant. Nearly half your house decimated by faceless cowards who could never fathom the valor shown by your brothers running up the stairs of the North Tower as countless others were running the other way. Just seeing the plaques in the downstairs garage was as inspirational as it was sobering.

Today I'm writing to you on behalf of the USAF Pararescuemen (PJs) and Combat Rescue Officers (CROs) and our PEDRO HH-60 Pavehawk Aircrew respectively of the 46th and 26th Expeditionary Rescue Squadron (ERQS) deployed here at Camp Bastion, Afghanistan. Back home we are part of Alaskan and Florida USAF Rescue Teams. Be it on alert in AK/FL or here in Afghanistan, we are always ready to respond. Our primary job here is the combat recovery, treatment and evacuation of downed and isolated Special Operations and coalition troops; by any means necessary, anytime, anywhere. Much like your team we are specialized and tested. We dive, freefall parachute, shoot, perform invasive medicine, extricate, use ropes, perform in confined space, collapsed structure, all to bring American and Coalition troops home safe. We strive every day to uphold the legacy set forth by rescue professionals such as you.

We wear different uniforms. We live in different worlds. But we live by similar creeds. We honor the memory of your fallen brothers today here in Helmand Province Afghanistan. In the only way fellow rescue specialists know how…Taking our shirts off, putting on some war paint and going into combat sporting the colors. It inspires the folks who know what it means and freaks out the bad guys that get in our way. It was a fun day. It pissed off the leadership something fierce but it was totally worth it.

It was 11 years ago today your house was dealt a tremendous loss. We've been at war ever since and taken many losses of our own. It's been a long time in between. Just know that we will never forget the courage your displayed and continues to uphold.

TSGT Jake Soignour, Aerial Gunner

These things we do that others may live…Hooya

The company received this letter in September of 2012. It was a clear message that the company's loss is still remembered by our nation's military.

The first major storm related incident started when Rescue 1 was assigned to a reported crane collapse at 2:33 p.m. Arriving with the first due units, they were faced with a collapsed tower crane atop a 75-story building on West 57th Street and Sixth Avenue. Battalion 9 ordered the company to reach the area of the collapse, approximately the 73-75th floor. With no other safe way to reach the location, Rescue 1 headed up the stairs. After the arduous climb, they reached their destination. They found the crane, the upper portion of which had collapsed in a side to side fashion, hanging dangerously over West 57th Street. With winds in excess of 50 mph, members of Rescue 1 donned safety ropes as they moved onto the roof area. As

Freeing worker trapped in mud at Second Avenue subway project, March 19, 2013.

Rescue 1's assessment of the crane's vulnerability was communicated, the collapse zone below was enlarged. (In all 34 buildings, including a 42-story hotel, and a 62-story high-rise multiple dwelling, were evacuated.)

The Rescue Battalion arrived. Using cell phone cameras, photos of the crane were taken from various vantage points then relayed to the command post. As the winds whipped dangerously around the top floors, members of Rescue 1 secured loose debris and other items in the area. Later, members of Rescue 1 tethered Building Department representatives with safety ropes, as they inspected the collapsed crane.

At 8:30 p.m., Swift Water #1 was sent to East 23rd Street to check on a car stranded in water with people possibly inside. The crew working in Swift Water 1 were: Lt. John Tobin and Firefighter Glenn Bullock both of Rescue 1, as well as Firefighters John Gaine and John Tew from Rescue 4, and Christopher DiBenedetto of Squad 18.

At the site the vehicle was checked and found empty. The team then moved to 14th Street to check on reports of people trapped. Several minutes later, a tremendous explosion occurred at the Con Edison plant only yards away from their location. Lt. Tobin ascertained from a Con Ed supervisor that there were 10 to 15 employees inside the plant, and that due to the explosion and the rising storm waters their safety was in serious question.

Tobin ordered all members of Swift Water 1 to don their water safety gear (dry suit, helmet, gloves, knife, flashlight strobe light and a personal floatation device PFD), then prepare to launch the boats. The removal of the boats from the rigs was difficult and dangerous, requiring the efforts of all six members to overcome the 70 to 80 mph winds. The boats were launched at 14th Street and Avenue A. Boat 1 was operated by FF Bullock and FF Tew; Boat 2 was operated by FF Lennox and FF DiBenedetto. Lt. Tobin and FF Gaine remained as back up after the unit was advised by SOC that there was no other Swift Water help available.

The boats motored down 14th Street in 12-foot deep water, battling the gusting winds and floating debris. As the boats continued on, FF Gaine waded through chest deep water and entered a nearby tenement to check on the occupants. These civilians were moved to higher floors. While Gaine was checking on these forty civilians his perspective and view of the Con Ed plant changed. He sent an urgent message stating that one of the four large concrete exhaust stacks at the plant was moving in the high winds.

Tobin relayed this information to the boats as they entered the plant area, and located a place to reach the stranded workers. FF Bullock left the boat, and entered the plant in search of the workers. He located, assessed and assembled the workers. A plan was devised to remove four workers at a time in each boat. The operation began as the Swift Boats moved back into the hurricane lashed streets. As the first boatloads of workers were making there way back, Lt. Tobin was informed that two MTA employees were trapped in a flooded vehicle on the FDR Drive, with a possible injury. Tobin requested a fire boat, but none were available. A second trip was made by the swift boats. Due to the severe conditions encountered on each round trip, it took 45 minutes to complete.

With all Con Ed workers accounted for, the team shifted to the MTA workers stranded on the FDR Drive. FF Lennox and FF Bullock told Tobin they believed, despite the worsening conditions, the search could be made. Tobin then deployed Boat 1, with Bullock and Lennox proceeding to the FDR north of the plant, and Boat 2 to maintain a position on 14th Street and Avenue C to monitor the swaying stack.

When Boat 1 reached the FDR Drive, FF Bullock exited the boat climbing up the ramp to a small elevated area. There he found the two men who'd been trapped for more than three hours. They were removed by Boat 1 and returned towards 14th Street, with team members checking each submerged vehicle they passed.

The members of Swift Water 1 operated at this particular incident for more than three hours. They rescued and removed 18 people from extremely dangerous conditions. For their heroic efforts they were awarded a Unit Citation.

A despondent tourist from Spokane, Washington tried to end his life by jumping from a pier into the chilly Hudson River, at 9:19 on the morning of January 30, 2013. His resolve apparently faded the second he splashed into the 39-degree water, as he immediately began screaming for help. Workers aboard the Intrepid Sea, Air & Space Museum dashed to his aid, tossing him a life preserver and calling 911.

Within minutes Rescue 1 arrived, responding from quarters only blocks away. Firefighter John McCann entered the water in dive gear, and was able to quickly pull the man to safety.

Two young men from the Bronx horsing around on the frozen Central Park Pond, set in motion a series of events that would end up with five people through the ice and into the freezing water. Despite the warning signs posted around the pond, on February 5, 2013 two young men ventured out to the middle of the ice. It was about 2 p.m.; they took pictures and were goofing around when suddenly the thin ice beneath them gave way, plunging them both into the water. One man pulled himself out, but the other was unable to free himself.

Witnesses called 9-11. Moments later Rescue 1 rolled towards the park with Lt. Tony Tarabocchia in command. While the FDNY was en route, park workers arrived at the scene. They attempted to help the man, but ended up going through the ice as well. A park police officer and worker attempted to throw a rope to the man in the water when the ice broke around them, plunging them both into the icy water. Another park worker came to help. He, too fell through the ice.

As first due units slid ladders across the ice to better distribute the weight, the various rescuers were helped

> He placed a rescue collar around the young man as firefighters on shore pulled him to safety. The young man later told reporters, "The fireman saved my life. Thank God for saving my life. I thought I would die."

from the icy water. Then Rescue 1 Firefighter Matt Murphy, wearing a dive suit, entered the twelve-foot deep water. He placed a rescue collar around the young man as firefighters on shore pulled him to safety. The young man later told reporters, "The fireman saved my life. Thank God for saving my life. I thought I would die."

On Tuesday evening March 19, 2013, a 27-year old construction worker, was working at the subway construction site at Second Avenue and East 95th Street in Manhattan. He, a member of Local 731, the excavator's union more commonly known as "Sandhogs", was walking by a piece of machinery when his pants leg caught on the edge. This sudden pull caused him to slightly stumble. His foot went off the temporary wooden flooring sinking into mud.

Other construction workers tried to free the man for several minutes without success. At 2033 hours (8:33 p.m.) the fire department was notified and a "Confined space rescue" alarm was dispatched for Manhattan Box 1233, Second Avenue and East 95th Street. This alarm matrix would send two engines, two ladders, Rescue 1, two squad companies, as well as the Hazardous Materials unit, Battalion 10, and the Special Operations Battalion.

The incoming FDNY units would be faced with a construction worker trapped in mud, 75-feet below street level, in a wide trench excavation dug for the subway extension. The nighttime conditions were frigid and damp, and the clay-like mud would prove to be an obstacle not easily overcome.

The first due truck attached a life saving rope to the man, and slung it up and over a high point to prevent his sinking any further into the mud.

Shortly after these actions were taken, Rescue 1 arrived and was directed by the Tenth Battalion to the 96th Street and Second Avenue entrance to the excavation site. Chauffeur Michael Cioffi positioned the rig as close to the site as possible, as the officer and a team sized up the problem and a cache of tools they believed would be needed in the trench below was established. The sandhog was stuck in the mud up to his waist. Members of Rescue 1, under the command of Captain Michael Smithwick (SOC), and Squad 41 began to dig around the worker with hand tools. This type of wet clay-like mud, known as Bull's Liver, consists predominantly of silt-size particles, but has little or no plasticity. (The capability of being molded, receive shape or being made into a desired form. It contains particles of quartz, ground to a very fine state by the abrasive action of glaciers.) It was like "moving in wet cement".

Rescue 1 began using a construction company air knife, but it was having little effect due to low air pressure. Despite the slow progress the rescuers continued. After an hour of messy, dogged work, it was determined that the man's leg was also pinned underneath sheets of plywood, now covered by the wet mud. The mud caused a tremendous suction affect on these submerged sheets of wood, and their removal would prove to be both difficult and time consuming.

As additional technical rescue help was called to the scene, several 36-volt sawzalls were brought down. Attempts to cut the plywood proved futile, as the wet clay slowed the cutting and gummed up the saws. A griphoist was placed in position, and using a J-hook members tried to pull or lift the plywood. The suction power of the wet clay could not be overcome, and the hook eventually broke off small pieces of the wood. (This would eventually prove to be the way to remove the plywood small piece after small piece.)

Battalion Chief Donald Hayde, from Special Operations Command arrived, and was placed in charge of rescue efforts directly in the trench. The 36-year veteran took in the scene around him. His firefighters were faced with sheets of wood covered by a cold, slippery slurry of wet clay-like mud, that was acting like quicksand and almost impossible to move due to the suction. Rescuers were getting stuck left and right, as they used hand tools to dig in the immediate area. Stanley pumps were being operated in a dewatering effort; the griphoist was being set and reset, pulling away sections of the imbedded plywood. With the operation taking longer than expected, it was decided to have a rescue trained Paramedic enter the trench to evaluate the workers condition.

An FDNY EMS Paramedic moved in, and evaluated his patient's condition. The worker, except for slight hypothermia, was actually in remarkable condition. The Paramedic was able to run an IV. After the workers torso was completely cleared, warm blankets were applied to stabilize his temperature. An EMS doctor also examined the trapped worker and monitored his vitals.

Above on the street, three rescue companies and three squad companies had joined in the effort, along with several other specialized units. The department compressor was positioned. It was able to supply the correct pressure to the SOC air knife. Three sump pumps were in operation. The Con Edison vacuum truck was positioned, and despite the great distance was able to remove some of the mud and water. The first griphoist was clogged with mud. It was placed out of service. A second griphoist was repositioned with a better directional pull, and the operation continued. Various SOC members rotated in and out of digging positions, trying to keep fresh hands at work.

A heavy equipment operator joined in. Following the directions of the rescue leader, he dug a trench adjacent to the trapped worker to help drain the soil. Learning how to overcome the extreme difficulties of the mud slurry, the rescuers were finally making good headway. When enough plywood was pealed away and digging by hand exposed the worker's leg, a Prusik cord was girthed around his leg just above the knee. The final removal of the entrapped leg was accomplished.

The worker was medically re-evaluated, then secured in a Stokes basket and hoisted towards the street in a construction basket. There a wave of flash bulbs ignited, and live news cameras caught the action. On both sides of Second Avenue, crowds of construction workers, neighborhood residents and interested New Yorkers broke into cheers when the muddy, but conscious sand hog emerged relatively uninjured. He was then rolled to a waiting ambulance.

More than 130 firefighters and other rescue workers were needed to accomplish this very unusual four-hour long rescue. Several firefighters were injured. They were also taken to the hospital with minor injuries. For their outstanding efforts the members of Rescue 1: Captain Michael Smithwick (SOC), Firefighters Michael Cioffi, Christopher Morgan, Daniel Hyland, John McCann and Carl Sheetz were awarded a Unit Citation.

Just after 5 o'clock on the afternoon of May 20, 2013, Rescue 1 responded to a reported person in the water at Box 799 the Hudson River at West 43rd Street. Being two blocks from quarters, the company was on scene in minutes. The divers quickly gearing up. Springing from the front seat, Lt. Thomas Donnelly was directed by civilians, who pointed to a man in the water 20 feet from the pier, he was visibly in distress. Donnelly, wearing a PFD (personal floatation device) and a rescue rope, hurried the 100-feet to the end of the pier. With no other fire personnel yet available, he handed the end of his rope to NYC Park worker and plunged into the water.

As the water rescue team emerged fully dressed from the rear of the rig, Donnelly swam towards the man. Reaching him, he wrapped his arms under and around the man to steady him and prevent his drowning. By this point Rescue 1 Firefighter Matthew Murphy, the primary diver, was in the water and swimming towards the pair. As Donnelly steadied the man, Murphy wrapped the rescue horseshoe collar around the victim.

As the rescue team prepared to lift the over 200-pound soaking wet man onto the pier, Marine One arrived. The rescue pair swam the man to the boat, and helped him onboard.

The Hearst Tower is a 46-story office building at 57th Street and Eigth Avenue in Manhattan. It is the world headquarters of the Hearst Corporation, and the home of *Cosmopolitan*, *Esquire*, and numerous other popular magazines. The iconic 6-story base of the structure was built by William Randolph Hearst in 1928. It was designed as the base for a skyscraper. The addition had to wait nearly eighty years before it was designed and built. The new steel and glass skyscraper soars 600-feet into the midtown skyline.

On the afternoon of June 12, 2013, a team of window washers were being lowered down the Eighth Avenue side of the building in a 30 mph wind. Apparently one of the lowering motors failed, causing the scaffold to buckle and fail in a "V-shape" on the 44th floor. The two workers were left dangling on their harnesses and safety lines, on the outside of the building, as the call for help was made.

Rescue 1 responded from quarters at 2:40. They were one of the first units on the scene. Rescue men could see the scaffold hanging dangerously between the 44th and 45th floors. The building had irregular features at the roof level, complicating the rescue effort. Lt. Thomas Donnelly split the company into two teams. Team 1 Firefighters William Owens, Carl Sheetz and Chris Gaulrapp were sent to the roof level to assess the damage and to get a safety rope attached to the dangling workers.

Team 2, Lt. Donnelly, Firefighters Joel Kanasky and Thomas Gayron proceeded to the atrium on the 44th floor. The area was almost two-stories high, with a 2-foot ledge near the top of the window. On the roof, Team 1 encountered 30 mph winds and a 25-foot high angled parapet wall with a 2-foot wide ledge. From this dangerous perch, they were able to lower safety lines to the workers.

Due to the high winds and obstacles on the roof level, it was decided the safest method of removal would be through the glass on the 44th floor. Team 2 began the difficult task of cutting through the 4-inch thick glass. It took nearly an hour to cut the proper sized hole. When that was completed, FF Gayron was attached to a FDNY safety line, climbed out the window, and onto the scaffold to assist the workers. FF Kanasky, also attached to an FDNY safety rope, straddled the window to help the workers passage from the damaged and moving "V-shaped" scaffold.

This complicated and dangerous transfer required the handling of two exhausted victims and numerous ropes, in and around a wind blown swaying scaffold 44 stories in the air. The work of the rescue men was accomplished smoothly and professionally, while being observed by numerous FDNY staff chiefs, intense media coverage, and a large crowd below. For their teamwork, the members of Rescue 1 received a Unit Citation.

The day tour of Thursday, July 11, 2013 started like most every firehouse day preceding it: roll call, tool and equipment check, and cups of coffee. The day would take a dramatic turn at 12:45 p.m., when Manhattan Box 217 was transmitted. Moments later a "10-75!" boomed across the airwaves. The members of Rescue 1, under the command of Captain Robert Morris, scrambled into position. The rig was soon racing downtown to 17 Pike Street, just off Henry Street, for a reported explosion and fire. At this location, as many as 24 "bug-bombs" (poisonous and highly flammable aerosol canisters) were being improperly discharged inside a first floor beauty salon. The dense, chemical fog cloud found an ignition source and exploded. This caused a localized collapse, igniting a fire that quickly began spreading.

Rescue 1 joined first due companies searching the building, which apparently had been illegally subdivided. Eight persons were rescued from the smoke-filled structure and rushed to nearby hospitals. Two persons were in critical condition, while two more were in serious condition. Firefighters then concentrated on cutting off and controlling the fast moving flames.

An hour later, after the secondary searches were complete and the building was made safe, the members of Rescue 1 assembled at their rig to change out air cylinders and check on their tools. Wet, tired, and dirty they began to realize this was probably the last fire their boss would work in New York City.

Today was the last tour for Captain Robert R. Morris, who after forty years in the FDNY would retire. Morris, who had reached the mandatory retirement age of sixty-five, could still do the job, as he had just proved at this difficult Chinatown fire. "I just got hit with a calendar. It kinda snuck up on me," Morris said. After being sworn in March 19, 1973, Morris worked in busy companies in Harlem and the Bronx, including Rescue 3, before being promoted to lieutenant. As a captain, he was placed in command of Ladder 28 in Harlem and served there until he took command of Rescue 1. This highly decorated officer led the members of Rescue 1 to fires and emergencies with distinction.

Effective 0900 hours, September 21, 2013 Captain Robert R. Morris Jr., became the commander of Rescue Company 1. For the first time in company history, and department history as well, a son followed immediately after his father as company commander.

On November 3, 2013 the FDNY communications office received a call at about 5 p.m. stating a man had fallen between two buildings. (This NYU student, had been missing for two days.) Units were dispatched to 80 Lafayette Street in lower Manhattan. There they found the 19-year old student, wedged in the 10-inch space between the walls of two buildings, NYU dorm and a parking garage. A rope was lowered, but the injured man could not even move his head. He was wedged in place. The company realized they could not remove the victim from above, but would have to operate laterally.

Setting up in the parking garage, Rescue 1 made a pilot hole through the wall. They found the wall was composed of two layers of cinderblock, separated by foam, and that the outer layer blocks were filled with rebar and concrete. Additional pilot holes were made, and the search-cam was used to pinpoint the man's exact location. Establishing a cutting location, Rescue 1 used a Partner saw with an Alpha blade to cut a triangle in the block. Two pneumatic chipping and breaking tools were then used, in conjunction with 7 lengths of 2-1/2 inch hose line provided by Engine 55. This hose was fed by Rescue's air compressor, and delivered the required pressure to a manifold at the cutting location.

Carefully the wall entrapping the student were breached, with care being taken to control any possible debris from falling on the already injured student. During the

Capt. Morris and his crew after his final job in the FDNY. An explosion and fire at 17 Pike Street on July 11, 2013.

At a little after eight o'clock on the evening of August 23, 2013, Rescue 1 received a phone alarm for a person in the water at Pier 45, Christopher and West Streets. The company rolled from quarters heading south as the dive team donned their gear in the rear of the rig. Upon arrival, a witness was interviewed, FF Richard Miranda, the primary diver, entered the black mirky water and began his search. Using a fan pattern search, fifteen feet from the pier, Miranda began swimming arches across the river bottom in 12-feet of water.

After a grueling twelve minutes in the pitch-black water, Miranda came upon a pier piling. Despite the added dangers of entanglement, he began to search beneath the pier itself. Within minutes, Miranda reported to his tender (via the underwater communications system) that he'd found the victim, a twenty-five year old man, and was in the process of returning to the surface.

For his heroic actions, Firefighter Richard Miranda was awarded a Class B.

The captain's spot in Rescue 1 remained open in accordance with department regulations, until all applications for the position could be evaluated. The official announcement of the new captain came in Supplement No. 66 to Department Order No. 62 dated September 18, 2013.

cutting Rescue 1 gained accesses to the patient's leg, and a doctor was able to start on ACPressure IV.

Finally, the rebar bar cutter removed the last obstacle. After 90 minutes, he was gently removed and turned over to EMS. The patient was treated for a possible fractured skull, pelvis and arm, as well as internal injuries.

At about 7:20 Sunday morning, December 1, 2013, a Metro-North Railroad train derailed on a curved section of track, under the Henry Hudson Bridge, near the Spuyten Duyvil Station. All of the seven cars of the train left the tracks, the first two plunging into a wooded area along the Hudson River. The lead car stopped only feet from the water. The next three cars were left on their sides. Cars five and six remained upright, although off the tracks. The seventh car was tilted at an extreme angle, still attached to the diesel locomotive that rested on its side, along an adjacent section of slightly elevated track.

The southbound train, with more than 100 persons aboard, was on its way from Poughkeepsie to Grand Central. The train left Poughkeepsie at 5:54 a.m., being pushed south by the diesel locomotive. Four people were killed and 67 were injured 11 critically. Three of the four persons killed were apparently thrown from the derailed train.

At 9:31 on the morning of March 12, 2014 a gas leak caused a massive explosion, and the collapse of two 5-story tenements, at 1644 & 1646 Park Avenue in the East Harlem section of Manhattan. The first FDNY units arrived two minutes later, and a second alarm and 10-60 were transmitted. Rescue 1 responded to the scene.

Rescue 1, under the command of Captain Robert R. Morris, Jr., arrived at the location and reported to Battalion 12. After conferring with the chief, Captain Morris split his company into two teams. One team (outside team) went to evaluate the stability and conditions of Exposure 4, while the other team (inside team) went to the Exposure 2 side to help remove an elderly victim.

After completing their assignment, the outside team placed portable ladders to the rear windows of a building on East 116th Street, to provide access to the rear of the collapsed building for FDNY members and hoselines. The inside team accessed the rear of the collapsed buildings through Exposure 4's lobby entrance, located on East 117th Street. At this point, all members of Rescue 1 met in the rear courtyard (exposure 3-side) of the burning collapsed buildings.

began a search, as Firefighters Geidel and Feeley hurried back to the rig for tools and medical gear. In full gear and wearing SCBA, the members of Rescue 1 climbed onto the debris pile, using the jagged sections of pipe and fire escape parts as hand holds.

The smoke condition on the top of the pile was extremely heavy. They searched by feel in zero visibility. Conditions resembled working on a roof during a cockloft fire. Crawling across the jagged debris, they searched every void, as the large calibre streams from tower ladders pounded into the burning pile around them. Working in these severe conditions with the five-story partially collapsed walls looming above, they located a critically injured woman. Despite her apparent mortal injuries, she was quickly removed from the pile as the search continued.

Fifty-feet away from the first victim, a second victim, a 67-year old woman was found semi-conscious and wedged in the rubble. Amidst the thick smoke, rescue men began to treat and extricate the woman. A medical assessment indicated she was suffering from severe head trauma, and multiple traumatic injuries to her body. As the removal continued, the streams from the tower ladders (unable to see the top of the pile through the smoke) were striking the victim and her rescuers. Members of Rescue 1 shielded her, as the captain radioed the situation to the members directing the streams. The remainder of the company arrived with a backboard and stokes basket. The victim was stabilized, packaged, and due to the heavy smoke condition, placed on air from an SCBA.

Members of Rescue 1 with President Obama.

Carefully, the members of Rescue 1 carried, slid, and dragged the stokes back to the edge of the pile. The woman was passed to other firefighters, then taken to an ambulance.

Back on the pile, Rescue 1 continued searching despite the dangerous conditions. About 15-feet from where the woman was found, the company located a deep void created by an "I-beam" that collapsed in a "lean-to" position. Inside the void was the remnants of a staircase, allowing rescue men to search down two additional levels. This search had to be cut short, due to building heat and smoke under pressure. A home owner's flashlight was found in the "on" position, indicating another possible victim. Captain Morris called for a line.

This area was far different than conditions found in the front. Here, in the rear, a huge section of 1646 Park Avenue had not completely collapsed. A 65-feet long, free-standing section of the five-story tenement loomed above the rescue men. The other building, 1644 Park Avenue, although fully collapsed did not spill into the rear yard, but rather came to rest as a jagged cliff, 2-3 stories high. Snapped floor joists, twisted and mangled fire escapes, pipes and other debris bristled through the brick pile. Thick black smoke blanketed the area, fed by the uncontrolled gas-fed flames below. No other members of the department had reached this dangerous area.

A radio transmission, from a nearby roof, indicated a possible victim visible in the collapse pile. Morris again split his team. The captain, Firefighters Morgan, Miranda and Hyland

Members of Rescue 1 placed two 20-foot straight ladders on the pile, to facilitate movement of members and the hoseline. Engine 83 moved in and directed their stream, hitting pockets of fire, as rescue men continued their searches. The safety battalion then requested an assessment of the partially collapsed 1646 Park Avenue. Captain Morris and a team of rescue men verified the stability of the structure, then conducted a search of floors two through five. All searches were negative.

The members of Rescue 1 operated under extreme conditions at this explosion, collapse, and fire. Under heavy smoke and with an unstable structure above them, they rescued a trapped woman, undoubtedly saving her life.

At 12:50 p.m. on November 12, 2014 Rescue 1 responded to Number 1 World Trade Center for a scaffold accident. Window washers were were being raised back to the roof when one of the cables snapped. The scaffold now hung dangerously at a 65 degree angle, 827-feet above the ground. The two workers clung tightly to the damaged frame, as the pleasant day rapidly cooled, pushed by the increasing north wind.

Rescue 1 arrived at the scene. They were advised that Capt. Brian Smith and Squad 18 were already at the roof level, lowering a 600-foot safety line. Lt. William Ryan and the men of Rescue 1 went to the unoccupied 68th floor. They accessed the area where the scaffolding was dangling just outside the window and began to set up equipment. This new building, America's tallest, soars 1,776 feet above the sidewalks of lower Manhattan. Opening for business a week earlier, the 104-story Port Authority building has above standard fire and life-safety systems and features. The huge glass tower stands on the northwest corner of the 16-acre World Trade Center site. Just to the south, across Fulton Street, is the National September 11 Memorial & Museum.

Rescue 1 Firefighters Christopher Gaulrapp, Renald Jean, and Kevin Kroth set up rigging for additional safety ropes and provided power for the tools. The window was covered with pressure sensitive tape to control loose shards. Firefighters Tim Geraghty and Matthew Murphy donned harnesses and dust masks, then readied the robo-pack saws. (These battery operated diamond tipped circular saws can also be electrically fed). Lt. Ryan conferred with Special Operations Battalion Chief Joseph Jardin, as the tools and ropes were set up.

Outside on the scaffold, the two workers attached FDNY safety lines and used a portable fire department radio that had been lowered to them. When everything was ready, Lt. Ryan checked with the workers. They returned a "thumbs up". On Ryan's order, the rescue men began cutting the thick double-paned glass.

As the autumn winds buffeted the scaffold, the two workers watched the rescue men methodically cut a 4 x 8-foot, door-size hole though the inner layer of 3/4-inch thick glass. This glass was cleared. Then work began on the 1/2-inch laminated outer layer of glass. On the street below, police closed down the sidewalks and streets beneath the scaffold. The National September 11 Memorial & Museum was temporarily cleared as a safety precaution.

When the last cut was made, rescue men handed a second safety rope to each worker. With a rescue man steadying the scaffold, each of the workers gingerly stepped through the opening. The workers briefly thanked the firefighters before being handed over to EMS for evaluation. The were both hospitalized for mild exposure.

Almost one hundred years after the start of Rescue Company 1, the officers and men stand ready to respond to all manners of emergency. From the smoky depths of sub-cellars, to the wind-blown tops of high-rise buildings, they have battled flames. They have saved people from swiftly moving rivers, extricated them from vehicular and mechanical accidents, and provided calm professional care wherever they've worked.

The end of this book only denotes a publishing deadline. The story of Rescue Company 1 continues to be written every tour, by the dedicated members of the company. We wish them continued success.

"Outstanding!"

The story of Rescue Company 1 continues to be written every tour, by the dedicated members of the company. We wish them continued success. – Outstanding!

Top left: Operating at 1 World Trade Center for a scaffold collapse on November 12, 2014. Middle left: Large section of thick glass is cut and removed, to rescue trapped workers. Bottom left: A diamond tipped saw was utilized to cut through the multi layered glass.

Rescue 1 Company

1914 Cadillac

1921 White

1924 Mack

1931 Mack

Apparatus

1939 Ward LaFrance

1939 Ward LaFrance A-frame

1948 Mack

Rescue 1 Company

1959 Mack

1959 Mack in Engine 65 firehouse. (Mike Dick)

1959 Mack dashboard (Mike Dick)

198

Apparatus

1971 Mack

1971 Mack after lettering

1979 Mack with door logo.

1979 Mack

Rescue 1 Company

1985 Mack

1996 HME/Saulsbury

1996 HME/Saulsbury

2002 EOne/Saulsbury

1985 Mack with A-frame.

Apparatus

2002 EOne/Saulsbury (Calderone)

2007 Pierce (Calderone)

2005 Mack Collapse Rescue 1

2011 Ferrara (Jeffers)

Rescue 1 Company

Rescue Company 1 in 1920. (l. to r.) Standing: William Fletcher, Jim Devine, Lt. Kilbride, Lt. Donohue, Frank Joseph, and John Conners. In rig front: William Dorritie, Walter Lamb, Frank Clark, and Charles Roggencamp. In rig back: William Hutcheon, Joe Horacek, and John Milward.

Firemen Charles Roggencamp, William Dorritie, Robert Tierney, Thomas Larkin, Lawrence Fullam, Louis Tischler, John Conners, and Captain Walter Lamb in 1926.

Members Through The Years

Firemen Dominico DiBenedetto, Daniel Kavanagh, Ed Cronin, Charles Kennedy, Henry Mulholland, William Dorritie, Louis Tischler, and Captain Cornell Garety in 1934.

Original Captain's badge design.

Rescue Company 1 in front of quarters in 1938.

Rescue 1 Company

Rescue 1 Company in 1949. (l. to r.) Back: unknown, Lt. Louis Werner, and Captain Patrick Green. Front: Walter Bronnekant, Stephen Huvane, Albert Temme, Allen Ostrow, unknown in mask, Alfred Jacobs and Timothy Sullivan.

Members Through The Years

1960 Rescue 1 officers Frank Yuskevich, Joe Rooney, William McMahon and Erwin Alexy.

Members in 1964. (l. to r.) Back: Lt. Alexy, Al Forsyth, Gordon Harrington, and Harold Andersen. Front: Joe Duffy, Paul Geidel and Frank Caltabellotta.

Firemen Geidel, Reres, Driscoll, Plauding, Peterson, Baldwin and Lt. McMahon taking a break in 1962.

Rescue 1 Company

Members in 1967. (l. to r.) Bo Southern, Herb Peterson, Ron McGhee, Marty Cunniff, John Driscoll and Paul Geidel.

Belt buckle with Lieutenant badge

Members in 1964. (l. to r.) Back: Captain Joe Rooney, Phil Prial, Tom Baldwin, Paul Geidel, Walter Bronnekant, and Al Forsyth. Front: Gordon Harrington, and Casimir "Lefty" Surdukowski.

Firemen Bessman, DeBellis and Martin backstage at Radio City Music Hall with ballet dancers on August 23, 1972.

Members Through The Years

Members in 1975. (l. to r.) Mike Maloney, Tony Limberg, Don Wilday, George McGann, Ronnie Foote, Lt. Geidel, Bob Burns, Jim Dowling and Hugh McGloin.

Michael Maloney was promoted to lieutenant and was working in Rescue Company 3 on March 19, 1975. While operating at a third alarm, Maloney and his men were forced from the blazing building by extreme heat and smoke. The officer collapsed outside and could not be revived.

Bob Burns, Anton Vardvarka, George McGann, Bill Bessman, Mike Maloney, and Lt. Paul Geidel in 1974.

Rescue 1 Company

Rescue Captain's badge

Taking a blow after battling a five-alarm hotel fire. (l. to r.) Front: Lt. Kalish (B8) and Bill Curran. Back: Bob Burns, Louis Garcia, Joe Angelini and John McAllister.

The senior crew in 1985. (l. to r.) Bob Burns, Dan Killoran, Bill Bessman, John Driscoll and Bill Riley.

Rescue 1 and Rescue 4 at LIRR drill in 1982. (Calderone)

Members Through The Years

Circa 1977 (l. to r.) Front: John "Spanky" McAllister, Jimmy McCarthy, and George McGann. Back: William "Moose" Curran, John Becker, and Frank DeBellis.

Back step with Bruce Newbery, Bill Riley, Bill Bessman, Norm Newkbk, Jim Corcoran and Lt. John Cerato in 1985.

Rescue 1 Company

After working the Seventh Avenue collapse on July 31, 1988. Jack Theobald, Captain Jack Calderone, Dave Williams, Harvey Harrell, Hank Molle and Ed Geraghty.

Comedian Richard Lewis in quarters for a live TV spot in 1989.

Captain Jim Rogers, Firefighters Hank Molle, Bruce Newbery and rescue men on Medal Day 1994.

Tim Kelly, Ray Phillips (R3), Paul Baldwin, Lt. Dennis Mojica, Joe Angelini and Neal Fredericksen.

Members Through The Years

Dan Duddy, Captain John Norman, Mike Montesi, Paul Hashagen, Lloyd Infanzon and Warren Forsyth in 1997.

Medal Day 1998 with medalists, Lt. Tony Errico, Stan Sussina, Lt. Mojica, and David Weiss.

August 1999, Joel Kanasky, George Healy, Dennis Mojica, Terry Hatton, Gerry Nevins, James Leavey, Bill Henry, Mike Montesi, Patty O'Keefe and Paul Hashagen.

Rescue 1 Company

Ed Myslinski, Patty O'Keefe, Lt. Mike Pena, Frank Fee, and Thor Johannessen after a tough job.

Tim Geraghty, Tony Tarabocchia, Kevin Kroth, Glenn Berube, Pat Neville, and Cliff Stabner.

Company photo taken for FDNY Millennium history book. A different photo was used.

Members Through The Years

Members on April 6, 2006. (l. to r.) Glenn Bullock, Lt. Tony Tarabocchia, Chris Mandeville, Cosmo DiOrio, Kevin Kroth, and Rob Roderka.

Glenn Bullock, Lt. Tony Tarabocchia, Chris Mandeville, Cosmo DiOrio, Kevin Kroth, Rob Roderka, and Lt. John Weisheit in 2006.

Military guest visits quarters in 2012.

Rescue 1 Captains, Robert "Rex" Morris, Jr. and Robert Morris on July 11, 2013.

Rescue 1 with Fire Commissioner Sal Cassano in 2013. (l. to r.) Frank Rush, William Owens, Comm. Cassano, Kevin Kroth, Tom Gayron, Joel Kanasky, and Lt. Tom Donnelly.

Rescue 1 Company

I. Rescue Company 1 FDNY Company Commanders

Captain John J. McElligott	1915-1916
Captain Edwin A. Hotchkiss	1916
Lt. Benjamin Parker	1916-1919
Lt. Francis Blessing	1919-1920
Lt. Thomas Kilbride	1920-1925
Captain Walter L. Lamb	1925-1930
Captain Cornell M. Garety	1930-1938
Captain George F. Hughes	1938-1942
Captain Raymond T. Millner	1942-1945
Captain Patrick Green	1945-1951
Captain James A. Adams	1951-1957
Captain John T. O'Hagan	1958-1960
Captain Joseph W. Rooney	1960-1973
Captain William Anderson	1973-1976
Captain Thomas Baldwin	1976-1979
Captain Brian O'Flaherty	1979-1991
Captain John Cerato	1991-1992
Captain Charles L. Kasper	1992-1993
Captain James Rogers	1994-1994*
Captain John Norman	1995-1999
Captain Terence Hatton	1999-2001*
Captain Fred LaFemina	2001-2002
Captain Robert R. Morris	2002-2013
Captain Robert R. Morris, Jr.	2013-present

* Died in the line of duty

II. Rescue Company 1 Firehouses

44 Great Jones Street

When Rescue Company 1 went into service on March 8, 1915, they were stationed in the quarters of Engine Company 33 at 44 Great Jones Street, Manhattan between the Bowery and Lafayette Street. This building constructed in 1898 was designed by the architects Flagg & Chambers. This firehouse is considered a Beaux Arts masterpiece. The building features a huge concave Beaux Arts arch bearing a cartouche. Engine 33 moved into the firehouse on June 1, 1899. The chief of department also maintained night offices in the building.

278 Spring Street

Rescue Company 1 was relocated to the quarters of Engine 30 on February 18, 1920. This 1904 Beaux-Arts firehouse is now the home of the New York City Fire Museum.

The architects, Ernest Flagg and Walter B. Chambers met in Paris and became partners in New York City in 1894. A number of their buildings have been designated as National Landmarks. Their works include: The Scribner Building on Fifth Avenue in Manhattan. The Washington State Capital, and the United States Naval Academy chapel, among many others.

243 Lafayette Street

The company responded to a fire and collapse on New Years's Eve 1946 and upon the completion of the grueling operation the next day, they backed their rig into a different firehouse than the one they left. They now occupied the quarters of Engine Company 20, who were disbanded that same morning. The department decided to move the rescue into these quarters rather than leave the building vacant and the area without a fire company. This firehouse was a little more than a half a mile from their previous quarters, but still left them in the middle of downtown Manhattan.

33 West 43rd Street

On May 1, 1960 Rescue 1 moved to midtown Manhattan. Here they would share the quarters of Engine Company 65, and be more centrally located in their response area. Manufacturing was moving out of lower Manhattan. Midtown was booming. The proliferation of large hotels, the numerous theaters, and close proximity to the garment district made midtown a good base of operations for Rescue 1.

530 West 43rd Street

When the quarters of the recently disbanded Engine 2 became available Rescue 1 was moved across 43rd Street to fill the void. This would give 65 Engine their house back and placed Rescue 1 alone, in their own firehouse. The move was made on November 25, 1982.

215 West 58th Street

As a result of the ten-alarm fire and the subsequent destruction of their quarters, the now "homeless" Rescue 1 spent the night of January 23, 1985 in the quarters of Engine 23.

440 West 38th Street

It was decided a better temporary location for the company would in the quarters of Engine 34 and Ladder 21. The rigs were re-arranged, bunks, lockers and the rescue office were moved in. For the next four years Rescue 1 shared this firehouse until new quarters were rebuilt on the same spot on West 43rd Street.

530 West 43rd Street

The officers and members of Rescue 1, moved back to their new quarters on 43rd Street on April 29, 1989. This was the first New York City firehouse built especially for a rescue company. The company was back on 43rd Street for the third time.

Appendix

III. Rescue Company 1 Awards

Just three years after the start of the paid firefighting force, the Metropolitan Fire Department began a system of recording the heroic deeds of its members. On November 22, 1868, the department's Committee of Appointments instructed the secretary to open a book to be called "The Roll of Merit M.F.D." Here a record of the valorous deeds performed by the officers and members of the department would be inscribed.

By 1915, the department, since 1870 known as the FDNY, had modified and refined the system that now included classifications of the meritorious acts. The breakdown is as follows:

Award Classifications
Class I – For Extreme Personal Risk
Class II – For Great Personal Risk
Class III – For Unusual Personal Risk
Class A – Involves Initiative and Bravery
Class B – Involves Initiative or Bravery

The department's Board of Merit (a board of experienced and respected officers, usually staff officers) meets quarterly and based on the facts presented in the reports they decide the degree of the award. Then once a year the Medal Board sits to decide which class awards will receive a medal of valor.

The following list is as complete as this writer was able to research. Department records officially document the awards, and hopefully each and every award will be included. If it's not perfect, I trust it's close.

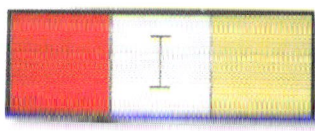

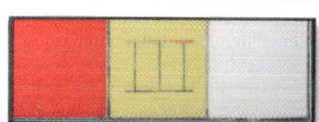

Individual award ribbons.

FDNY Roll of Merit
Member of Rescue Company 1

In the year ending December 31, 1915, the Board of Merit reviewed the record of Rescue 1 and awarded each member a Class A for the exceptionally hazardous service.

1915
Capt. John J. McElligott, Class A
Lt. Edwin A. Hotchkiss, Class A
Fr. Frank C. Clark, Class A
Fr. Alfred V. Henretty, Class A
Fr. William A. Dorritie, Class A
Fr. Thomas Kilbride, Class A
Fr. Alfred Kinsella, Class A
Fr. Walter A. O'Leary, Class A
Fr. John P. Ryan, Class A
Fr. John F. Mooney, Class A
Fr. James Shaw, Class A
Fr. Francis Blessing (E93, detailed to R1), Class A

October 25, 1916
Fr. Thomas Kilbride, Class I

1916
Capt. John J. McElligott, Class A
Lt. Edwin Hotchkiss, Class A
Fr. Francis Blessing, Class A
Fr. Frank C. Clark, Class A
Fr. John W. Donohue, Class A
Fr. William A. Dorritie, Class A
Fr. Alfred V. Henretty, Class A
Fr. Thomas Kilbride, Class A
Fr. Alfred Kinsella, Class A
Fr. John F. Mooney, Class A
Fr. Walter A. O'Leary, Class A
Fr. John P. Ryan, Class A
Fr. James Smith, Class A

1917
Lt. Benjamin F. Parker, Class A
Lt. Francis Blessing, Class A
Fr. Frank C. Clark, Class A
Fr. John C. Conners, Class A
Fr. John W. Donohue, Class A
Fr. William A. Dorritie, Class A
Fr. Thomas Kilbride, Class A
Fr. Alfred Kinsella, Class A
Fr. John Mayr, Class A
Fr. John P. Ryan, Class A
Fr. James Smith, Class A

January 16, 1918
Lt. Benjamin Parker, Class I
Fr. John W. Donohue, Class II
Fr. John C. Conners, Class II

April 11, 1918
Fr. John W. Donohue, Class II
Fr. John C. Conners, Class II
Fr. John P. Ryan, Class II

October 5, 1918
Lt. Francis Blessing, Class I
Fr. Thomas Kilbride, Class I
Fr. John W. Donohue, Class I
Fr. John P. Ryan, Class II
Fr. John Mayr, Class II
Fr. Frank C. Clark, Class II
Fr. James Smith, Class II

1919
Lt. Benjamin F. Parker, Class A
Lt. Francis Blessing, Class A
Fr. Frank C. Clark, Class A
Fr. John C. Conners, Class A

Fr. John W. Donohue, Class A
Fr. William A. Dorritie, Class A
Fr. Thomas Kilbride, Class A
Fr. William T. Hutcheon, Class A
Fr. Alfred Kinsella, Class A
Fr. John Mayr, Class A
Fr. John B. Milward, Class A
Fr. John P. Ryan, Class A
Fr. James Smith, Class A

February 17, 1919
Lt. John W. Donohue, Class A
Lt. Thomas Kilbride, Class A
Fr. John P. Ryan, Class A
Fr. John C. Conners, Class A
Fr. William A. Dorritie, Class A
Fr. William T. Hutcheon, Class A
Fr. James Smith, Class A

July 24, 1919
Fr. Charles C. Roggencamp, Class B
Fr. Paul C. Maron, Class B
Fr. John P. Ryan, Class B
Fr. Joseph Horacek, Class B

August 9, 1919
Lt. Francis Blessing, Class A
Fr. John B. Milward, Class A

September 13, 1919
Lt. Francis Blessing, Class A
Fr. Alfred Kinsella, Class A
Fr. John Kistenberger, Class A
Fr. William R. Fletcher, Class A
Fr. Walter Lamb, Class A
Fr. James A. Devine, Class A
Fr. Charles C. Roggencamp, Class A

Appendix

FDNY Roll of Merit – Member of Rescue Company 1 (continued)

October 17, 1919
Lt. Thomas Kilbride, Class A
Fr. Paul C. Maron, Class A
Fr. Alfred Kinsella, Class A
Fr. William A. Dorritie, Class A

June 23, 1920
Lt. Thomas Kilbride, Class A
Fr. Frank C. Clark, Class A
Fr. Walter L. Lamb, Class A
Fr. Charles C. Roggencamp, Class A
Fr. John Kistenberger, Class A
Fr. Frank Joseph, Class A
Fr. Joseph Horacek, Class A

July 18, 1921
Fr. Charles C. Roggencamp, Class I
Lt. Thomas Kilbride, Class II
Fr. Charles A. Kennedy, Jr., Class II

November 29, 1921
Lt. John A. Coffey, Class A
Fr. William Hutcheon, Class A
Fr. William A. Dorritie, Class A
Fr. John C. Conners, Class A
Fr. Joseph D. Sullivan, Class A
Fr. James Devine, Class A
Fr. Joseph Horacek, Class A

June 23, 1922
Fr. Charles C. Roggencamp, Class A

September 26, 1923
Lt. Thomas Kilbride, Class A
Fr. Peter F. Walsh, Class A
Fr. Robert A. Tierney, Class A
Fr. William R. Fletcher, Class A
Fr. Joseph D. Sullivan, Class A

October 11, 1924
Capt. Walter L. Lamb, Class B
Fr. William A. Dorritie, Class B
Fr. John B. Milward, Class B
Fr. Charles C. Roggencamp, Class B
Fr. John Kistenberger, Class B
Fr. William R. Fletcher, Class B
Fr. Charles A. Kennedy, Jr., Class B

December 11, 1925
Capt. Walter L. Lamb, Class II
Fr. Bela Varga, Class II
Fr. Cornell M. Garety, Class II

January 27, 1927
Lt. Thomas Kilbride, Class II
Fr. Bela J. Varga, Class II
Fr. William T. Hutcheon, Class II
Fr. John B. Milward, Class II
Fr. James E. Walsh, Class II
Fr. Charles A. Kennedy, Jr., Class II
Fr. Edward Cronin, Jr., Class II
Fr. Peter Doyle, Class II
Fr. John Mayr, Class II

January 6, 1929
Fr. William A. Dorritie, Class II

February 19, 1929
Lt. Thomas Kilbride, Class A
Fr. William A. Dorritie, Class A
Fr. John C. Conners, Class A
Fr. Lawrence F. Fullam, Class A
Fr. Charles C. Roggencamp, Class A
Fr. Robert A. Tierney, Class A
Fr. Henry M. Mulholland, Class A
Fr. Louis Tischler, Class A

March 5, 1929
Fr. William A. Dorritie, Class II

June 20, 1930
Fr. Edward Cronin, Jr., Class I

August 11, 1930
Fr. Bela J. Varga, Class I
Fr. Charles A. Kennedy, Jr., Class III
Fr. Charles C. Roggencamp, Class III
Fr. Lawrence F. Fullam, Class III

September 14, 1930
Fr. William A. Dorritie, Class III
Fr. Henry M. Mulholland, Class III
Fr. Peter Doyle, Class III
Fr. Charles A. Kennedy, Class III
Fr. Edward Cronin, Jr., Class III
Fr. John C. Conners, Class III

April 30, 1931
Fr. Henry Mulholland, Class A
Fr. Robert A. Tierney, Class A
Capt. Cornell M. Garety, Class A

September 29, 1931
Fr. William A. Dorritie, Class II
Lt. Thomas Kilbride, Class A
Fr. Edward Cronin, Jr., Class A
Fr. Daniel J.J. Kavanagh, Class A
Fr. Henry M. Mulholland, Class A
Fr. Henry Tischler, Class A
Fr. John C. Conners, Class A

May 26, 1932
Capt. Cornell M. Garety, Class I
Fr. Charles C. Roggencamp, Class III
Fr. James E. Walsh, Class III
Fr. Dominico A. DiBenedetto, Class III
Lt. George H. Friel, Cambridge, Massachusetts FD, Class III

August 1, 1932
Lt. Thomas Kilbride, Class A
Fr. Charles C. Roggencamp, Class A
Fr. Edward Cronin, Jr., Class A
Fr. John C. Conners, Class A
Fr. William A. Dorritie, Class A
Fr. Thomas A. McCarthy, Class A
Fr. Louis Tischler, Class A

May 4, 1933
Lt. Theodore J. Beliakoff, Class A
Fr. Thomas A. McCarthy, Class A
Fr. Edward Cronin, Jr., Class A
Fr. John C. Conners, Class A
Fr. Robert A. Tierney, Class A
Fr. Charles A. Kennedy, Jr., Class A
Fr. Daniel J.J. Kavanagh, Class A

August 1, 1933
Lt. Thomas Kilbride, Class A
Fr. Charles C. Roggencamp, Class A
Fr. Edward Cronin, Jr., Class A
Fr. John C. Conners, Class A
Fr. William A. Dorritie, Class A
Fr. Thomas A. McCarthy, Class A
Fr. Louis Tischler, Class A

September 13, 1933
Lt. Theodore J. Beliakoff, Class B
Fr. William A. Dorritie, Class B
Fr. Edward Cronin, Jr., Class B
Fr. Dominico A. DiBenedetto, Class B
Fr. Henry M. Mulholland, Class B
Fr. Charles A. Kennedy, Jr., Class B
Fr. George J. Nelson, Class B

October 10, 1934
Lt. George Hughes, Class A
Fr. James E. Walsh, Class A
Fr. Charles A. Kennedy, Jr., Class A
Fr. Edward Cronin, Jr., Class A
Fr. Edward L. Lyons, Class A
Fr. Thomas A. McCarthy, Class A

July 15, 1935
Fr. Robert A. Tierney, Class B (VD)

September 3, 1936
Lt. Henry M. Mulholland, Class III
Fr. Daniel J.J. Kavanagh, Class III
Fr. James E. Walsh, Class III
Fr. George Planding, Class III
Fr. Christian A. Conrad, Class III
Fr. Michael F. Horan, Class III

March 4, 1937
Lt. Henry M. Mulholland, Class A + B (VD)
Fr. William J. Anthony, Class A
Fr. Herman Maier, Class A
Fr. Edward L. Lyons, Class A
Fr. Robert A. Tierney, Class A
Fr. Harry Pokorny, Class A
Fr. Christian A. Conrad, Class A
Fr. George C. Versfelt, Class A

June 26, 1938
Fr. Edward L. Lyons, Class A
Fr. James Ferguson, Class A

January 23, 1939
Fr. Christian A. Conrad, Class III
Fr. William J. Anthony, Class III
Fr. Michael F. Horn, Class III
Fr. Martin D. J. Kelly, Class III
Fr. William F. Mosich, Class III
Fr. James Ferguson, Class III
Fr. Joseph Donohue, Class III

Appendix

FDNY Roll of Merit – Member of Rescue Company 1 (continued)

October 10, 1939
Capt. George F. Hughes, Class B
Fr. Louis E. Werner, Class B
Fr. George Planding, Class B
Fr. John A. Stanek, Class B
Fr. Walter Bronnekant, Class B
Fr. William F. Morish, Class B
Fr. Edward J. Barbour, Jr., Class B

January 1, 1940
Fr. James Ferguson, Class A (VD)

June 29, 1940
Fr. Michael J. Donohue, Class A
Fr. Charles Sadera, Jr., Class A

September 3, 1940
Fr. Charles Sadera, Jr., Class I

April 18, 1942
Lt. Patrick T. Green, Class III
Fr. William J. Anthony, Class A
Fr. Joseph Donohue, Class A
Fr. Herman Maier, Class A
Fr. John A. Stanek, Class A
Fr. Timothy J. Sullivan, Class A
Fr. James E. Walsh, Class A

April 30, 1943
Fr. Joseph Donohue, Class A

June 7, 1944
Fr. James Ferguson, Class II

September 23, 1944
Lt. John J. Loretan, Class A
Fr. John F. Seibert, Class A
Fr. Stephen J. Barry, Class A
Fr. John P. MacHaffie, Class A
Fr. Francis X. Lantier, Class A
Fr. Vincent C. Gallo, Jr., Class A
Fr. George Tollefson, Class A
Fr. Allen Ostrow, Class A

September 28, 1944
Fr. Carl F. Reidway, Class B (VD)

April 7, 1945
Lt. Joseph W. Schick, Class B
Fr. Walter Bronnekant, Class B
Fr. Allen Ostrow, Class B
Fr. George Planding, Class B
Fr. Harry Pokorny, Class B
Fr. John H. Thompson, Class B
Fr. Edward L. Lyons, Class B

July 8, 1945
Lt. Louis E. Werner, Class III
Fr. John R. Donovan, Class III
Fr. Michael O. Glynn, Class III

July 28, 1945
Lt. Louis E. Werner, Class B
Fr. John H. Thompson, Class B
Fr. Michael O. Glynn, Class B
Fr. Allen Ostrow, Class B
Fr. George Planding, Class B
Fr. Harry Pokorny, Class B

Fr. George F. Voigt, Class B
Fr. Joseph Donohue, Class B
Fr. Walter Bronnekant, Class B

February 11, 1946
Lt. Louis E. Werner, Class A
Fr. George Planding, Class A
Fr. Timothy J. Sullivan, Class A
Fr. Edward L. Lyons, Class A
Fr. John H. Thompson, Class A
Fr. Joseph V. Senese, Class A
Fr. Edward J. Costello, Jr., Class A
Fr. Allen Ostrow, Class A
Fr. Walter Bronnekant, Class A

December 31, 1946
Capt. Patrick T. Green, Class I
Lt. Joseph W. Schick, Class II
Fr. Joseph Donohue, Class II
Fr. Edward L. Lyons, Class III
Fr. Fred H. Darmstadt, Class III
Fr. Mathias Olsen, Class III
Fr. John A. Stanek, Class III
Fr. Hugh T. Early, Class III
Fr. George F. Voigt, Class III
Fr. Allen Ostrow, Class III
Fr. Edward Barbour, Jr., Class III
Fr. Harry Pokorny, Class III
Fr. Timothy J. Sullivan, Class III
Fr. Walter Bronnekant, Class III

January 1, 1947
Fr. Walter Bronnekant, Class III

January 10, 1947
Fr. Joseph Donohue, Class A
Fr. Harold B. Andersen, Class A
Fr. Walter Bronnekant, Class A
Fr. Edward J. Costello, Jr., Class A
Fr. Albert E. Temme, Jr., Class A
Fr. George Planding, Class A
Prob. Fr. Arthur L. Moran, Class A

May 14, 1947
Capt. Patrick T. Green, Class I
Fr. Hugh T. Early, Class I
Fr. Edward J. Barbour, Jr., Class I
Fr. William F. Martorano, Class I
Fr. John R. Donovan, Class I
Fr. William J. Anthony, Class I
Fr. John A. Stanek, Class I
Fr. Timothy J. Sullivan, Class I
Fr. Joseph W. Rooney, Class I

July 21, 1947
Lt. Joseph W. Schick, Class III
Fr. James Ferguson, Class A
Fr. William F. Martorano, Class A
Fr. Joseph W. Rooney, Class A

November 28, 1947
Lt. Michael J. Donohue, Class III
Fr. Alfred B. Jacobs, Class III
Fr. John A. Stanek, Class III
Fr. Timothy J. Sullivan, Class III
Fr. Allen Ostrow, Class III

Fr. William F. Martorano, Class III
Fr. Edward L. Lyons, Class III
Lt. Joseph W. Schick, Class A
Fr. Harry Pokorny, Class A
Fr. Albert E. Temme, Jr., Class A
Fr. John R. Donovan, Class A
Fr. Harold B. Andersen, Class A + A (VD)
Fr. Charles Sadera, Class A

August 26, 1948
Lt. Louis E. Werner, Class A
Fr. George Planding, Class A
Fr. Edward L. Lyons, Class A
Fr. Joseph Donohue, Class A
Fr. Albert E. Temme, Jr., Class A
Fr. John R. Donohue, Class A

December 27, 1947
Fr. Hugh T. Early, Class III

May 13, 1949
Capt. Patrick T. Green, Class II
Lt. Michael J. Donohue, Class A
Lt. Louis E. Werner, Class II
Fr. Edward J. Barbour, Jr., Class II
Fr. Joseph Donohue, Class II
Fr. John R. Donovan, Class II
Fr. John J. Ryan, Class II
Fr. Allen Ostrow, Class II
Fr. Edward J. Fox, Class II
Fr. Stephen P. Huvane, Class II
Fr. Edward F. Courtney, Class II
Fr. Edward J. Costello, Jr., Class II
Fr. Walter Bronnekant, Class II
Fr. William A. J. Beck, Class II

October 14, 1949
Lt. Louis E. Werner, Class A
Lt. Michael J. Donohue, Class A
Fr. Joseph W. Rooney, Class A
Fr. John F. Seibert, Class A
Fr. Albert E. Temme, Jr., Class A
Fr. George Tollefson, Class A
Fr. Joseph W. Ryan, Class A
Fr. Charles Sadera, Jr., Class A
Fr. Edward J. Costello, Jr., Class A
Fr. Stephen P. Huvane, Class A
Fr. John R. Donovan, Class A
Fr. Timothy J. Sullivan, Class A
Fr. George Planding, Class A
Fr. Casimir S. Surdukowski, Class A
Fr. William J. Anthony, Class A
Fr. Hugh T. Early, Class A

November 23, 1950
Lt. Michael J. Donohue, Class A
Fr. Albert E. Temme, Jr., Class A
Fr. Joseph W. Ryan, Class A
Fr. Harry Pokorny, Class A
Fr. Warren M. Wykel, Class A
Fr. Edward J. Barbour, Jr., Class A
Fr. William J. Anthony, Jr., Class A

November 24, 1950
Lt. James Ferguson, Class A
Fr. George Planding, Class A

FDNY Roll of Merit – Member of Rescue Company 1 (continued)

Fr. Edward J. Fox, Class A
Fr. Alfred B. Jacobs, Class A
Fr. Edward J. Costello, Class A
Fr. Joseph W. Ryan, Class A
Fr. Taras T. Kinasewitz, Class A
Fr. Hugh T. Early, Class A (VD)
Fr. Allen Ostrow, Class A (VD)
Fr. Joseph W. Rooney, Class A

March 7, 1951
Lt. Michael J. Donohue, Class B
Fr. Edward J. Barbour, Jr., Class B
Fr. Casimir S. Surdukowski, Class B
Fr. William J. Anthony, Class B
Fr. Joseph W. Rooney, Class B

September 5, 1951
Capt. James A. Adams, Class A
Fr. William J. Anthony, Class A
Fr. George Planding, Class A
Fr. George J. Straub, Class A
Fr. Timothy J. Sullivan, Class A
Fr. George M. Tollefson, Class A

February 6, 1953
Fr. Charles Sadera, Jr., Class A
Fr. Hugh T. Early, Jr., Class A
Fr. Taras T. Kinasewitz, Class A
Fr. John T. O'Rourke, Class A

April 17, 1953
Fr. Hugh T. Early, Class A

April 13, 1954
Lt. Michael J. Donohue, Class A
Fr. Edward J. Barbour, Jr., Class A
Fr. Edward J. Fox, Class A
Fr. Warren M. Wykel, Class A
Fr. John F. Seibert, Class A
Fr. Thomas F. Harper, Class A
Fr. Harold B. Andersen, Class A

December 28, 1954
Fr. Hugh T. Early, Jr., Class I
Fr. Charles Sadera, Jr., Class I
Lt. John P. Mitchell (L20 det. R1), Class II
Fr. John J. Ryan, Class II
Fr. Cecil C. Southern, Jr., Class II
Fr. Walter Bronnekant, Class II

April 30, 1955
Lt. Joseph W. Ryan, Class I
Fr. John R. Donovan, Class I
Fr. John T. O'Rourke, Class A
Fr. John J. Ryan, Class A
Fr. George C. Planding, Class A

September 7, 1955
Fr. Thomas D. McMahon, Class III

September 21, 1955
Fr. Edward J. Barbour, Jr., Class I
Fr. Timothy J. Sullivan, Class A

October 14, 1955
Fr. John R. Donovan, Class I

August 18, 1956
Lt. Joseph W. Ryan, Class B

September 26, 1956
Lt. Harold A. Cochard, Class A

February 21, 1957
Lt. Joseph W. Ryan, Class A (VD)

February 14, 1958
Capt. John T. O'Hagan, Class III + Class A (VD)
Lt. Harold A. Cochard, Class III
Lt. Charles A. Brienza, Class III
Lt. Joseph W. Ryan, Class III
Lt. Frank Yuskevich, Class III
Fr. John R. Donovan, Class III
Fr. George Planding, Class III
Fr. Victor A. Miozzi, Class III
Fr. James J. Duffy, Class III + Class A (VD)
Fr. John P. Delury, Class III
Fr. John J. Ryan, Class III + Class A (VD)
Fr. Warren M. Wykel, Class III + Class A (VD)
Fr. John F. Seibert, Class III
Fr. George M. Tollefson, Class III
Fr. Frank E. Smith, Class III + Class A (VD)
Fr. John T. O'Rourke, Class III + Class A (VD)
Fr. Walter Bronnekant, Class III
Fr. Casimir S. Surdukowski, Class III
Fr. Joseph M. Duffy, Class III + Class A (VD)
Fr. Leonard Smith, Class III
Fr. John P. McBride, Class III + Class A (VD)
Fr. Edward J. Fox, Class III
Fr. Thomas F. Harper, Class III
Fr. John C. Farragher, Class III + Class A (VD)
Fr. Alfred W. Hankin, Class III
Fr. Robert W. Cramatte, Class III
Fr. William J. McMahon, Class III
Fr. Harold B. Andersen, Class III
Fr. Gordon E. Harrington, Class III
Fr. Alan R. Smith (L9), Class III
Fr. Thomas P. Baldwin (L161), Class III
Fr. William C. Anderson (L16), Class III

March 19, 1958
Capt. John T. O'Hagan, Class III
Fr. John T. O'Rourke, Class III
Fr. Harold B. Andersen, Class A

April 15, 1958
Fr. Joseph M. Duffy, Class III

September 16, 1958
Lt. Joseph W. Ryan, Class B
Fr. Charles Sadera, Jr., Class B
Fr. Harold B. Andersen, Class B
Fr. Cecil C. Southern, Jr., Class B
Fr. Gordon E. Harrington, Class B
Fr. Victor A. Miozzi, Class B
Fr. Philip J. Prial, Jr. (L9), Class B

June 9, 1959
Fr. John P. Delury, Class B (VD)

January 6, 1960
Lt. Frank Yuskevich, Class II
Fr. Frank E. Smith, Class A

November 7, 1960
Fr. John D. Smith, Jr., Class B (VD)

December 16, 1960
Lt. William J. McMahon, Class B (VD)
Fr. Thomas W. Bonamo, Jr., Class B (VD)
Fr. John C. Farragher, Class B (VD)
Fr. John T. O'Rourke, Class B (VD)
Fr. Herbert C. Peterson, Class B (VD)

December 19, 1960
Lt. William J. McMahon, Class II
Fr. Thomas W. Bonamo, Jr., Class II
Fr. Timothy P. Costello, Class II
Fr. Frank L. Caltabellotta, Class A + Class B (VD)
Fr. Casimir S. Surdukowski, Class B (VD)
Fr. Alfred W. Hankin, Class A
Fr. George C. Planding, Class A
Fr. John C. Farragher, Class A

October 1, 1962
Fr. William J. Curran, Class I

October 3, 1962
Lt. William J. McMahon, Class B (VD)
Fr. Ronald J. McGhee, Class B (VD)
Fr. Paul E. Geidel, Class B (VD)
Fr. William J. Curran, Class B (VD)
Fr. Frank L. Caltabellotta, Class B (VD)
Fr. Walter F. Clarke (L7), Class B (VD)

October 30, 1962
Lt. William J. McMahon, Class B
Fr. Thomas P. Baldwin, Class B
Fr. William J. Curran, Class B
Fr. Paul E. Geidel, Class B
Fr. George Planding, Class B
Fr. Joseph J. Guido, Class B
Fr. Herman H. Kroger, Class B

December 1, 1962
Fr. Paul E. Geidel, Class III

March 22, 1963
Fr. Thomas W. Bonamo, Class B

February 22, 1964
Fr. Paul E. Geidel, Class A

May 8, 1964
Fr. Joseph A. Reres, Class A

June 22, 1964
Lt. Erwin J. Alexy, Class II
Fr. Thomas W. Bonamo, Jr., Class III
Fr. Ronald J. McGhee, Class III
Fr. Alfred W. Hankin, Class III
Fr. William A. Cooper, Class III
Fr. James J. Dowling, Class III
Fr. William F. Wilson, Class III

October 20, 1964
Fr. William A. Cooper, Class A

May 24, 1965
Fr. Paul E. Geidel, Class A

Appendix

FDNY Roll of Merit – Member of Rescue Company 1 (continued)

January 27, 1966
Lt. Erwin J. Alexy, Class A
Fr. William F. Wilson, Class A
Fr. James J. Dowling, Class A
Fr. Raymond M. Brown, Class A
Fr. Alfred W. Hankin, Class A
Fr. Martin J. Cunniff, Class A
Fr. Francis J. Fehling, Class A

December 22, 1966
Fr. Raymond M. Brown, Class I
Lt. Erwin J. Alexy, Class II
Fr. William J. Curran, Class III
Fr. Alfred W. Hankin, Class III
Fr. Joseph M. Duffy, Class III
Fr. Edward J. Vomero, Class III

February 14, 1967
Fr. Alfred W. Hankin, Class III

May 31, 1967
Fr. Michael A. Maloney, Class B

February 15, 1968
Fr. Paul E. Geidel, Class III

November 7, 1968
Fr. George A. McGann, Class B

December 19, 1968
Fr. Robert D. Wilday, Class B

February 25, 1969
Fr. Martin J. Cunniff, Class I
Fr. William B. Bessman, Class A
Fr. John J. Driscoll, Class B (VD)

July 18, 1969
Fr. Francis J. Fehling, Class B (VD)

December 5, 1969
Fr. William B. Bessman, Class A
Fr. George A. McGann, Class A

February 26, 1970
Fr. John D. Becker, Class B

March 6, 1970
Fr. William M. Moclair, Class A
Fr. John J. Harney, Class A
Fr. James T. McCarthy, Class A
Fr. Robert L. Burns, Class A

March 8, 1970
Lt. Thomas P. Baldwin, Class B
Fr. Hugh M. McGloin, Class B
Fr. William J. Curran, Class B
Fr. William B. Bessman, Class B
Fr. John J. Driscoll, Class B
Fr. Ronald J. McGhee, Class B
Fr. Francis J. Fehling, Class B
Fr. William A. Riley, Class B
Fr. Robert D. Wilday, Class B
Fr. Michael J. Walsh, Class B
Lt. James P. Leddy (B8), Class B
Fr. Edward J. Tuite, Class B
Fr. Max Siegel (L2), Class B

March 16, 1970
Fr. James J. Dowling, Class A

December 4, 1970
Lt. William A. Cooper, Class III
Fr. John J. Driscoll, Class A
Fr. Ronald J. McGhee, Class A
Fr. Robert W. Johnson, Jr., Class A

December 29, 1970
Fr. Robert D. Wilday, Class A

July 7, 1971
Fr. John J. Driscoll, Class A
Fr. William J. Curran, Class A

August 5, 1971
Fr. Dennis Dale, Class A

October 14, 1971
Fr. John J. Driscoll, Class A

February 25, 1972
Fr. Robert L. Burns, Class B (VD)
Fr. Frank J. Fehling, Class B (VD)

March 22, 1972
Fr. James T. McCarthy, Class I
Lt. Raymond M. Brown, Class III
Fr. John R. McAllister, Class III
Fr. Hugh M. McGloin, Class III
Fr. John J. Driscoll, Class A
Fr. Philip J. Prial, Jr., Class A
Fr. William M. Moclair, Class A

April 2, 1972
Fr. George A. McGann, Class B (VD)

April 15, 1972
Fr. Ronald J. McGhee, Class B
Fr. John P. McBride, Class B
Fr. William M. Moclair, Class B

April 28, 1972
Fr. John D. Becker, Class B

July 14, 1972
Fr. Michael A. Maloney, Class A

November 24, 1972
Fr. Michael A. Maloney, Class B

August 3, 1973
Lt. Thomas P. Baldwin, Class A
Fr. William B. Bessman, Class A
Fr. Joseph R. Bryant, Class A
Fr. William J. Curran, Class A
Fr. Francis J. Fehling, Class A
Fr. Anthony P. Limberg, Class A
Fr. William A. Riley, Class A

August 23, 1973
Fr. Michael J. Walsh, Class B
Fr. Philip J. Prial, Class B

January 14, 1974
Fr. Daniel J. Killoran, Class A
Fr. John J. Driscoll, Class A

January 26, 1974
Fr. Ernest M. Andreacchi, Class B

October 2, 1975
Fr. Henry C. Gonzalez, Class A
Fr. William A. Riley, Class A

November 16, 1975
Fr. Dennis J. Dale, Class A

December 23, 1975
Lt. Paul E. Geidel, Class III

January 7, 1976
Fr. Robert D. Wilday, Class A

October 28, 1976
Fr. John J. Driscoll, Class III
Fr. James J. Dowling, Class B
Fr. Dennis Dale, Class B
Fr. James D. Rogers, Class B
Fr. Ernest M. Andreacchi, Class B
Lt. Thomas Fried (B8), Class B

December 17, 1976
Fr. James D. Rogers, Class A

May 13, 1977
Fr. Stephen J. Casani, Class B (VD)

May 25, 1977
Fr. Robert L. Burns, Class A

March 7, 1978
Fr. William M. Moclair, Class A
Fr. Henry C. Gonzalez, Class B

June 7, 1978
Fr. James D. Rogers, Class II

August 15, 1978
Fr. William A. Seigel, Class A

November 18, 1978
Fr. James D. Rogers, Class A

December 4, 1978
Fr. James D. Rogers, Class B

April 24, 1979
Fr. Joseph J. Angelini, Class B
Fr. John R. McAllister, Class B

May 29, 1979
Fr. Stephen J. Casani, Class B (VD)

August 2, 1979
Fr. James D. Rogers, Class B

October 21, 1979
Fr. Stephen J. Casani, Class B (VD)

December 15, 1979
Fr. Joseph M. Kilbra, Class B

February 8, 1980
Lt. James J. Curran, Class II
Fr. John R. McAllister, Class II

219

Appendix

FDNY Roll of Merit – Member of Rescue Company 1 (continued)

February 12, 1980
Fr. Henry C. Gonzalez, Class B

February 29, 1980
Fr. Robert L. Burns, Class A

June 30, 1980
Lt. Anthony P. Limberg, Class B (VD)

February 9, 1981
Fr. Norman L. Newkirk, Class A
Fr. Henry C. Gonzalez, Class B

March 29, 1981
Fr. Thomas F. Fitzpatrick, Jr., Class B

May 20, 1981
Fr. James D. Rogers, Class A

August 31, 1981
Lt. John Cerato, Class B (VD)
Fr. David J. Williams, Class B (VD)
Fr. William A. Riley, Class B (VD)
Fr. Richard M. Martinsen, Class B (VD)
Fr. Thomas F. Fitzpatrick, Jr., Class B (VD)

September 28, 1981
Fr. Joseph R. Bryant, Class B

November 1, 1981
Fr. Thomas H. Baker, Class B

January 21, 1982
Capt. Brian E. O'Flaherty, Class III

January 29, 1982
Lt. James J. Curran, Class III

February 18, 1983
Capt. Brian E. O'Flaherty, Class A

March 13, 1983
FF William B. Bessman, Class II

May 13, 1983
FF Thomas H. Baker, Jr., Class B

July 13, 1983
FF Joseph J. Angelini, Class B (VD)

April 4, 1984
Lt. James J. Curran, Class III
FF Michael Fitzgerald, Class III
FF Richard Cody, Class III

November 3, 1984
Lt. Joseph H. Dirks (B8), Class III
FF John R. McAllister, Class III

November 8, 1984
FF James T. Emery, Class A

November 23, 1984
FF Thomas H. Baker, Jr., Class III
FF Paul F. Hashagen, Class B
FF Patrick Hyland, Class B

April 26, 1985
FF Paul F. Hashagen, Class III
FF John W. Boyle, Class A

October 8, 1985
FF John J. Driscoll, Class A

November 3, 1985
FF John J. Driscoll, Class B
FF Thomas H. Baker, Jr., Class B

September 30, 1986
FF Paul F. Hashagen, Class II

October 22, 1986
FF Paul F. Hashagen, Class II

January 9, 1987
FF Norman Newkirk, Class III

February 24, 1987
FF Norman Newkirk, Class B

February 27, 1987
Lt. Stephen J. Casani, Class A

August 4, 1987
FF Paul F. Hashagen, Class B

February 22, 1988
FF John Theobald, Class A

June 25, 1988
FF Robert L. Burns, Class B

January 16, 1989
FF Raymond M. Brown, Jr., Class A

September 20, 1989
FF Carl Feilmoser, Class III

July 17, 1990
FF Raymond M. Brown, Jr., Class A

May 14, 1991
FF Kevin F. Shea, Class I

September 12, 1991
FF Joseph J. Angelini, Class III

September 28, 1991
Lt. James P. Ellson, Class B

January 31, 1993
FF Henry G. Molle, Class III
FF Bruce H. Newbery, Class III

February 26, 1993
FF Harvey Harrell, Class B (VD)

August 31, 1993
FF Thomas J. Reichel, Class B

April 7, 1995
Lt. Stephen J. Casani, Class A
FF Paul T. Baldwin, Class B
FF John W. Boyle, Class B

May 22, 1995
FF Thomas F. Sullivan, Class A
Lt. Dennis Mojica, Class B

January 7, 1997
FF Stanley J. Sussina, Class II

August 6, 1997
Lt. Dennis Mojica, Class III

March 18, 1999
FF Gerard T. Nevins, Class II

March 22, 1999
FF Patrick J. O'Keefe, Class B

July 25, 1999
FF Michael G. Montesi, Class B

November 21, 1999
FF Gerard T. Nevins, Class A

June 22, 2000
FF John M. Flatley, Class B

February 7, 2001
FF Michael G. Geidel, Class B

2005
FF Sean G. Cummins, Class A
FF Christopher R. Mandeville, Class A
FF Michael F. Schunk, Class B

2006
Capt. Robert R. Morris, Class B

2007
Lt. Thomas P. Donnelly, Class A
FF Frederick J. Ill, III, Class A
FF Francis W. Rush, III, Class A
FF James D. Hodges, II, Class B

2009
FF Carl C. Gelardi, Jr., Class A
FF Francis W. Rush, III, Class A
FF Timothy Sullivan, Class A

December 31, 2009
FF William J. Owens, Class B

2010
FF Glenn S. Bullock, Class B
FF Stephen B. Katz, Class B

2011
FF Glen Merkitch, Class A

2012
FF Brian D. Burik, Class B

2013
FF John J. McCann, Class B
FF Christopher Morgan, Class B
FF Matthew J. Murphy, Class B

August 23, 2013
FF Richard I. Miranda, Class B

Appendix

IV. Rescue Company 1 Unit Citations

Starting in 1958 the New York City Fire department began awarding Unit Citations for meritorious worked performed by companies at fires and emergencies. Then, in 1975 the department instituted chest insignias for individual and unit awards. The original insignias for a unit citation only included engine and ladder companies and used the department colors of red, white, and yellow. Members of the rescue companies hoped to change this. The the company's union representative, Fireman Dennis Dale (Rescue 1 member 1970-81), went to headquarters and spoke to the chief in charge of personnel. Dale convinced the chief that rescue men were not orphans, and should have their own ribbon and they would even pay for them to be made.

Two hundred ribbons were made. The colors of the Rescue Unit Citation was red, white, and blue. When the chief asked, why blue instead of yellow? Dale replied, "There was no yellow in Rescue." The chief agreed.

Unit Citation ribbons.

✴September 7, 1966
Box 5-5-831
SS Hanseatic, Pier 84

✴October 18, 1969
Box 75-831
228 W. 47th Street
Lt. William A. Will
Fr. James J. Dowling
Fr. John J. Harney
Fr. Joseph R. Bryant
Fr. James Dunscomb (E21)
Fr. James P. Mauser (L16)

✴August 9, 1971
Box 728
40th Street &
Galvin Avenue

✴August 3, 1973
Box 75-365
673 Broadway

✴January 17, 1974
Box 75-872
810 Seventh Avenue

✴June 6, 1974
Box 33-2739
862 Jennings Street

✴February 13, 1975
Box 33-70
1 World Trade Center
Lt. Martin Cunniff
Fr. William Moclair
Fr. Henry Gonzalez
Fr. William Curran
Fr. Edward Noonan
Fr. Michael Walsh
Fr. Robert Burns

✴January 7, 1976
Box 55-532
173 Atlantic Avenue
Capt. John O'Connor (D3)
Fr. Robert Wilday
Fr. John McAllister
Fr. Dennis Dale
Fr. William Riley
Fr. William O'Keefe (L4)

✴February 21, 1977
Box 426
691 FDR Drive
Lt. Anthony Limberg
Fr. Stephen Casani
Fr. Christopher Glianna
Fr. Dennis Dale
Fr. John McAllister
Fr. James Dowling

✴June 17, 1977
Box 75-797
325 W. 43rd Street
Lt. Salvatore Russo
Fr. Robert Burns
Fr. William Curran
Fr. Christopher Glianna
Fr. Felix Mullen
Fr. George Symon (L4)

✴February 25, 1978
Box 22-412
145 Attorney Street
Lt. Paul Grassi (B6)
Fr. William Bessman
Fr. John Bornemeier
Fr. William Moclair
Fr. George Kreuscher
Fr. Dennis Dale

✴September 8, 1979
Box 33-812
Grand Central Station
Capt. Anthony Bruno (D3)
Fr. Ernest Andreacchi
Fr. Richard Martinsen
Fr. Joseph Bryant
Fr. John Driscoll
Fr. Michael Fitzgerald (L4)

✴February 8, 1980
Box 75-851
545 W. 49th Street
Lt. James Curran
Fr. William Curran
Fr. Norman Newkirk
Fr. John McAllister
Fr. Richard Martinsen
Fr. Patrick Hyland

✴February 12, 1980
Box 22-833
522 W. 47th Street
Lt. Frank Miale (B8)
Fr. Henry Gonzalez
Fr. Richard Martinsen
Fr. Dennis Horigan
Fr. Christopher Glianna
Fr. Barry Meade

✴June 23, 1980
Box 55-845
299 Park Avenue
Lt. James Curran
Fr. Henry Gonzalez
Fr. Norman Newkirk
Fr. Christopher Glianna
Fr. Joseph Bilboa
Fr. Edward Wysocki

✴April 17, 1981
Box 55-689
Hotel Statler
401 7th Avenue
Lt. Norman Kalish (B8)
Fr. William Curran
Fr. Joseph Angelini
Fr. John McAllister
Fr. Robert Burns
Fr. Louis Garcia

✴August 10, 1983
Box 44-747
500-512 7th Avenue
Lt. James Curran
FF Richard Martinsen
FF Richard Cody
FF Thomas Baker
FF James Corcoran
FF John R. McAllister

✴November 3, 1984
Box 33-1157
1264 Lexington Avenue
Lt. Joseph H. Dirks (B8)
FF John McAllister
FF John W. Boyle
FF Richard Cody
FF James Corcoran
FF Carl Feilmoser

✴January 29, 1985
Box 22-1161
525 E. 86th Street
Lt. James J. Curran
FF Robert Burns
FF James Corcoran
FF Alfredo Fuentes
FF Paul Hashagen
FF Carl Feilmoser

Appendix

Rescue Company 1 Unit Citations (continued)

✴ **February 28, 1985**
Box 44-471
500 7th Avenue
Capt. John J. Fanning (D15)
FF Alfredo Fuentes
FF Carl Feilmoser
FF John W. Boyle
FF Robert Burns
FF Bruce H. Newbery (L25)

✴ **April 26, 1985**
Box 8169
East River at 34th Street
Lt. James J. Curran
FF Paul Hashagen
FF John Boyle
FF Norman Newkirk
FF Joseph Angelini
FF William Bessman

✴ **August 20, 1985**
Box 22-281
154 Forsyth Street
Lt. John Cerato
FF John Driscoll
FF Thomas Reichel
FF Thomas Prin
FF Raymond M. Brown Jr. (L113)
FF Keith Monzillo (L4)

✴ **October 8, 1985**
Box 22-662
66 Madison Avenue
Lt. Anthony P. Limberg
FF Paul Hashagen
FF Thomas Prin
FF James T. Emery
FF John J. Driscoll
FF Barry Meade

✴ **October 22, 1986**
Box 8192
Pier 86, Ft. of 46th Street
Capt. Brian E. O'Flaherty
Lt. John Cerato
FF Paul Hashagen
FF George R. Kreuscher
FF John J. Driscoll
FF John Theobald
FF Thomas H. Baker
FF Michael McLoughlin (L4)

✴ **April 8, 1987**
Box 22-2185
2645 Third Avenue
Bronx
Lt. Stephen J. Casani
Lt. James P. Ellson (L124)
FF Thomas H. Baker

FF Alfredo Fuentes
FF Barry J. Meade
FF Henry G. Molle
FF Bruce Newbery
FF Thomas J. Reichel
FF Donald Sollecito (L4)

✴ **May 29, 1987**
Box 22-781
351 W. 42nd Street
Lt. James P. Ellson (L124)
FF Joseph J. Angelini
FF John W. Boyle
FF Carl B. Feilmoser
FF Michael J. Fitzgerald
FF Paul Hashagen
FF John Theobald

✴ **November 11, 1987**
Box 359
177 Sullivan Street
Lt. James P. Ellson
FF Raymond M. Brown, Jr.
FF John R. McAllister
FF Henry G. Molle
FF Donald Sollecito
FF Joseph Pierotti (E23)

✴ **December 3, 1988**
Box 22-239
269 East Broadway
Lt. James P. Ellson
FF Joseph J. Angelini
FF Paul Hashagen
FF Henry G. Molle
FF Paul A. Schmidt
FF David J. Williams

✴ **June 2, 1989**
Box 75-1506
135 W. 128th Street
Lt. Jay Fischler
FF Thomas Baker
FF John Carroll
FF Neal Fredericksen
FF Edward Geraghty
FF George Kreuscher
FF Daniel Killoran

✴ **September 3, 1989**
Box 22-195
92 Bowery Street
Lt. Stephen J. Casani
FF Daniel J. Killoran
FF Thomas H. Baker
FF Henry G. Molle
FF Edward F. Geraghty
FF Ronald D. Bucca

✴ **March 12, 1990**
Box 1041
1207 Broadway
Capt. Brian E. O'Flaherty
Lt. Jay Fischler
FF Raymond M. Brown, Jr.
FF Ronald D. Bucca
FF James T. Emery
FF Paul Hashagen
FF David J. Williams
FF Bruce H. Newbery

✴ **August 14, 1990**
Box 86
170 William Street
Lt. Jay Fischler
Lt. James P. Ellson
FF Joseph J. Angelini
FF Raymond M. Brown, Jr.
FF Paul Hashagen
FF John McAllister
FF Neal Fredericksen
FF Patrick J. O'Keefe (L35)
FF Edward Mauro (SQ1)
FF Peter Martin (R2)

✴ **May 13, 1991**
Box 44-1358
230 W. 113th Street
Lt. James P. Ellson
FF Gary P. Geidel (R5)
FF Harvey Harrell
FF Edward J. Mauro
FF Bruce H. Newbery
FF John Moran (L4)

✴ **May 14, 1991**
Box 33-837
723 7th Avenue
Lt. Patrick Brown (SOC)
FF Kevin Shea
FF Bruce H. Newbery
FF Patrick O'Keefe
FF Patrick Barr (L45)
FF Kevin Dowdell (R2)

✴ **July 25, 1991**
Box 1493
3200 Broadway
Capt. John Cerato
FF Ronald Bucca
FF Gary Geidel
FF Edward Mauro
FF John Hopkins (R3)
FF Eric Wiener (L111)

✴ **August 28, 1991**
Box 22-556
E. 14th Street & Union Square
Lt. James J. Corcoran
FF Bruce Newbery
FF Joseph Angelini
FF Kevin Shea
FF Warren Forsyth
FF Richard T. Muldowney, Jr. (L7)

✴ **March 29, 1992**
Box 55-865
226 W. 50th Street
Lt. Stephen J. Casani
FF David J. Williams
FF John W. Boyle
FF Edward Mauro
FF Kenneth Kaasmann
FF Eric M. Wiener (L111)

✴ **November 2, 1992**
Box 33-1563
2121 Madison Avenue
Lt. Kevin Williams (SOC)
FF Paul Hashagen
FF Henry G. Molle
FF Neal Fredericksen
FF Stanley Sussina
FF Joseph Angelini
FF Alfred Benjamin (L104)

✴ **January 31, 1993**
Box 88-827
280 Park Avenue
Lt. Stephen Casani
FF Bruce H. Newbery
FF Henry G. Molle
FF Kevin Shea
FF Edward Mauro
FF Lloyd D. Infanzon

✴ **June 13, 1993**
Box 33-8200
Hudson River at W. 57th Street
Capt. Shaun Reen (SOC)
FF Paul Hashagen
FF Harvey Harrell
FF Bruce Newbery
FF Kevin McGeary
FF Patrick O'Keefe

✴ **May 11, 1994**
Box 785
250 W. 43rd Street
Lt. Kevin Williams (SOC)
FF Thomas Baker
FF Dennis S. Amodio
FF John P. Theobald
FF Paul T. Baldwin
FF Michael G. Montesi

Appendix

Rescue Company 1 Unit Citations (continued)

★July 1, 1994
Box 1247
1867 Second Avenue
Lt. Kevin Williams (SOC)
FF Paul Hashagen
FF Joseph Angelini
FF Kenneth E. Kaasmann
FF James E. Smith
FF Michael Montesi

★November 7, 1994
Box 44-537
501 West Street
Lt. Stephen Casani
FF Paul Hashagen
FF John Theobald
FF Neal Fredericksen
FF Stanley J. Sussina
FF Alfred Benjamin
FF Warren J. Forsyth

★May 22, 1995
Box 841
318 E. 48th Street
Lt. Dennis Mojica
FF Gary P. Geidel
FF Thomas P. Sullivan
FF Michael J. Conboy (R3)
FF John P. Bergin (R5)
FF Victor R. Diz (L20)

★June 21, 1995
Box 75-847
1251 Avenue of Americas
Lt. Anthony M. Errico
FF David J. Williams
FF Warren J. Forsyth
FF Thomas F. Sullivan
FF Lloyd D. Infanzon
FF Paul T. Baldwin

★July 7, 1996
Box 460
800 East 14th Street
Lt. Dennis Mojica
FF Henry G. Molle
FF Warren J. Forsyth
FF Lloyd D. Infanzon
FF Joseph A. Morstatt
FF William L. Henry

★November 4, 1996
Box 403
151 Norfolk Street
Lt. Kevin C. Dowdell (SOC)
FF Timothy J. Kelly
FF Joseph J. Angelini
FF Gerard T. Nevins
FF Henry G. Molle
FF Steven J. Mockler

★January 7, 1997
Box 33-909
1 Lincoln Plaza
Lt. Dennis Mojica
FF Paul Hashagen
FF Warren J. Forsyth
FF Patrick J. O'Keefe
FF Stanley J. Sussina
FF Salvatore Civitillo (R2)

★September 29, 1997
Box 937
Queensboro Bridge
Capt. Phil Ruvolo (SOC)
FF Paul F. Hashagen
FF Joseph J. Angelini
FF Gerry Nevins
FF Steven Mockler
FF James C. Leavey

★February 18, 1998
Box 642
26 West 26th Street
Capt. John Norman
FF Ed Myslinski
FF Neal Fredericksen
FF Joe Angelini
FF Gerry Nevins
FF Brian Foy (L26)

★June 26, 1998
Box 795
4 Times Square
Lt. Stephen Spall (SOC)
FF David Williams
FF Gary Geidel
FF Michael Montesi
FF Thomas Sullivan
FF John Schoff (E41)

★May 16, 1999
Box 137
310 Greenwich Street
Lt. Dennis Mojica
FF David J. Marmann
FF Steven J. Mockler
FF James C. Leavey
FF Gary P. Geidel
FF Brian J. Foy

★October 12, 1999
Box 929
315 West 57th Street
Capt. Terence S. Hatton
FF Kevin G. Kroth
FF Gerry Nevins
FF Joe J. Angelini
FF Thor A. Johannessen
FF David Weiss

★May 2, 2000
Box 722
222 East 40th Street
Capt. Terence S. Hatton
FF Paul F. Hashagen
FF Joseph J. Angelini
FF Alfred Benjamin
FF Dave J. Marmann
FF Thor A. Johannessen

★June 2, 2000
Box 943
10 Columbus Circle
Lt. John D. Kiernan
FF David J. Williams
FF John M. Flatley
FF Michael G. Montesi
FF James C. Leavey
FF David M. Weiss

★August 4, 2000
Box 79
77 Fulton Street
Lt. George A. Hosle (SOC)
FF Gary P. Geidel
FF Dave J. Marmann
FF Patrick J. O'Keefe
FF Kenneth J. Marino
FF James T. O'Conner (SQ 252)

★January 19, 2001
Box 729
320 West 36th Street
Lt. Dennis Mojica
FF Kevin G. Kroth
FF Joseph J. Angelini
FF Alfred Benjamin
FF Kenneth J. Marino
FF Anthony T. Tedeschi

★March 21, 2001
Box 897
Lt. Peter C. Martin (R2)
FF Kevin G. Kroth
FF Anthony T. Tedeschi
FF Michael G. Geidel
FF Kenneth J. Marino
FF James C. Leavey

★October 24, 2001
Box 479
215 Park Avenue South
Lt. Steve Turilli (B18)
FF Joel T. Kanasky
FF Glenn S. Bullock
FF Alfred Benjamin
FF Edward W. Myslinski
FF Todd Smith (L159)

★February 6, 2004
Box 723
64 West 35th Street
Capt. Robert Morris
FF Jason Faso
FF Cosmo DiOrio
FF Robert Rufh (L30)
FF Frank Rush (L37)
FF Chris Mandeville (L40)

★July 24, 2005
Box 10
State Street & Whitehall Street Station
Lt. Thomas Donnelly
FF Jason Faso
FF Robert Roderka
FF Glenn Bullock
FF Vincent McMahon
FF Carl Scheetz (E62)

★October 11, 2006
Box 44-1031
530 E. 72nd Street
Lt. Antonio Tarabocchia
FF Francis G. Fee, Jr.
FF Michael G. Geidel
FF Christopher R. Mandeville
FF Cosmo DiOrio
FF Glenn S. Bullock

★December 26, 2006
Box 75-1358
Capt. Robert R. Morris
FF Jason H. Faso
FF Michael G. Geidel
FF Michael Anson, Sr.
FF Brian D. Burik
FF Christopher P. Reynolds
FF James D. Hodges (SQ41)

★March 27, 2007
Box 33-973
Lt. Antonio Tarabocchia
FF Kevin Kroth
FF Glenn Bullock
FF Christopher Mandeville
FF William Owens
FF Richard Miranda

★July 18, 2007
Box 775
East 41st Street & Lexington Avenue
Lt. Antonio Tarabocchia
FF Jason Faso
FF Sean Cummins
FF Frederick Ill
FF Michael Cioffi (L4)
FF Richard Miranda (L120)

223

Appendix

Rescue Company 1 Unit Citations (continued)

✴**March 15, 2008**
Box 44-861
305 E. 50th Street
Lt. Thomas Donnelly
FF Glenn Bullock
FF Sean Cummins
FF Matthew Beatty
FF Carl Gelardi
FF Michael Schnarri (L47)

✴**April 9, 2009**
Box 77-866
840 Eighth Avenue
Capt. Robert Morris
FF Joel Kanasky
FF James Feeley
FF Francis Rush
FF Christopher Mandeville
FF Glen Merkitch

✴**February 24, 2010**
Box 33-78
Capt. Robert Morris
FF Jason Faso
FF Francis Rush
FF Christopher Mandeville
FF William Owens
FF James Hodges

✴**June 7, 2010**
Box 75-619
Lt. Thomas Donnelly
FF Joel Kanasky
FF Frank Rush
FF Sean Cummins
FF Al Benjamin
FF John Bardak

✴**January 10, 2011**
Box 22-132
28 James Street
(Also awarded FF Thomas Elsasser Medal)
Capt. Robert Morris
FF Alfred Benjamin
FF Michael Cioffi
FF Sean Cummins
FF Jason Faso
FF Francis Rush

✴**March 22, 2012**
Box 1527
Capt. Robert R. Morris
FF Alfred Benjamin
FF Jason H. Faso
FF John M. Bardak
FF Christopher Morgan
FF Thomas Cosgrove, Jr.

✴**June 10, 2012**
Box 22-686
Capt. Robert R. Morris
FF Kevin G. Kroth
FF Joel J. Kanasky
FF Francis W. Rush, III
FF Timothy P. Geraghty
FF John M. Bardak

✴**July 17, 2012**
Box 1063
Capt. Lawrence E. Tompkins
FF Joel Kanasky
FF Christopher Morgan
FF Michael Cioffi
FF Thomas Cosgrove, Jr. (L28)
FF John W. Norman (L111)

✴**October 29, 2012**
Box 44-916
"Hurricane Sandy"
Lt. Thomas Donnelly
FF Joel Kanasky
FF Matthew Murphy
FF Francis Rush
FF Michael Cioffi
FF Thomas Cosgrove

✴**March 19, 2013**
Box 33-1233
Capt. Michael Smithwick (SOC)
FF Michael Cioffi
FF Christopher Morgan
FF Daniel Hyland
FF John McCann
FF Carl Sheetz

✴**June 12, 2013**
Box 75-915
Lt. Thomas Donnelly
FF Joel Kanasky
FF William Owens
FF Carl Sheetz
FF Chris Gaulrapp
FF Thomas Gayron

✴**November 3, 2013**
Box 160
Lt. Antonio Tarabocchia
FF Joel J. Kanasky
FF Richard I. Miranda
FF John J. McCann
FF Andrew Dinkle
FF Renald Jean (L107)

Appendix

V. Medals Awarded to Members of Rescue Company 1

1916
Lt. Thomas Kilbride
Department Medal

1918
Lt. Benjamin Parker
Kenny and Department Medals

Lt. Francis Blessing
Bennett and Department Medals

Fr. Thomas Kilbride
Department Medal

Fr. John Donohue
Department Medal

1921
Fr. Charles Roggencamp
Prentice Medal

1927
Capt. Walter L. Lamb
Stephenson Medal

1930
Fr. Edward Cronin, Jr.
Kenny and Department Medals

Fr. Bela Varga
Scott and Department Medals

1931
Fr. William A. Dorritie
Prentice Medal

1932
Capt. Cornell Garety
Bennett and Department Medals

1940
Fr. Charles Sadera
Crimmins and Department Medals

1946
Capt. Patrick T. Green
McElligott and Department Medals

1947
Capt. Patrick T. Green
Bennett and Department Medals

Fr. Hugh T. Early
Bonner and Department Medals

Fr. John A. Stanek
Department Medal

Fr. Allen Ostrow
Department Medal

Fr. Edward J. Barbour, Jr.
Department Medal

Fr. William J. Anthony
Department Medal

Fr. John R. Donovan
Department Medal

Fr. Joseph W. Rooney
Department Medal

Fr. Timothy J. Sullivan
Department Medal

Fr. William Martorano
Department Medal

1954
Fr. Hugh Early
Roosevelt and Department Medals

Fr. Charles Sadera, Jr.
Stephenson and Department Medals

1955
Fr. Edward J. Barbour, Jr.
Third Alarm Association and Department Medals

Lt. Joseph W. Ryan
Commerce & Industry and Department Medals

Fr. John R. Donovan
Crimmins and Department Medals

1960
Lt. Frank Yuskevich
Cronan Medal

Lt. William McMahon
Crimmins Medal

1962
Fr. William Curran
Kenny Medal

1964
Lt. Erwin J. Alexy
Delehanty Medal

1966
Lt. Erwin J. Alexy
Delehanty Medal

Fr. Raymond M. Brown
Trevor-Warren Medal

1969
Fr. Martin J. Cunniff
Brummer Medal

1972
Fr. James T. McCarthy
Trevor-Warren Medal

1977
Fr. Christopher V. Glianna
Lane Medal

1978
Fr. James D. Rogers
Prentice Medal

1980
Lt. James J. Curran
Johnston Medal

Fr. John R. McAllister
Scott Medal

1981
Fr. Norman L. Newkirk
American Legion Medal

1982
Capt. Brian E. O'Flaherty
Kane Medal

Lt. James J. Curran
Brummer Medal

1983
FF William Bessman
Bonner Medal

1984
Lt. James J. Curran
Columbia Association Medal

FF Michael J. Fitzgerald
Steuben Association Medal

FF Richard H. Cody
Company Officers Association Medal

FF Thomas H. Baker, Jr.
Fire Marshal Benevolent Association Medal

FF John R. McAllister
Williams Medal

1985
FF Paul F. Hashagen
Tuttlemundo Medal

1986
FF Paul F. Hashagen
Trevor-Warren and Police Honor Legion Medals

FF Paul F. Hashagen
Crimmins and Burn Center Medal

Capt. Brian E. O'Flaherty
Burn Center Medal

Lt. John Cerato
Burn Center Medal

FF John Driscoll
Burn Center Medal

FF George Kreuscher
Burn Center Medal

FF Thomas H. Baker
Burn Center Medal

FF John Theobald
Burn Center Medal

FF Michael McLoughlin (L-4)
Burn Center Medal

1987
FF Norman L. Newkirk
Wagner Medal

Lt. Stephen Casani
UFOA Medal

1991
FF Kevin Shea
Bonner Medal

FF Joseph Angelini
Goldman Medal

1993
FF Bruce H. Newbery
Dolney Medal

FF Henry G. Molle
Dougherty Medal

1997
FF Stanley J. Sussina
Bennett & NYS Honorable Chiefs Medals

Lt Dennis Mojica
Brookman Medal

1999
FF Gerard Nevins
Kenny Medal

FF Gerard Nevins
Fiedberg Medal

2003
FF Cosmo DiOrio
DeFranco Medal

2005
FF Francis G. Fee, Jr.
Trevor-Warren Medal

FF Christopher R. Mandeville
Delehanty Medal

FF Sean G. Cummins
Lane Medal

2007
FF Frederick J. Ill, III
Brummer Medal

2011
Capt. Robert R. Morris
Elsasser Memorial Medal

FF Francis W. Rush, III
Elsasser Memorial Medal

FF Alfred Benjamin
Elsasser Memorial Medal

FF Sean Cummins
Elsasser Memorial Medal

FF Jason H. Faso
Elsasser Memorial Medal

FF Michael J. Cioffi
Elsasser Memorial Medal

Index

A

Adams, James A. 214, 218
Adamson, Robert 7, 10, 11, 18, 19
Alexy, Erwin 93, 97, 205, 218, 219, 225
Alfonso, Danny 4, 157, 163, 164
Allbaugh, Joe 175
Amodio, Dennis 151, 222
Andersen, Harold 67, 81, 205, 217, 218
Anderson, William 108, 115, 214, 218
Andreacchi, Ernest 117, 219
Angelini, Joseph 136, 137, 138, 139, 144, 146, 147, 155, 157, 158, 162, 165, 166, 168, 169, 170, 171, 172, 208, 210, 219, 220, 221, 222, 223, 225
Anson, Michael Sr. 223
Anthony, William 61, 67, 216, 217, 218, 225
Anzelone 42
Archer 18, 22, 23, 26, 34, 35, 36, 37, 38, 40, 41, 43, 48, 49, 55, 56, 58, 63, 68, 70
Ashe, Shawn 172

B

Baden, C. 58
Baker, Thomas 126, 133, 136, 140, 146, 151, 220, 221, 222, 225
Bala, Thomas 126
Baldwin, Paul 151, 154, 155, 210, 220, 222, 223, Thomas 101, 103, 104, 205, 206, 214, 218, 219
Baltz, Steven 86
Barbour, Edward 58, 60, 67, 76, 217, 218, 225
Bardak, John 185, 186, 187, 224
Barr, Patrick 143, 222
Barry, Patrick 176, Stephen J. 217
Bassman, Jacob 68
Beake, Gunther 70
Beame, Abraham 117
Beatty, Matthew 182, 224
Beck, William A. J. 217
Becker, John 209, 219
Beliakoff, Theodore J. 216
Belnavis 162
Benjamin, Alfred 147, 151, 154, 155, 163, 164, 165, 171, 172, 185, 186, 222, 223, 224, 225
Bennett, Bill 4, James Gordon 24, 35, 50, 67, 157, Michael 65
Bergin, John P. 223
Berube, Glenn 212
Bessman, William 4, 101, 102, 106, 111, 116, 123, 139, 206, 207, 208, 209, 219, 220, 221, 222, 225
Bilboa, Joseph 111, 117, 120, 219, 221
Binns 20, John 28, 31
Blessing, Francis 9, 13, 20, 21, 22, 23, 24, 25, 214, 215, 225
Blume 116
Blumenthal 78
Bollon, Vincent 134
Bonamo, Thomas 4, 81, 82, 83, 86, 88, 95, 123, 218
Bonner 67, Hugh 123, 143
Boyle, John 125, 126, 131, 136, 139, 146, 148, 154, 155, 180, 220, 221, 222
Braxmar, G.C. 10
Brienza, Charles A. 218
Brodey, Milton 62
Bronnekant, Walter 204, 206, 217, 218
Brown, Joseph 40, Patrick 130, 139, 142, 143, 144, 146, 165, 168, 170, 222, Raymond 97, 98, 219, 225, Raymond Jr. 134, 137, 168, 170, 220, 222, Tim 4, 167
Brummer 102, 123
Bruno, Anthony 118, 221
Brusati 78
Bryant, Joseph 102, 115, 219, 220, 221
Bucca, Ronald 131, 132, 134, 140, 168, 170, 222
Bullock, Glenn 171, 172, 177, 178, 181, 182, 185, 190, 191, 213, 220, 223, 224
Burik, Brian 186, 220, 223
Burns, Robert 112, 115, 117, 139, 207, 208, 219, 220, 221, 222
Bush, George 147
Butler, Robert 134, William 173
Byrnes, Owen 123

C

Calderone 201, 208, Jack 4, 141, 210
Callagy, Arthur 29
Caltabellotta, Frank 88, 91, 205, 218
Campbell, Dennis 4, Edward 82
Cannon, Don 4
Carey, Hugh 117
Carroll 139, John 140, 222
Carter, Jimmy 117
Caruso, Enrico 141
Casani, Stephen 115, 117, 118, 134, 135, 136, 137, 139, 140, 146, 148, 152, 154, 155, 219, 220, 221, 222, 223, 225
Cassano, Sal 213
Cavanagh, 229, George 49, 50
Cerato, John 104, 133, 134, 137, 139, 140, 144, 209, 214, 220, 222, 225
Chambers, Walter B. 214
Cioffi, Michael 176, 181, 185, 188, 191, 192, 223, 224, 225
Civitillo, Salvatore 223
Clark, Frank 8, 9, 19, 21, 22, 26, 202, 215, 216
Clarke, Walter 91, 218
Clements, Katy 4
Clinton, Bill 160
Cochard, Harold A. 218
Cody, Richard 125, 126, 139, 220, 221, 225
Coffey, John 24, 25, 27, 28, 29, 30, 31, 34, 36, 216
Collins 110
Conboy, Michael J. 223
Conklin 102
Conners, John 21, 23, 28, 30, 40, 48, 202, 215, 216
Conrad, Christian A. 216
Conran, William F. 83
Cooper, William 108, 218, 219
Corcoran, James 126, 144, 209, 221, 222
Corrigan, John B. 16
Cosgrove, Thomas 186, 188, 224
Costello, Edward 217, 218, James 97, Timothy 88, 218
Costner, John 85
Coumo, Mario 143
Counes, John 28
Courtney, Edward F. 217
Cousteau, Jacques-Yves 81
Cramatte, Robert W. 218
Crawley 31
Croker, Edward 3, 25
Cronin, Edward 42, 47, 48, 203, 216, 225, Jeremiah 65
Crossman, Wayne 4
Culkin, Macaulay 159
Cummings, John 16
Cummins, Hanna 178, Maureen 178, Sean 173, 175, 176, 178, 181, 182, 185, 220, 223, 224, 225, Tara 178
Cunniff, Martin 101, 102, 112, 206, 219, 221, 225
Curran, James 112, 117, 119, 221, 122, 123, 125, 126, 131, 219, 220, 221, 222, 225, William 91, 106, 115, 208, 209, 218, 219, 225

D

Dale, Dennis 4, 114, 115, 116, 219, 221
D'Amico, Joe 119
Daniels, Fred 119
Darmstadt, Fred H. 217
Daugherty 43
David, George 89
DeBellis, Frank 104, 206, 209
Deeken, Julian 118
DeFranco, Dan 129, David J. 140, 176
Delehanty 93, 97, M. J. 178
DelMaestro 155
Delury, John P. 218
Demarest, Charles S. 10
Devine 78, James 216, James A. 30, 215, Jim 202
Dewey 36
DiBenedetto, Dominico 4, 50, 203, 216
DiBennedetto, Christopher 190
Dick, Mike 4, 198
Dinkle, Andrew 4, 224
DiOrio, Cosmo 172, 175, 176, 179, 180, 213, 223, 225
Dirks, Joseph 125, 126, 220, 221
Diz, Victor R. 223
Dolney, Robert R. 148
Donaghey, John 20
Donnelly, John 186, Thomas 4, 176, 178, 179, 181, 182, 185, 192, 213, 220, 223, 224

Index

Donohue, John 16, 21, 22, 23, 24, 202, 215, 217, 225, Joseph 61, 216, 217, Michael 217, 218
Donovan, John 24, 67, 75, 217, 218, 225, Richard 54, 57
Dornacker, Jane 133
Dorritie, William 23, 24, 30, 40, 45, 46, 48, 49, 53, 202, 203, 215, 216, 225
Dougherty, Thomas 40, 50, 148
Dowdell, Kevin 151, 222, 223
Dowling, James 102, 115, 207, 218, 219, 221
Downey, Raymond 137, 158, 159, 168, 170
Downs 123
Doyle, Peter 42, 47, 48, 216
Drennan, Thomas 20, 29
Dreyfous, Albert 4, 11
Driscoll, John 4, 101, 103, 106, 108, 111, 133, 139, 140, 205, 206, 208, 219, 221, 222, 225
Duddy, Daniel 164, 165, 171, 211
Duffy, James J. 218, Joseph 81, 205, 218, 219
Dugan, Joseph 64
Dunn, Vincent 144, 150, 151
Dunscomb, James 102, 221

E

Early, Hugh 61, 66, 67, 75, 217, 218, 225
Egan 42
Eisner, Harvey 4, 124, 128, 136
Ellison 137, 139
Ellson 136, 137, 138, 140, 142, James P. 220, 222
Elorde, Gabriel "Flash" 94
Elsasser, Thomas 185, 224
Emery, James 220, 222
Errico, Anthony 211, 223
Esposito, James 185
Eysser, Herb 4, 141

F

Fagan, Francis 97
Fanning, John J. 222
Farley 18
Farragher, John 88, 89, 90, 218
Faso, Jason 166, 173, 176, 178, 180, 181, 183, 185, 186, 223, 224, 225

Foy, Harry 97
Fee, Francis 170, 171, 172, 173, 176, 178, 212, 223, 225
Feehan 170
Feeley, James 180, 194, 224
Fehling, Francis 103, 219
Feilmoser, Carl 126, 137, 140, 220, 221, 222
Ferguson, James 55, 72, 216, 217
Finn, Thomas 50
Fischler, Jay 139, 140, 142, 222
Fitzgerald, Michael 125, 137, 220, 222, 225
Fitzpatrick, Thomas F. Jr. 220
Flagg, Ernest 214
Flatley, John 162, 170, 171, 172, 220, 223
Fletcher, William 36, 40, 202, 215, 216

Foley, Maurice 29, 30
Foote 110, Ronnie 111, 207
Ford, Gerald 111
Forgeard, Noel 175
Forsyth, Al 83, 205, 206, Warren 144, 157, 211, 222, 223
Fox, Edward 42, Edward J. 217, 218
Foy, Brian 223, Harry 97
Fredericksen, Neal 139, 140, 144, 147, 152, 156, 170, 210, 222, 223
Freed, Fred 90
Friedberg, William 162
Fried, Thomas 219
Friel, George 50, 216
Fuentes, Alfredo 136, 168, 170, 221, 222
Fullam, Joseph 43, Lawrence 48, 49, 216, 202
Fuller, Jack 90
Fusco, Chief 146

G

Gaine, John 190
Gallone, Robert 158
Gallagher 42
Gallo, Vincent C. Jr. 217
Gammandella, Ellen 108
Ganci, Peter 160, 168, 170
Garcia, Louis 208, 221
Garety, Cornell 41, 47, 49, 50, 51, 53, 54, 55, 203, 214, 216, 225
Gates 123
Gaulrapp, Christopher 192, 195, 224
Gayron, Thomas 192, 213, 224
Geidel, Gary 142, 144, 146, 148, 149, 158, 159, 162, 164, 167, 170, 171, 172, 222, 223, Michael 4, 157, 194, 220, 223, Paul 4, 91, 98, 99, 100, 110, 114, 170, 205, 206, 207, 218, 219

The devastating effects of the fire inside the Holland Tunnel on May 13, 1949.

Index

Firemen remove an injured woman rescued from a collapsed tenement building at 137 Pitt Street in Manhattan. Rescue 1 members tunneled and shored their way to those trapped on May 18, 1957.

Gelardi, Carl 180, 182, 220, 224
Geraghty, Edward 139, 140, 168, 170, 210, 222, Timothy 187, 195, 212, 224
Gerus 75
Gill, John Lee 4, 120, 121, 128, 129
Giuliani, Rudolph 172, 175
Glianna, Christopher 115, 116, 120, 221, 225
Glynn, Michael O. 217
Goldman, Edith B. 144
Gomez, Michael 4
Gonzales 186
Gonzalez, Henry 112, 120, 219, 220, 221
Grane, John 42
Grant, U.S. 19
Grassi, Paul 116, 221
Grasso, Joseph 156
Gray, Alexander 42, Harry F. 30
Green, Patrick 61, 63, 65, 66, 67, 204, 214, 217, 225
Greene, James 50
Grimes, William 119
Guido, Joseph J. 218

H

Hampton, Lionel 156
Handschuh, David 4, 166, 167
Hankin, Alfred 88, 98, 100, 218, 219
Hardina, Louis 50
Haring, Tom 132
Harnett 50
Harney, John 102, 219, 221
Harper, Thomas F. 218
Harrell, Harvey 139, 140, 142, 147, 150, 168, 170, 210, 220, 222
Harrington, Gordon 205, 206, 218
Hashagen, Joanne 4, Paul 126, 131, 132, 133, 137, 138, 139, 140, 147, 150, 152, 155, 156, 157, 158, 164, 165, 171, 172, 211, 220, 221, 222, 223, 225
Hatton, Beth 172, Kenneth 175, Terence 156, 157, 159, 160, 162, 163, 164, 165, 166, 167, 168, 170, 171, 172, 174, 175, 211, 214, 223, Terri Elizabeth 172

Hayde, Donald 187, 191
Hayes 18
Hazrick, Walter 45, 46
Healy 171, Daniel 30, George 211
Heaney, John 69
Hearst, William 192
Heeg, Christian 97
Heffernan, William 49
Helm, Henry 26, 31, 34, 41, 42
Hendrik, Walt 138
Henretty, Alfred 8, 9, 215
Henry, William 162, 166, 167, 170, 171, 172, 211, 223
Herold, John 55
Herrmann, Fred 157
Hesline 43
Hickey, Brian 165
Hodges, James 180, 183, 220, 223, 224, Joe 154
Hogan, 45, William 65
Ho, Lin H. 142
Hopkins, John 222
Horacek, Joseph 23, 26, 30, 215, 216, 202
Horan, Michael F. 216
Horigan, Dennis 120, 221

Horn, Michael F. 216
Hosle, George A. 223
Hotchkiss, Edwin 8, 9, 11, 12, 18, 214, 215
Hughes, George 54, 58, 61, 214, 216, 217, James 39, Thomas 176
Hurley, Tom 4, 164
Hutcheon, William 23, 27, 30, 31, 40, 42, 47, 49, 202, 215, 216
Huvane, Stephen 204, 217
Hylan, Mayor 35
Hyland, Daniel 192, 194, 224

I

Ill, Frederick 180, 181, 220, 223, 225
Infanzon, Lloyd 147, 148, 155, 161, 211, 222, 223

J

Jacobs, Alfred 114, 204, 217, 218
Jardin, Joseph 195

228

Index

Joy, John 10
Joun, Ronald 195, 224
Jeffers, Ron 186, 201
Johannessen, Thor 162, 171, 172, 212, 223
Johnson, Robert 219, Stephen 126, Thomas 97
Johnston, Albert S. 119
Jones 29, 60
Joseph, Frank 26, 202, 216
Joyce 176

K

Kaasmann, Kenneth 146, 147, 148, 222, 223
Kaiser, John 40
Kalish, Norman 208, 221
Kanasky, Joel 161, 171, 172, 176, 185, 187, 188, 192, 211, 213, 223, 224
Kane, Vincent J. 122
Kasparian, Arsen 179
Kasper, Charles 148, 168, 170, 214
Katz, Stephen 172, 220
Kavanagh, Daniel 203, 216
Kelly, Martin 216, Timothy 147, 156, 210, 223
Kenlon 7, 8, 10, 11, 13, 18, 19, 20, 22, 23, 24, 25, 35, 37, 42
Kennedy, Charles 28, 29, 34, 36, 41, 42, 48, 53, 203, 216, John F. 85
Kenny, Edward 29, Thomas 21, 24, 91, 160
Kiernan, John 157, 223
Kilbride, Thomas 8, 9, 18, 19, 21, 22, 23, 24, 25, 26, 27, 29, 32, 36, 37, 40, 42, 43, 46, 47, 49, 202, 214, 215, 216, 225
Killoran, Daniel 111, 118, 139, 140, 208, 219, 222
Kinasewitz, Taras 74, 218
King, Martin Luther Jr. 100
Kinsella, Alfred 8, 9, 12, 24, 43, 45, 215, 216
Kirkham, William 50
Kistenberger, John 26, 40, 215, 216
Kleehaas, John T. 125
Klein 42
Kocher, John F. 20, 21
Kreuscher, George 115, 116, 117, 118, 125, 133, 139, 140, 181, 222, 225
Kroger, Herman H. 210
Krull, Kevin J. 162, 171, 177, 180, 181, 187, 195, 209, 213, 223, 224

L

LaFemina, Fred 172, 175, 214
LaGuardia 51, 58, 59, 60
Lamb, Walter 26, 36, 37, 41, 45, 47, 202, 214, 215, 216, 225
Landers, James 36
Lane, Denis 116, 178
Langford, Thomas 71
Lantier, Francis X. 217
Larkin, Thomas 34, 45, 49, 202
Laufer 106
Leavey, James 158, 171, 211, 223
Leddy, James 104, 219
Lener, George W. 152
Lennox 190
Lenz, Charles 16
Lerch, Jack 4
Lewis, Harry 30, Richard 210
Lidle, Cory 180
Limberg, Anthony 115, 118, 207, 219, 220, 221, 222
Lindsay, John 105
Lopez, Michael 154
Loretan, John J. 217
Lowery, Robert O. 105
Lyons, Edward 55, 216, 217

M

MacArthur 60
MacHaffie, John P. 217
Mahoney, Patrick 70, Philip 70
Maher, Patrick 21, 55
Maier, Herman 61, 216, 217
Mainzer, Robert 7, 22, 23, 42
Maloney, Donald 63, Michael 108, 207, 219
Mancuso, Nick 134
Mandeville, Christopher 176, 177, 178, 181, 183, 213, 220, 223, 224, 225
Mannion 176
Marino, Kenneth 167, 170, 171, 172, 223
Marmann, David 4, 157, 171, 223
Maron, Paul 23, 24, 27, 215, 216
Marquardt, Charles H.
Martin, 206, Joseph 16, 21, 24, 25, 26, 29, 30, 31, 32, 36, 38, 42, 48, 125, Peter 222, 223
Martinson, Richard 119, 170, 175, 220, 221
Martorano, William 67, 217, 225
Matthau, Walter 90
Matthews 104
Mauro, Edward 142, 146, 148, 222
Mauser, James P. 221, John 102
Maye, Danny 4
Mayer, Louis B. 42
Mayr, John 21, 22, 42, 215, 216
McAllister, John 110, 114, 115, 116, 119, 125, 126, 137, 139, 149, 208, 209, 219, 220, 221, 222, 225
McBride, John 89, 136, 218, 219
McCann, John 101, 102, 220, 224
McCarthy 42, James 107, 108, 209, 219, 225, John 61, Thomas A. 216
McClusky, John 133
McCormack, Raymond 143
McDermott, John 85, 143
McElligott, John 4, 7, 8, 9, 10, 11, 12, 14, 18, 19, 36, 51, 51, 65, 214, 215
McGann, George 4, 102, 207, 209, 219
McGeary, Kevin 222
McGee 78
McGhee, Ronald 91, 106, 206, 218, 219
McGinn, Billy 167
McGloin, Hugh 207, 219
McGovern, Peter 50

Commissioner Cavanagh discusses tactics at Wooster Street collapse on February 14, 1958. For many hours, despite heavy snow and the bitter cold, Rescue Companies 1 & 2 tunneled through walls and debris at extreme risk to recover the dead.

Index

Somber members of Rescue 1 carry one of the twelve firefighters lost at the 23rd Street collapse. Manhattan Box 55-598 occurred on October 17, 1966.

McGuire 11, John 65
McInzer, Wilmer 20
McKavanagh 177
McKee 104
McKenna 18
McKeogh, Charles 95, 97
McLoughlin, Michael 133, 222, 225
McMahon, Peter 71, Thomas 218, Vincent 178, 223, William 86, 88, 90, 91, 94, 95, 205, 218, 225
McNally, Tom 16
McNamee, John P. 16
Meade, Barry 120, 134, 136, 222
Meehan, Thomas 54
Melahn, Fred 4
Merkitch, Glen 220, 224
Miale, Frank 120, 221
Miles, Barney 14
Millner, Raymond 61, 62, 214
Milward, John 23, 31, 32, 34, 40, 42, 47, 202, 215, 216
Miozzi, Victor 60, 84, 93, 102, 218
Miranda, Richard 4, 177, 180, 181, 193, 194, 220, 223, 224
Mitchel, John Purroy 18

Mitchell, John 218
Mockler, Steven 158, 161, 223
Moclair, William 107, 112, 116, 117, 219, 221
Mojica, Dennis 157, 158, 166, 167, 170, 171, 172, 210, 211, 220, 223, 225
Molle, Henry 136, 137, 139, 140, 147, 148, 152, 154, 210, 220, 222, 223, 225
Monet, Claude 81
Montesi, Michael 151, 158, 159, 161, 162, 164, 166, 167, 170, 171, 172, 211, 220, 222, 223
Monzillo, Keith 222
Mooney, John 8, 9, 16, 215
Moore 101
Moran, Andrew 16, Arthur L. 65, 217, John 142, 168, 170, 222
Morgan, Christopher 186, 187, 188, 192, 194, 220, 224, J. P. 27
Morris, Robert 176, 182, 183, 185, 186, 187, 192, 193, 213, 214, 220, 223, 224, 225, Robert Jr. 193, 194, 213, 214
Morstadt, Ronald 155
Morstatt, Joseph A. 223

Mosich, William F. 216, 217
Muldowney, Richard 144, 222
Mulholland, Henry 48, 49, 54, 57, 203, 216
Mullen, Felix 115
Mulvaney, James 28, 29
Murphy, Frank 63, 66, Matthew 191, 192, 195, 220, 224
Murrah, Alfred P. 155
Murtagh 21
Murtha, Thomas 34
Myslinski, Edward 171, 172, 179, 212, 223

N

Nardone 159
Narvaes, Frankie 94
Nast, Thomas 19
Naudet, Gedeon 4, Jules 4
Nelson, George J. 216
Neville, Pat 212
Nevins, Gerard 158, 160, 162, 164, 165, 166, 167, 170, 171, 172, 211, 225, 220, 223
Newbery, Bruce 126, 136, 139, 142, 143, 144, 148, 150, 152, 170, 172, 209, 210, 220, 222, 225, David 172

Newkirk, Norman 118, 121, 131, 134, 209, 220, 222, 225
Nigro, Daniel A. 4
Niver, W.A. 16
Nixon, Richard 106
Noonan, Bill 4, Edward 111, 112, 114, 221
Norman, Dave 168, John 4, 156, 168, 171, 188, 211, 214, 223, 224

O

Obama 194
O'Brien 171
O'Conner, Edward 75, James 223
O'Connor, John 114, 221
O'Dea, Pete 4, 146
O'Flaherty, Brian 122, 133, 134, 137, 139, 141, 168, 170, 214, 220, 222, 225
O'Hagan, John 81, 97, 105, 115, 214, 218
O'Keefe, Patrick 143, 157, 162, 164, 165, 166, 167, 169, 170, 171, 172, 211, 212, 220, 222, 223, William 114, 221
O'Leary, Walter 8, 9, 16, 40, 215

Index

Oliver, David 28, 29
Olsen, Mathias 217
Ono, Masaru 152
O'Rourke, John J. 117, 129, John T. 81, 218
Ostrow, Allen 67, 204, 217, 218, 225
Owens, William 177, 181, 182, 183, 192, 213, 220, 223, 224

P

Parker, Benjamin 18, 21, 23, 24, 214, 215, 225
Pate, William 133
Pearl, Rachel 178
Peever 34
Pena, Michael 4, 159, 161, 162, 171, 212
Pepin, Jaques 164
Peterson, Herbert 86, 94, 98, 111, 205, 206, 218
Petrocelli 130
Petrone, Beth 172
Pfeifer, Joseph 167
Phillips, Ray 168, 210
Pierotti, Joseph 123, 137, 222
Pierson, William H. 18
Pinkham, Gary 4
Planding, George 88, 205, 216, 217, 218
Poggi, Anthony 38
Pokorny, Harry 216, 217
Pratt, William 50
Prentice, John H. 49, 117
Prial, Philip 86, 115, 206, 218, 219,
Prin, Thomas 144, 222

Q

Quayle 66

R

Reagan, Nancy 134, Ronald 134
Reen, Shaun 222
Reichel, Thomas 131, 136, 220, 222
Reidway, Carl F. 217
Remar, James 130
Reres, Joseph 89, 205, 218
Rewkowski 149
Reynolds, Christopher 223
Rice 65
Riley, William 4, 104, 110, 115, 118, 139, 208, 209, 219, 220, 221
Rittmeyer 138
Rivers, Carlos 142
Roche 50
Roderka, Robert 176, 178, 179, 213, 223
Rogan 43
Rogers, James 112, 116, 117, 125, 137, 153, 210, 214, 219, 220, 225
Roggencamp, Charles 23, 26, 28, 29, 30, 31, 32, 41, 48, 50, 202, 215, 216, 225
Rooney, Joseph 65, 67, 93, 105, 205, 206, 214, 217, 218, 225
Roosevelt, Teddy 19
Rufh, Robert 176, 223
Rush, Francis 176, 180, 181, 183, 185, 187, 213, 220, 223, 224, 225
Russo, Salvatore 115, 117, 221
Ruth, Babe 141
Ruvolo, Philip 156, 158, 223
Ryan, John J. 50, 217, 218, John F. 8, 9, 11, 19, 21, 22, 23, 213, Joseph 70, 74, 217, 218, 225, William 195

S

Sadera, Charles 57, 75, 217, 218, 225
Sammon, Francis 85
Santoro, Anthony 97
Sarrocco 183
Scharr, Michael 182
Scheetz, Carl 178, 186, 223
Schick, Joseph W. 217
Schiller, Samuel 64
Schmid 78
Schmidt, Paul 139, 222
Schnall, Harry 45, 46
Schnarri, Michael 224
Schoff, John 158, 223
Schoppmeyer, John 32
Schunk, Michael 172, 179, 220
Scott, Walter 48, 119
Segal, Max 104
Seibert, John F. 217, 218
Seigel, William A. 219
Seigneur, Jake 189
Senese, Joseph V. 217

One of the twelve firefighters killed on October 17, 1966 is carefully placed in an ambulance. This fire and collapse was the greatest tragedy in FDNY history until September 11, 2001.

Index

FDNY members are seen operating at the scene of a fire and collapse of the Waldbaum's supermarket at 2892 Ocean Avenue in Brooklyn. Rescue 1 joined Rescue 2 in a difficult and dangerous search for trapped firefighters.

Sere, Ed 4
Shapiro, Larry 4, 180
Sharkey, W. J. 21, 22
Shaw, James 8, 9, 16, 215
Shea, Kevin 143, 144, 148, 149, 150, 220, 222, 225
Sheetz, Carl 192, 224
Sheppard, Mike 186
Siddons, Robert 97
Siegel, Max 219
Simmons, Clayton 61
Simonetti 29, James 28
Smith, Alan 218, Brian 195, Edward 42, Frank 218, James 16, 21, 22, 23, 148, 215, 223, John 218, Leonard 218, Matthew 174, Todd 171, 172, 173, 223
Smithwick, Michael 191, 192, 224
Sollecito, Donald 136, 137, 222
Soltner, Andre 164
Southern, Bo 206, Cecil C. Jr. 218
Spak, Steve 4, 137
Spall, Stephen 158, 159, 223
Spinatto, Joseph 134
Stabner, Clifford 156, 212

Stanek, John 60, 61, 67, 217, 225
Stephenson 45, 75
Stiefel, Bella 126
Stirnweiss, George 82
Straub, George J. 218
Strauss, Ken 150
Stravinsky, Igor 141
Sullivan, Joseph 30, 31, 36, 40, 216, Thomas 147, 158, 159, 220, 223, Timothy 60, 61, 67, 204, 217, 218, 220, 225
Surdukowski, Casimir 83, 88, 206, 217, 218
Sussina, Stanley 144, 147, 157, 211, 220, 222, 223, 225
Sweeney, Brian 42, 166, 168, 170, 171
Sykes, Joseph 154
Symon, George 115

T

Tarabocchia, Antonio 175, 177, 178, 179, 180, 181, 191, 212, 213, 223, 224
Taskowsky, Felix 21

Taubert, William 55
Tedeschi, Anthony 171, 223
Temme, Albert 75, 204, 217
Terilli, Steve 172
Tew, John 190
Thalberg, Irving 42
Theobald, Jack 210, John 133, 137, 139, 148, 151, 220, 222, 223, 225
Thompson, John H. 217
Tierney, Robert 36, 49, 51, 53, 55, 202, 216
Tischler, Henry 216, Louis 202, 203, 216
Tobin, John 185, 190
Tollefson, George 4, 217, 218
Tompkins, Lawrence 188, 224
Tracy, Joseph 39, 78
Trevor, Emily 97, 108, 132, 143, 176, 225, George 21, 22
Tubridy, James 57
Tuite, Edward 104, 105, 219
Turi, Al 146, 150
Turilli, Steve 223
Turner 137

U

Urbanowicz, Gary 4

V

Vardvarka, Anton 207
Varga, Bela 41, 42, 47, 48, 49, 216, 225
Versfelt, George C. 216
Vincent, James 21
Voigt, George F. 217
Vomero, Edward J. 117, 219, Russell 151

W

Wagner, Susan 134
Walsh, James 36, 42, 47, 50, 61, 216, 217, Michael 104, 106, 112, 117, 219, 221, Patrick 31, 61, Peter 39, 40, 216, Winfield 65
Walters, John 179
Warren, Mary B. 97, 108, 132, 143, 176, 225
Webb, Dick 173
Weir, Harry 123
Weisheit, John 171, 172, 173, 213
Weiss, David 161, 162, 163, 166, 167, 168, 170, 171, 172, 211, 223
Werner, Louis 70, 75, 76, 204, 217
Westbrook, Carl 4
Whitleson 14
Wiener, Eric 146, 222
Wilday, Robert "Don" 104, 111, 114, 207, 219, 221
Will, William 102, 221
Williams, David 139, 146, 147, 148, 151, 152, 158, 162, 177, 210, 220, 222, 223, Henry 4, 58, 60, Kevin 147, 151, 222, 223, Wesley 126
Wilson, William F. 218, 219
Wykel, Warren M. 217, 218
Wynn, Howard 68
Wysocki, Edward 221

Y

Yard 126
Yeager, George 112
Young, Andrew 117
Yuskevich, Frank 83, 85, 205, 218, 225